Portrait of an American Rabbi:
In His Own Words

Portrait of an American Rabbi: In His Own Words

Rabbi Lance J. Sussman, Ph.D.

Copyright © 2023 by Rabbi Lance J. Sussman, Ph.D..

Library of Congress Control Number:		2023909359
ISBN:	Hardcover	978-1-6698-7791-2
	Softcover	978-1-6698-7790-5
	eBook	978-1-6698-7789-9

All rights reserved. No part of this book may be reproduced or transmitted in any form or by any means, electronic or mechanical, including photocopying, recording, or by any information storage and retrieval system, without permission in writing from the copyright owner.

As often as possible, this book follows the Hebrew transliteration guidelines of the CCAR Press.

Print information available on the last page.

Rev. date: 06/14/2023

To order additional copies of this book, contact:
Xlibris
844-714-8691
www.Xlibris.com
Orders@Xlibris.com
850774

To my grandchildren

דּוֹר לְדוֹר יְשַׁבַּח מַעֲשֶׂיךָ

One generation shall praise Your works to another.

—Psalm 145:4

CONTENTS

Introduction xiii

PART 1
In the Beginning, 2001–2006

Getting Started, 2001–2006 1
In the Beginning, My Story 3
The World Jewish Condition Today: Europe 5
You Went to Germany? 15
A Red Thread: Uncommon Threads 25
The Roadblock to Peace 27
Half Empty or Half Full: Judaism in America 37
American Jews and Israel: The Doctrine of Interdependence 45
Twenty-Five Years in the Rabbinate 55
Where Are the Borders of Jewishness? 57
Israel Defense Forces: Heroes of the Jewish People 59
Gaza 61
Iraq: What Do You Think? 69
Yizkor 79
Hanukkah: The Right Light 83
Tikkun Torah 85
Why I am a Jew! 95

PART 2
A Little Religion Is a Good Thing 2007–2011

In the Rear View Mirror, 2007-2011 107
A Little Religion Is a Good Thing 111
Israel at 60 119

Justice, Justice You Shall Pursue..129
Sin 131
Rabbis and Imams...139
I Believe in Prayer 141
Abraham's Other Son: Jewish-Muslim Relations Today.....................149
Judaism and the Difficult Question of Race 157
My Synagogue..167
On the Road Again: Maryland Jewish Heritage Tour.........................173
My Munich Report: The German Jewish Heritage and
American Judaism 175
HUC-JIR Founders' Day Talk..177
Jewish Dance? 179
The Statute of Liberty and the New York Mosque Controversy 181
Shamang Israel: Israel's Recent Conversion Crisis..................................183
No Place Like Home...185
I Love Israel 191
Reform Judaism..197
Yizkor..207
Transcending an "Artless Tradition": The Birth of a Modern
Jewish Art Movement 209
Generations: My Dad, Charles Sussman, z"l 217

PART 3
A Night of Watching
2012–2016

A Night of Watching, 2012-2016 221
Passover Report: Seeing Oneself Going Forth From Egypt.................223
You Can't Go Home Again? President Obama's Peace Proposal........225
Taking Syria Seriously...227
Rabbi's Journal: *The Feminine Mystique* at 50.......................................229
Rabbi's Journal III: My Cup Overfloweth..231
Why Hanukkah?..233
Zimmerman Trial 235
A Blessing for Everything...243
The Blessing of Peace..249
The Blessing of Love...255
The Blessing of Memory...261

Faith in Art: Visual Culture and the Future of Judaism 263
The New Union Haggadah: Exodus as a Theme in American
History and Culture 265
Second Isaiah: "A Light to the Nations" and the Mission of
Reform Judaism..269
Ahavat Yisrael: Love of Israel..281
Malachi: Healing, Comfort, and the Hearts of the Children............291
Ezekiel: Renewal and Awakening...299
Acharei Mot K'doshim: The Battle of Baltimore..................................301
Seeing Is Believing: Visual *T'filot* and the Future of Jewish Worship 303
The Confirmation Revolution: Then and Now 307
Back to Ohio: Revisiting My First Pulpit 311
Rabbi, What Do You Believe? 315
A Sacred Event: Social Justice, *Chesed*, and Reform Judaism...............317
Rabbi Joseph Krauskopf, Reform Triumphalism, and the 1885
Pittsburgh Platform..327

PART 4
Crossroads, Conflicts, and Challenges
2017–2022

Crossroads, Conflicts, and Challenges 2017-2022.........................333
Strangers and Neighbors: The Golden Rule Today 339
The Fight Against BDS: Israel's Battle for Legitimacy......................349
Not by Might: Jews, Guns, and Violence..357
Celebrating Hanukkah: To Decorate or Not to Decorate, That
Is the Question!..365
Neglect: The Hidden Crime 367
Between a Rock and a Hard Place: Navigating the Book of Leviticus 369
It All Depends: Finding the Middle of the Torah 373
The 13 *Midot*: God is Ethical and So Are We 377
You Are What You Eat: The New World of Kosher Food 381
What We Can Confirm: The Path of Torah 385
Judaism, Medical Science, and Spirituality: A Brief History............389
Liberty and Freedom from Religion in America................................393
Finding Our Moral Compass: Reflection on Charlottesville 397
Personal Strength: Am I Strong Enough? 401
Jewish Unity.. 407

Staying Strong: American Anti-Semitism Today 415
Chazak, Chazak v'Nitchazeik: Keeping our Synagogue Strong............423
Yizkor: Staying Strong in the Shadow 431
I Still Believe: Rereading Anne Frank 433
Mazal Tov: The KI Puppets are 13! 437
Marines 439
The Final Review: Philip Roth, 1933–2018 441
An Emblem of the Land I Love: Reform Jewish Reflections on
Flag Day 445
The Wine Was Good: Another Look at the *Trefa* Banquet 449
Bibi: The Cheltenham Years 453
Why We Need Good Sermons Now More Than Ever 457
I Cannot Forgive You 461
The Voice for Justice 469
An English Hanukkah 477
Walls: American, Israeli, and Mexican 481
A Bold Centrist: Remembering Isaac M. Wise 485
Siding with Science: Reform Judaism, Evolution, and the
Environment 489
The Coronavirus Pandemic and the Future of Organized Religion 493
Ordinary Citizens: Lessons from the Pandemic of 2020 497
Lessons Learned: Historical Pandemics and the Philadelphia
Jewish Community 501
Grant Us Peace: An American Reform Jewish Classic Prayer 505
Closing Our Shuls, Opening Our Homes: A Jewish Response to
COVID-19 509
An Old Hatred and New Challenges: Jews, Blacks, and White
Supremacy in America 511
A Long History: American Jews and the NAACP 515
Monumental Questions: A Rabbinic Reflection for July 4, 2020 519
What Is Being Asked of Us? 521
The Right to Vote—*Shof'tim* 16:15–21:9 525
Rest in Peace: Remembering Justice Ruth Bader Ginsburg, a"h
September 24, 2020 529
The Attack on America 533
Back to Work: Step by Step, Inch by Inch 537
The Unbearable Middle: The Public, the Police, and Life in
America Today 539

Alaska and the Holocaust: An Unknown Story 541
Huddled Masses: Sanctuary for Afghans in America 545
In Situ: A View of The Landau Windows from the Pulpit of
Reform Congregation Keneseth Israel 549
What's in a Name? Thoughts on Jewish Identity 555
Anti-Semitism and the Taking of Hostages: A Tragic and
Undeniable History 559
In the Crosshairs of History: The Jews of Ukraine 563
Spiritual Roadmap: The Hidden Battle for the Soul of Reform
Judaism 567
From Now On, No Distinction 571
My Last Day at Sunday School (JQuest): A Few Final Thoughts 579
Five Special Moments 583

Acknowledgments 587
About the Author 591

Introduction

On June 30, 2008, Professor Marc Saperstein, the world's leading scholar of sermons and rabbinic addresses in the Jewish tradition, gave a talk to a gathering of rabbinic graduates of the Leo Baeck College in London. He began by asking a disquieting question, "Is the sermon on its deathbed?" His comments were subsequently published in *European Judaism* (March 2009); and although he tactfully did not answer his own question, Saperstein ended with the following recommendation: "So I urge all rabbis: whatever you write, keep your papers safely stored away for future use, and leave instructions that the texts of your sermons not be tossed into the rubbish bin, but sent for safekeeping to an appropriate archival collection." He then provided a gratifying rationale. "The sermons you give," he assured his audience, "plant seeds in the minds and souls of your congregants, but they are also part of the historical record of our people."

This book is an attempt to comply with Saperstein's dictum by providing a published record of select sermons and articles I wrote during my twenty-one years as Senior Rabbi of Reform Congregation Keneseth Israel (KI) in Elkins Park, Pennsylvania, from 2001 to 2022. Far from the complete record suggested by Dr. Saperstein, they are hopefully representative of the many themes and literary genres that constituted the core of my rabbinic work and writing during the second half of my career. Ordained at the Hebrew Union College–Jewish Institute of Religion (HUC-JIR) in Cincinnati, Ohio, in 1980, I previously published a book of sermons, *Sharing Sacred Moments* (1999), taken from my first nine years as rabbi of Temple Concord in Binghamton, New York.

The seed of producing a book of sermons and other rabbinic writings in my life actually goes back to my days as a rabbinic student. For my rabbinic thesis, under the guidance of Dr. Jacob R. Marcus, I wrote on the sermons of Isaac Leeser (1806–1868), the leading Jewish religious leader in the United States in the decades prior to the American Civil War. In fact, Leeser was the primary Jewish religious leader (he was not an ordained rabbi nor ever claimed to be) who pioneered the tradition of preaching in the American synagogue. He ultimately published ten five-hundred-page volumes of *Discourses*. I read, studied, and indexed all of them and can honestly report that they were almost entirely theological treatises of little or no entertainment value. However, they did constitute an intellectual diary of American Jewish religious life during the Antebellum Period in which the influence of Protestant, Bible-centered religiosity was the dominant form of spirituality in the United States. Leeser himself believed that his sermons were his most important contribution to American Jewish life and, at the end of his long career, taught homiletics at Maimonides College in Philadelphia, the first rabbinic school in the United States, which he established in 1867.

While I admired Leeser's erudition and persistence, I also recognized that preaching in a synagogue at the end of the twentieth century and the beginning of the twenty-first century would require storytelling, humor, and a kind of emotional accessibility Leeser could not provide. Certainly, contemporary American Jews were not interested in forty-five-minute addresses, which featured sentences with an average of 250 words. Already a rabbinic student in Richmond, Indiana, I received my first warning about "baling all hay" from a synagogue president who literally timed my Shabbat talks and reported back to my supervisors at HUC-JIR that I tended to "wax eloquent." I learned my lesson early and actually received the College's Mrs. Arthur Hays Sulzberger Prize in Homiletics for the Best Short Sermon when I graduated from rabbinic school. However, I must admit that as the years passed, I would occasionally give a "Leeser length" sermon for the High Holy Days. Some of those remarks are included in this volume.

Learning to write and deliver sermons was a major part of HUC-JIR's curriculum in the 1970s. My homiletics professor was Dr. Ed Goldman. The basic sermon, as he presented it, included an engaging introduction; a Biblical verse (only used in a positive way); three major points, which could be sequential or dialectical; and a compelling, comforting conclusion. I internalized that outline early in my career, and it has served me well.

The spoken word was taught by Professor Lowell McCoy, a kind, caring, insightful instructor. Over and over, McCoy reminded us to "react to the meaning of your words." I believe I repeated those same words to a thousand or more b'nai mitzvah students and confirmands.

Again, taking my cue from Dr. Saperstein, this book includes more than actual sermons, quite literally selections of "whatever" I wrote and shared with the congregation during the last two decades. While sermons are the main entries in this book, there are also weekly e-messages, quarterly synagogue bulletin columns, and articles published in print and online journals. Because I published a collection of my poetry, *The Kindness Response* (2021), I did not include any poems in this book or any of the hundreds of ephemeral invocations, benedictions, prayers, and eulogies I penned over the years. For the record, much of my public speaking was extemporaneous including my hundred-plus PowerPoint lectures on Jewish history and art. What is included in this book is actually only a fraction of the over two thousand pages of my typed talks exclusive of *b'nai mitzvah* comments, wedding addresses, and well over one thousand eulogies. Judaism is a literary tradition, and for over four decades, my life and work have been anchored in the written and spoken word.

Because I also trained as a historian and earned a PhD in American Jewish history at HUC-JIR, I have taken the liberty of dividing the material in this book up into four periods representing the early days of my work at KI, the middle years, and my final six years on the pulpit before health concerns resulted in a slightly premature retirement. Each of the four sections has its own historical introduction. Having been granted extra years, I was determined to get a selection of my words on record for posterity, especially for my family as well as any future scholar interested in American Jewish life at the beginning of the twenty-first century precisely at the moment when the role of preaching in the American synagogue pulpit was radically transformed by unprecedented trends in popular culture and technology.

During my first ten years at KI, our Friday night services were broadcast live on AM radio. I had exactly twenty-two minutes to deliver my message. Thereafter, KI began streaming services; and although the technical time limit was removed, my messages generally became shorter because of the nature of "Zoom sermons" to the point where I actually received feedback that my High Holy Day sermons could have been a little longer. From a rabbinic perspective, that is almost proof of the existence of God!

Having reread my own work, I became aware of a number of themes that characterized my work as a preacher or darshan. Unlike Leeser, I frequently shared personal and autobiographical information to help connect with "my people." I spoke regularly on social justice, Israel, contemporary events, and Reform Judaism. I also gave numerous talks promoting synagogue programs and initiatives. My sermons contain more "history" than average, reflecting my academic interests. Like all pulpit rabbis, I had to make decisions about giving political talks and, influenced by ancient Israel's prophetic tradition, occasionally took a stand on a controversial talk with intense instant feedback being offered every single time I felt I just had to give my views on Iraq, Iran, and gun violence. Fortunately, I did not have to defend my right to "freedom of the pulpit," although early in my time at KI, I had to adjust the level of intellectual content in my remarks to match the culture of the congregation. Slowly but surely, the congregation became accustomed to my style of rabbi-professor preaching! Much safer were the reports on my travels, international and domestic, and on Jewish art, another personal interest.

As a child growing up in Baltimore, I was blessed to have had outstanding rabbis in my life. In particular, my Senior Rabbi Abraham Shaw and his Assistant, Martin Weiner, were both powerful orators. Their words and measured delivery still resonate with me. Rabbi Shaw had the mellow voice of an FM radio announcer. He embodied wisdom and empathy in everything he did and said. Rabbi Weiner had a powerful presence and as a tall man could stretch his arms out dramatically to make a point and make us feel close to him despite the immense size of the synagogue's main sanctuary. Whatever aspects of my own preaching that has impacted positively on my congregants ultimately were derived from their shining examples of what an effective pulpit rabbi could do by speaking from the heart with well-chosen words shared in authentic, caring voices.

Honestly, I am worried about the future of the sermon. When I first started out as a young rabbi, I felt that the biggest challenge was television and its short segments punctuated by commercials. Online communication, cell phones, tiny text messages, and storytelling by TikTok have made successful preaching even more difficult. Fortunately, for forty-two years on the pulpit, twenty-one of them at KI, I also learned that a good sermon could still move people; and with the final amen, a buzz could fill the sanctuary with the sounds of approval and engagement. Feedback could continue for days, including comparisons, happy and insidious, with other area rabbis.

Judaism has long maintained that there are two Torahs: written and oral. The written Torah was given by Moses, and the oral Torah was provided by the ancient rabbis. We need both. We need compelling written testimony about our faith in our time, and we need the living spoken word of Judaism to make our tradition come alive, prod the minds, and move the hearts of our people. I do not know if the sermon will survive, but I believe it has played a vital role in making Judaism a vital tradition for centuries. If my words have contributed in any measure to that legacy, then I will take my leave and join voices with the psalmist who declared, "Happy are those who dwell in Your house, they will praise You forever!" (Ps. 84:5).

Part 1

In the Beginning, 2001–2006

Getting Started, 2001–2006

Although the early rabbis warned the ancient Jewish community not to speculate about what happened before creation, my arrival at Reform Congregation Keneseth Israel (KI) had a significant prehistory. For several months before I officially assumed my duties, I regularly drove from Binghamton, New York, to Philadelphia to meet with several dozen focus groups from the congregation including religious school families, clusters of members living in large apartment buildings, and major financial supporters of the synagogue. The purpose was to get to know one another so that I could "hit the ground running." Although I met several hundred people before I gave my first sermon, I continued to introduce myself from the pulpit for several years by sharing autobiographical information on a regular basis. Some of those talks are included here in Part 1.

But my arrival at KI was anything but normal. Just a few weeks after I began my rabbinic duties, 9/11 occurred, and the whole world changed. In addition to dealing with the magnitude of the event, I was at a loss as I simply did not know my new congregation or my clergy colleagues, Jewish and non-Jewish, in the area. My instinct was to connect with as many people in the area to build a broad base of mutual support in the community. The result was the founding of the Cheltenham Area Multifaith Council to continue the interfaith work from my previous pulpit. By the second anniversary of 9/11, I was able to organize a massive memorial service attended by three thousand people at KI. My interfaith work not only continued but also intensified during the following years.

The 9/11 incident had tremendous consequences for America, Israel, and the world; and sermons with an international scope became a significant part of my pulpit repertoire. In particular, I felt the need to provide rabbinic insights into American military involvement in Iraq and Afghanistan and the repercussions for the Jewish State. Despite the disruptions of the moment, I was able to initiate a program of world travel including Israel and Central Europe and gave regular reports to the congregation. I was also able to reestablish myself as a rabbi-scholar and with the consent of the congregation taught Jewish Studies classes at Rutgers University more than an hour north of Philadelphia. At the same time, I began to preach and teach regularly on the American Jewish experience, my academic area of expertise.

The drama and complexity of the years 2001 to 2006 also required that I provide pastoral messages to the congregation. From the beginning of my work at KI, I focused on Yizkor (memorial) messages, especially on Yom Kippur and Shemini Atzeret. Perhaps the spiritual highlight occurred in the little Austrian town of Eisenstaedt, fifty miles south of Vienna. In the course of touring the town, we visited a long-abandoned synagogue in the town's former Jewish ghetto. In the Ark, someone had left a scrap of parchment, the remains of a Torah scroll. The group from KI I was traveling with asked me to read and translate it. The moment was electric. The Jewish past, present, and future were all present. We were at one with our heritage. Four thousand miles from Philadelphia, I was finally at home at KI. To celebrate my newfound spiritual home, I created the KI Puppets, featuring myself as Torah Turtle, for our preschool. The KI Puppets instantly became a significant part of the KI brand.

In the Beginning, My Story

August 2001 KI Bulletin

In the beginning, there were phone calls, and the relationship was unformed and void. Then the search committee said, "Let there be an interview," and it was good. And the committee distinguished between viable and not-so-viable candidates. And the spirit of God hovered over the face of the highways and airways.

On the second day, the committee said, "Let there be references and due diligence and questions of every kind." Day and night, information flowed, and résumés covered the boardroom table. And it was good.

On the third day, the committee said, "Let us travel and go north and see and listen for ourselves." So they journeyed across the mountains of creation and went to services and listened and observed. They had discussions of every kind and exchanged questions of every species and returned to their homes.

On the fourth day, the committee said, "Let us give an invitation to the candidate and ask him to speak in our place of worship and show us how he can preach and teach in our midst and let him bring his wife to our house so that she can see something of how we live and pray together." And it was so.

On the fifth day, the committee said, "Let us make an offer so that our candidate can be one of us and move his family across the mountains of creation and cast his lot with us so that we can be together." And the candidate said yes and spoke with his family and friends. And it was good.

On the sixth day, there were boxes and trucks and packing tape and strong men lifting heavy pieces of furniture. And the candidate taped messages on 800 numbers and said, "Let there be water and light and oil and electricity in our new home." And it was so. The committee then said that it was not good for our candidate to be alone, so they created parlor meetings under every vine and fig tree. And the candidate learned how to drive in Philadelphia and locate food stores, pharmacies, and Barnes & Noble.

On the seventh day, the committee rested and said, "Let there be Shabbat services and a study group and a new committee called Transition." And it was so. And the candidate became the Senior Rabbi of KI and ascended the bimah and looked out at the huge sea of welcoming faces and souls and said, "It is good." And his spirit rested and was refreshed. And the congregation said, "Behold, it is good and pleasant when we dwell together." And they dwelt together in the land of Elkins Park for a very long time.

THE WORLD JEWISH CONDITION TODAY: EUROPE

September 6, 2002, Rosh HaShanah Evening 5763

This past year has been one of the most difficult twelve-month periods in recent memory for the United States, the Jewish people, and the world community. The year 5762 began with the demonic attacks of 9/11, then saw an intensification of the violence in the Middle East, a terrifying series of pediatric kidnappings and murders, and a massive erosion of liquid wealth in the world stock markets. On top of all that, ethical failures at the highest levels of business and commerce brought ruin to several major corporations. The ripples in the financial pond were felt from shore to shore. Family fortunes shrank, pensions were devastated, and questions about the ethics of business, instead of the business of business, abounded.

The year 5762 was difficult for all of us. But it was a year of some measured good as well. Patriotism, long dormant in this society, came back to life. Young people, widely perceived as apolitical, suddenly took interest in local, national, and global affairs. Interfaith, generally a low communal priority, was rediscovered and reaffirmed in a multitude of magnificent ways. Indeed, in just five days, this sanctuary will be the venue for the largest multifaith gathering in the Commonwealth of Pennsylvania, in memory of those who perished on 9/11 in New York City, western Pennsylvania, and Washington, DC. If we learn only one thing from 9/11, let it be that this country is a community of communities, the most ethnically inclusive, the most religiously tolerant, and the most democratic society on the face of this planet. Next Wednesday night, September 11,

2002, please join all your neighbors—Jewish, Christian, Buddhist, Bahá'í, and others—in a reaffirmation of national hope and global unity.

Reviewing the previous year and accounting for where we have traveled individually and globally is a central part of what the High Holy Days are all about. In Hebrew, we call it *Heshbon HaNefesh*, taking stock of the soul. But there is another aspect of our lives we need to consider at this turn of the year. And that is, where are we as Jews at this moment in our own lives and in the history of the Jewish people? For those who have gathered here this evening to reaffirm their ties to Torah, Judaism, Israel, and this synagogue, the grand themes of the High Holy Days, which echo back and forth between the intensely personal and the universal, are also distinctly punctuated by the specifically Jewish.

Over the course of these High Holy Days, I would like to share with you my thoughts on "The World Jewish Condition Today." Each of my three talks this holiday season will be focused geographically on a major sector of contemporary Jewish life. Tonight, I will share with you some reflections on Jewish life in Europe, the immediate past center of Jewish life. Tomorrow, we will turn to Israel and its many trials and tribulations; and finally, on the eve of Yom Kippur, pressed between our two recitations of Kol Nidrei, I want to talk to you about contemporary Jewish life in this country, in this region, and in this synagogue.

Perhaps the leading Jewish woman writer of our time, Cynthia Ozick, once remarked that if you want to make a great sound with a shofar, you blow into the narrow end. If you try to sound the wider end, nothing happens. The same is true with us as Jews. We are people, we are Americans, but we are also Jewish. To understand who we are and to make our greatest sound, we need to understand the specifically Jewish dimension of our lives. Armed with that self-knowledge, we will enable our souls to sound a great *tekiah gedolah* and restore ourselves as people and as Jews.

The sounds of the shofar can serve as a paradigm for understanding each geographical area of Jewish life today. The European Jewish experience is like a *teruah*. It is the distinctive sound of the shofar, and it is a warning. The European Jewish experience, as we shall see, serves as a warning to what can become of us in modern times if we do not provide for ourselves spiritually and physically.

The Israeli experience is *tekiah*. *Tekiah* is a call to action, courage, and strength. It is a summon to redemption. Israel and the world Jewish community need to hear the sound of tekiah today.

In America, we sound the third and final shofar note, *shevarim*. *Shevarim* is a variant of *teruah*, a broken sound, a series of alternating notes between high and low. Jewish life in America is uneven, alternating between great successes and depressing failures. It is ambivalent, affirming, unsure, broken, and, because we remain Jewish, hopeful.

We begin our discussion of the World Jewish Condition Today with a look at the situation in Europe. European Jewish history and life constitute our *teruah* note—the foundation note, the place where the distinctive Jewish sound was basically articulated for us. *Teruah* is a somber, perhaps terrifying, note of warning. For almost a thousand years, Europe was the center of Jewish life in Spain, Germany, and Poland. Our basic Ashkenazic articulation of Talmudic Judaism is European. Judaism flourished in Spain. Yiddish began in Germany and transplanted itself to Eastern Europe. By the sixteenth century, Poland was the international center of Jewish learning. In the eighteenth century, Hasidism emerged in Ukraine. Jewish modernity began in Europe too. Jewish enlightenment, the three major branches of modern Judaism, the academic study of Judaism, and most recently, Zionism all are expressions of the intersection of Judaism and European cultures.

But a dark shadow was always cast over European Jewish life, even in the best of times. As much as Judaism flourished in the Rhineland, Lithuania, and Iberia, so did vicious strains of anti-Semitism. Even the term itself, anti-Semitism, is European. A brutal inquisition, murderous pogroms, and, finally, and most catastrophically, the Nazi Holocaust chopped the tree of European Judaism down to a mere stump. A thousand years of Jewish life, culture, and spirituality literally went up in smoke in twelve terrifying years from 1933 to 1945. The *teruah* sound of European Jews—once so proud, once so bold—was muffled by an unthinkable continent-wide program of genocide.

This summer, I had the honor and pleasure of escorting forty-two individuals, thirty-six of them from our congregation, to Central and Eastern Europe. Our trip took us to southern Poland, central Slovakia, eastern Austria, and the central area of the Czech Republic. It was a remarkable journey of discovery and learning. What we learned about was the rich history of Jewish life in Europe: its triumphs, its sorrows, its near-total destruction, and the fledging attempts to begin anew. It was abundantly clear to all of us that proud synagogues, once filled with the blast of the shofar, are now simply gone, in ruins, or monuments to the past. The shofar sounds no more in most of the places we went—no *tekiah*, no *teruah*, no *shevarim*.

Evidence of a glorious Jewish past abounded everywhere we went. In Kazimierz, the medieval Jewish center of Krakow, several major synagogues still stand, monuments to Jewish life. At one end of the market was a Renaissance-period brick synagogue, now a museum of Jewish life in Poland. At the other end of the square was the smaller Remuh synagogue, the synagogue of the great scholar, Moses Isserles, whose commentary on Judaism's basic code of law continues to define the contours of Ashkenazic orthodoxy. Several blocks farther up on Honey Street, we visited "The Temple," one of the finest Reform synagogues in Eastern Europe. Its tasteful beauty, now fully restored, pointed to another apex in modern Polish Jewish life just a century ago.

In Budapest, we saw the great Dohany Street synagogue, a beautiful gilded Moorish building, the largest synagogue in Europe, restored to perfection. In its heyday, it was the pride of Hungarian Jewry. Three thousand seats and multiple balconies fill its immense central space. Its ornate Ark, once the focus of a hundred *Avinu Malkeinus* and endless blasts of the shofar, testified silently to a muted past of one of Europe's great Jewish communities.

In Prague, our last stop, we were privileged to walk through the beautiful streets of the Old Jewish Quarter. The Jewish city Town Hall, with its Hebrew-faced clock, still stands there. Synagogues stretching back to the deep Middle Ages are open for public inspection. We learned about the great Maharal and the legend of the Golem of Prague. We toured the surreal Jewish cemetery of Prague, stepping back in time.

In a little village thirty miles south of Vienna, we visited the tiny former Jewish ghetto of Eisenstaedt. When Napoleon razed the gates to Jewish ghettos across the European continent, his soldiers somehow missed the entrance to the Jewish quarter of this village, where a famous rabbinical Yeshiva once operated in the shadow of the palace of the Esterhazys and the studio of their court musician, Joseph Haydn. Inside the ghetto, we climbed up narrow ramparts and found our way to the private synagogue of the town's court Jew. Someone had left a torn Torah on the reader's desk. I read the *Sh'ma* and the *V'ahavta* to our group, an echo of sounds long gone, echoes of the sound of *teruah* inside the gates of Eisenstadt.

The signs of Judaism's entrance into modernity also punctuated our trip wherever we went. In Budapest, a marker in the synagogue indicated the spot where Theodor Herzl's childhood home once stood. From there, Herzl went on to found the World Zionist Movement in the wake of the infamous Dreyfus trial. A Jewish officer in the French Army, Dreyfus was betrayed by a member of the Esterhazy family, whose palace we saw in Eisenstaedt. In Vienna, we visited the Stadttempel, whose lobby included a memorial to Salomon Sulzer, one of the two principal architects of the grand music of classical Reform Judaism. In Prague, we learned about the life of Franz Kafka and his struggle with the Judaism of his father's generation. European Judaism variously experimented with assimilation, reform, and nationalism in search of a new sound, a new *teruah* to adjust itself to the new order of modern Jewish life.

But modernity failed the Jews of Europe, and that failure was most poignantly depicted in the monuments of Vienna's Judenplatz. At one end of the square was a handsome statue of Gotthold Ephraim Lessing, the great advocate of reason in Central Europe's Enlightenment. Lessing was among the first who believed that Jews could become full citizens of the new European state. The personal example he pointed to was the brilliant Berlin Jewish philosopher Moses Mendelssohn. Lessing was right. Jews were able and deeply wanted to be citizens of Europe's emerging nation-states of France, Germany, and Austria. But ultimately, enough reactionary, xenophobic Europeans did not want either Jews or Judaism in their midst. They did not want to hear the sound of the shofar in the courtyards of Krakow and Budapest and Prague. And so they organized themselves to drown out our sounds in our screams and our blood.

Other modern Europeans were simply indifferent. The people of Oświęcim could look across the main rail line of their town and see the killing camp at Birkenau. In Cracόw, a single gentile, a pharmacist, elected to remain in the ghetto established by the Nazis to minister to the medical needs of the unwanted Jewish populace. And on the other side of town, we stood in front of Oscar Schindler's famous factory, the most daring rescue effort in that city, a site that still does not have a marker to testify Schindler as a righteous gentile.

A group of thirty-six people from KI and six other friends also stood with me at the end of the tracks deep inside Birkenau, the killing camp in a tri-part complex known as Auschwitz. Situated on a large plain, Auschwitz II, as it is commonly known, is a city of the dead. It is vast, and it is ghastly. Barbed-wire fences still stretch around its perimeter. A thousand broken chimneys still stand where barracks once housed hundreds of thousands of slave laborers. Piles of collapsed bricks still mark the spot where four crematoria stood and spewed the ashes of the children of Israel into the sky and fields of southern Poland. In an age that rejects absolutes, Auschwitz stands as a monument to absolute evil, a place of absolute silence, where no *teruah* is heard.

Remarkably, as we gathered for a brief memorial service inside the camp, a group of wild foxes came out of the woods behind us. In my mind, an Aggadic passage from the second century came rushing forward. The rabbis were in mourning, Jerusalem was in ruins, and the mountain where the Temple stood was desolate—so desolate that foxes played where sacrifices had once been offered. Now, foxes played on the killing fields across from the village of Oświęcim and its indescribable memory of horrors.

Nowhere, however, did the reality of European Jewish life strike us more than in the remote Bohemian village of Telč. We had been traveling from Vienna to Prague and, by arrangement, had stopped for lunch in this beautiful baroque town. Nothing on the itinerary or in any guidebook suggested there was a Jewish dimension to Telč. From a discussion in broken English with a saleslady in the town's bookstore, I learned that the police station, two blocks off the main square, had once been a synagogue. Only a broken Jewish star on the iron railing betrayed the building's original purpose. A visit to the town's museum resulted in more information. The entrance to the village's church had a Holocaust Memorial. We went there as a group. A sheet of marble with the names of the last sixty Jews of the town, and the concentration camps where they perished, stared us in the face. We read their names aloud. We didn't know any of them, but we cried as if we were saying Kaddish for members of our own family.

Our bus driver learned that a Jewish cemetery had been left intact on the outskirts of Telč. Our group found its way to a wooded area in a distant field. There, behind high brick walls, the ancient Jews of Telč slept for eternity. But the gate was locked, and we couldn't get in to read the inscriptions. Symbolically, the youngest member of our group, our son Judah, climbed the wall and took pictures of everyone from the inside. We are not to be denied our heritage.

Two weeks later, a kind of miracle happened. We had returned to the States, and I had taken Judah to the Jewish summer camp where our family has gone for the last thirteen years, in the Hudson Highlands near West Point, New York. One night, an Israeli scout came to visit us. Sixteen years old, brilliant, and lively, Sheked needed a night of "family bonding"; and our door is always open. He told us about his life in Herzliya, north of Tel Aviv, and how his father's family had come from Russia. "What about your mother's family?" I asked.

"Oh," he said, "you won't know where they came from."

"Try me," I replied.

"They come from a little village in the former Czechoslovakia. My grandfather recently went back to the village he grew up in."

"What's it called?" I asked.

And Sheked answered, "It's called Telč ."

From the town's walled cemetery, from its abandoned synagogue, from the names of its Jewish martyrs on the wall of St. James, the distant sound of the shofar pierced my being.

One last scene from our trip this summer. Our final excursion was to the Terezin concentration camp north of Prague. Terezin had been a walled city garrison before the Holocaust. Originally built as a Hapsburg fort, it was used by the Nazis as a showcase concentration camp, the place where the Nazis successfully duped the International Red Cross about the real purpose of German concentration camps.

Terezin is also the place where the famous "Butterfly Poem" was written by one of the young people interred there. I read these words, written by Pavel Friedman, to our group in front of the restored crematoria at Terezin:

> The last, the very last,
> So richly, brightly, dazzlingly yellow.
> Perhaps if the sun's tears would sing
> Against a white stone.
> Such, such a yellow,
> Is carried lightly way up high.
> It went away I'm sure because it wished
> To kiss the world goodbye.
> For seven weeks I've lived in here,
> Penned up inside this ghetto
> But I have found my people here,
> The dandelions call to me
> And the white chestnut candles in the court.
> Only I never saw another butterfly.

That butterfly was the last one.
Butterflies don't live in here,
In the ghetto.

Terezin is also the place where the great rabbi Leo Baeck accompanied the last Jews of Berlin to their deaths, ministered to them, and wrote a classic work, *This People Israel: The Meaning of Jewish Existence*. Even in Terezin, with his own home and home synagogue destroyed, Rabbi Baeck continued to teach the meaning of *tekiah*, *teruah*, and *shevarim*.

So much happened to us at Terezin in just a few hours, it remains unimaginable. After holding our brief memorial service, a survivor of Terezin, now a resident of Great Britain, joined our group and talked with us about his time there. As we accompanied Joseph to the bus, butterflies flew out of the woods and into our path. There are butterflies again at Terezin.

Our guide then asked us if we wanted to see something extraordinary. Of course, we did. She took us to a street of row homes in the residential part of the village and talked to the owner of one of the houses. He let our group pass through his modest garden and enter his garage. A painter had discovered some Hebrew writing on the wall there; and after a little more investigative work was done, it was determined that this garage, in the heart of Terezin concentration camp, was a secret synagogue, organized and decorated by a group of Jewish craftsmen. On the wall, above where the leader of the prayers stood, was an inscription from the prayer "*R'tzei*" which we recite every Friday night here at KI. "May our eyes behold your return to Zion in mercy," the Hebrew said. Prayer, the sound of the shofar, hope was intoned even in a concentration camp.

From across the miles and over the sea, the sound of the shofar—the sound of a muted alarm, the sound of *teruah*—echoes in the dark. Jewish life in Europe has been decimated. And although there are still pockets of strength in England, France, Russia, and now Germany, Europe is no longer the center of Jewish life. In Poland, where over three million Jews still lived in 1939, there are now fewer than five thousand Jews, most of them elderly. In all of Poland, there is only one Jewish kindergarten today. The Talmud teaches that even if it can be repaired, a badly damaged shofar is no longer valid.

Jewish life in Europe is broken. The center of Jewish life there has been transplanted to Israel and to America, where the sound of the shofar calls to action and continues to warn us of the physical and spiritual dangers of modern Jewish life.

In Europe, the sound of *teruah* is now mostly the sound of a eulogy. In today's world, the shofar is now on the lips of young soldiers in the land of our ancestors and in the hands of our children in America. Tomorrow, we shall discuss the sound of the shofar in Israel and its call to courage. Then, on Yom Kippur Eve, we will explore how *shevarim*—the broken, ambivalent note—has come to characterize Jewish life in North America, Philadelphia, and perhaps many of our homes.

The question before us is, what kind of shofar sound can we make this New Year? Does our soul break into pieces like *shevarim* before the challenges of Jewish life? Are we worried like a *teruah*? Or are we ready to move on and recommit, to blast our Jewish declaration that we are prepared to rebuild the house of Israel in America? Together, we will explore all these possibilities. Together, we will search for the way to sound a *tekiah gedolah*, a call to return, to *tikkun olam*, to redemption, in our own age, and in our own lives.

On this eve of the new year 5763, may you be blessed with renewed Jewish resolve. May you learn to discover the great shofar of return in your hearts. May you sound the clarion call of *tekiah* in your private and your public lives. May you be blessed with health, well-being, and peace in the year ahead.

Amen.

Shabbat Shalom. Shana Tova.

You Went to Germany?

September 26, 2003, Rosh HaShanah Evening 5763

From the moment I proposed a congregational trip to Germany two years ago, I encountered doubt, resistance, and even a little anger from numerous individuals who had heard about it.

"You're going where?"

"Why are you going there?"

"I wouldn't spend a dime on anything German!"

"They don't deserve a visit from you or anybody else."

"They should all rot."

And those were the nice reactions.

Even when I shared the idea with a seasoned travel agent, she warned that Germany was a bit of a stretch. "I've been in the business a long time," she told me, "and I haven't sent a Jewish group to Germany yet."

"We'll see," I said, with a little bravado.

"On the other hand," the agent began to reason like a Talmudic scholar, "not many Jewish people from this area have gone to Germany, and maybe there's a little market niche there."

"We'll see," I said.

The fact of the matter is that most American Jews instinctively don't like Germany or things German. It is more than understandable. The Holocaust is still a living memory. We have many survivors in our midst. We also have many veterans who served in the European theater during World War II. It is almost inconceivable to think about normalizing German-Jewish relations, at least at this point in history. Maybe in another twenty-five or thirty or forty years, when there is no living connection between the horrors of the Nazi past and the present, it will be possible.

There are also other deep reasons at work here, which explain how most American Jews feel about Germany.

If you turn the clock back fifty years or more, there were widespread tensions within the American Jewish community between East European Jews and the old German Jewish guard. Many of you remember how those communal and social dynamics played out. Mixing East European and German Jews was like mixing oil and water.

There is also a nagging suspicion, but on close analysis, a very hurtful proposition that "the German Jews of the 1920s and 1930s brought it on themselves." "They wanted to assimilate," you hear over and over. "They wanted to be Germans. They are to blame for the Holocaust themselves."

Buried deep in this (outrageous) allegation is a painful recognition that we in the American Jewish community look a great deal like the German Jewish community of pre-1932.

We are, as a community, totally at home in this country. Indeed, the statistical benchmarks of assimilation, as reported in the 1990 and the 2000 National Jewish Population Surveys, are even greater here and now than they ever were in Germany during the Weimar Republic. Alarmists among us even talk about a "bloodless Holocaust" in America, as assimilation and social absorption into American culture steadily erode Jewishness and Judaism in this country.

Sometimes I feel we don't want to look at the German Jewish experience, particularly the modern German Jewish experience with its remarkable record of Nobel Prize winners, artists, musicians, actors, writers, leading business leaders, department store owners, newspaper publishers, athletes, doctors, lawyers, professors, and social activists because we can see too much of ourselves in them.

The fact of the matter is that the basic paradigm of modern Jewish life was worked out, almost completely, with all its problems and challenges, as well as with its remarkable accomplishments, in Germany. In many ways, any Jew who speaks the vernacular of the society in which he or she lives as the primary language, dresses like the people around him or her, and participates in the contemporary world of athletics and entertainment but still views him or herself as a Jew is a cultural descendant of German Jewry.

Modern Jewish life was born in Germany.

Reform Judaism was born in Germany.

The modern academic study of Judaism was born in Germany.

Simply put, we as American Jews walk in the cultural pathways pioneered by the Jews of Germany a century or more ago.

But there is more—much more—to this story.

If we push our collective memory further back, way back to the beginning of the Middle Ages, we discover that Ashkenazic Jewish culture, the dominant expression of Jewish life in Europe and America, first emerged in Germany and then, only centuries later, spread to Poland, Russia, and Ukraine.

The Yiddish language first emerged in Germany. The practice of saying the Mourners' Kaddish and observing Yahrzeit first emerged in Germany. The bread we use on Friday nights for *HaMotzi* is of German origin. The basic melodies of many of our prayers are of German origin. "*Adon Olam*" is based on a bell song from German churches, the tune to "*Ein Keloheinu*" is from a German beer-drinking song, and "Rock of Ages," the magnificent Hanukkah hymn we sing during the Festival of Lights, was an old tune also used by Martin Luther. Even the idea of seminary-trained "preaching" rabbis is German.

To understand ourselves as modern Jews, we need to know the basics about the German Jewish experience. I would add that to fully appreciate the Holocaust and modern anti-Semitism, it is also necessary to encounter Germany, to confront firsthand the unimaginable coexistence of a modern country with impressive cities, universities, museums, and opera houses with the most barbaric chapter in all of human history. The total evil called Nazism cannot be measured until it is placed against the background of Goethe, Beethoven, Schiller, and Einstein.

It is not just that Nazism resulted in the murder of six million Jews, 1.5 million of them children, and that Germany was responsible for a world war in which innumerable millions of people were killed, maimed, or permanently uprooted from their places of birth; but it is the insane fact that some of the most advanced, cultured, intellectual, scientific people in the world were responsible for these unprecedented crimes against us and against humanity.

To go to Germany is to stand in the middle of the greatest contradiction in human history. Think about what happened during the course of the twentieth century to all of humanity, not just the Jews but the whole human race. Think about the incredible advances in science, medicine, transportation technology, communications, engineering, computers, and miniaturization. We sent a man to the moon and launched satellites into the deep recesses of outer space. Think about all those wonderful accomplishments, our own high standard of living, and the incredible bounty we enjoy and then balance that picture against the fact that the twentieth century was also the bloodiest century in history.

More than one hundred million people were killed in war from 1900 to 1999. Weapons of mass destruction were developed. Chemical warfare was used for the first time. Dictatorial states were established not only in Germany but also in Russia and China and North Korea, more brutal and cruel than anything that ever preceded them. Even the Holocaust itself is decidedly modern because it took a modern state to industrialize death on a scale the Inquisition or pogromists could never have imagined.

Nowhere is the greatest contradiction in history, the most perplexing enigma of all, more palatable, more pressing, more bothersome than in modern Germany, and nothing is more contradictory, more tragic, more hopeful than the Jewish experience in Germany.

The enigma called Jewish existence is again being reenacted in Germany today, unlike anywhere else on the planet. If you had told me twenty-five years ago that Jews would begin moving back to Germany in large numbers, that Germany would become the fastest-growing Jewish community in the world, that more Jews would choose to settle in Germany than in Israel on an annual basis, and that it would become statistically probable that the pre-Hitler level of the Jewish population would ever be restored in Germany, I would have told you that you were crazy. But that is exactly what is happening in German today. I needed to see this latest chapter in the unfolding of Jewish history for myself, and I wanted to take as many of you along for the ride as possible.

But my interest in German Jewish life is not just historical or rabbinic. It is also personal. My mother, who is here today with my father, was born in Germany, in a little town in the geographical center of Europe. Bamberg was no different than any other town in Germany. Its Jewish community, barely a thousand people at its height, was nearly a thousand years old. Over the centuries, fifty-three different Torah scrolls were accumulated and placed in the city's beautiful Moorish-style synagogue. Jews prospered there, helped improve the civic quality of their town, and fought for their "homeland" in wars against the French, the British, the Russians, and even the Americans. They were part of the warp and woof of daily life, and they openly practiced Judaism.

And then came the Nazis. In a matter of just a few years, the Jews of Bamberg were systematically deprived of their rights, their property, and their lives. They were terrorized, humiliated, arrested, tortured, exiled, quarantined, and, finally, murdered.

Not one single Jewish family from before World War II remains in Bamberg today. Except for a historical marker here or there, there is virtually no visible sign of Jewish life left to the untrained eye in this little city on the northern edge of Bavaria.

Only a tiny skeletal community of survivors, Displaced Persons, and their children stayed on after the war. For a meeting place, they were given a small room in the center of town without any external Jewish markings.

And then, out of nowhere, with the fall of Communism in 1989, Jews began moving back to Germany, back to Bamberg, back to places where Jewish life had been destroyed a generation earlier. Today, because of immigration, there are as many Jews in Bamberg as there were before Hitler came to power. And slowly, surely, Jewish life is being restored in Berlin, Frankfurt, Munich, and in smaller cities across the map of Germany.

Jews have become preferred immigrants in Germany. The country is unwilling to impose a quota on Jewish immigration, and Jewish immigrants are afforded the full benefits of Germany's extensive social service system. Indeed, at least within various levels of government, from the local level to the federal government in Berlin, there is even an eagerness to restore Jewish life. The eastern city of Leipzig is actually building a synagogue in anticipation of Jews resettling there.

What has been happening in Bamberg and throughout Germany is nothing short of absurd and miraculous, and that absurd miracle has physically and spiritually touched my family.

Approximately seventy-five years ago, my grandfather purchased a silk factory in Bamberg. It was profitable and respected in the community and the thread industry. In 1938, the business was Aryanized, and the building and its machinery were confiscated by local Nazi officials. My mother was sent to America alone. Her parents and brother lived for a few more agonizing months in the belly of the beast until fleeing and reuniting a year later in New York. The factory itself sustained only light damage during the war, but the building was intact.

After the war, there was a reparations trial, and a minimal settlement was made. The factory officially passed into other hands, and my family's connection to it ended forever, or so we thought. In 1953, fifty years ago, the factory was closed. The machinery was removed, and the building began to deteriorate. It was given to the Bavarian Jewish Council, but they had no use for it. It stood empty for fifty years—until last year.

Every time we return the Torah to the ark, we sing, "Return us, Lord, restore us to how we were in former times." Those words were not lost on the leader of Bamberg's Jewish community. Heinrich Olmer was born in Bamberg after the war. His parents were survivors from Poland. They were settled in the large DP camp near Bamberg but never moved on. Somehow, they instilled a sense of Jewish pride and purpose in their son.

An economics teacher by training, Heinrich spearheaded an effort to build a new synagogue in Bamberg for its burgeoning Jewish community. The old prewar synagogue was destroyed on Kristallnacht. The flames of the burning temple were visible from my grandparents' home. The leading Jewish citizen of the community of the prewar period, Willy Lessing, an industrialist and former city council member, ran to the synagogue and begged the storm troopers to give him just one of the fifty-three Torah scrolls. Just one scroll, so Jewish life could go on, even in the midst of Nazi persecution. His request was met with a vicious beating with iron bars brought to the scene by the Nazi thugs to tear the synagogue to pieces. Lessing never recovered and died two months later from his wounds. Thirty of us from KI stood at his grave this summer in silent tribute to this Jewish hero.

Before we arrived in Bamberg, we had already toured the Rhineland and visited the sites of medieval rabbinic academies, ancient Jewish cemeteries, and semi-restored neighborhoods that had been Jewish ghettos in the twelfth, thirteenth, and fourteenth centuries. We already developed a basic understanding of the complex history of the German Jews and firsthand knowledge of what contemporary general life is like in Germany.

By the time we left our hotel in Bamberg and walked one block up Willy Lessing Street, the main thoroughfare of Bamberg so renamed after the war, we were no longer strangers in Germany. And when we learned that both the current Jewish community room and my grandfather's factory were located on Willy Lessing Strasse, we knew we were in for something extraordinary.

Detail by detail, we learned from Heinrich Olmer how he had successfully lobbied the Bavarian Jewish Council, the mayor of Bamberg, the president of the Bamberg University, executives at the local Bosch factory (the largest employer in Bamberg), and numerous individuals to rebuild my grandfather's factory on Willy Lessing Strasse as the new synagogue and Jewish Community Center of Bamberg. Later that day, in a private meeting in his office, he also proceeded to tell me how he envisioned the new synagogue to be the great interfaith center of Bamberg, a place of meeting for the whole community, a place whose mission was to advocate tolerance and promote healing.

Late on Friday afternoon, July the Fourth, we stood in front of the factory, now mostly a construction site, and said prayers of rededication with Heinrich. That night, we joined the local Jewish community for Shabbat services. The house was full, and a special Oneg Shabbat had been prepared. When Olmer introduced my mother to the congregation and explained her connection to the factory, and soon-to-be synagogue, the room broke out in sustained applause.

At the Oneg, we were absorbed into the crowd. To our surprise, we met an Israeli family who had come to the area to study the production of beer. We also met a Jewish dentist from Long Island who had settled in Bamberg, and most remarkable of all, we met the town's piano tuner, a Jewish man from Philadelphia and a graduate of Central High School. There were Jews from Russia, Ukraine, and other parts of Germany. There were converts to Judaism and non-Jewish spouses who identified with the reborn Jewish community of Bamberg. There were even Jewish children in a place where, not so long ago, all the local Jewish children had been marked for extermination.

In Bamberg, we came face-to-face with the full sweep of the tragedy and miracle of Jewish existence. Twenty-five centuries ago, the prophet Isaiah compared the Jewish people to a tree that had been cut down to a mere stump and to a fresh, tender new shoot that again grew out of the stump. The new shoot of the Jewish tradition was literally growing on the site of my grandfather's old factory. Collectively, we knew that we had witnessed the miracle of Jewish survival.

A day later, we were on our way south to Munich with a stop at Nuremberg. Nuremberg, as you know, was the spiritual center of Nazism. It is not a place where many tourists go. An immense stadium built by Hitler for a quarter of a million storm troopers still stands there in an area now used exclusively for sports and family recreation. We went to that awful place to explore the heart of Nazism. Our bus pulled up to the huge marble grandstand built by Hitler, where forty thousand party officials once stood behind the speaker's box to lead the sea of storm troopers in repeated chants of Sieg Heil! We shivered from historical memories in the grayness of that summer day.

Sitting in our bus with the doors closed before we left the rally ground, we listened to an audio recording of Hitler and Goebbels at one of the Nuremberg rallies. The whole demonic force of that place pierced us. Images of quaint, charming Bamberg, the graves of martyrs, the faces of the new immigrants, the memorial markers that stood in naked plazas where synagogues once stood, all streamed through us, rendering us speechless and drained and more knowledgeable about Germany, the Holocaust, and the meaning of Jewish existence than we ever imagined we could be. After Bamberg and Nuremberg, none of us were the same people who had left Philadelphia a week earlier.

The last few days of our trip were spent in Berlin, where Germany's imperial past still collides with Weimar culture and where the physical remnants of the Nazi era and the Communist period are retreating behind massive efforts to recast Germany as a modern, postindustrial democracy. We climbed the spiral steps of the new Reichstag and explored the hallways of the city's striking new Jewish Museum. We listened to a lecture at the Wansee Conference Center, where, in a matter of an hour and a half in January 1942, in a disconcertingly beautiful lakefront palace, the Nazi high command worked out the plans for the Final Solution and its goal of eleven million Jewish deaths.

As a group, we also went to the first general conference of Reform Judaism in Germany since 1928 and visited the campus of the University of Potsdam, where the first liberal rabbinic school in Central Europe is now being created by a handful of visionaries in the very place where Reform Judaism first emerged in history.

But more than anywhere else, the site of the New Synagogue in downtown Berlin seemed to capture the moment for us. Built in the 1860s, it was absolutely massive, with three thousand permanent seats in the sanctuary, considerably larger than this room as it is configured this morning. The building was topped with the finest dome of any synagogue in the world. The greatest rabbis and cantors in Germany led services from its marble bimah. And then it was destroyed. The sanctuary was demolished. The dome caved in, and only the front facade remained.

Today it is a partly restored building. The dome is back, and the front of the synagogue is restored. But the space where the sanctuary once stood is now an open-air memorial. In an outside rock garden, fragments of the stone Ark stand where active worship once took place.

The Great Synagogue of Berlin is a massive monument to what was the glory of Jewish life in Germany. It is also a stark reminder of what was lost and, in its own way, a beacon of what might yet be brought back to that place and throughout the world.

Standing in the huge hollow space of the Oranienburgerstrasse Synagogue in Berlin, my mind began to wander until it came to thoughts of home. The juxtaposition of contemporary Jewish life in Germany and America was leaving me with an uneasy feeling. There in America, in this land of freedom and constitutionally protected rights, our synagogues have massive exteriors and their interiors are in good repair, but there are generally more memorial plaques than active worshippers. In one place, the glory of Israel was destroyed by hate. On the other, it is on the edge of collapse from indifference, institutional failure, and Jewish illiteracy.

On this Rosh HaShanah, let us learn again to heed the call of Emil Fackenheim, one of the great Jewish philosophers of the twentieth century and an exiled German Jew, who taught us about the 614th commandment. Fackenheim, who died just a few days ago, once observed that, according to the Talmud, there are 613 commandments, *Taryag Mitzvot* in Hebrew. But the 614th commandment—the commandment of our time, he taught—is not to give Hitler a posthumous victory.

It is very easy to take exception to everything German and denounce Nazism and anti-Semitism and the destruction of European Jewish life. It is much more difficult to come to terms with the very real challenges to Jewish life in this country and in this community.

I learned a great deal in Germany this summer. I learned about the relentless anti-Semitism of the Middle Ages. I learned about the many achievements of the German Jewish community before the Nazis came to power. I learned how, in town after town, the Nazis eradicated Jewish life so thoroughly that all that remains today are a few broken stones where proud synagogues once stood. I learned about where my family came from, and I learned about the miracle of Jewish self-renewal—about how one person in a small isolated community is making his Jewish dream come true of not letting a thousand years of Jewish life perish without a fight.

I learned about the little green shoot on the stump that Isaiah described in Jerusalem so long ago.

I learned something about the Jewish spirit, which was instilled in me by my parents, teachers, and rabbis. I learned about the historical moment we are all living and our place in it.

As a people, we have suffered endless degradations, violence, and merciless slaughter. We also have never given up, never allowed the eternal light of hope to go out, never abandoned the fundamental Jewish belief—that the world must hear—that the human being is the crown of creation and it is our job to repair the broken crown.

We have a message that must be preserved for the sake of humanity. We have kept the heritage of Torah alive in the worst of circumstances. Now we are bringing Torah back to places where it was desecrated and brutally crushed.

We also have the opportunity, without any external constraint, to make Judaism thrive in this country, in this city, in this building. If the Jews of Bamberg can do it just fifty years after the fall of the Third Reich, then the members of Reform Congregation Keneseth Israel can do it too in the birthplace of American freedom.

At the beginning of this new year, let us vow to fill these halls with the voices of children and their parents and their grandparents, with the sounds of our tradition, with messages of hope and compassion, with a renewed determination to be of service to our larger community, with pride in being the children of an ancient people, and with the conviction that our heritage should live and thrive and proclaim its mighty truths for all to hear—to do justly, to love mercy and to walk humbly with our God.

Amen.

Shabbat Shalom.

A good year.

A Red Thread: Uncommon Threads

2003

Fabric and, more specifically, thread has been a big part of my life. Before our family fled and resettled in the United States, my mother's father, Max Sacki, produced silk thread products in his factory in Bamberg, Germany. Today, his factory has been renovated and is the new Jewish Community Center of Bamberg, complete with a synagogue, *mikvah* (ritual bath), Hebrew school, and an interfaith learning center.

In 1992, when I went to Bamberg for the first time, I located the then-abandoned factory. (It still had a hole in the roof from an American bomb dropped from an airplane.) It was a very strange, even eerie experience. The building was completely empty but still worth exploring. I combed all of it and decided to go into the basement. I found one free-standing closet downstairs with its doors ajar. When I opened the closet, I was amazed to see red silk spools lined up on the shelves. I took as many of them as I could carry.

When I got home, the family gathered around my parents' dining room table. Without saying a word, I took the spools out of my luggage and set them on the table. It was a rare moment when my childhood house was silent. But the sight of the spools brought everything and everyone to a total stop. "Where in the world did you find them?" someone barked. I explained. They were amazed. No one had seen such a spool in over fifty years.

"I didn't know they even existed anymore," someone whispered.

My mother then told us that when she had left Germany alone as a child in 1938, her parents had taken empty spools, wrapped money around the central axis, and then, by hand, wound the silk so that they looked like business samples. Thus, they provided my mother with financial resources for the road. If not for a red thread, I would not be reporting this story.

Along the way, I learned about a kabbalistic practice of wearing a red thread. Peddlers sell them at the Western Wall in Jerusalem. The first time I purchased a red Jerusalem thread, the seller told me I should wear it because it would bring me good luck. "You bet your life," I said as I put it on my wrist and then proceeded to go to the Wall to give thanks for my family whose life literally hung by a thread.

The Roadblock to Peace

October 3, 3003, Yom Kippur Evening 5764

Yesterday's devastating news from Israel came as no surprise. A young Palestinian woman walked into a well-known restaurant in Haifa, an establishment frequented regularly by both Arabs and Jews. She shot and killed the security guard and then detonated an explosive belt wrapped around her body. The carnage was horrifying and massive. People on the street, positioned just beyond the blast's deadly range, rushed to the scene to help. But there were few survivors to accept their aid. Nineteen dead were scattered on the restaurant's floor; four of them were little children.

Three weeks ago, a similar explosion rocked a café in a Jerusalem suburb. Among the dead was David Applebaum, a medical doctor and American immigrant to Israel. Also killed was his twenty-year-old daughter, Nava. Nava was to be married the next day, September 11. The two were having coffee just to spend time together before the big day. Dr. Applebaum had just returned from a lecture tour in the United States. Ironically, his specialty and the theme of his lecture series were emergency room procedures and triage in the treatment of large numbers of critically wounded victims. Everyone who knew Dr. Applebaum, including the American Medical Association in their press release, referred to him as a "hero of humanitarianism."

The sickening reality of life in the Middle East today is that the roadmap to peace has again been blocked by a reign of terror, violence, and visceral hatred. The plan released by the Bush administration only six months ago is now just another scrap of paper in the dustbin of plans.

Accords and interim steps have failed to bring even a measure of peace and normalcy to Israel and the Middle East. If it wasn't so tragic, it would be laughable to think that phase one of the roadmap, an end to terrorism by May 2003 and the creation of the infrastructure of a Palestinian state, at the present time was anything more than a pipe dream. The American invasion of Afghanistan and Iraq, and their promise of disrupting the global network of terrorism, has not changed the dynamics of the Arab-Israeli conflict. As this morning's news shows, terrorist training camps still operate openly in Syria with recruits from around the world in their programs. Indeed, in the Arab-Israeli conflict, terrorism has continued to intensify, seeking ever new levels of depravity and finding theologically sanctioned justifications for murder.

The reason the roadmap has not led to peace for Israel and her neighbors is the fact that a primarily historical and willful roadblock to peace still exists in the Middle East. That roadblock is the widespread belief, among Palestinian leaders as well as within the general Palestinian population, that Israel and Zionism can be defeated. Call it the Crusader thesis, that a long war of attrition will eventually drive the enemy out, or "revolutionary romanticism" or "religious triumphalism." The roadblock is mobile, deadly, and capable of blocking every or any effort to make peace with Israel.

It is no small coincidence that the ideological father of the contemporary global suicide bomber movement and a principal mentor of Osama bin Laden is the late Abdullah Azzam, a Palestinian born in Jenin in 1941 and, later, leader of the Afghan Jihad movement. Indeed, the greater the diplomatic activity in the direction of peace, the greater the countereffort to block the road to peace in the Palestinian camp. In my opinion, the failure to curb Palestinian extremism is not just a matter of power and organization but also the reflection of a fundamental ambivalence among the Palestinian people, who are seemingly more dedicated to the destruction of Israel than to the creation of a viable Palestinian state.

On numerous occasions, whether it was a pre-State of Israel discussion on binationalism, the 1947 Partition of Palestine into autonomous Jewish and Arab sectors, the Oslo Accords, or the subsequent Barak Plan, it has always been one side and one side only that has been willing to trade land for peace—and that is the Israeli side.

In the 1920s and 1930s, the Arabs rioted to try to drive the Jews out of British Palestine. Their leader, the Grand Mufti of Jerusalem, Haj Amin al-Husseini, had not openly aligned with the Nazis and their genocidal policies but served as the Nazis' chief propagandist to the Arab world.

In 1947, the Arab world launched a guerilla war and then a multistate invasion to destroy Israel.

In 1967, Nasser dreamed of driving the Jews into the sea. When he was soundly defeated, the PLO and the Arab world circled their wagons in Khartoum in Sudan and declared to the world that they would never recognize Israel's right to exist. To this day, they have never properly retracted that statement.

In 1974, Yasser Arafat stepped up to the podium of the UN with a pistol strapped to his belt, and five years later, in Resolution 3379, the organization designed to represent the whole of humanity officially adopted the position that "Zionism is Racism," the modern equivalent of a medieval blood libel. At the same time, the Saudi regime has worked diligently to disseminate the fraudulent Protocols of the Elders of Zion and its preposterous claim of a criminal Jewish conspiracy to rule the world.

In 1988, the First Intifada erupted. The Hamas movement was born to challenge and resist any effort to reconcile with Israel and to terrorize anyone they deemed to be collaborators. Hamas came into existence to destroy Israel and counter any attempt at Arab-Israeli reconciliation.

All this and still deep within Israeli society a yearning for peace remained alive. Children sang songs of peace. A peace movement was born; and great generals, Rabin and Barak, for pragmatic reasons, embrace the Oslo Accords and offered even more generous plans of their own.

What was the response in the Palestinian community to the Oslo and Rabin-Barak initiative? To seize upon the brazen grandstanding of Ariel Sharon in his march to the Temple Mount and to launch a Second Intifada with murderous results. Since the High Holy Days of the year 2000, just three years ago, nearly 2,500 Palestinians and 900 Israelis have been killed in sustained and vicious violence.

Hidden in those statistics is a grim reality. Among the Palestinian dead, eighty-four of the 2,500 who died have been women. Among the Israeli victims, 258 out of nearly 900, not including the most recent attacks, have been noncombatant women. In other words, the numbers verify what is already known. The Israeli struggle is to preserve a state and to attack military and strategic targets. The Palestinian struggle is to destroy a people, principally by attacking noncombatants— women, immigrants, and children.

In my opinion, there is no moral parity between Israel's efforts to defend itself and Palestinian attempts to destroy the Jewish state. That is why, when *Newsweek* magazine linked together a murdered Israeli teenager and her Palestinian female killer as equals, there was such a hue and cry. And that is also why, when the Israeli writer and peace activist Amos Oz wrote in an op-ed piece in the *New York Times* this summer that Sharon and Arafat were equally cowards, he was forced to retract his statement in shame.

There is no moral parity in the Arab-Israeli conflict, and as American Jews, we should never doubt the validity of Israel's right to exist and defend itself. That is not to excuse every action taken by the State of Israel or individual Israeli citizens. The invasion of Lebanon was a disaster. Baruch Goldstein was a murderer when he shot up a congregation of Muslim worshippers in Hebron on our holiday of Purim. The Jewish assassin who killed Yitzhak Rabin is a criminal. But as horrible as these and other incidents really are, they do not represent the basic commitment of the State of Israel to a comprehensive peace with its Arab neighbors.

By contrast, all the opinion polls confirm that the majority of Palestinians have not renounced the 1967 Khartoum Platform and have not abandoned their hope that the Jewish state will one day be destroyed. That, in short, is the real roadblock to peace.

Deeper than the question of the settlements, the precise location of the new security wall, the ultimate status of Jerusalem, and the Palestinian "right of return" is the question of whether or not the Palestinians can acknowledge the legitimacy of the State of Israel, of whether or not a Jewish Israel and an Arab Palestine can coexist.

I personally came to understand this problem several years ago when Hanan Ashrawi spoke on the campus of Binghamton University. It was the most disingenuous, duplicitous speech I have ever heard. Yes, she said, she believed in a two-state solution, Palestine and Israel. But, she added, the right of return would have to be invoked in Israel proper. In other words, she wanted her state—and the Jewish state too—to be open to Palestinian resettlement. Not a word was mentioned about the dispossession of hundreds of thousands of Jews, fully absorbed by the young State of Israel, who had been forced to flee their homes from Egypt, Iraq, Yemen, and other Arab countries. Not a word was mentioned about the right of Jews to settle in the sector she called Palestine.

Some of you may still be asking yourselves, "Do the Jews really have a claim to any part of the land of Israel in modern times? Isn't Israel really an Arab land?"

The answer is the Jewish people have a claim to a part of the land of Israel today, yesterday, and tomorrow. Jewish people have been on the land since time immemorial. Moreover, the same exact ideology that helped define Arab nationalism at the end of the nineteenth century and then led to the breakup of the multinational Ottoman Empire and the expulsion of the French and English in the twentieth century also helped define the modern nationalism of the Jewish people. The Jewish people have an equal and inalienable right to a homeland in part of Israel for solid historical, political, and cultural reasons. Indeed, if the Jewish claim to Israel is not valid, then no modern movement for national sovereignty is legitimate.

It is also important to understand that the widespread notion that the Jews, as a group, do not have the right to self-government, the basic premise of modern anti-Zionism, is, in essence, classical anti-Semitism in contemporary dress. In the Balfour Declaration and at the UN, the right of the Jewish people to establish a state in their historic homeland has been affirmed by the family of nations and repeatedly rejected by those who would seek to deny the Jewish people their historic national rights.

After both World War I and World War II and, most recently, in September 2000, when an Arab State to be called Palestine was envisioned by diplomats and statesmen, the possibility of a limited Palestine was rejected by Arab extremists and intellectuals as well as shopkeepers and farmers. In the words of Abba Eban, "The Palestinians never miss an opportunity to miss an opportunity." And the results have been catastrophic for the world, for Israel, and, most of all, for the Palestinians themselves.

Without question, this last Intifada, now three years old, is no different. Thousands are dead and wounded in the Palestinian camp. Their already-weak economy has further eroded. Schools have been closed more than they have been open for three years. The Israeli military has strategically reentered areas they once left for diplomatic reasons. The infrastructure of a future Palestinian state is in considerably worse shape than it was three years ago. There are more checkpoints, settlements, and prisoners than before. In short, nothing is better, and just about everything is worse. Worst of all is that hope has faded into the distance, and the possibility of peace seems further away than ever.

Instead of dealing with the real roadblock to peace, some Palestinian leaders have recently focused on the Security Wall that Israel is now building along the borders of the West Bank and Gaza and attempted to make it the central issue in the historic conflict. The Security Wall is actually more than a wall. It is a complex system of fences and security apparatuses. The idea for a separation wall was hatched in response to the relentless suicide bombings initiated by Hamas and Islamic Jihad during the current Intifada. Something needed to be done to impede the movement of would-be bombers from their lairs in the territories. The result was the security fence and all the controversy that surrounded its construction.

Personally, I do not believe that a fence can solve a security problem. Moats rarely worked during the Middle Ages. The Maginot Line did not hold the Germans back. The Bar Lev Line did not stop the Egyptian forces from crossing the Suez Canal and taking up positions in the Sinai.

However, what the fence can do, and is doing, is begin the process of defining a border between the State of Israel and the future State of Palestine. The Palestinian leadership knows what is at stake and is, therefore, contesting every dunam of land the wall is encapsulating. On the other hand, rabid anti-Semites, including cartoonists engaged by the *Philadelphia Inquirer*, use the wall for fodder in their despicable anti-Israel propaganda. Shame on the *Philadelphia Inquirer* for running such a libelous political cartoon of a barbed-wire fence in the shape of a Jewish star!

Israel's biggest long-term problem is not terrorism or even the irrationality and intransigence of Yasser Arafat. It is demographic. The Arab birth rate in the Middle East reportedly exceeds the combined growth rates in natural increase and Jewish immigration to Israel. Even in the short run, the Jewish character of the State of Israel is clearly compromised by the growth of the Arab population. It is a simple Malthusian equation. The natural response to poverty and despair is fecundity, and unless Israel does something to separate from the Arab population in its midst, it will be destroyed from within. The security fence is Israel's first opportunity to define, strategically and demographically, the defensible borders for itself in the years to come.

Today, the most controversial part of the security fence involves the large settlement of Ariel in the north-central sector of the West Bank. It is a thriving town in the heart of the biblical Jewish homeland, ten miles or so past the 1967 border. For all the debate today about Ariel, even the Barak plan of 2000 called for its retention along with the city of Ma'ale Adumim, just to the east of Jerusalem. I personally would not want to live in Ariel or Ma'ale Adumim, but I also understand that it was long-term Arab intransigence that created the settler movement among Israelis.

On the other hand, the Sharon government has ordered the demolition of a number of outposts in the territories, particularly the smaller settlements located in essentially indefensible positions. Sharon has shown a willingness to stand up to YESHA and other settlers' groups if he has solid military reasons to do so. My hunch is that more settlements will be uprooted in the future, if and when a genuine peace process develops. The example of Yamit is instructive. Yamit was a Jewish settlement in the Sinai, and when the order came to dismantle it, the army complied, even in the face of significant civil disobedience.

Israel, in my opinion, needs to continue to position itself strategically and pragmatically in preparation for the day when the two-state solution is finally implemented. Holding on to all of the lands of Israel is even more dangerous than not letting go. The idea of a massive transfer of Arab populations out of a greater Israel is unlikely, and it is both mostly wrong and politically impossible. The goal of Zionism is not to uproot an entire people but to root itself in part of its historic homeland. Those who point to Pakistan or the resettlements of various ethnic groups within Stalinist Russia and even the ethnic policies of ancient Assyria should think about how poorly those plans have worked in other places before advocating transfer in the case of modern-day Israel.

Israel needs to remain strong—not only strong on the ground and in the air but also strong in spirit. The goal of the current intifada is to wear Israel down and break the spirit of the Jewish state. Its strategy is to make "Israeli suffering" intolerable, even if it means sustained, unbearable suffering for the Palestinian people. It is a strategy, not unlike the Russian response to French, German, and other invaders, that we have more bodies than you have bullets. It is a dangerous and potentially successful strategy and a strategy that not only Israel but also the whole Jewish world must resist.

Israel is the most important experiment in modern Jewish life. It is the embodiment of the Jewish nation's will. It has revolutionized Jewish life in our time, recreated the Hebrew language as the vernacular of the Jewish people, and given Jews everywhere a harbor in any storm. It has more problems and issues and controversies than any other place I know of. It is simultaneously exciting, desperate, hopeful, modern, and ancient.

There is much we can do. We can support Israel politically and financially. We can encourage cultural, sports, and youth exchanges. We can fly the flag of Israel in Jewish institutions throughout the Diaspora. We can stay in touch with Israeli families and friends. We can keep ourselves informed on a daily basis and be ambassadors of the Jewish people in the circles of life in which we travel. And for those who are willing, we can go and visit there to express our solidarity with the State of Israel at the specific request of the Israeli government. If enough members of this synagogue are willing to participate in a congregational trip to Israel during the course of the next few months, we will provide the rabbinic leadership to staff it.

What is at play here is the Jewish principle of *Ahavat Yisrael*, the love of the Jewish people. If you love Israel, if you love the Jewish people, find a way, your way public and private, to demonstrate your support in the days and weeks ahead.

On this Yom Kippur, my mind goes back to this date, the Day of Atonement, thirty years ago. I had just returned home from part of my junior year at the Hebrew University of Jerusalem. The summer of 1973 was a golden time in the history of the Jewish State and in my life. I lived in a brand-new neighborhood along the water line where Jerusalem meets the Judean desert. From my room, I could see the Old City. I regularly walked its streets, ate in Arab cafés, and went to the Western Wall at will. For the first time in my life, I studied Hebrew in a serious fashion, and I made many Israeli friends. In the summer of 1973, Israel became my spiritual home, and I learned to walk around the streets of Jerusalem as if it were my hometown.

And then I returned to the States for my senior year. Early on the morning of Yom Kippur, my father woke me up with startling news. The Egyptians had crossed the Canal. Reports of casualties were staggering. In the days to come, I learned of the deaths of numerous young men I had befriended that summer. The person I considered my best friend at that time in my life was in a helicopter that had been shot down in Syria. The Syrian soldiers in that sector were under orders not to take prisoners and pumped multiple rounds into the bodies of all the survivors of the crash.

My friend survived, but like Israel, he had to endure years of depression and private anguish and pain. When we met again, he forced me to look at his wounds and dozens of wounds and amputations evident among other students at the Technion. That struggle has yet to cease. The road to peace is still blocked deep in the heart of the enemies of Israel. The roadblock to peace is the true front line in Israel's fight for survival and in the fight for the survival of Judaism and the Jewish people in our time.

On this Yom Kippur, let us vow to be resolute, firm, and courageous. Affirm your love of the Jewish people. Together, let us rehearse the words of Israel's national anthem, *"HaTikvah,"* in our hearts of hearts, *"Od lo avda tikvateinu."* We have not given up hope for Israel; for the Jewish people; for a way around the roadblocks; and for a time when there will be peace, security, and justice for all the children of Abraham.

Amen.

An easy fast.

HALF EMPTY OR HALF FULL: JUDAISM IN AMERICA

September 16, 2004, Rosh HaShanah Morning 5765

Three hundred fifty years ago this September 1, Jewish settlers arrived in New Amsterdam. Twenty-three Jews—displaced by the Portuguese reconquest of the Dutch city of Recife, Brazil—were in search of refuge and believed the Dutch colony on the Hudson River could serve as their haven from the storm. At first, local government and religious leaders worked to prevent them from unpacking and rooting in the community. However, the refugees eventually won the right to settle; applied for permission to do business; joined the local militia; and, in a year's time, wrote to Holland asking the Jews in the Dutch homeland to secure a Torah for them and send it to the New World.

None of these original twenty-three settlers could have imagined that they were the beachhead of what would become the most affluent, legally secure, and largest Jewish community in history. But slowly, other Jews came. By 1776, the Jewish population of the new United States had reached 2,500. By the time the Civil War broke out in 1861, that number had grown to 150,000. Within twenty years, a wave of Jewish immigrants from Tsarist Russia began moving toward the United States, resulting in the largest transfer of the Jewish population in history. By the time the gates to America closed because of restrictive legislation in the mid-1920s, only Poland had a greater Jewish population than the United States. In the wake of the Holocaust, the Polish center of Jewish life was almost totally destroyed, and the United States found itself with the largest Jewish population of any country in the history of the Jewish people. Today, about 5.5 million Jews live in the United States, and as many as another 3 million individuals view themselves as being of Jewish descent. By contrast, the second largest Jewish population center in the world, Israel, only has 4.2 million Jews.

Why did so many Jews decide to settle in the United States? What are the factors in American history that have nurtured Jewish life in this country? Last night, I discussed three of these factors: (1) our marketplace economy, which hopefully places profit over prejudice; (2) the American constitutional doctrine of the separation of church and state, which has afforded both Jews and Judaism an equality of rights heretofore unprecedented in the history of the Diaspora; and (3) the relatively low level of American anti-Semitism because of the diversity of our society. Compared to Russia or Germany or Spain, American anti-Semitism has been mercifully light. Furthermore, even at the height of public anti-Semitism in America, Jewish immigration from East Europe continued to swell until blocked by congressional legislation.

For these and many other reasons, America quickly evolved from a haven to a home for its Jewish citizens. In short, Jews have thrived in America as in no other location in the Diaspora. Think back to the lives of your ancestors in Germany, Poland, Russia, Lithuania, Hungary, Romania, and other places in the Old World. Could they have imagined a country in which multiple Jews have served on the Supreme Court of the land? In which Jewish men and women are elected, in significant numbers, to the House of Representatives and the Senate? Where Jews have become presidents of nearly every leading research university in the country? Where Jews can attend medical schools and practice medicine in the hospitals of their choice? Where Jews can be engineers and chemists, generals and admirals, and movie producers and TV stars? Where Jews can sit at the top of the Federal Reserve system, guide major financial institutions, and publish leading newspapers and journals of opinion? From Louis Brandeis to Barbara Streisand to Samuel Gompers and the AFL, to Adolph Ochs and the *New York Times*, to the Guggenheim family, to Julius Rosenwald of Sears and Roebuck, Jews as individuals and as families have had an incredible run in America.

Not so long ago, there used to be a standard question that was asked in the Jewish community about new government programs, changes in foreign policy, and the construction of new apartment buildings. Very simply, the question always asked was "Is it good for the Jews?" If we were to ask, "Has America been good for the Jews?" the answer would have to be a resounding—indeed, a thundering—yes. America has been good for the Jews as individuals and families.

But if we took the same question and rephrased it just a bit, and instead of asking of "Has America been good for the Jews?" we would ask a more cultural question, "Has America for the last 350 years been good for Judaism as a faith community?," we would be confronted with a very different set of data to consider.

Instead of looking at Jewish individuals, if we begin to consider institutions and communal support of institutions of higher Jewish culture, the picture begins to change. It took nearly a hundred years of settlement in this land before a synagogue was built, and when it was built, it was a very modest structure and unevenly supported by the community. It took nearly two hundred years of Jewish life in America before a properly ordained rabbi was enticed to settle here and serve a congregation. Tragically, soon after his arrival, Rabbi Rice felt compelled to quit his post and go into dry goods because of conflicts with his congregation. The level of Jewish education in the United States, until very recently, has been crushingly low. In a survey of Jewish education in New York about a century ago, it was discovered that less than 10 percent of Jewish children of school age were enrolled in Jewish education programs in that city. Today, places like metropolitan New York and Los Angeles continue to have synagogue affiliation rates that drop as low as the single digits in outlying areas. And as everyone knows, Hebrew illiteracy is rampant in the United States. Every little shtetl in Poland was able to train its boys in Hebrew. By contrast, few American Jews can read Hebrew with comprehension, let alone speak or write in the basic language of our tradition. I doubt that in a world with at least six million Hebrew speakers, there are even twenty thousand American Jews who have a real command of Hebrew.

What happened, and why is Judaism so culturally weak in the United States? First and foremost, the American Jewish community was very slow to develop. It was isolated, cut off from Europe by an ocean. For much of its early history, it was considered to be a frontier area. Moreover, in America a one-two combination of radical individualism coupled with pressure to conform to a "Yankee" model of American culture dramatically curtailed the open expression of Jewishness in the United States from 1654 to 1964.

Judaism in America also began in modern times when religious belief, in general, began to weaken and a great premium was placed on being part of contemporary society. As in the broader Zionist movement, the old was widely rejected and the new was idealized. Judaism was viewed as part of the past, and America was the land of the future.

Of course, not everything was lost; and despite the warnings of numerous Jeremiahs that Judaism was bound for extinction, the tradition has endured although in highly transformed modalities. Tradition itself maintained a momentum of its own that modernity could not stop. Numerous inspirational leaders rose up at various, critical junctures in American Jewish history like the biblical Elijah or the heroic Judah Maccabee to provide the means for Jewish renewal in this society. Gershom Mendes Seixas, a native-born New Yorker, provided religious leadership during the Early National Period and forged the first and enduring interfaith connections with clergy of other faiths. In the decades prior to the Civil War, Isaac Leeser of Mikveh Israel here in Philadelphia was the first to envision the full potential of American Judaism, translated the Bible into English for American Jews, founded the first Jewish newspaper, and established the first rabbinic school in the United States. Leeser was followed by the indefatigable Isaac Mayer Wise, who organized the first designated branch of American Judaism, the Union of American Hebrew Congregations, in 1875. He was followed by Solomon Schechter, a fine scholar who came from England to shape the American Conservative movement in Judaism. Simultaneously, at the turn of the century, numerous Orthodox rabbis and scholars began giving institutional expression to American Judaism's most traditional branch.

Their efforts were reinforced by the general status of organized religion in the United States. As many Jews assimilated and started to drift away from their ancestral faith, they discovered that the broader American public was more religiously committed than they themselves often realized. Seeing their Christian neighbors supportive of their churches, loyal Jews felt compelled to return to their synagogues and made sure that the synagogue as well as the church was fully represented on Main Street, USA.

This general feeling for the necessity of religious affiliation as an expression of American-ness became increasingly intense during the Cold War, which witnessed the vast expansion of the suburbs. Suburbia quickly became home to the largest number of new synagogues ever built in the history of the Jewish people. At the same time, the founding of the State of Israel and knowledge of the Holocaust further bolstered American Jewish identity, although, in general, they tended to strengthen the commitment to the Jewish Federations and their network of social services and international support for far-flung Jewish communities across the globe.

Off the radar for most American Jews in the years just after World War II was the transplanting of a number of major Hasidic and Yeshiva communities to the United States. As Holocaust survivors determined to rebuild their traditional way of life, they quickly built schools and rebuilt their families. By the beginning of the new millennium, a new phenomenon had developed in American Judaism, a vigorous ultra-Orthodoxy, which not only was successfully recreating the lifestyle of the ancestors of the majority of American Jews of East European descent but also attracting and influencing Jews and their religiosity in the mainstream of American Judaism.

Personally, I have visited many of these enclaves of ultra-Orthodox Judaism in America from the Satmar community near Monroe, New York, to the nearly frum communities of Monsey and New Square, to the largest Lithuania-style American yeshiva in Lakewood, about an hour's drive from here. Today, there are thousands of Orthodox rabbis in the United States, and tens of thousands of Yeshiva students are studying in Hebrew and English on these shores.

Finally, a Jewish renewal movement has reshaped much of Reform and Conservative Judaism during the last few decades in this country. It emphasizes Jewish crafts, folk music, informality, and the interior experience of religion and draws eclectically on Kabbalah. Only in America could someone named Madonna transform herself into someone named Esther. Who would ever have thought that something as foreign to Judaism as tattoos would find a Jewish application in American life?

How then do we add up the pluses and the minuses? How do we weigh the relative impact of those forces that diminish Jewish life in this country against those that sustain it and help negotiate our ever-changing cultural landscape? It is not an easy job. In part, it depends on whether you understand the cup of Jewish life to be half empty or half full. Is Jewish life evaporating in America, or is it being replenished?

On Rosh HaShanah, while we do not have the ability to reshape Jewish communal religious policy, we have the power and the mandate to make some decisions about the place of Judaism in our own lives. One of the greatest virtues of life in this county is that, especially in areas of personal conviction, we are free to do as we choose.

May I suggest a few simple ways of observing the 350th anniversary of Jewish life in this country, which will help replenish the cup of Jewish life in this land? First, make sure your homes have a mezuzah. It's this big! But like a tiny drop of ink in a large glass of water, it colors the whole airspace and serves as a powerful reminder of the mandate of having a Jewish home.

Second, and more difficult, light Shabbat candles. They are this big! Lighting Shabbat candles establishes the rhythm of Jewish life, a beat that is very different than the beat of life all around us. They bring holiness into a home, a bit of sacred light, which casts a beautiful glow in our space.

Three, observe yahrzeits. In recent years, the tradition of saying Kaddish, particularly within the Reform movement, has weakened. Kaddish is a powerful prayer. It too has a rhythm that transcends time. It has a sound that only works when said with others. It's an affirmation of community, even as it is a balm to the grieving heart.

Fourth, find ways to be part of Jewish educational efforts. We have programs galore in this congregation and community for Jewish adults. You can read a book of Jewish content or go online to a Jewish universe of electronic discourse I simply call the Veb. Root your kids and grandkids in Jewish educational programs both formal and informal. Youth groups, summer camps, and travel programs have demonstrated longitudinal effects on Jewish kids. Offer incentives to choose Jewish electives at college. Sometimes synagogues help defray the cost of textbooks for a Jewish course at school with a grade of C or better! I've seen it work both for enrollment and improved performance.

Fifth, and finally, play some Jewish music at home or in the car. Music is always good for the soul, and Jewish music can make the Jewish heart sing for joy.

In my opinion, we no longer need to talk about Jewish survival. We are going to survive as a people and as a tradition. The real question is scope. How many of us will practice Judaism? How many of our descendants will adhere to our faith and to what extent? Jewish survival, in my opinion, is a theological, not a sociological, proposition decided by our ancestors and God a long time ago. Jewish vitality is the piece we need to be concerned with or not!

We need to preserve Judaism for ourselves, for our families, and for the benefit of mankind. Judaism brings a sane message of justice, mercy, and hope to a very sick world. Judaism emphatically believes that all people are created equal in the image of God, and Judaism believes that it is possible—indeed, it is necessary—that one day, somehow, all the nations will learn to live together, that the lion will lie down with the lamb, and that the swords will be beaten into plows. Our tradition actually has something to say to humanity, and it has a permanent place in your hearts if you let it in.

When you bring your kids or grandkids to Hebrew school or decide to support your synagogue or light Shabbat candles, you are doing something big, something huge. You are not just preparing for a *bar mitzvah*. You are nurturing a soul. You are not just clearing another piece of paper off your desk. You're keeping the *ner tamid*, the eternal light of faith, alive. You are not just adding a nice, aesthetic touch to your home. You are bringing light to the world.

Judaism has stumbled and bumbled and run and leaped in this country for three and a half centuries. As a community, we have filled our collective Kiddush cup halfway.

On this Rosh HaShanah, 350 years since our first ancestors stepped onto these shores, let us resolve to replenish the cup of Jewish life until our cup runs over with life, joy, and hope.

Shanah Tovah.

A good year!

American Jews and Israel:
The Doctrine of Interdependence

September 24, 2004, Yom Kippur Evening 5765

My personal relationship with the State of Israel began in 1962 when I was eight years old. That was the year my grandmother's brother from Haifa came to visit us. He brought us all gifts. My gift was an oversized Passover Haggadah wrapped in blue velvet and illustrated with watercolor scenes of modern Israel. Somehow that book, those images, and my name inscribed on the title page bonded me to the Jewish State.

I went to Israel for the first time in December 1969, on the first-ever teen travel program sponsored by Camp Harlam where so many KI kids go today. I have a number of distinct memories. The first was at Kennedy Airport when we boarded our El Al aircraft. I didn't see it coming, but the fact that I was on a Jewish airplane, a Jewish jet, a Jewish thing with real power, made me fill up with some primal feeling I hadn't experienced before in my life.

Many hours later, I remember seeing the coastline of Israel come into focus as our plane descended through a winter cloud cover. At the time, I didn't know that Agnon, one of the greatest modern Hebrew writers and winner of the Nobel Prize for Literature, had once said that "I was born in Jerusalem—my mother just happened to give birth to me in Poland." When I first heard that, it wouldn't have made much sense to me. But since landing at the old Lod Airport my first time, I have felt that a piece of me has always been a resident in Jerusalem.

I have been to Israel a total of fifteen times. I spent a part of my college years there. I returned for the first year of rabbinic school. I met Liz there. I've been there with my oldest child and hope to take some of my other children with me this December as part of our Old York Road Kehillah trip.

My relationship with Israel has changed over the years, always deepening, always more complex, and always more fundamental to my being. I've tried to learn to speak Hebrew, visit all the historic and religious sites of the country, and befriend Israelis as a matter of personal principle.

My bar mitzvah took place one week after the Six-Day War in 1967. My coming of age and my pride in being Jewish were forever intertwined with the miracle of Israel's swift victory that June thirty-seven years ago.

I too was crushed by the news of the surprise attack on Yom Kippur in 1973, then worried about the incursion into Lebanon, horrified by the first intifada, elated by the peace efforts of Rabin, Peres, and Barak. I was crushed again by the murder of Yitzhak Rabin and disgusted by Arafat's betrayal of the Oslo Accords. Like so many others of my generation, American and Israeli, who grew up on songs of peace, I was forced to come to the horrible conclusion that we had no partner at the table.

Like most of you, I have watched the images of the lingering Intifada on TV and in the papers with great sadness. How many more bus bombers? How many more hotel seders as killing fields? How many more pizza shops and coffee shops? How many doctors, children, and soldiers? How many more? How many more could the people of Israel endure to lose? When I received a surprise phone call late last Spring that I had been picked to be part of a special program sponsored by the Sochnut, the Jewish Agency, to go to Israel to learn about various curricular issues pertaining to Israel in the American Jewish education system, I had a strange feeling that it was time to go again. So I said yes.

I went to my orientation meeting for NACIE (North American Coalition for Israel Engagement) at Gratz College. There were nine of us from across the Philadelphia area. We would join four or five similar groups from around the United States in Israel in July.

NACIE had been organized in the wake of the recognition that Israel was no longer at the center of American Jewish education. Spirituality, changes in American constructs of ethnicity, and endless violence all seem to be moving American Jews emotionally away from Israel. What could be done to stem the flow and turn the tide back to Israel?

Almost no one I knew wanted me to go. Don't go on the buses! Don't go to Ben Yehuda Street, Jerusalem's central business district! And, most of all, "Don't go!" were repeated to me over and over. But I hadn't been in Israel since moving here to KI, and it was time to go again. I've long believed that you can't understand Israel without being there. How could I report to you if I didn't see, hear, and feel for myself?

Our group left for Israel at the end of the day of Tisha B'Av. Tisha B'Av, the ninth of Av, is a fast day that commemorates the destruction of the Temple in Jerusalem and other calamities in Jewish history. Rumor had it that in deference to the religious people on the flight, there would be no movies. Eleven hours, I thought to myself, with no movies and maybe very little or no food.

It wasn't true. There were movies and plenty to eat. The Orthodox on the flight simply waited longer into the night before taking their meals. Something was going on here I didn't expect. It was very relaxed onboard. There were all the baby sounds, Hasidim patrolling the aisles and self-absorbed businessmen (without neckties) that you normally find on an El Al flight. Still, it was a little different.

When we landed at Ben Gurion, the airport was incredibly busy. There were people everywhere. Passport control took forever. Outside, the suburbs of Tel Aviv seemed to go about everyday life without a second thought. The highway up to Jerusalem was bumper to bumper. At first, I didn't even want to sit near a window or look around. "Don't do this" and "Don't do that" echoed in my head. But everyday life was going on all around me and calling out to me.

We checked into our hotel across from Mount Zion. From the hotel, I could see the walls of the Old City and the new security wall in the distance tracing the peak line of the Mount of Olives. The sun was shining brilliantly and equally on everything that noon. Israel, I thought to myself, has always been a country of walls.

We had a bit of free time before our first official meeting, so I decided to go to the pool. If nothing else, I was planning to sit by the pool and get some Middle East sun on my face. The pool was filled with Ethiopian teenagers, fifteen years old or so, like our confirmation class, several dozens of them wearing nice swim gear, playing and speaking flawless Hebrew. They were totally Israeli, totally at home; and suddenly, in that special sunlight of Jerusalem, I started to relax a bit in body and soul.

As time went on, our tour only got better. We were guided through the Mount Scopus campus of the Hebrew University where I had once studied.

I took a walking Ulpan course, which toured the streets of Jerusalem with lectures in Hebrew for American-style Hebrew speakers. We went to Israel's new Supreme Court building, endowed by the Rothschild family as a gift to the Jewish people, and learned of Israel's remarkable comparative law system. We drove north on Israel's new super highway, Highway 6, which, in the middle of the country, follows the security fence right along the Green Line for miles, with Jewish towns on the left and Arab villages on the right. We went to a kibbutz center for nontheistic expressions of Jewish spirituality. We visited the fresh grave of Naomi Shemer, Israel's modern muse and grandchild of the first kibbutz, and looked out across the waters of the Kinneret, the Hebrew word for a harp-shaped lake. We went to Massuah, a Holocaust research center and museum south of Netanya, which studies how the Holocaust is taught in Israeli schools.

Of course, the emotional high point of our trip was spending Shabbat in Jerusalem. On Friday night, I walked with a group of people to the synagogue of Shlomo Carlebach, the outstanding Jewish religious songwriter of the twentieth century. The modest synagogue was in the middle of a middle-class neighborhood. It had seats for about one hundred men and fifty women. But by the time we got to the Psalms of Kabbalat Shabbat, the small shul was packed with several hundred young people, average age twenty or so, all singing the songs of Shlomo Carlebach. Exactly a month later, I went to a Friday night service in the largely restored synagogue of the Westend in Frankfurt, Germany, with the students from our KI exchange program. The same music lifted up from the voice of the bar mitzvah student leading the service there. I guess in the language of physics, it was like being a part of a spiritual "unified field."

Shabbat morning in Jerusalem, I went to Kol HaNeshama, a Reform synagogue in the same neighborhood as the Carlebach Shul. The synagogue had its own building with a glass dome over the entire congregation. Because it was Israeli Reform, the whole service was in Hebrew. We sat nearly in the round, informal, yet intent. A *bar mitzvah* boy was called to the Torah. His shirt tail was out, and he was wearing sneakers; but when he chanted in his native Hebrew, he nearly had me in tears. Then he thanked his family and told them how they had come to Israel, escaping the Nazis by going to the four corners of the earth before coming home. The family, clearly secular, beamed with pride. The father, a man who had only come to synagogue in his capacity as a father, gave his charge; and then he gave the rabbi a kiss on the cheek. It was totally compelling. The service ended with a song, Psalm 150, which included the name of the synagogue, calling on all humanity to pay homage to God, and then a final prayer for peace in Hebrew and Arabic. The sun was brilliant, the congregation was devout until the last note was sounded, and the prayers drifted heavenward like the smoke of the ancient sacrifices of ancient Jerusalem. A moment of peace, in a city called peace, which is so far from receiving the blessing of peace.

That night, intoxicated with the Shabbat and air of Jerusalem as my elixir, I went to Ben Yehuda Street, against all the pretrip advice I had received. The whole shopping area had been secured by the police, who were, to say the least, *en garde*. The promenade was so packed with people one could barely walk. I hadn't seen Jerusalem so alive, even in the halcyon summer months of 1973, when I feasted on pizza and ice cream every week after Shabbat "went out," as they say in Hebrew. The words of my teacher struck me that evening: "Everywhere else in the world," she said, "you have to bring Shabbat into you. In Jerusalem, you enter Shabbat." I could now see Shabbat departing from Jerusalem and the youth filling its streets with song just as it is envisioned in the seventh and final wedding blessing.

Just as returning to Jerusalem reconnected me to the ancient spirit of our people, so our time in Tel Aviv helped me reattach myself to Israel of today.

In Tel Aviv, I took an elective architectural tour of the city concentrating on the Bauhaus tradition there. Tel Aviv, now a World Heritage Site, has the most Bauhaus structures, over 4,400, of any place in the world. Designed by German Jewish architects displaced by Hitler, these starkwhite buildings are among the finest statements of architectural modernity, its vision and its hopes, in the world today.

However, the centerpiece of our time in Tel Aviv was a visit to Israel's Independence Hall. Because our group was from Philadelphia, we were chosen to do our presentation piece there. I had the privilege of being our group spokesman. For the occasion, I took the liberty of recrafting the American Declaration of Independence to fit the occasion. I called my text "American Jew and Israel: A Declaration of Interdependence."

Standing just a few feet from where Ben Gurion proclaimed the reestablishment of the Jewish state, I summarize our mission's purpose in these words:

When in the course of human events, it becomes necessary for the Jewish people to reaffirm the bonds which have connected them to one another, and to assume among the peoples of the earth a separate and equal station to which the laws of humanity and their own heritage entitle them, a decent respect to the opinions of mankind requires that they should declare the causes which impel them to maintain their essential unity and common future as American Jews and as citizens of the Jewish State.

We hold these truths to be self-evident: that all people are created in the divine image; that all are endowed by the Creator with certain inalienable rights, that among them are life, liberty, security and the maintenance of their way of life; that to secure these rights and goals, a state and communities are instituted, deriving their authority from the force of tradition and the consent of the people; that whenever social, cultural or political forces become destructive of these ends, it is the responsibility of our people to counter them and to institute new structures, laying their foundation on such principles and reorganizing themselves in such form, as to most likely effect their continued existence and cohesiveness as a people.

Prudence and respect will dictate that traditions long established should not be changed for light and transient causes; and accordingly, all experience hath shown that people are more prone to suffer, while challenges and problems are sufferable, than to right themselves by countering the problems which besiege them in radical ways.

For a whole host of reasons, which invariably combined to reduce and divide up by circumstance or by malice, it is now our duty, our obligation, to provide for our future unity and our wellbeing as a people.

Such has been the reality of our people in modern times and is such now the necessity of which impel us to alter our current communal and national policies, practices and priorities.

This history of the Jewish people in modern times is a history of disruptions, disintegration and dispossession and renewed determination.

To prove this, let our history be submitted to a candid world, which despite its profound indifference and rising malice, remain obliged to hear us state our cause:

We have traveled together as a people for more than three dozen centuries, since we first emerged on the stage of history.

We spawned a new vision of human society and human potential in prophetic word and deed.

We evolved a nation from our family of origin to tribes, and finally, to a monarchy in the Land of Israel.

We survived the destruction of our national state and then developed viable Diaspora communities without ever despairing of our return to our homeland.

We preserved in the Diaspora the language, customs and memory of our people on every continent and in every age.

We incurred cruel persecution by kings, peasants, religious fanatics and tyrants of every stripe.

We survived the broadest and most diabolical program of genocide which has ever stained the earth with blood and tarred humanity with ignominy.

We fought in modern times for enlightenment and emancipation and humanitarian causes for the benefit of all people.

We envisioned, through the Zionist movement, a return to our ancient homeland based on the principle of our heritage and affirmed by international law and the agreement of the family of nations.

We gathered the remnants of our people from the four corners of the earth and reacquainted them with their land, their language, and their national pride.

We have resolved to exercise our reborn power with restraint, integrity, and hopefulness.

We have pledged to work together in the many lands of our domicile as a single people assembled into many politics and communities, to provide for our mutual wellbeing and common spiritual nourishment.

We have witnessed in recent years a disengagement of many of our people and have confused sovereignty with isolation and security and affluence with destiny.

We have allowed, at this time, too many centrifugal forces to weaken Jewish life from within, reduce our ties to one another, and in the final analysis, imperil our common future.

We therefore, the Philadelphia representatives of the North American Coalition for Israel Engagement, assembled at Independence Hall in Tel Aviv, appealing to the People of Israel in North America and in the State of Israel, solemnly state and declare our perpetual mutual interdependence; that our communities ought to be interdependent, and that all connections between us shall be strengthened and preserved; and that as a global people we should establish economic programs, cultural exchanges, and institutional ties which will bind us together in perpetuity.

And for the support of this Declaration, with a firm reliance on our tradition and ourselves, we hereby pledge to each other our bond of fellowship, our communal resources and our sacred future as one people of a common heritage and a shared future.

But the absolute high point of our trip was the last night. It was a beautiful, relatively cool, star-laden night. A large group of people from our tour walked the short block to the beach. We had agreed to go to a sing-along nightclub on the water's edge, which specialized in the songs of modern Israel before the advent of Hebrew hip-hop/Naomi Shemer songs and Hebrew songs that sound like clones of Edith Piaf pieces from the cafés of Paris. There were nearly a thousand people there, sitting on the beach in plastic chairs, singing the songs of Israel throughout the night. Groups of kibbutzniks, families celebrating birthdays together, and even a few tourists. We sang, and the waves of the Mediterranean kept beating about twenty yards behind us.

That night, I reflected deeply on what my trip had done for me. I knew I was lucky because I had come to Israel during the longest lull in years—several months of quiet, perhaps brought on by the security fence, the relentless attacks on the leadership of Hamas, or sheer exhaustion. Who knows? But it was clear that the old Israel had a chance to come out from behind the sandbags—the old dream of the Jewish people living in the land of our ancestors, singing the songs of our people in the most ancient language of our people, of living quietly, normally, contentedly.

My whole trip to Israel this summer was a prolonged song, the song of the yearning of the people of Israel for shalom and shalvah, peace and quiet. A reminder that the Zionist dream was never meant to be a landscape of nightmares and horrors but a different dream for a revival of an entire people and the opportunity to be normal, like everyone else, living in their place, singing their songs, rejoicing with their children, and not being afraid that someone who despised the very fact of their existence was going to come and kill them. I am not delusional. I know the moment I experienced was the exception. I know that there are terrible conflicts and irresolvable problems. I know that life in Israel is complex beyond description and that just behind where we sat on the beach, in some apartment, somewhere down the block, there were only the sounds of pain, loss, and death and mothers and fathers who will never feel whole again.

We can debate the fence- I'm for it. We can debate the pullout from Gaza- I'm for it. We can debate the settlements—I'm against aggressive nationalism and religious zealotry. We can debate all that, but what we can't debate is our interdependence with Israel, Israel's right to exist, and most of all, the dream of Israel being restored.

We have a choice. We can understand the essence of Israel in terms of Tisha B'Av, in terms of national tragedy, suffering, and powerlessness. Or we can understand modern Israel in terms of the spiritual possibilities of a Sabbath in Jerusalem or a night of song on the beach in modern Tel Aviv.

Years of Intifada have warped the view of too many American Jews.

Too many of us have become the weepers of Tisha B'Av. In Israel, they know they have no choice but to continue to sing the songs of Zion, to give their children strength, and to stand behind their soldiers. They have no choice, and we need to choose to be with them and let them know, especially in these dark times, "We are one."

We have our own deep national problems and challenges, but we also have our Jewish responsibilities.

On this most solemn night of the year, let us resolve to stand with Israel, to sing with Israel, to pray with Israel. And until the day comes when the lion lies down with the lamb, swords are beaten into plowshares, and the security fence crumbles from neglect and uselessness like a thousand other abandoned ancient walls all across the landscape of Israel, let us remain steadfast, united, and confident about the absolute justice of Israel's cause.

Adonai ohz l'amo yitain, Adonai y'vareich et amo va'shalom.
May God give our people strength,
May God bless us, with the greatest blessing of all,
The blessing of peace.
Amen. Shabbat Shalom and an easy fast.

Twenty-Five Years in the Rabbinate

2005 KI Bulletin

This spring, I will celebrate the silver anniversary of my ordination. Twenty-five years ago, I was called along with my classmates before the Ark at the Plum Street synagogue in downtown Cincinnati. The president of Hebrew Union College–Jewish Institute of Religion (HUG-JIR) raised his hands above my head and pronounced a blessing, making me a rabbi. It was a sacred moment for me, a moment amplified by the soaring music that filled that Civil War–era sanctuary as soon as the last of my class was ordained. I carry those feelings of pride, inspiration, humility, and deep responsibility wherever I go.

I always wanted to be a rabbi. I never really seriously considered doing any other work, except to append a significant commitment to academic study to my rabbinate.

I have been the luckiest of all people. I have had the chance and continue to have the chance to do both. The long hours take their toll on the body and mind but not the spirit. I remain "in my work." I felt I was called to the rabbinate as a child. I am still responding without hesitation to that call.

In the course of twenty-five years, longer if you include my three years in a student pulpit (mine was in Richmond, Indiana), you see life—all of life, in all of its dimensions, complexities, and variations—almost on a daily basis. Although much of what I am currently doing might be classified as administrative or managerial because of the needs of our congregation, the core of my rabbinate remains pastoral. The biggest thing I've learned about the rabbinate, despite my personal love of learning, is that what the congregation needs is personal emotional access to the rabbi and to the transcendent. Some need it every day; some need it once a year. But beyond the programs, the services, the campaigns, the initiatives, and more, it's really very simple: people need to feel the power of the tradition in their hearts and through that power of the tradition, a hit, an echo of the ineffable. My job is to help you connect to the sacred within you. There is nothing I would rather do.

At every turn in the road of life—at birth, at the beginning of a child's education, *bar* or *bat mitzvah*, marriage, family crisis, a moment of accomplishment, a health issue, even death—there is a moment to connect. And sometimes it's something you read or saw on a trip or thought about while commuting on the train. It doesn't matter. That moment of spiritual opportunity is always there, always ready to break through and then share.

For the next twenty-five years, I just want to continue being there for you, to continue learning and teaching, dreaming and building, doing my part in that very long, very noble generational baton race we call Judaism and KI. Remember the movie *Chariots of Fire* when the Scotsman just puts his head back and runs on the beach with the wind? That's what I wanted to do in a spiritual way on the unknown road that lies in front of me. It's the joy of simply being and running and feeling the wind and the spirit.

Thank you for helping me to be who I want to be. Thanks for bringing *you* to me.

May we all go from strength to strength.

Where Are the Borders of Jewishness?

May 5, 2005, eKI

I was privileged to sit in on the culminating session of a special conference on Jewish Literature this week at the University of Pennsylvania. Leading scholars from all over the world were present. The papers they delivered were insightful. The discussion which followed was lively. At the core of the discussion was a nagging question about exactly what makes a given piece of literature Jewish or not Jewish. Here at KI, I recently reflected on this same problem inherent in the work of Philip Roth, who is Jewish, often writes on Jewish topics and insists that he is not a writer of Jewish literature! The topic even came up in a recent Confirmation Class when we discussed Jewish group self-consciousness at (regular) school and how it compares, for example, to African American group self-consciousness.

Where are the borders of Jewishness in our lives? Where are those borders clearly demarcated. Where are they porous? These questions are part of a larger complex of issues inherent in the tension between this week's Torah and Haftarah portions and the line between Jewish and non-Jewish in our lives. The Torah teaches us "to love our neighbors as we love ourselves" (Lev. 19:18), which seems to be a universal dictum. But what if "neighbor" primarily refers to someone who is Jewish and not gentile? Do we love the Jewish person more? If not, what happens to the whole philanthropic basis of Jewish communal life and, most particularly, its social services. Furthermore, the Haftarah from Amos (9:7) teaches us that in the eyes of God, Jews and Ethiopians are alike and that there is no divine priority in favor of the Jews. To draw the map of our lives and delineate exactly the Jewish borders- morally, culturally, and spiritually- is not an easy task. Rather it is a task we need to explore together. We need to figure out what is Jewish in our lives, to what extent the core of our existence is Jewish, and what we are supposed to do about it. Obviously, one's humanity and one's Jewishness cannot be fully separated. But "where the Jewish begins" and what the implications of our Jewishness may be is not so easy to determine. Together, we need to look deeply into this matter. Shabbat Shalom!

ISRAEL DEFENSE FORCES: HEROES OF THE JEWISH PEOPLE

August 18, 2005

As I write this column, the disengagement from Gaza is in full swing with a little more than half of the settlers evacuated from their homes. The clearest, most important message coming out of Gaza right now is that the Israel Defense Forces (IDF) is doing a spectacular job. For more than a year, everyone in the Jewish world has been worried about this moment and its impact on the soldiers. Would they break rank and refuse their orders? Could they effectively remove the settlers without violence? Would the control-and-command chain hold in the IDF?

We have our answer, and it is spectacular. More than forty thousand unarmed Israeli soldiers and police marched into Gaza, kept to their game plan, remained firm, were not incited, and removed the settlers one by one. They were taunted, spit at, and even hit, but they did not flinch. Young recruits and seasoned officers alike held their ground, stayed at their posts, and did their jobs. If you ever had any doubt about the IDF, go back and look at the media pictures from this last week: tough, strong, disciplined, sensitive, caring, and respectful. Was there ever a military operation like the Gaza disengagement where the military might of a nation under siege was employed with gentle hands and broken hearts?

Many of the settlers and their radical supporters did things to provoke, intimidate, and break the soldiers' will. They did themselves, Israel, and the Jewish people a great disservice. They are entitled to protest in a democracy. Unfortunately, they overstepped the boundaries of loyal dissent on too many occasions in an attempt to create inflammatory images and engage in the political theater of the most calculated kind. In the end, they only made the IDF look better. The IDF carried out the will of the majority in the State of Israel with great dignity. Wherever you are in the political spectrum in Israel, you should feel very proud of the young people in IDF uniform. Once again, they are the heroes of the Jewish people.

Shabbat Shalom.

GAZA

October 4, 2005, Rosh HaShanah Morning 5766

Without question, the biggest Jewish news story of the last year, a year filled with incredible headlines, was Israel's withdrawal from Gaza. The Jewish community the world over was braced for the worse possible outcome: Jew fighting Jew. Throughout the year, both international Jewish and local Israeli opposition to the withdrawal mobilized and stirred deep emotions. Orange became the Jewish color of discontent this summer. Orange shirts and banners were everywhere. Everyone was braced for the worst internecine Jewish violence since the last days of Jerusalem in the Roman period.

From their vantage point, the Palestinian community watched with great skepticism. "They will never leave," they said, and "If they leave, what difference will it make? The Israelis will still control the sea, the sky, and the economy."

For their part, many in the European community, obsessed with their hatred of Ariel Sharon, openly questioned Israeli motives and the probable outcome of the process. In much of Europe, Israel is viewed as a mega-colonial power, the most racist state on the planet, and doggedly irredentist.

Except for the Israeli government and the Israeli army, which discreetly and unpretentiously rehearsed the evacuation, no one knew what to expect, except something bad. Then, on August 15, at midnight, the borders of Gaza were sealed. Two days later, the army began removing settlers. Quietly, systematically, forcefully, but with great sensitivity, the IDF dismantled twenty-one settlements, evacuated nine thousand settlers, and, finally, withdrew its own forces. All this was achieved with cameras rolling and the whole world watching. All this was done without serious injury, except for self-inflicted wounds, and without deaths caused by violence. All this was done ahead of schedule and with exceptional efficiency.

As far as I know, there is no historical parallel of a sovereign state giving up land it captured in war, land contiguous with its sovereign homeland, in the name of peace and justice.

There is no historical parallel of an army removing its own civilian population, against the will of that population, with such incredible discipline, precision, and compassion.

There is no historical parallel of a unilateral action of land for peace.

In short, Israel's unilateral withdrawal from Gaza was unprecedented, breathtaking, and courageous. The withdrawal now stands with the Six-Day War, the bombing of Iraq's nuclear power plants, and the raid on Entebbe as one of the signature actions of the Jewish state.

We have much to be proud of today as Jews and supporters of the State of Israel. We can be proud of Israel's resolve, its democratic character, its Jewish values, and its willingness to take reasonable risks and bold actions in the name of peace. We should be proud of its young people and its soldiers for their passion, discipline, and devotion. If you ever doubted that the spirit of Israel is as strong today as it was forty years ago, look at the pictures of the soldiers of Israel during the disengagement and how they discharged their duties. It was truly inspirational!

The story of the withdrawal from Gaza was essentially a modern-day reenactment of this morning's Torah portion. Abraham was commanded to sacrifice Isaac as a test of his devotion to God. Modern Israel felt commanded to sacrifice its hold on Gaza as a sign of its commitment to peace and its willingness to take bold actions to defend itself. Abraham was then ordered by God not to slay the child. Modern Israel also showed tremendous restraint by not hurting the settlers when they were removed from their homes. We can only hope that at the end of the day, Israel and the Gaza settlers will be able to walk together just as Abraham and Isaac walked off together toward Beersheba at the conclusion of the horrifying *akedah* epic.

Like *Akedat Yitzchak*, the question of Gaza is complicated. Gaza is a small flat coastal territory. Only 135 square miles—one-fifth the size of Montgomery County, Pennsylvania—it is home today to almost 1.5 million Arab residents and, until the third week of September 2005, approximately

9,000 Jewish settlers. Some of it is very beautiful. Its land mostly supports light agriculture. It has resort-quality beaches but lacks a true natural port.

Gaza sits at the juncture of the world's two largest continents, Asia and Africa. It straddles what was called the Via Maris in the ancient world, the great caravan system connecting Egypt and Mesopotamia. Gaza has never been particularly rich, but it has almost always been unstable.

During the conquest of Canaan in biblical times, the ancient Israelites failed to take control of Gaza even though it was promised to the tribe of Judah. Instead, it was taken over by the Philistines, an Aegean people displaced by the Trojan Wars. Samson, a tragic figure and judge during the tribal period of ancient Israel, was deceived by Delilah and met his fateful end in a pagan temple in Gaza. David rose to prominence in ancient Israel when he slew the gigantic Philistine warrior, Goliath. The Hasmoneans, the successors of the Maccabees, were the only Jews to subdue Gaza in ancient times, but they held it for less than a century. In the year 635 CE, Gaza fell to the Arabs and was both Arabized and converted to Islam. In the ensuing centuries, only small pockets of Jews have lived there.

I would argue that part of the reason Ariel Sharon determined he could leave Gaza is that it has never really been part of the Jewish homeland. Although some revisionist maps might include it in Greater Israel, it does not have definitive Halachic status as such. It is neither truly Eretz Yisrael, the land of Israel, of *chutz la'aretz*, outside the land. Ultimately, its Jewishness is debatable; and therefore, its disposition was negotiable by the Israeli government.

In 1947, Gaza, with a total population of fewer than sixty thousand, was promised by the UN to the Palestinians as a region in their national homeland. But during the War of Independence, it came under Egyptian control. Although Egypt never formally annexed Gaza, it did retain administrative control over it until the 1967 War.

Israel began to place settlers in Gaza by the end of 1967. It also retained control of Gaza in the wake of the 1973 Yom Kippur War, and Anwar Sadat, perhaps with clairvoyant powers, decided not to take Gaza back under Egyptian control as part of his peace agreement with Menachem Begin. It was as if a time bomb with a long fuse was now set and burning down to an inevitable explosion. Hamas, a radical Palestinian Islamic resistance movement, was founded in Gaza in 1987, the same year that saw the beginning of the First Palestinian Intifada. Inspired by Iranian-style terrorists, Hamas quickly gained massive backing on the Arab street in

Gaza and linked itself with international anti-American terrorism. Lest we forget, Hamas was also linked to the first bombing of the World Trade Center in New York in 1993. Despite the radicalization of Gaza's Arab population—and, perhaps, because of it—Israel continued to build and expand its infrastructure in Gaza until two years ago.

What led Ariel Sharon—an architect of the settler movement, an opponent of Labor's "land for peace" policy, and a tough military commander—to change his mind about Gaza? The main factor was demographic. Although the numbers are disputed by the Zionist Organization of America and other right-wing pro-Israel groups, common wisdom in Israel today is that the Palestinian birth rate greatly exceeds the Jewish birth rate. It is only a matter of time, save another huge influx of Jewish immigrants from abroad, until Israel, combined with the territories, will have a majority Arab population. In the not-too-distant future, every reasonable demographic projection suggests, the combined Arab population of Arab Israelis, Arabs in Gaza, and Arabs in the West Bank and Jerusalem will constitute a clear majority in the Land of Israel west of the Jordan River.

By ceding Gaza, Sharon helped preserve the Jewish character of Israel. Not so remarkably, throughout England and Europe, Sharon was taken to task for this so-called racist goal. They even dared to call the disengagement "ethnic cleansing." In fact, the opposite is true. Arabs were not removed from their homes. Jews were. Arabs were not denied their rights; their autonomy was actually augmented. Only those irrefutably opposed to the existence of a Jewish state in the first place could have opposed Sharon's decision.

In a certain sense, Sharon actually saved the settlers from the consequences of their own miscalculations about the State of Israel, the Land of Israel, and Jewish sovereignty. Israel actually has a number of internal demographic issues to deal with, including the population profile of Galilee, Jerusalem, and sectors of the Negev. To some extent, the relocation of Gaza's nine thousand settlers will help in some of these equations.

Sharon was also motivated by security concerns. Fighting Arab terrorists and protecting Jewish settlers in Gaza was no easy task. Force and restraint needed to be combined at all times. Border crossings needed careful monitoring. Internal roads needed to be protected. Meanwhile, the

Israeli military and civilian presence, as Sharon himself pointed out, only made the situation with the Arabs worse.

In 2004, at the Herzliya Conference sponsored by Israel's Institute for Policy and Strategy, Sharon unveiled his disengagement plan. He met with tremendous resistance from within his Likud party and from the religious Right. The majority of his own coalition was threatened. The Prime Minister hopscotched back and forth, keeping both himself in power and the disengagement plan alive. Meanwhile, the army began to figure out how it would organize itself internally with the object of removing the settlers while assuring that it would not be split apart by insubordination. As late as December 2004, a new coalition with Labor was formed to keep the disengagement plan alive.

It doesn't take a great deal of insight at a purely human level to understand the huge display of emotion that accompanied the eviction of the settlers from their homes. "Home" is more than a physical place. It is a web of many networks. It is a place of being, which takes years to develop. To uproot an entire community is difficult even if you are hostile or neutral to the population being affected. Imagine what it must be like to evict your own countrymen, people you either respect or know. Imagine closing schools and synagogues and post offices and doctors' offices and every nook and cranny of what we call daily life.

On top of that, add a long tragic history of Jewish evictions and evacuations, of Jews fleeing from Poland and being chased out of Morocco and Iraq. Imagine being on the other side of the evacuation.

Think about the centrality of land in the Zionist dream, of living in the land of Israel as a free and independent people. Think about the contraction of that dream and the loss of land, the redemptive agent in the life of your people.

Think about your own families, most of whom live only thirty or forty miles away from the action. They look like the settlers. Talk like the settlers. Eat like the settlers. Pray like the settlers. In their faces, you see your face.

Some of the settlers misbehaved horribly. Some are in jail for their actions. Throwing chemicals on your own soldiers is a crime. Placing Jewish stars on the clothing of little children so they look like they are Holocaust victims is morally repugnant. No one was being shot or gassed. The government was and is willing to spend vast sums of money to help the Gaza settlers rebuild their lives. Too many of the protests were "over the line" and harmful to the well-being of the State of Israel.

No one knows what the long-term benefits of disengagement will be. In the short term, Israel's demographic challenge was solved. Israel was supported by the United States, numerous European countries (much to their own surprise), and even the United Nations. The disengagement was an immense political success, at least in the short run.

By contrast, the initial Palestinian reaction was truly ugly. Various terrorist groups tried to get a jump on some first-class real estate. Israeli hot houses and other businesses were instantly looted. Palestinians poured over the Egyptian border. Worst of all, the abandoned synagogues of Gaza were razed to the ground by angry mobs. The world was completely silent as these atrocities were carried out. When Jewish mobs attacked mosques in the North of Israel recently, we know what happened. The authorities jumped in and took action. Perpetrators were arrested. Law and order were restored, yet Israel was nevertheless criticized!

We know the Palestinian situation is complex. The Palestine Authority is uneven in its performance and determination to control terrorism. Hamas and Islamic Jihad continue to push the envelope. Civil war on the Arab street in Gaza is a real possibility. Assassinations and political murders are rampant. The shelling of Israel from within Gaza has resumed and, most worrisome, the prospect of an influx of a huge number of Palestinians from Lebanon and perhaps Jordan is possible. Talk of vast economic development in Gaza seems empty with the PA still largely not in control and the various factions and gangs within Abbas's own organization still out of control.

In his speech of May 18, 2005, Sharon correctly declared that "now the Palestinians bear the burden of proof. They might fight terror organizations, dismantle its infrastructure and show sincere intentions of peace in order to sit with us at the negotiating table." The Prime Minister continued, "The world awaits the Palestinian response, a hand offered in peace or continued terrorist fire. To a hand offered in peace, we will respond with an olive branch. But if they choose fire, we will respond with fire, more severe than ever."

Israel's response to renewed Qassam rocket attacks has shown that Sharon will keep his word and, hopefully, will also show that Israel can use its superior firepower in the air and even on the ground against Hamas in Gaza if they need to. It won't exactly be the equivalent of shooting fish in a barrel, but we can all be assured Israel will not suffer terrorism lightly.

What can we do to help? Israel is a strong, independent democracy, but it still needs our support. Israel enjoys a special political relationship with our country, but we must continue to advocate for that relationship.

We can also invest in Israel directly through business or through bonds or through charitable conduits like Federation.

We can go to Israel as tourists. Tourism continues to rebound, and American Jews need to be part of that trend. Hopefully, within the next year or so, we will be able to reestablish the tradition of Confirmation and high school trips to Israel, once a regular part of our education program prior to the two Arab intifadas.

We can strengthen our pro-Israel programming here at KI. We have an Israel committee, and it needs your help and involvement. As many of you know, our synagogue was recently maligned in the *Exponent*, and the ghosts of sixty years ago were resurrected despite decades of pro-Israel advocacy at KI. Help us help Israel and help us keep KI identified with Israel.

You can also vote for ARZA (The Association of Reform Zionists of America) and the Reform movement in the upcoming international World Zionist Organization vote. You can help strengthen Israel by broadening its Jewish religious spectrum and giving Israelis the choices they need and want in spiritual matters.

Finally, and most importantly, make Israel part of the life of your children and grandchildren. Make your families "Israel-in-the-news aware." Display Israeli art in your homes. Hang a picture of Jerusalem in a prominent spot where you live.

The survival of the Jewish people over the centuries remains a mystery. Although our survival is essentially miraculous, it is also based on solidarity and loyalty. Israel is the greatest experiment in Jewish life in modern times. It is an incredible country, which has done more to rebuild the Jewish people and the Jewish spirit than any other agency in our collective life.

Before we sing the *"Birkat HaMazon,"* our grace after eating, we sing a psalm of *Shivat Tzion*, of returning to Zion.

When we end our seders on Passover, we say, "Next year in Jerusalem!" And when we conclude a wedding, we pray that "there will ever be heard the sounds of children at play in the holy city."

As we begin this new year, keep Israel and Jerusalem in your prayers just as our people have done for centuries.

May the one who makes peace in the heavens above make peace for us and for all of Israel, and we say amen and Shana Tova.

Iraq: What Do You Think?

October 12, 2005, Yom Kippur Evening 5766

Her name was Lori. She was from Arizona. She was twenty-three. She was a divorced mother of two children, ages four and three. She served in the 507th Army Maintenance Unit. Her grandfather served in WWII and her father in Vietnam. Her unit, including a better-known soldier Jessica Lynch, was ambushed in Iraq. Lori stood her ground and died firing her weapon. She was the first Native American woman to die in combat in service to the United States. She is buried on the Indian reservation near where she grew up.

His name was Nolan. He was twenty. He was an average kid who faced a number of personal challenges growing up near Spartanburg, South Carolina. He dreamed of being a Marine. He served in the First Battalion, Second Marine Regiment. His unit came under enemy fire near the southern Iraqi city of Nasiriya. Air cover was ordered but was miscalculated. Nolan was killed by so-called friendly fire.

Wednesday, September 28, 2005. Two weeks ago, exactly. What were you doing? I was in New York City. Every Wednesday, I teach at my rabbinic school, HUC. I remember getting out of the subway one stop early so I could walk through the open-air market in Union Square. It was sunny. People were relaxed, even in New York. I don't recall seeing a single political button or T-shirt or student handing out leaflets. Another great day to be alive, to be enjoying one's work, to be traveling around the country on trains and subways with relative ease and modest expense.

Wednesday, September 28, 2005. Somewhere near Ramadi, Iraq. A Bradley fighting vehicle staffed with soldiers from the First Battalion, 108th Infantry Regiment, Twenty-Eighth Infantry Division, Pennsylvania Army National Guard found itself in a deadly firefight. It was a bad day for our Commonwealth and its soldiers. Staff Sergeant George, thirty-nine, of Carbondale; Daniel, twenty-seven, a Staff Sergeant from Montrose; Sergeant Eric, twenty-one, of Township; Specialist Lee, twenty, of Hallstead; and PFC Oliver, nineteen, also of Carbondale, were all KIA (killed in action).

We have a lot to think about tonight as a nation and a people. Although not many of us feel it directly and few of us have been compelled to sacrifice for it, we are at war, a war that is staggering in its cost to human lives and materiel. No one really knows how many people died in the second Iraq war. The official American number of casualties is 1,956 dead and nearly 14,000 wounded. Add to the coalition losses, civilian contractors, Iraqi security forces, Iraqi citizens, and insurgents killed in action, the total number is staggering, maybe 100,000, maybe 200,000, or maybe 600,000.

The materiel costs of the war are mounting. Congress is now allocating in the hundreds of billions. We have no timeline for an exit of coalition forces. We have no plan for the rebuilding of the country of Iraq and no final dollar amount to attach to it. We are urged to "stay the course." From one point of view, I think we can all understand why staying the course is a necessary political and military option. Simply put, we have soldiers in the field, and we can't cut them off from behind. But from another point of view, I imagine most of us can also understand why staying the course is not a feasible strategy for the United States because of the lack of goals and the enormity of the potential cost in lives and materiel.

We have a lot to think about tonight as a nation and as a people, as Americans and as Jews. Yom Kippur is meant for serious reflection. One way or another, by assent or silence or opposition, we are all part of the story of America's war in Iraq. We can play the role of the ostrich and pretend that we have no connection to the fighting. But that is a dangerous delusion. Indeed, whether we are a military family, Republican enthusiasts or card-carrying Democrats, we are part of the history of our times. We can even choose to be bystanders, but that is a position too, and it is far from morally or politically neutral.

On this night of ultimate self-assessments, I would urge you to dig deep into your consciences and "personal news databases" and consider where we are as a nation in Iraq, where we are headed, what the goals are, and how we can conclude our business there. It is confusing. There are other issues at hand. But Iraq is now central to who we are as a nation and a people.

The list of questions about the war in Iraq is long, growing, and increasingly complex and painful:

- Was Saddam Hussein a direct threat to the United States?
- Was he tied to 9/11? Was he tied to international terrorism? Did he possess weapons of mass destruction? Did he violate one too many UN Security Council resolutions?
- Were we obliged to come to the rescue of victims of human rights abuses in Iraq? How important is Iraqi oil to our national interests?
- Are we spreading democracy in the Middle East by fighting in Iraq? Can we fight democracy by fighting Baathists and jihadists but not corrupt monarchies, the historic target of most democratic revolutions?
- Did we need to fight a big war? Do we need to continue to maintain an army of occupation?
- Did we understand the three-part sharing of power in Iraq—Kurdish, Sunni, and Shiite—before we destroyed the regime of Saddam Hussein?
- Do we support the concept of American unilateralism? How important is our relationship with our allies, especially in Europe, on this matter?
- Is the war justified because of the absolute necessity of a victorious outcome in both the military and the political arenas in Iraq and beyond? What are the consequences of not challenging Islamic terror and Baathist fascism in Iraq?
- Is this a war that was launched with good reason but not pursued with adequate force or post-invasion planning?
- How are we going to pay for the war in Iraq? Rebuild the American Gulf Coast, keep vital services intact in this country, and keep a cap on taxes?
- Are military enlistment levels falling to dangerously low levels? Is a backdoor draft fair? What is the international role of our National Guard?

These are just some of the banner questions we need to consider about America's involvement in Iraq. But that is not the end of the matter for us as American Jews. As American Jews, whether we like it or not, and independent of how we prioritize our own personal Jewishness and Americanness, we are also involved in the general discussion about the war in Iraq in yet another set of dimensions specific to our group within American society.

Almost exactly one year ago, the great American Jewish novelist Philip Roth published his counterfactual story, *The Plot Against America*. Many people understood it as something more than a "what if" scenario that landed Charles Lindbergh and not a third-term FDR in the White House. They understood it as more than even an insightful exploration of Jewish insecurities and American anti-Semitism in the late 1930s and early 1940s in the United States. Many people understood Roth's work as a historical parable about the Bush administration and the war in Iraq and specifically about a so-called Jewish motivation for the war. In the years prior to America's entrance into World War II, many isolationists and "American First" types led by Charles Lindbergh argued that Jews were leading America into war against Germany for their own interests but not in the best interest of this country. In the end, of course, Roth's *Plot Against America* affirms that we fought World War II for the best interests of the United States and the free world, not because of Jewish interests.

Do not delude yourselves. There are dangerous voices both on the right and the left of the political spectrum today, both opposed to the war in Iraq, who view Jewish involvement in the launching of the Iraq War in the most nefarious of terms. On the left are Cindy Sheehans and others who explicitly complain that America is fighting the Iraq War for the benefit of Israel. Outside the United States, those voices are even louder and are generally tied to radical anti-Israel groups and causes.

Not unlike in the late 1960s and early 1970 when parts of the Civil Rights movement were morphing into Black Nationalism and some anti-Vietnam organizations were not just protesting the war but also advocating extreme anti-American, anti-Israel viewpoints, many American Jews critical of the war in Vietnam found themselves essentially political orphans in the peace movement. How do you hold hands with someone who hates someone you love? Do you compartmentalize in the name of a higher morality, or do you stop holding hands with the enemy of your friends?

I am convinced that tens of thousands of American Jews are ready to speak up against the war in Iraq. But with whom can they partner? People who are calling for the destruction of Israel on the flip side of their anti-Iraq protest signs? The former radical SDS leader Rabbi Arthur Waskow might be willing to march with one hundred thousand anti-war activists on a Shabbat in Washington, DC, and Ismar Schorsch, the retiring chancellor of the Conservative movement's New York-based Jewish Theological Seminary, might be willing to come out and openly call the war a mistake, but they are rare exceptions in today's American Jewish community.

The result has been a painful self-stifling of many voices in the American Jewish community. Remarkably, I can't even find a single major statement by our own Reform movement, which is broadly liberal in most policy areas, on the war in Iraq within the past two years. Similarly, if you go to Hillel sites on the web, they will direct Jewish college students to publications that begin with the question, "Confused about Iraq?" and then launch into Jewish texts that illuminate and complicate ethical questions about war in general.

The situation on the right wing of American politics is no better. I looked at David Duke's website recently. He was very quick to pick up on Cindy Sheehan's comments about Israel. "Cindy is right," he declared. "Iraq is a Jewish war."

Even inside the "respectable spectrum" on the American right, voices like Pat Buchanan are ringing out charges of "it's their war, a Jewish war, not an American war." Even a congressional representative from Virginia recently echoed similar sentiments in public. Buchanan, as demonstrated in an article in *Time*, was focusing on and exaggerating the views and powers of the so-called neoconservatives in contemporary American political life. In fact, though, American neoconservatism does have some roots in the American Jewish community of the late 1960s, which found itself caught in a contradiction pitting its anti-Vietnam dovishness against its hawkish pro-Israel views. Norman Podhoretz, the editor of *Commentary*, was one of the first left-wing Jewish intellectuals to move to the right on a number of foreign policy issues and develop a single coherent, unilateralist view of America's role in the global community and thereby help lay the foundation for neoconservatism.

Today the list of Jewish neoconservatives is extensive and includes both Irving and William Kristol, Elliot Cohen, Elliot Abrams, Nathan Glazer, Paul Wolfowitz, and even a local opinion maker, Daniel Pipes.

Intellectually, much of the neoconservative philosophy has been traced back to the prolific writings of a German Jewish intellectual displaced in America during the 1930s, Professor Leo Strauss.

Of course, not all neoconservatives or all American unilateralists are Jewish. That is preposterous. And to think that President Bush, Vice President Cheney, Donald Rumsfeld, and Condoleeza Rice are all intellectual puppets in the hands of Jewish political theorists is paranoid. But paranoia is debilitating, and some early Jewish proponents of the war have grown quieter over time as the specter of conspiratorial anti-Semitism increasingly looms overhead in political circles in this country.

On the other hand, many neoconservatives and some other Jewish advocates of the American campaign in Iraq have held their ground and remain publicly committed to an American military victory in Iraq. Noah Feldman's 2003 book, *After Jihad: America and the Struggle for Islamic Democracy*, is unrepentant in its belief that we are on the right course as a nation. Other neoconservative voices, such as the editor of our local Jewish community's weekly *Exponent*, have become shrill in their denunciations of antiwar activists and intellectuals but rarely spell out the reasons for their pro-Iraq views or goals, except that "it's good for Israel."

Israel itself is in a very peculiar position vis-à-vis American involvement in Iraq and, in my opinion, has won points for not returning fire when Iraqi scuds hit Tel Aviv in the first Iraqi war. Recently, even Pakistan's president softened his public statements on Israel, but that was mostly to curb the growing connections between Israel and India and a nascent anti-Muslim Jewish-Hindu alliance.

Many Israelis I have spoken with would not mind if American tanks kept rolling west and into the streets of Damascus. On the other hand, if Iraq collapses into civil war and a broader Sunni-Shiite conflict develops in the Middle East, anti-Israelism could easily be used by either side to curry favor with their supporters in a broader fight. Most ironically, Israel's disengagement from Gaza happened during the second Iraqi war, an action contrary to the wishes of American Jewish and Israeli hawks who vociferously support American actions in Iraq, in large part because they believe that the destruction of the Hussein regime was good for Israel.

In the face of this complicated mess, it's no small wonder that most American Jews are very quiet about Iraq in public. Why make noise now? Isn't this situation going to run its course and self-correct?

I'm reminded of the jam American Jews found themselves in this country just prior to the outbreak of the Civil War. By the mid-1850s, nearly every religious community in the United States had split over the question of slavery and radicalized one way or the other. American Jews had stayed quiet and would have stayed quiet longer had not they been challenged by outside voices to take a stand. What followed was a brief but intense internal debate over slavery in the American Jewish community. A few Jewish abolitionists spoke up, as did apologists for slavery. One of the few rabbis who openly attacked Southern slavery was KI's David Einhorn, and to this congregation's eternal credit, he was not stifled by his officers or trustees.

American Jews did not speak up in significant numbers about slavery until the eve of the Civil War. Nor have most of us been terribly public about our views on Iraq until this point. But we are approaching a critical marker in the history of the struggle over Iraq. The approval or rejection this coming weekend of a national constitution in Iraq, which grants significant political and economic advances to the Kurds in the north and the Shiites in the south, is now upon us. In any event, if the constitution is adopted and takes root, or is adopted and does not take root, or is vetoed by the requisite three provinces, it is time, in my opinion, to lay out a clear exit strategy. Either our political objectives will have been met or not. If the Iraqis, especially the Sunni Iraqis, are ready for democracy, then so be it; and let's leave the work of democracy to them. If they reject democracy, it is even more urgent to leave, lest we see our casualties spike from nearly two thousand to three thousand to God knows how high.

In my opinion, it is almost impossible to have a clear simple definition of success in this situation. How ironic it would be if our expedition to Iraq resulted in a democratically elected pro-Iranian Shiite theocratic state! How tragic it would be if Iraq disintegrated into total civil war.

On this most sacred of nights, we need to challenge ourselves and ask all those hard and awful questions, beginning with, are the vital interests of the United States served by staying in Iraq, or do we cut our losses and go home, sad, hurt, and a little wiser? Do we draw a line in the sand in Iraq in the war on terror, or do we find another more pointed way to combat jihadism? Do we continue the work of advancing democracy alone or in a multilateral fashion? These are not easy questions, and we are not exempt from trying to answer them either as Americans or as American Jews.

Twenty-five hundred years ago, a Jewish poet sat down on the banks of the Euphrates River. Without reflecting on the birth of the Jewish people near the headwaters of that mighty stream and without knowledge of the great rabbinic academies which would thrive in Mesopotamia in later antiquity, he lamented in Psalm 137, "By the waters of Babylon, there we sat down and wept." Today thousands of American tears are flowing into the waters of Babylon, and tens of thousands of American troops are dreaming of returning home to their Zion.

In my opinion, we cannot continue to go about our national life as if we live in normal times. We do not live in normal times. We are cursed, as an ancient Chinese saying goes, to live in "interesting times." It is not right to walk around on sunny afternoons in the park or the mall as if the whole world was on holiday when thousands of nineteen-year-olds from upstate and down the street, carrying the flag of our country, are in harm's way. It is not right to assign the total burden of war to a volunteer military community as if it is their duty, their responsibility, their choice. A flag in a lapel or a flag hanging from a front porch are good things, but they are not enough. There is no parallel commitment to sacrifice.

Our Jewish tradition is brutally realistic about war. It despises war as the greatest tragedy and sin we can inflict upon one another. It also understands that the time comes when we must defend ourselves or be vanquished by our enemies. There is a time for war and a time for peace, we are taught. There is a time to beat swords into plowshares and a time to beat plowshares into swords.

The great rabbi-scholar-activist Abraham Heschel once remarked that a prophet is a person who knows what time it is! On this Yom Kippur, ask yourself about the historical minute in which we are now living. Is it a time for war or a time for peace? A time to gather stones or a time to cast stones? A time for swords or a time for plowshares?

In my opinion, it is no longer a time to be silent but a time to think and a time to speak. "I have set before you the blessing and the curse," the Torah tells on this holiday of holiday, "life and death." In a world of uncertainty and uncertain consequences, every option is frightening. The only option not available is to simply stand by silently.

There are times when we are called upon to choose. May we choose wisely for our nation and the world, and may God help us make our choices for what is right and true. If only the road to the Promised Land wasn't so long and so difficult. But that is our fate, and that is our responsibility.

As the New Year begins, let us find the strength to respond to the shofar and its call to personal responsibility. May our intentions be pure, our actions just, and our work enduring. Then Lori and Nolan and Daniel and Oliver and George and Eric and Lee and 1,949 others will not have died in vain.

Amen. An easy fast.

Yizkor

October 13, 2005, Yom Kippur Afternoon 5766

In the Jewish tradition, we call memorial services Yizkor. In its original literary setting in the Hebrew, Yizkor literally means "may God remember." Personally, I render Yizkor as "God will remember." Spiritually, I am comforted by the fact that "God will remember." The phrase "May God remember," on the other hand, includes an element of doubt, petition, and unsureness. Of all the services I lead or attend, Yizkor is the one I experience without any doubt at all. I know that I will remember my loved ones who are no longer with my family. There is no way I can forget them. They are with me every day. Just as in life, sometimes their presence is active and sometimes it's dormant. But they are there in my heart, in my mind, in my memory, in my soul. Without question, I remember them—Yizkor—and God remembers them too.

When we come to Yizkor, we don't need help remembering. We need something much deeper from one another, from God, and from ourselves. We need comfort. We need something to touch the pain of loss inside us like a doctor putting pressure on a bleeding wound. For some of us, the wound is new and deep and refuses to close. For some of us, that wound is old but still aches. We need a firm but unseen hand to put tender pressure on those wounds. Comfort is not the same as healing. It is a much more modest emotional goal. It is possible to find comfort. It is less likely to be fully healed. That's why we call out for Yizkor—for God to remember our loved ones, to give us some sense that their lives have been validated by the great primal force in the universe. We need to know that their lives were good, even if their deaths were unfair, untimely, or even inexplicable.

Many times, when we lose someone unexpectedly or too early in life, death violates us like a thief robbing us at gunpoint or slithering into our homes in the shadows and taking away what rightly belongs to us. According to the rabbis, the commandment not to steal actually refers to kidnapping, the stealing of people. Death is that thief. Death is that kidnapper. But there is no court of law or appeal to prosecute death or compensate for grief.

Sometimes grief is expressed in anger.
Sometimes grief is experienced like a punctured wound.
Sometimes grief evokes irrepressible feelings of guilt.
Sometimes grief is experienced as a violation of our own persons.
Sometimes grief cripples us.
Sometimes grief forces us to retreat into ourselves.
Sometimes grief forces us into the embrace of others.
Sometimes grief forces us to look at life differently.
Sometimes grief teaches us to love more fully and with less reservation.

Grief is never a good thing, but sometimes good things can come from a grieving heart.

When I come here to Yizkor, I know that my grandmothers and uncles and in-laws are not forgotten in the heavens above or here below. They are totally remembered. What I do want is for God to remember me and my hurts and my losses and my brokenness and my terrible sense of incompleteness.

Death can teach us to live fully. Sometimes, when we are lucky, we loved someone completely in life and continue to love them after they are gone. Complete love lives on.

On the other hand, if we allow it, broken love can continue to break lives. But broken love can also admonish us to repair the emotional breaches or at least learn to deal with them more kindly. Grief can teach us not to waste a moment in life because in experiencing death, we learn that there is no such thing as excess time. Time is precious; and not taking time to love, to help, to forgive, to extend kindness, and to yield to someone else—all these human shortcomings are very expensive in the great scheme of things.

At Yizkor, I pray for guidance and strength to live. I owe that to those who have gone before me. I need to live for them. I need to live for me. I need to live for those who love me and depend on me.

For some of us, the last year has been brutal. The thief called death visited us and stole away a piece of our life. We are crushed and hurt and angry and incomplete. I lost a favorite uncle unexpectedly this year. He hadn't been sick. He was so important to all of us, and then, he was gone. His death instantly placed me and keeps me in a world of surreal grief.

Many of you are part of that same broken landscape. Some of us have traversed it together. Some are here in hope of finding a comforting word. We all want some measure of comfort, some proof of undying love, some hint of healing.

I believe that God will remember our departed loved ones just as God will remember us in our hour of pain. May this be a time of comfort, of forgiving, and of turning to the future. May God remember all of us, the departed and the living, for the good. May these moments of remembrance help us to keep our memories of them alive and our spirits strong within.

Amen.

HANUKKAH: THE RIGHT LIGHT

December 22, 2005

Last week at our KI Center City's Lunch 'n' Learn (we meet the third Thursday of every month at a different location for lunch and a text study), we took a close look at the Talmud's discussions (Shabbat 21a) of how to light and place the Hanukkah menorah (*hanukkiyah*). One of the issues not discussed in the original Talmudic presentation on Hanukkah is whether or not the first candle should be placed on the extreme right or the extreme left of the *hanukkiyah* and to proceed to add candles nightly from that point. It's not an easy question to answer, as you will see.

Of course, we could simply say it's a tradition or majority practice to light from the right. There is also the explanation that the candles follow the "direction of Hebrew writing" or what one commentator calls "our way of doing things." But there is more to this story—much more! Let me explain! First of all, Hanukkah is a rabbinic, not a Torah-based, holiday. By any reckoning, the first Hanukkah took place in 165 BCE, hundreds of years after the completion of the Torah. The rabbis, however, invoking Deuteronomy 17:11, which teaches that we must follow the "authorities of our own time," declared that the practice of Hanukkah is a "mitzvah" just like the "mitzvot of the Torah." Hence, in the first blessing, we say *v'tzivanu*—that is, "we are commanded"—to light the lights of Hanukkah.

But which light do we light first? Now it gets complicated. The Talmud, we learned in our study group, says that originally the Hanukkah menorah was placed on "the doorpost" at the entrance of our homes as part of the instruction to display the *hanukkiyah* so that the public can see and we can "share the miracle." However, we know that the mezuzah is already on the doorpost! So should we place the menorah above or below the mezuzah? Actually, neither works. We can't place the menorah above because it would trump the mezuzah, and we can't place it below because it would make the menorah inferior. Better, the sages taught, we should place the menorah across from the mezuzah on the other doorpost and be "surrounded by commandments."

Now, the tradition determined that the mezuzah should be on the "right side of the door as we enter our homes based on a grammatical reinterpretation of your homes" as "arriving at your homes." We now know that the only place the *hanukkiyah* can be placed is on the left side of the doorway "as people arrive." Combine that with the Talmudic ordinance (Shabbat 21a) to share the miracle with the public, and it is clear that the newest light should be placed at the outermost position on the menorah—that is, we begin lighting on the "most right position" and "add to the left" each night, lighting the newest candle first. Centuries later, the posting of the menorah on the doorpost fell out of use, but the procedures for lighting the menorah remained in place. Not surprisingly, when I checked the Code of Jewish Law, particularly some of the commentaries on the basic *Shulchan Aruch* (sixteenth century), I discovered that some Jewish communities in Austria started on the left, not the right! The overwhelming majority light the candles beginning on the right!

What can we learn from all this? First, there is a logic to how our tradition has developed over time. Our Judaism is not impetuous or nihilistic. Rather, it is based on a combination of great principles and time-honored legal precedents. Indeed, Hanukkah keenly illustrates how all this works.

The great underlying principle here is that we are to share the story and miracle of Hanukkah with the world. We perform the mitzvah of lighting our menorahs from home but we share their light with the world. Why? First, we should be proud of our tradition and ourselves as descendants of an ancient and worthy tradition. Second, Hanukkah and Judaism have a message for the world—that we can never allow darkness to prevail over light, injustice over justice, or despair over hope. The light of Hanukkah is the light of loyalty, strength, and eternal faith. The light we light on Hanukkah is the right light for ourselves and for humanity. The bigger question then is exactly as the Talmud phrases it, namely, not *how* we do Hanukkah but *why* we do Hanukkah. The answer shines as bright as our menorahs.

Shabbat Shalom and Happy Hanukkah.

TIKKUN TORAH

September 22, 2006, Rosh HaShanah Evening 5767

The other day, I was in an office at the Bildner Center for Jewish Studies at Rutgers University. The director of the program had just received a copy of *The Annual Assessment* of the Jewish People Policy Planning Institute of the Jewish Agency and was eager to share it with me.

The *Annual Assessment*, the most comprehensive of its kind, ran 672 pages. It contained data and analyses of every Jewish community in the world as well as a global perspective. Demographics, generational trends, philanthropic trends, affiliation patterns, and more—everything was in this report. Everything except an assessment of Jewish belief today.

In my opinion, beyond all the numbers and theoretical models and initiatives and policy recommendations is the basic question of belief. If we can't answer the question, "What do we believe?" then how can we plan for the Jewish people? And if we do not hold Judaic values and beliefs of any stripe, then, ultimately, there will be nothing to plan for. People neither support nor "do" things they don't believe in for very long.

Jewish belief is classically divided into three categories: God, Torah, and Israel. The question of whether or not there is a God, and if so, what kind of God is God is not necessarily a Jewish question although Judaism has produced numerous understandings of God of its own.

The question of Israel, or Jewish peoplehood, is actually the most straightforward and least problematic of the three. Few Jewish people today deny being Jewish; most are very or extremely proud of it. Jewishness, to any degree, is the easiest of the three categories.

The biggest Jewish challenge today, theologically speaking, has to do with the idea of the Torah. We know we are Jewish (or not), and we generally know if we believe in God or not. But how do we connect with God? Is it through Jewish ritual and literary sources, or is it through some generic spirituality? Does Torah provide us with a secular ethnic script, or is it a valid religious pathway?

Let me begin with an image provided by a Jewish mystic, Isaac Luria, who lived in Israel in the sixteenth century in Safed. He theorized that when God created the world, there was light—pure light—an intense ray of light that shot out of the Creator and was aimed at cosmic vessels then available. But the vessels couldn't contain the light, and they exploded. Little pieces of primal light were then scattered throughout the universe, and according to the mystics, the final redemption would be the gathering of these shards of light. They called this process *tikkun olam*.

By analogy, the Jewish tradition created a powerful concept called Torah. Torah is our original beam of light. But in modern times, we do not always have the "belief vessels" to contain it. With modernity, our views of the Torah shattered, leaving each of us with the task of collecting fragments of the Torah for our own use. Perhaps this process might be called *tikkun Torah*.

What is Torah for modern Jews? Where does Torah come from? How does it inform my life? Is Judaism a vast collection of customs, or is it something more—something metaphysical, something with authority in our lives?

Granted, these are not everyday questions. We generally do not talk about the origins of Torah while at the mall or over lunch or at a business meeting or while on vacation. But they are important questions, especially at the beginning of the New Year on the Jewish calendar, questions that make sense to ask and, perhaps, to answer.

Let's begin by considering Torah on a small scale. Several times a year, someone comes to my office and brings me old Judaic items for safekeeping. Yellowed tallises, old tefillin with cracked straps softened by age and use, musty prayerbooks with crumbling pages, and a miniature Torah scroll wrapped in a white skirt. The little scroll is too brittle to open but too sacred to discard.

People feel instinctively that it is wrong to discard a sacred object, so they bring them to me, and I hold on to them until I have accumulated enough of them to take them to a cemetery or the Rose Garden here at KI and give them a proper burial. *K'lay koeosh*, the sacred objects we use in the Jewish tradition to help bring holiness into our lives, like the human beings they enrich, deserve special, gentle treatment, especially at the end of their earthly course.

Sometimes I will hold on to one of these items for a while because I can use them for educational purposes or because their former beauty still echoes in them or because their holiness seems undiminished, even if they are beyond their practical usefulness. I put them aside, but I never forget them.

It is interesting to note that one of these objects, the little miniature Torahs, never had any practical usefulness at all. From the beginning, they were meant to be a symbolic pediatric statement about the revered place of the Torah in the Jewish tradition.

Three weeks from now, we will gather in this sanctuary for the holiday of Simchat Torah when we complete reading the Torah and start the scroll over again. With song and dance, we will parade all our Torah scrolls around this great sanctuary and then call our youngest and newest students up to the Ark and have them recite the sacred words of the *Sh'ma*. Into their little hands, we will place miniature Torahs dressed in white skirts. The students will hold on to them and then show them to their parents and grandparents and uncles and aunts and give them a place of honor on a shelf in their bedrooms and keep them for years and years. They are remarkably enduring Judaic keepsakes. Everybody can accept and love a little Torah.

These little Torahs are given to us to mark the beginning of our Jewish education. They are scaled down so that they are accessible to us as children. But as we grow, the Torahs we learn from and about also begin to grow in content, complexity, and size.

At age thirteen, we are called upon to read and interpret a passage or two from a complete adult Torah. Like a cobbler's apprentice, we are asked to produce a "Torah masterpiece" that reflects our spiritual and intellectual development at the edge of adulthood. Being called to the Torah for the first time is so important in our tradition that our parents commit us to years of study and preparation and themselves to years of shlepping just to stand there with us at the moment when we make the ancient words of Torah sing with our own voices. Family and friends will cross continents to hear us chant a three-thousand-year-old text. Elderly relatives who normally would not risk walking up a steep flight of marble steps will ascent to the *bimah* with determination.

Somehow, as families circle around their *b'nai mitzvah* and watch them move through their portions with a Hebraic competence they themselves did not always achieve, the whole tradition of Torah begins to make more sense to us, at least for a moment. Generations long gone seem to take their place next to us. Images of Passover seders and flickering Shabbat candles and old-world grandparents and Hanukkah menorahs dance in and out of memories of toddlers taking their first step, tricycles, first-day-at-school jitters, and Little League and dance competitions. Ancient chanted words and living family memories intersect and are woven together for a moment, perfectly matched in their sanctity and importance to us.

For some of us who were not raised in the Jewish tradition, a family *bar* or *bat mitzvah* is often our first up-close exposure to the Torah scroll and its extraordinary role in the lives of Jewish families. There is much common ground to be found in family loyalty, in universal ethical teachings, and in the mutually safe zones of the Jewish tradition where our spirits can meet and be at ease.

Many of us return to the Torah as a sacred symbol and meta-script in our lives just before we marry. In a wonderful custom called *aufruf*, a couple comes to the synagogue on a Shabbat prior to their *chuppah* and receive a blessing before the Ark. In so doing, they link their covenant of love with the covenant of faith, which has kept our people wedded to its heritage for centuries.

There is even a custom about a second *bar* or *bat mitzvah*. According to the Psalms, our lifespan is "three score years and ten," or seventy years. Thus, when we reach the age of eighty-three, or seventy years plus *bar mitzvah*, we are called back to the Torah to reenact or experience anew our *bar* or *bat mitzvah*. In Judaism, the slopes of Sinai are never too steep for us to scale, not even at age eighty-three or more. Rather, the Torah, as it itself tells us, is in our mouths that we may speak it and in our hearts that we do it, whenever and wherever we choose.

Imagine for a moment the Torah scenes of consecration, *b'nai mitzvah* of all ages, and pre-wedding blessings unfolding across dozens of generations and hundreds of locations. Torah readings in wooden synagogues in Poland and Russia, in great temples in Germany, in modern *battei midrash* in Israel, in the immigrant shuls of Philadelphia a century ago, and in the synagogues of our youth. All these scenes become real in the eye of memory and in our hearts. Ivory pointers and silver crowns, Torah skirts of every color, crowns of silver, and breastplates with lions and commandments.

Symbols everywhere, shining, glowing, responding to some deeper reality in our lives.

Isaac Luria, the mystic who created the concept of *tikkun olam*, also had a specific insight as to the nature of Torah. He taught that there are, in fact, two Torahs. The *Aleph Torah*, he taught, is eternal and incorporeal. Its abode is in the heavens above and beyond time and space.

Then there is the *Bet Torah*, the material Torah of words, ink, cloth, and silver. The *Bet Torah*, Luria taught, is only a case, a shell, a garment around the *Aleph Torah*. It is our best human attempt to represent pure Torah.

"*Dibrah Torah bilshone adam*," the rabbis taught. "Torah speaks in human language" because pure Torah is not accessible to us. Like radio waves, which are transformed into music by our electronic technology, so pure *Aleph Torah* is made accessible to us only by the words and songs and artifacts that encase our sacred tradition. The Torahs in our Ark and the little Torahs we place in our little children's hands are symbols and repositories of an even greater more essential Torah.

What is Torah? Torah is more than an object called Torah. Torah literally is divine instruction, a sacred path, and the specifically Jewish path to truth, justice, kindness, holiness, and life itself as our tradition believes it should be lived.

For sure, our Torah, the Torah of Moses, is not the only Torah in this world. There is the Torah of Zen. There is the Torah of Dao. There is the transformational Torah of Christianity. Islam follows the Torah of Mohammed. The Mormons follow the Torah of Joseph Smith and Brigham Young. Each tradition has its own Torah, its own path, its own response to and exploration of a higher, purer, undifferentiated and, ultimately, unknowable *Aleph Torah*.

In Judaism, we love our Torah and use our Torah as the guiding text in our life, *not* because our Torah is truer or better than anyone else's but because it is ours, culturally specific, and historically tested in our religious and historical continuum. Jews have lived Torah, learned Torah, and bequeathed Torah for dozens of generations. It is our channel, our tool, to make our lives holy.

The exact origins of Torah as literature and as an artifact are shrouded in the mists of time. Tradition, of course, assigns the authorship of Torah to Moses. By contrast, modern biblical scholars, whether or not they view

Moses as a historical figure, believe that the compilation of the Five Books of Moses extended from the tenth to the fifth centuries BCE.

The Torah scroll is even later in its development. First, a parchment technology needed to be developed. Second, the Hebrew alphabet, as we know it, did not take shape until the Greco-Roman period. Ironically then, the *Sefer Torah* is a combination of Israelite and Hellenistic elements, of theories of revelation and reason.

The Torah itself does not offer an explanation of its origins. "In the beginning," it commences, "God created the heaven and the earth." I once asked a seventh-grade class who was the narrator in that passage and who they think the intended audience was. One very bright student fired back, "The narrator is the universal third-person male."

"And who is the audience?" I asked again.

"We are," said one of the kids.

Indeed, both answers were right on the mark!

To make things even more complex, the rabbis of the Talmud believed that there were actually two Torahs, written and oral; and they understood that every verse in the written Torah of Moses has at least seventy meanings, which were cultivated orally in the rabbinic institutes of Israel and Mesopotamia and then preserved in the Talmud.

How can we be any less expansive and inclusive about our understanding of Torah than the rabbis of two millennia ago?

The medieval Jewish philosophers also understood that Torah is more than an object and more than a narrowly constructed narrative that contains specific laws, complex genealogies, and the national story of ancient Israel. As rationalists, they believed that "the truth" can always be derived both by reason and by prophecy. From Saadia Gaon to Moses Maimonides, our philosophers sought to demonstrate that the Torah of Moses and the Torah of Aristotle reflected the same higher truth, the same rational *Aleph Torah*, the same essence, the same ultimate reality. The controversial statement recently issued by the pope actually includes insight and challenging comments on the relationship of faith and reason in monotheism.

The Reform movement came along exactly two hundred years ago and eventually *historicized* our understanding of Torah. Torah, the founding of our movement taught, evolves over time, taking many different forms and shapes over the centuries. It began with Moses on Sinai but changed again because of historical need in Roman times and then again during the Middle Ages and yet again with modernity and the rise of a scientific worldview. To the early Reformers, the codifying of the Torah scroll was the beginning of a dynamic process that continues to adapt and innovate and apply itself in every generation in the history of our people in the Pentateuch itself, in rabbinic literature, and in modern critical Torah scholarship.

Modern Jewish thinkers like Martin Buber, Franz Rosenzweig, and Abraham Joshua Heschel, without denying the historical evolution of Torah in Judaism, pointed to the possibility of reintroducing holiness in our lives through their existentialist Torah-based philosophies. According to Buber and others, Torah, whether an echo of Sinai or a moment of spiritual discovery in Philadelphia, is genuine and transformational in our lives. These modern thinkers assure us that the divine presence can be just as real to us as it was to the generation of the Exodus or to Rashi or the Baal Shem Tov. Each generation, Buber and others teach us, creates its *Bet Torah* its own way. Torah, these philosophers assure us, is always a genuine religious possibility.

Torah, the rabbis across the centuries taught, is generally expansive with respect to ideas but, more often than not, specific with respect to actions. Beliefs about creation, revelation, and providence run the gamut in Judaism. However, with respect to human actions and behaviors, Torah can be, and generally is, very specific. "*Naaseh v'nishma*," the Torah declares, "we will do, and then we will listen." We will do the commandments that speak to us first, and then we will speculate on their origins and meanings.

In the Jewish tradition, each specific Torah action is called a *mitzvah*, a commandment, a good deed. By traditional reckoning, there are 613 commandments in the Torah, 613 *mitzvot*. The familiar word *mitzvah* can mean many things. It literally means a "commandment" in Hebrew. However, when used as a word in Yiddish, it means a "good deed." As Reform Jews, the term *commandment* may be theologically out of reach for many of us while a *good deed*, although comfortable intellectually, may be religiously incomplete.

From the perspective of modern Judaism, I would describe a mitzvah as a "personal Torah action," an existentially nonnegotiable imperative in our lives including the universal mitzvot like "you shall not steal" as well as the specifically Jewish commandment to mark the beginning of the new year by listening to the sound of the shofar. Both are *mitzvot*. The *mitzvot* we feel compelled to do are our personal way of writing our own personal Torah with our lives.

In my opinion, one actually writes his or her own personal Torah through the doing of *mitzvot*, ethical living, moral business practices, and devotion to family; observing the Sabbath and holidays; supporting institutions of learning; caring for the sick, the elderly, and the poor; and studying and pursuing justice. In thousands of ways and in tens of thousands of acts, we can actualize the *Aleph Torah* of our lives and create a *Bet Torah*. Some of us do it in a more traditional way. Some do it in a modern and even secular fashion. But the presence and power of Torah are evident everywhere around us, in our lives, in our families, and in our community.

There is also the very real possibility of helping to write an actual *Sefer Torah*, a Torah scroll, a powerful symbol of our heritage and the principal repository of the teachings, values, and practices of our ancient faith. No matter which Judaic ideology informs the listing and explanations of the commandments, it is universally held that the 613th mitzvah, the final mitzvah, is to write your own Torah by adding a letter in your own hand to the work of a trained scribe.

During the course of this coming year, we are going to write our own Torah and complete the "ultimate mitzvah" together as a congregation. In writing a Torah, we will learn a great deal about Torah, its letters and words, its inks and its parchment. By writing a KI Torah, we will ground ourselves in the larger concept of Torah.

Several summers ago, I led a group of about forty individuals from KI on a tour through several countries in Central and Eastern Europe. One of our destinations, Eisenstaedt, a small town in Austria near the Hungarian border, held particular historic significance for us and an unexpected religious opportunity.

During the eighteenth century, Eisenstaedt emerged as a particularly important center of Torah study. Typical of the time and place, the community's leader, Samson Wertheimer, built a synagogue in his home in the middle of the town's old Jewish ghetto.

When we visited the long-abandoned Wertheimer synagogue in Eisenstaedt, we found a nearly empty room of what was once a grand architectural statement in marble and stone. The infixed stone Ark no longer had a curtain. Nor was there an eternal light above it. What it did have was a piece of parchment in it, a fragment of what was once a complete

Torah scroll. A strange relic. A partial script. A piece of a destroyed past, which somehow still resided in this sanctuary.

We sat down as a group, and it was my job to read and translate a few lines from this Torah fragment. The unknown scribe had a good hand. The letters were square and neat and easy to read.

The words from the parchment began to resonate in the room and inside all of us who were assembled there. Somehow memories we never had as individuals but retained in our larger group consciousness began to emerge. In our hearts, we could hear a Hazzan singing across the gap of 2.5 centuries since the synagogue was first built. In our minds, we could hear the rabbis of the town's famed yeshiva planting vines of thoughts in the rich soil of each Torah term. In short, for a moment, we experienced the meaning of *Tikkun Torah*, the repair of the Torah in modern times.

This little torn piece of parchment left in a long-ago abandoned synagogue had surprising transformational powers to each and every one of us. It was an echo from the past, a whisper of what was, and a reminder of what we must do in our lives as modern Jews seeking to nurture and preserve our tradition.

Each of us in this sanctuary brings their own Eisenstaedt Torah fragments to this place, connecting memories and resonating texts to be stitched together, to be completed, not only to be adorned with beautiful cloths and silver crowns but, more importantly, to be crowned with the voices and lives of an engaged, living Jewish community.

Torah has power, even if it is only a single torn column. It calls out to us and says, "Here is your spiritual homeland, portable and transcendent, inscribed in an ancient hand in black ink on a piece of vellum and filled with the stories and laws and customs that define who you are among all the peoples of the earth."

Torah is Judaism's sacred path. Torah is the essence of our tradition and the details of its teachings. It is a multifaceted concept including the totality of Judaism, an object in the synagogue, a work of literature, and a cosmic possibility that hope, love, and truth are real and not merely utilitarian concepts. Torah is a gift and a challenge, a standard and a goal.

Judaism is Torah. One way or another, Torah is at the center of who we are and what we do as Jews. Torah is the path and the mountaintop, our home and our destination as individuals and as a people.

As this New Year begins and we hear the resonant tones of the *shofar* calling us home to our inner selves, let us resolve to live a life of Torah and *mitzvot*, each in his or her own way, and together as a community. Let us recall the little white Torahs of our youth and let us strengthen our hold on the wooden staves of our full-size adult Torahs. Then we can begin to rediscover Torah's highest teachings and richest details; and most of all, we will then be able to pass on the heritage of Torah, the glory of the people of Israel, to the next generation of our families and our people.

"It is a tree of life to those who hold it fast," we sing as we return the Torah to the Ark, "and all who cling to it find happiness." We then conclude, "Its ways are ways of pleasantness and all its paths are peace."

May the year ahead be a year of pleasantness and peace, happiness and health, and learning and doing, a year of good deeds and a year of Torah.

Amen.

Shana Tova and Shabbat Shalom!

WHY I AM A JEW!

October 1, 2006, Yom Kippur Evening 5767

This semester I am again teaching a lecture course at Rutgers University in New Brunswick, New Jersey, on Modern Jewish History. I have thirty-nine students and five adult auditors. Most of the students are juniors and seniors who are taking the course as an elective. We meet in a basement classroom of a large dormitory overlooking the Raritan River.

It is a good class. A majority of the students are "seekers"—that is, young Jewish adults trying to understand their heritage. One of the leading Jewish academics of our time, Jacob Neusner, once complained that he wished he had students searching for something other than themselves. I am actually quite happy that I have students searching for themselves. It's an important part of a liberal education.

I'm also of the conviction that the only way that the majority of Jewish kids growing up today will remain rooted in Judaism is if they study it in a critical fashion at the university level, the same way they study everything else at a university, and come to informed decisions about who they are, how Judaism developed, and their place in it. Of course, I don't advocate anything Jewish or Judaic in class. That would be wrong and not in accordance with the mission of the university. Nor do I have to. The students are free to personalize or distance themselves from our shared topic. My sense of the class is that most of the kids are taking their studies personally, and that is just fine with me.

One of the most important themes in my class on Modern Jewish History is the history of Jewish political emancipation, the story of how newly formed modern states late in the eighteenth and early nineteenth centuries struggled to redefine their Jewish populations from permanent alien residents and, for all intents and purposes, a foreign criminal class and instead make them citizens of France and Germany and the United States.

It was not always a happy story. Even here in Pennsylvania, at the moment of national independence in July 1776, Jews were not granted full citizenship. Neither the Quakers nor the Lutherans of the time were interested in enfranchising non-Christians as equals in their Commonwealth. Jews in Pennsylvania had to wait a few years until the adoption of the United States Constitution to achieve that status, at least in theory.

The most important discussion about the place of Jews in the modern state did not take place in the United States. Rather, it was with the Enlightenment and the American Revolution in mind that the French debated what would become known as the Jewish Question. In its most precise form, the Jewish Question challenged just everyone to define the primary political allegiance of Jews in their various countries of domicile. In other words, the Jewish Question asked if Jews who were born in France primarily viewed themselves as Jews or Frenchmen who happened to be of the Jewish religious persuasion. The corollary to the Jewish Question was, why should emancipated Jews remain Jewish if they were no longer compelled to do so?

For about fifty years, European Jews, politicians, and intellectuals of every stripe and every flavor debated the Jewish Question. Internally, the Jewish community also struggled to find compelling reasons to remain Jewish and not be swept away by the developing centrifugal forces of emancipation and assimilation.

People became so obsessed with the Jewish question that the following joke eventually developed:

A professor of zoology required his class to write a paper on the elephant and how it has been studied in different countries.

The German student submitted a paper on "An Introduction to the Bibliography of the Scientific Literature on the Elephant."

The French student wrote a paper on "Romance and the Elephant."

The American student wrote "Breeding Bigger and Better Elephants."

And finally, the Jewish student prepared a paper entitled "The Elephant and the Jewish Question."

In the summer of 1806 and continuing into that Fall, the French emperor Napoleon convened what he called an "Assembly of Jewish Notables" to answer his Jewish Questions. Less important than the predictable answers the Jewish notables politely and tactfully supply to Napoleon was the symbolism of the moment. Napoleon, the great liberator, was going to break down the last vestige of medieval legal discrimination against the Jews of his empire, declare the Jews of his realm to be citizens, and redefine Judaism as valid faith in the eyes of the French state.

Two hundred years later, the drama of the French Assembly of Jewish Notables should not be forgotten. Whether they wanted to be liberated or not, the Jews of France would become French citizens and Judaism would become a confessional community in France controlled by, not compelled by, the state. Today, almost exactly two hundred years later, the Assembly of Jewish Notables can be viewed as a symbolic beginning of Jewish modernity.

Modernity came with a heavy price for the Jews of France. They had to give up their status as an autonomous community. The basic forces that shaped a person as a Jew shifted from external to internal. It was not the state but the individual who now needed to figure out why they should remain in the Jewish community.

Of course, redefining the political status of Jews in France, Germany, and other places did not instantly snuff out a thousand years of European anti-Semitism. Many Europeans deeply resented the enfranchisement of Jews into their society.

In France, the Dreyfus Affair, in which a Jewish officer in the French Army was charged with treason, exploded on the French scene eighty-eight years after the Assembly of Notables was convened. It dramatically demonstrated the depth of official and grassroots anti-Semitism in modern Gaul. Ironically, the Dreyfus Affair also served to crystallize the Zionist response to the Jewish question. Listening to the reactionary clerics and establishment military bigots, Theodor Herzl came to the conclusion that Jews in France were, indeed, Jews living in France and not Jewish Frenchmen but ex-patriate Jewish nationals. His goal was to create a new Jewish state, a homeland. Israel became that state in 1948.

For the majority of the Jews in France at the turn of the century, Herzl's conclusion did not result in a decision to emigrate from France. They wanted to live in France, and they wanted to be Frenchmen of the Jewish religious persuasion. Now they needed to figure out answers to a new and enduring set of Jewish questions: Why remain a member of a tiny often-disliked religious community? Why uphold an ancient religious heritage that seemed, on the surface, incompatible with living a modern life? Why eat funny food? Why drink bad wine? Why employ nasal and guttural languages like Yiddish and Hebrew when one could communicate in the beautiful language of French? In short, why be Jewish?

In the Middle Ages, Jews had no trouble answering that question. The state told them they were Jewish. The church told them they were Jewish. There was no reason to doubt that God had made them Jewish, punished them for the sins of their ancestors, and sent them into exile. Besides, everybody hated the Jews, and what choice was there really except to be Jewish?

But in modern times, after the liberal democracies and newly formed republics declared Jews to be equals and urged them to acculturate if not assimilate and lose their national identity, what would keep Jews Jewish? Within ten years of the assembly, French Jews began to retreat The rate of conversion soared, and Judaism began to retreat in the lives of French Jews, English Jews, German Jews, and American Jews.

On the other hand, in each place, voices could be heard making the claim that it was not "all or nothing," that one could be both modern and Jewish and that there was nothing in Judaism or Jewishness that contradicted the basic tenets of modernity. Jews could be French citizens and loyal members of the Jewish community along religious lines. In fact, it was exactly this historical circumstance that led to the formation of Reform Judaism in Germany in the early decades of the nineteenth century.

One of the most passionate of the voices exhorting French Jews to remain Jewish and to combine their Judaism with their personal modernity was a young French Jew by the name of Edmond Fleg. Fleg, born in 1874, a successful playwright, had drifted away from Judaism as a young adult. Then, traumatized by the Dreyfus Affair and the ugly anti-Semitism it unleashed and inspired by the early Zionist Congresses, Fleg returned to Judaism. He subsequently refocused his considerable literary talents on the exploration of Jewish literature and identity and searched for reasons to keep the increasingly cosmopolitan French Jewish community Jewish.

The most remarkable of all Fleg's publications is a short essay entitled "Pourquoi je suis Juif" or "Why I Am a Jew," which appeared in the late 1920s. Fleg's essay is actually a reflection on a letter he wanted to address to his "little unborn grandson." Fleg's own children at the time were only fourteen and nineteen, but he was already concerned that given the realities of modern Jewish life, it was possible that his grandchildren would drift away from Judaism. He was worried that his children's children would not be able to articulate a clear, compelling inner argument as to why they should remain Jews in their adulthood, decades deep into the twentieth century. It is an anxiety many people in the contemporary Jewish community continue to share.

In many ways, Fleg's essay is exactly the kind of text each of us needs to ponder on Yom Kippur. It begins as a confession and concludes as an affirmation. It is beautiful. It is moving. It is deep, both emotionally and existentially. It speaks to the modern Jewish condition.

"I ought to have attached myself," Fleg says of his own failure to secure a Jewish education as a youth, "to something that would be myself and more than myself. I reproach myself," he continued, "with not having understood the Jewish wisdom of which [my father] talked to me and which lived in him AND with no longer finding, by my own fault, anything in common between Israel's past and my own empty soul."

Fleg then asks his personal set of questions. What is Judaism? What ought a Jew to do? How to be a Jew? Why be a Jew? His response to these questions has become one of the classic formulations of what it means to be a Jew in modern times. He provides us with eleven affirmations of faith or reasons to be Jewish.

The first two of Fleg's responses are autobiographical.

"I am a Jew because being born of Israel and having lost her," he starts his statement, "I have felt her live again in me, more living than myself."

"I am a Jew," Fleg continues, "because being born of Israel and having regained her, I wish her to live after me, more living than myself."

Fleg then lists five reasons for being a Jew: "I am a Jew," Fleg tells the unborn generations of his family, "because the faith of Israel demands of me no abdication of the mind."

"I am a Jew," he continues, "because the faith of Israel requires of me all the devotion of my heart."

"I am a Jew," he writes, "because in every place where suffering weeps, the Jew weeps."

"I am a Jew," Fleg affirms, "because at every time when despair cries out, the Jew hopes."

"I am a Jew," he reminds us, "because the word of Israel is the oldest and the newest."

Finally, in his remarkable reaffirmation of his heritage, Fleg ends by demonstrating the universality of the Jewish faith.

"I am a Jew," he asserts in his eighth affirmation, "because the promise of Israel is the universal promise." Turning to the future, Fleg declares, "I am a Jew because, for Israel, the world is not yet completed. We are completing it."

"I am a Jew," he continues in his universalistic argument, "because above the nations and Israel, Israel places man and his unity."

Then, only in the eleventh and ultimate affirmation does he turn to the theological and the metaphysical. "I am a Jew," he writes, "because above man, image of the divine unity, Israel places the divine unity and its divinity."

In a postscript, Fleg again wonders if the future generations of the Jewish people will remain true to their people and their creed. If they "wish to abandon it," he says, "let it be for a greater truth, if there is one." But then he assures himself, "Whether you abandon [Judaism] or whether you follow it, Israel will journey on to the end of days."

I have read Fleg's essay and affirmation of faith many times. Recently, I began using it as the final text I review with our Confirmation class. We talk about each of Fleg's affirmations and whether or not we agree with them, disagree with them, or need to modify or add to them. I also ask the students to write their own version of Fleg's "I am a Jew."

Their statements would have been reassuring to Edmond Fleg. Here is a sample of what fifteen-and sixteen-year-olds at KI were able to say about themselves as Jews:

I am a Jew because I say so.
I am a Jew because I was born into a Jewish family.
I am a Jew because I feel a connection to Judaism.
I am a Jew because I want to be.
I am a Jew because it is part of me.
I am a Jew because I feel comfortable in my beliefs.
I am a Jew because I like to question things.
I am a Jew because I care about the Jewish people.
I am a Jew because I love Israel.
I am a Jew because I care about *tikkun olam*.
I am a Jew because I believe in one God.

This classroom exercise has also given me the chance to think about my personal Jewish affirmations—affirmation I need to remember and embrace again and again.

"Pourquoi je suis Juif?" Edmond Fleg asks me. "Why am I, Lance Sussman, a Jew?"

I am a Jew because I spent years of my life searching for a God I could believe in and eagerly traveled the spiritual trails of Judaism until I learned that the answer is in the journey and not in the final destination.

I am a Jew because my family escaped from Nazi Germany.

I am a Jew because I traveled to Auschwitz as an adult and stood at the end of the railroad tracks and was overwhelmed with images of my heritage and the realization that a whole nation had determined to erase those images from the face of the earth.

I am a Jew because my childhood memories are filled with warm scenes of Jewish holidays and family gatherings.

I am a Jew because I have always wanted to learn about Judaism from when I first learned to read until today and am never weary of learning more Torah.

I am a Jew because I have always loved Hebrew and the Hebrew language helps me express my innermost religious feelings and convictions.

"*Lamah ani Yehudi?* Why am I, Lance Sussman, a Jew?"

I am a Jew because the first time I saw the coast of Israel through an airplane window on an El Al plane at the age of fifteen, my eyes moistened and my throat constricted with emotion.

I am a Jew because every time Israel is attacked, I feel attacked.

I am a Jew because I once traveled underground in the former Soviet Union and met with refuseniks in their homes and experienced their pain and fear up close and personal.

I am a Jew because I have witnessed new *olim* from Russia—old and young, in families and all alone—descend from planes on the runway of Ben Gurion Airport and come home.

I am a Jew because Shabbat has provided the beat in the essential rhythm of my life, six days of work, and one day for ancient blessings.

Why am I a Jew?

I am a Jew because I have witnessed hundreds of couples under the *chuppah* link their covenant of love to Judaism's covenant of faith and destiny.

I am a Jew because I feel my heritage renewing itself every time I help give a baby his or her Hebrew name.

I am a Jew because I have stood at the Torah with thousands of people over time for bar and bat mitzvahs and experienced the unbroken generational train of our tradition with many different families.

I am a Jew because I have stood graveside with innumerable mourners and watched them hold on to tradition and the words of the Mourners' Kaddish for strength, comfort, and hope.

I am a Jew because I believe that the synagogue is the sanctuary of Israel.

I am a Jew because I believe that Judaism understands that between mercy and justice there is a path of righteousness.

I am a Jew because I believe that the "saving of a life" is an urgent *mitzvah*.

I am a Jew because I believe Judaism believes that education is an urgent *mitzvah*.

I am a Jew because Judaism rejects the belief that it is superior to other traditions and makes its claim on me only because it is already mine.

I am a Jew because in Judaism all of God's children are equally God's children and every life is sacred.

I am a Jew because Judaism believes that existence is not an accident and has meaning.

I am a Jew because Judaism recognizes holiness in everything beautiful, kind, and just in this world.

I am a Jew because Judaism is my spiritual home, and from my home, I can share in the beauty and delights of all creation.

I am a Jew because Judaism believes in personal responsibility, forgiveness, and hope.

I am a Jew because Judaism values my humanity above my ethnicity and enables me to become a better person by becoming a better Jew.

I am a Jew because Judaism recognizes that the world is not complete and that all of us have deep responsibilities in completing it and thereby complete ourselves as human beings and as Jews.

On this Yom Kippur, the holiest of days on the Jewish calendar, take a moment and think about your response to the statement "I am a Jew because . . ."

Are you Jewish as an accident of birth or as a matter of conviction?

Is Judaism at the core of your life or is it marginal?

Is Judaism, in any way, compelling to you because of its values, beliefs, or practices or largely foreign to you intellectually or distant to you emotionally or behaviorally?

Does being Jewish obligate you to do and not do certain things?

Does Judaism inform your view of the world and your critical ethical choices, or is it a limited culinary option you find little pleasure in?

If you were called upon to prepare your statement of Jewish belief and intent to be sealed for a generation and then read aloud to a still-unborn generation of your family, would you ask them to follow in your footsteps? Would you ask them to quicken their Jewish pace, or would you give them the option of deviating from the path?

What would you write in your Jewish book of life on this Day of Atonement?

Exactly two hundred years ago, the Jewish Notables of France were called together by their emperor and challenged to make the case that they should be allowed to live as Frenchmen and promise that their Jewishness would not interfere with their ability to function in society. Instead, the Notables made a statement that not only embraced modernity but also made the case that their remaining Jewish was a matter of reasoned choice.

We can be modern, we can be American, we can be French, and we can remain Jewish as a matter of principle. That is what the Reform movement is all about. That is what Edmond Fleg urged. Hopefully, for those of us assembled here tonight, that is what we believe as well.

May God open your minds and hearts to the heritage of Israel.

May you be inspired to teach and bequeath its values and truths to all the generations of your families.

May the heritage of Torah bring joy, depth, and satisfaction to your life.

May you be inscribed in the Book of Life for a year of health, happiness, and peace.

Amen.

An easy fast.

Part 2

A Little Religion Is a Good Thing
2007–2011

In the Rear View Mirror, 2007-2011

By the beginning of my sixth year at KI, the process of transition and integration to the Elkins Park synagogue was complete, and I was fully operational as the congregation's Senior Rabbi. By this time, it was also clear to me and the synagogue leadership that we were facing significant demographic challenges. Elkins Park, once the home of the largest concentration of Jews in the Philadelphia area, was now rapidly becoming a more diverse neighborhood. When I first arrived, I was frequently told that the area's public schools had been 90 percent Jewish, probably an inflated number, but now had very few Jewish students. The implications of this demographic change were monumental. The membership base of the synagogue was eroding, and we needed to do something about it! Three strategies emerged. First, create a satellite operation in another area that was attracting young Jewish families. Two, develop new and attractive programming at our large Elkins Park facility; and three, run an endowment campaign to help secure the financial future of the synagogue. It was of little comfort to know that the Reform movement in Judaism was facing the same challenges across the country.

As I look in the rearview mirror, it eventually became clear that the first strategy, a new location, did not succeed although we did open a campus in Blue Bell, Pennsylvania, and operated it for ten years. On the other hand, our efforts to intensify programming in Elkins Park and find creative new ways of expressing ourselves were hitting the mark! Most importantly, we found a way to use visual technology during services and then committed to transforming our sanctuary and chapel at tremendous expense into "live broadcast studios" complete with drop-down screens, projectors, cameras, monitors, flexible lighting, and a new sound system. Curiously, the iPhone appeared in the middle of all these changes in 2007. With great determination, we became a truly twenty-first-century synagogue and later found ourselves well-positioned when COVID struck years later, and we had the right technology in place. Gratefully, the transformation of our sacred space was made possible by several successful financial campaigns despite the massive downturn in the American economy in 2008.

My second quinquennial period at KI was also coterminous with a sea change in American politics. In January 2009, Barack Obama was inaugurated as the first African American president of the United States. For the majority of my congregants, Obama's election was a happy, historic milestone for our country, and optimism swept through the congregation about a number of his initiatives, domestic and foreign. On the other hand, my politically conservative members, typical of the American Right wing, were greatly alarmed, and the polarization of American politics, already deep and dangerous, became even more profound. For a preaching rabbi, it proved to be a perilous moment, which, tragically, only became more problematic as the years went by. What issues could I speak about from the pulpit? What could I say in my weekly electronic messages? One side wanted me to speak up. The other side asked that I be as judicious as possible.

The religious culture of the United States was also in flux during the years 2007–2011. On the one hand, religious fundamentalism was growing in the United States and becoming increasingly political in its orientation. For related but different reasons, the Reform movement, politically and religiously liberal, was also shifting toward more traditional practice (but not more traditional theology). On the other hand, a number of books were published during this rearticulating and sharpening arguments for atheism and against organized religion. Years earlier, I learned that the Native American name for the Hudson was "the river that flows two ways [salt and fresh water]." It was a "Hudson moment" for me as a religious leader.

At the national level, I served as the Chair of the Central Conference of American Rabbis' Press and had the honor of helping to publish the first volume of the Reform movement's new prayer book, *Mishkan T'Filah* (2007), which had encountered significant business and production problems before I was invited to join the publication committee. Subsequently, I was involved in the early stages of launching the High Holy Day prayer books *Mishkan HaNefesh*, which did not appear until 2015. In 2009, I served as one of three editors of *New Essays in American Jewish History* in honor of Dr.

Gary P. Zola, Executive Director of the American Jewish Archives, along with Professors Pamela S. Nadell and Jonathan D. Sarna. The following year, I published my first article on Jewish art, a new field of scholarly interest for me, in *Reform Judaism* magazine (March 2010).

On a very personal level, this period at KI included the death of my father, Charles Sussman (1925–2010) on October 27, 2010. A native of Baltimore, Maryland, my father was a decorated veteran of World War II who experienced 144 days of continuous combat including fighting in the Battle of Bulge. After World War II, my father obtained both a Bachelor's and a Master's Degree from Johns Hopkins. A lifelong educator and guidance counselor, my father taught me to read as a six-year-old and instilled an enduring interest in history in me. In his declining years, we spoke regularly on the phone, often when I was driving home from officiating at a funeral. However, those talks did not adequately prepare me for his death, which had a profound spiritual effect on me and deepened my ability to provide grief counseling and preach on death and dying although I had already officiated at hundreds of funerals. In the wake of my father's death, I believe I became a better rabbi. For their part, members of KI responded to Dad's death with a huge outpouring of empathy and support, which deeply moved me.

A Little Religion Is a Good Thing

September 12, 2007, Rosh HaShanah 5768

I hear it all the time: "Rabbi, I'm not really religious." "Rabbi, I wasn't raised in a religious home." "Rabbi, my family was Workmen's Circle. I'm not religious." "Rabbi, I grew up in a traditional home, but I'm not religious anymore." "Rabbi, I'm an agnostic." "Rabbi, I'm an atheist." "Rabbi, I'm a cultural Jew." "Rabbi, I'd love to talk, but I have a yoga class to go to right now." "Rabbi, I'm not really religious. My religion is Israel." "Rabbi, I really believe in God, but I'm not connected to Judaism." "Rabbi, I'm really into Judaism, but I'm not sure about God." "Rabbi, I'm a member but not really active." "Rabbi, I love the synagogue and come to everything, but I'm not really a believer." The reports go on and on, and just when I think I've heard of every religious-cultural-spiritual-ethical-Jewish combination, someone comes along and tells me a new one.

They are all expressions of our times and our current spiritual condition. They are all by-products of modernization, secularization, and, to some extent, even the re-ethnization and re-Judaization of the Jewish community, which has taken place in parts of the Jewish world in recent years. Few topics are more interesting or important to me.

For the last few years, I have taught a class at Rutgers on Modern Jewish History and will be doing so again next year for the Boston Hebrew College's Adult Jewish Learning Program in Cherry Hill. Last spring, I also offered an adult ed class here at KI on "Three Jewish Philosophers: Maimonides, Spinoza, and Mendelssohn" to explore the nexus of faith, reason, and science in medieval and modern Jewish thought.

Without question, the class here at KI that drew the most attention was the lecture on Spinoza, the great seventeenth-century Dutch Jewish philosopher, who was excommunicated by rabbis of Rembrandt's Holland but then did not convert to another religion. To some, Spinoza's philosophical rationalism made him the last of the medievals. To others, his scientific worldview made him the "first of the moderns." In time, he became an icon for Jewish freethinkers and rebels who saw themselves in him and his break from tradition. Indeed, all across Eastern Europe, in the shadow of the great yeshivas, there were Spinoza Societies that traded Talmud for ethical treatises and portraits of bearded rabbis for pictures of a clean-shaven Dutch Jew.

When over a hundred people showed up on a Sunday morning at KI last June to listen to a ninety-minute talk on Spinoza, I had to wonder, is this good or bad for Judaism? My answer? Very good. Spinoza represents the point of departure, the beginning of all those questions: Can I believe in God? To what extent can I call myself a religious Jew? Can't I be "just Jewish" like Spinoza and leave it at that?

Three hundred years later, Spinoza's views on God, the universe, free will, and other lofty topics helped define the religious views of yet another great Jewish scientist and thinker, Albert Einstein. On several occasions, Einstein was challenged and asked to explain his theology. Einstein saw himself as a disciple of Spinoza and regularly maintained, like his predecessor, that God and nature are the same things. Einstein insisted that he was not an atheist but a person who recognized that the vastness and complexity of the universe are far greater than our ability to understand it. From that reality, he drew spiritual inspiration.

Einstein, like Spinoza, was an enigma: a kind of nonreligious religionist who stood in awe of existence not because of miracles but because of our collective human capacity to understand enough of the world we live in to also recognize its poetry. At the same time, Einstein remained a proud Jew and an active Zionist who even received an offer to become the President of the State of Israel. Like so many of the people who report their personal Jewish condition to me on a regular basis, Einstein had a universal, cosmic, nontheistic spirituality combined with a strong Jewish identity.

"Rabbi," I hear all the time, "I'm just like Einstein."

"Of course," I reply with a smile.

On this eve of the New Year, when so many of us in the Jewish community choose to come to synagogue, to renew our ties with our community, and to test our faith (or lack thereof) against the official texts and practices of our tradition, I think it is important, perhaps essential, for us to take a moment and examine our beliefs about God; about faith; about organized religion, in general; and, last but not least, our understanding and commitment to Reform Judaism.

Despite the current and somewhat fashionable return to tradition in the Reform movement, my sense is that the majority of Reform Jews are actually more like Spinoza and Einstein, religious nonbelievers—that is, people who recognize the poetry in existence itself and the beauty of our tradition but from the vantage point of limited faith.

Although most of the official theologies, platforms, and prayer books of Reform Judaism are theistic—that is, religious systems that simply assume the existence of God—my sense is that, deep down, most Reform Jews and others just like us are less than 100 percent convinced about the existence of God. We vacillate between faith and fear of faith, between a sincere desire to uphold and maintain the faith of our ancestors and a genuine worry that religion also carries the seeds of insanity in it.

A true story: When Liz and I were engaged thirty-one years ago, we traveled between New York and Baltimore visiting different members of the family. One of the visits I remember most clearly was to the Jersey Shore. Liz's aunt and uncle from Elkins Park had a lovely home on the beach in Ship Bottom. We arrived, changed, went down to the water's edge, and parked ourselves next to her aunt and uncle's accountant, a well-known figure in the local Jewish community. He introduced himself to me by asking, "Are you the rabbinic student we have been hearing about?"

"Yes, I am," I responded with a touch of pride.

"Tell me something," the CPA demanded. "How much of that garbage do you really believe?" Prompt intervention by our hosts saved me from having to give a real answer to the question.

During the last few years, powerful, well-publicized, and much-debated antireligious literature has found its way onto Best Sellers lists, which I believe has amplified the inherent ambivalence about religion for many of us. In 2005, a Stanford graduate student, Sam Harris—the child of a Jewish mother and a Quaker father, a man who had refused to be bar mitzvah as a thirteen-year-old—published an important book called *The End of Faith: Religion, Terror and the Future of Reason*. In it, Harris revived the ancient atheist critique of the belief in God and participation in organized religion by raising the specter of Christian fundamentalism and Islamic extremism as the ultimate outcomes of religious belief.

Richard Dawkins—a well-known Oxford professor, native of Kenya, evolutionist, and atheist—was so impressed he suggested that copies of Harris's book be placed in every hotel room next to, or instead of, the Gideon Bible. Dawkins's own atheism, so powerful that it earned him the nickname of "Darwin's rottweiler," found expression in a 2006 book *The God Delusion*, which argued against any form of theism from the perspective of a scientist and evolutionary biologist.

This year, Christopher Hitchens, an Oxford-educated writer, completed the trilogy with his controversial best seller, *God Is Not Great: How Religion Poisons Everything*. A British American matrilineal Jew, a former Trotskyite turned neoconservative, he too maintained that the current appeal of fundamentalism, of all shades, is the ultimate outcome of religious belief. Religion—argue Harris, Hitchens, and Dawkins—should be exorcised, uprooted, destroyed, or abandoned in the name of goodness and the future of humanity.

Theists growled, agnostics cowered, and atheists cheered all around the world. How should we respond as Reform Jews? Where does this onslaught against the basic philosophical and psychological assumptions of religion leave us? What options are left for us by these descendants of Karl Marx, Sigmund Freud, and Jean-Paul Sartre?"

First, I believe, we need to level the playing field a bit. Religion's loudest critics today often create a clay-pigeon model of religious life, which emphasizes its worst aspects and conveniently forgets other more compassionate and modest expressions of the spirit. It is easy to criticize that which is despicable and evil. It is easy to criticize fanatics and murderers. It is easy to criticize those who use the shield of their faith to block and deflect every assumption behind modern science. It is easy to criticize and reject all those whom I call the "religious pirates" of our age. They are not travelers on the sea of faith; they are barbarians and killers whose banner of faith is really a standard of psychosis, extreme narcissism, and delusional thought. The monsters who attacked this country on 9/11 six years ago were no more representative of religion than were Nazis who did medical experimentation representative of physicians in general. Both perverted their callings into something cynical, sinister, and utterly horrific.

Second, the esteemed club of Harris, Dawkins, and Hitchens equates religious faith with scriptural literalism. While it is true that modern fundamentalists hold a view of the sacred text as inerrant, not all religionists do. Classical Talmudic Judaism believed that every verse of the Torah had at least seventy meanings. Modern Bible scholars and many Reform Jews understand the text of the Torah as multi-authored, complex, and edited, not as the one-dimensional word of God but as our ancestors' best effort to understand that which defies full understanding.

I was once on a panel of rabbis in Binghamton, discussing the idea of the Torah. Playing on a teaching of the great modern Jewish philosopher, Abraham Joshua Heschel, I responded that "Torah is a Midrash on the unknowable word of God." My friend, the local Orthodox rabbi, actually started to cry. He was so upset with my lack of faith in an inerrant Torah.

Third, we need to reject the view that religion stands or falls on whether or not one believes in Creation or the Big bang or creationism or evolution. If we hold a modern or postmodern understanding of the Biblical, we are not compelled by any stretch of the imagination to defend narrow literal interpretations of the text of the Torah.

When I read the story of creation, I'm not reading a scientific report. I'm reading an inspired response by my ancestors to the wonder of existence, to its order, to its immensity, to its beauty, and, most of all, to its inherent goodness. Other ancient people viewed the universe's origins in terms of malevolent chaos. In the Jewish narrative, an uncreated Creator looks out and says, "It is good. It is very good." According to a review in this last Sunday's *New York Times*, a recent scholar of Freud, one of modernity's leading Jewish atheists, believed that even the Viennese doctor, as an older gentleman, saw some good in Judaism's concept of an invisible, indivisible, uncreated Creator God. Einstein—much more than Freud, as we have seen—believed that a spiritual response to the order, size, and poetry of the universe was a valid, if nontheistic, faith.

Fourth, we need to affirm that human beings are inherently spiritual creatures. Going beyond Einstein's spiritual response to the vastness and orderliness of nature is the spiritual response to our lives as humans. Every time I do a baby naming, I sense a primal need to do something transcendent to welcome a new life into this world. Every time I officiate at a bar or bat mitzvah, I see a deep need in parents, grandparents, and family to create a rite of passage for their adolescents and for themselves. At every wedding, I see much more than the completion of a civil document. I see couples trying to infuse their union with something transcendent and their parents trying to balance their infinite blessings with a growing sense of finitude in their own lives. Most of all, sitting in family circles with the bereaved, listening to your stories, watching you interact and support one another, observing you resisting the reality of your own powerlessness in the face of death, and trying to help you maintain your loyalty to the dead, I am convinced of a natural primal need to recognize something more than life itself in recognition of its miraculous nature. I'm not talking about formal beliefs in the afterlife or concepts of God. I'm talking about love.

Fifth, it is time to stop thinking of religion and science as opposites. Good religion is not bad science. Science cannot provide spiritual guidance or support. Religion and science are best when they are respectful partners.

Thirty years ago, when I was a student rabbi in Richmond, Indiana, the local community hospital decided to look into a chaplaincy program. There was a great deal of resistance from the medical community: the priest and pastors would be in the way. They would compromise spirituality, and they have nothing real to do with healing. How different the situation is today!

Similarly, in the Reform movement, we had long done away with prayers for healing and almost with petitionary prayer, in general. Then Debbie Friedman's *Mi Shebeirach* prayer song arrived.

At first, like everyone else, I resisted. It's nonsense. It's delusional. It can't help. But it did help, and I, like many others, began to accept the emotional validity of that prayer. I always wondered what good a hospital visit or phone call from me would do. I have no power. I have no medical training. Slowly, it dawned on me that empathy counts. That prayer might not heal, but it can comfort you. That a visit might not end suffering, but it can slip a pillow under it. Sometimes it's just good to know someone cares, someone who has seen a lot of life—a lot of pain, a lot of joy—and really does want to share. You can't put it in the chart. But you can put it in the heart where it really counts.

All the studies about healing, prayer, and placebos are beside the point. I'm not talking about faith healers and other frauds. Forget them! I'm not talking about control groups of one hundred people praying in the hospital chapel and six patients on the floor and whether or not the prayers of the group of one hundred were efficacious. That's bad science and bad religion. I'm only talking about a word of encouragement, a smile, a song, a poem, or a prayer. We have to know our limits. Love and concern can't reset a broken bone or stop a raging cancer. But they can smooth the path, ease the heart, steady the soul.

Finally, there is something else religion can do. It can help us be happy people. When I say *happy*, I mean something like "contentment." The Greek term for *happiness* means "a good spirit." Somewhere around the year 350 BCE, Aristotle stated that happiness, or good spirit, is the only emotion that humans desire for its own sake. He observed that we seek riches, honor, and even health, not for our own sake but for happiness and contentment.

Sadly, most people do not associate Judaism with happiness. Usually, when we think about religion and happiness, we think about Buddhism. But Judaism has a lot to say about happiness. At a folk level, we say, "We should only see one another at *simchas* (happy events)." We call the holiday when we complete and restart the reading of the Torah Simchat Torah or "rejoicing with the Torah." And in the Torah, it is written, "You shall be happy with all the good God has given to you." Happiness is not just Jewish—it is the goal of Judaism. Happiness, deep contentment, satisfaction, and inner peace in this world and perhaps in the next, are not only Judaism's promises. They are the goal, in my opinion, of all religious life.

The sharp critics of religion today don't have it all wrong. Too many people sin in the name of religion. And religion, in general, has a lot to repent for. But religion is not a pathology. It is not only a submissive response to authority, and it is not just bad science. In small doses, it can actually be helpful in building community, inculcating kindness, helping people in pain, and helping us in our search for a modicum of happiness in this life.

In short, I believe, a little bit of religion is a good thing whether or not you fully embrace the idea of God. I believe that Reform Judaism should accept this approach and help its adherents translate their deep inherent religious needs with the symbols and practices of our ancient tradition. Reform understands that not only does it have to adapt as part of its cultural dance, but it also has to choose and create in order to complete its mission to help modern Jews, the children of Spinoza, and the disciples of Einstein to stay on course, to see the poetry written into the cosmos, and to help one another on the road to contentment with kindness, with concern, and with love. Every once in a while, somebody comes to me and says, "Rabbi, I'm so glad I'm Jewish." "Rabbi, I'm lucky. I have what I need. I have what I want." And I smile and count my blessings too.

On Rosh HaShanah, the *shofar* is sounded. It stirs our ancient souls. It reminds us of where we came from, and it sounds our rallying call for the future. Go forth into the new year with spiritual openness, kindness, pride, and joy.

May the new year bring you happiness, may the new year bring you good health, may the new year bring all of us peace.

Amen.
Shana Tova.
A good year.

Israel at 60

September 13, 2007, Rosh HaShanah Morning 5768

For one week this summer, I went to Cincinnati to work at the American Jewish Archives on the campus of Hebrew Union College. The purpose of my trip was to collect footage for a documentary I'm producing with Dr. Gary Zola for my rabbinic organization's conference this coming March. It will be called *Great Voices* and will include scenes of Stephen Wise denouncing Father Coughlin at one of his Carnegie Hall rallies in New York City; Reform rabbis at the inaugural ceremonies of Eisenhower, Kennedy, and other recent presidents; and Rabbi Joachim Prinz speaking at the Lincoln Memorial minutes before Dr. Martin Luther King Jr. gave his "I Have a Dream" speech.

Probably the oldest footage is of Joseph Krauskopf, a member of the first ordination class of HUC, at a graduation ceremony at Delaware Valley College just before his death in 1923. He was also the longest-serving rabbi of KI.

Only one piece of footage was missing: the speech by Abba Hillel Silver before the United Nations at Lake Placid, New York, in November 1947, calling for the partition of Palestine and the creation of a Jewish state. Everyone has heard the subsequent roll call vote and Ben Gurion's declaration of the establishment of the State of Israel. No one had ever seen the film footage. After weeks of searching, we finally located the missing film at Rabbi Silver's temple in Cleveland! It is sure to become one of the basic iconic images of modern Jewish history.

Remarkably, it was an American Reform rabbi Abba Hillel Silver who, on behalf of the Jewish Agency, Israel's pre-state government, put the question to all of humanity: sanction the establishment of a Jewish state in British Palestine!

It was almost fifty years to the day after the First Zionist Congress in Basel, Switzerland, and now almost sixty years since that moment when seventeen centuries of Jewish statelessness, landlessness, and powerlessness were brought to an end.

This year we have much to celebrate in the Jewish world: sixty years of Israeli statehood and forty years of reunification in Jerusalem.

Israel is one of the smallest countries in the world. Yet it has developed a first-class infrastructure, one of the greatest militaries in history, excellent medical care, and one of the most important high-tech clusters in the world.

Israel has gathered millions of Jews from around the world, fed them, educated them, taught them Hebrew, and trained them to be self-reliant.

This year, I received an alumni publication of Hebrew University that shared the fact that in the last five years, six faculty members of Hebrew University have received the Nobel Prize—an incredible accomplishment for any university, let alone one representing a national population that is smaller than metropolitan Philadelphia.

Most remarkable of all, despite constant military aggression and terrorism against its population, Israel has remained a democracy with a tradition of vigorous parliamentary debate, a free press, and an incredibly independent judiciary.

This December, I will be taking a group from KI to Israel to see what Israel has accomplished "on the ground" to bring back our report and to further cement our own ties to the Jewish state. We still have a few seats left if you want to come along.

Last summer, this congregation responded to the Hezbollah war in an extraordinarily positive way. Within a few weeks, half the congregation rallied and collected over $150,000 for emergency medical services in Israel. Subsequently, we reactivated our Israel Committee, which is now a permanent committee of the congregation. Our religious school has created a tie with an elementary school in Haifa. Via closed-circuit TV, our fifth-grade students and their Israeli counterparts talk face-to-face without ever leaving their respective school libraries.

We also have a rare special opportunity here in Philadelphia to attend a national AIPAC conference in Center City to learn about Israel's diplomatic and military situation and to find out how to help. I am very proud that our members Harriet and Larry Weiss are two of the principal sponsors of this event. Keynote speakers include Elie Wiesel and Natan Sharansky.

Of course, there is also Hadassah, Israel Bonds, the Reform movement's ARZA, and all other channels of support for Israel right here in our own community. Today Israel is stronger than it has ever been. But paradoxically and sadly, it has never been in a more difficult situation. During the last year or so, the military situation has changed, the nature of the conflict between Israel and its neighbors has changed, and the enemies of Israel and the Jewish people have found new and dangerous sources of support around the world.

What follows is a global look at Israel's mortal challenges from the Golan to the halls of Oxford and Harvard Universities. The most important military and diplomatic issue at this moment for Israel is Syria. Syria is strategically located between Iraq and Lebanon. Its eastern border has been more than porous with respect to the flow of arms to Hezbollah and the movement of anti-American guerilla fighters to Iraq. At the same time, tens of thousands of Iraqi refugees are streaming into Syria, many without work, further aggravating the situation and further destabilizing the region. Last week, the Israeli Air Force struck Syrian arms depots along the Iraqi border to disrupt that supply. It was not a knock-out punch, and the larger structural issues remain.

All this comes on the heels of an aborted discussion about Israel removing troops from the Golan to send them south to the Gaza border. With the United States pressing to isolate Syria diplomatically, there is currently little chance of progress. For sure, the Olmert government will need to think, prepare, and act strategically as it continues to monitor its dangerous enemy in Damascus.

Syria is tied directly to the Islamic Republic of Iran, the single greatest existential threat to the Jewish State. Officially, a radical Shiite state since the revolution of 1979, Iran is a large country with over seventy million inhabitants and 640,000 square miles of territory. Since coming to power two years ago, Iran's current president has sponsored both a World Without Zionism and a revisionist Holocaust conference. Allied to Venezuela, Cuba, and Russia, Iran's government is sworn to the destruction of Israel. As early as the sixth century BCE, the Persians sought and fought for control of the entire Middle East from Africa to Mesopotamia to the eastern shore of the Mediterranean Sea. It is hard to imagine the current regime in Iran in terms other than the ancient Persian/Iranian bad guy Haman, the evil vizier to King Ahasuerus and an early architect of an anti-Jewish government-sponsored program of annihilation.

Perhaps the biggest change in recent years in Israel's fight for existence is the emergence of Hezbollah, Iran's proxy army in Lebanon, as an effective ground force. The various investigations that looked into Israel's performance during last summer's war all concluded that neither the army nor the executive branch of government performed adequately. The last-minute rally on the ground showed Israel still has the capacity it needs, but it was too little too late. Intelligence reports now claim that Hezbollah is completely rearmed if not stronger than before. It is doubtful that even a high-tech rocket interception system can fully protect Israel's population if another round of hostilities were to begin. The biggest consequence of the Hezbollah war is the doubt it casts over the idea of a two-state solution with the Palestinians. The current internal struggle between Abbas and Hamas has served to strengthen U.S. and European support for Abbas. Even Israel is taking extraordinary steps right now to strengthen the Palestine Authority. Only in the context of the Middle East could the Authority be viewed as moderate. Like the old joke about a man who died without any redeeming qualities, compelling the rabbi to say at the funeral, "All I can say about this man is that his brother was worse," the PA's "moderation" is relative at best.

The problem is very simple, but the stakes are high. If a Palestinian state were set up in the West Bank and the PA lost control to Hamas, you could be sure that the Palestinians would imitate their Shiite cousins in Lebanon and move thousands of short-range rockets into their territory, rockets that could easily strike Tel Aviv, Jerusalem, and Beersheba. Haifa is already "in range" of Hezbollah.

Since I was old enough to follow the news from Israel, I always favored a two-state solution. My main concern was demographic. The Arab population is swelling, and its size compromises the democratic character of the State of Israel. The possibility of a truly demilitarized state in the West Bank is more of a pipe bomb than a pipe dream at this point. Israel has few options other than to hang tough and encourage diplomacy.

Viewing Israel's situation more broadly, the last year has only deepened the fact that it is no longer an Arab-Israeli or an Israel-Palestinian conflict but part of the larger struggle between radical Islam and the rest of the world. The struggle is global and not just the West versus Islam, as Islam also figures in the politics of India and even Western China.

Scholars debate the nature of Islamic fundamentalism. Most believe its principal goal is the reestablishment of a caliphate—that is, an Islamic state in the Middle East. Second, it is clear that Muslim radicals want to overthrow various regimes in countries with Muslim majorities that are not yet Islamified, especially the Saudi monarchy. Most scholars would argue then that the liberation of Palestine and the creation of a theocratic Islamic state there is only a third on their hit list.

I really doubt it. Radical Islamic hatred of Israel is deep and wide. When a terrorist operation was recently unearthed in Germany, the symbol of the organization featured a red map of Palestine right in the middle of its logo. The liberation of Palestine is not third on their list—it is first. Just as the Nazis flipped their priorities and continued to murder Jews in 1945 against their own strategic needs, so too will the Islamic radicals who hate Israel continue to target the Jewish state's destruction as their number one strategic and emotional goal.

Until moderate voices in the Islamic community can be heard, until there are deep economic reforms in Arab countries, and until the Iranian people overthrow Khomeinism, this hatred is not going to be tempered.

One might think that the century-old Sunni-Shiite split in the Muslim world could be to Israel's strategic benefit. Perhaps, in the short run, it does serve as a diversion of sorts. But more profoundly, it only serves to destabilize the entire Middle East. This is an old and irreconcilable struggle from the very beginning of Islamic history. Our own country has stepped into the sectarian abyss, and we now know firsthand something about the internecine Islamic struggle.

Could a reconciled Islamic world also reconcile with Israel? They can't even come to terms with their cousins, let alone their most hated foe.

If all this isn't enough for one small country to endure, there is yet another factor to consider, a global factor reaching deep into the world of the American opinion makers that helps put the whole struggle for Israel's survival into perspective. During the last year, perhaps to the greatest extent since the UN's passage of Resolution #3379 in 1975, which declared that Zionism was racism, the vilification of Israel, Zionism, and the friends of Israel has reached new and unprecedented proportions. The center of the storm has mostly been in England. No longer just the antics of London's loudmouthed anti-Semitic mayor Ken Livingston, British anti-Zionism has spread like a communicable disease among British academics.

Two different academic unions in England voted in 2005 and 2006 to boycott Israeli universities. The first was to protest connections between Haifa University and Bar Ilan with colleges in the West Bank. The second was to force Israeli dissidents to compel their institutions to protest Israeli control of the West Bank. Representing a counterintuitive alliance of leftists and Muslims, the boycott movement drew its inspiration from efforts to boycott South Africa during the long period of apartheid there. At its core, the boycott efforts were based on the belief that Zionism is a racist ideology and a colonialist, capitalist tool. More recently, the two unions combined to form the "University and College Union," in which anti-Zionist efforts continue to flourish.

England is not alone in this matter. The anti-Zionist virus has spread to American college campuses and the mainstream of American politics as well, although grassroots support for Israel seems to be holding up in the general American population.

The best-known anti-Zionist tract to appear in the last year was Jimmy Carter's *Palestine: Peace, Not Apartheid*, published in November 2006. The mere use of the term *apartheid* by the thirty-ninth president of the United States instantly set the Jewish world on edge. Moreover, Carter's insistence that the term Palestine only referred to the territories and not to pre-1967 Israel did little to calm the storm, nor did his appearance on various American college campuses or his open letter to the American Jewish community. A closer reading of the book reveals a completely lopsided view of the controversy and the selective and questionable use of facts.

Carter's book, however, was just the tip of the new anti-Zionist literary iceberg floating in American academic waters. For the past few years, American writers like Paul Findley have been pumping out anti-Israel books, especially *They Dare to Speak Out* (2003), which presents a maximalist view of the Israel lobby in the United States. Similarly, Binghamton University sociologist Professor Emeritus James Petras, a Marxist, published *The Power of Israel in the United States* in 2006. The headline grabber in this area, however, was John Mearsheimer and Stephen M. Walt's recent *The Israel Lobby and U.S. Foreign Policy*, published earlier this year (2007). Building on an article they had previously published in a British journal, Mearsheimer of the University of Chicago and Walt of Harvard's John F. Kennedy School of Government have attempted to discredit the idea that Israel has both "shared values" and "strategic value" to the United States. They have rallied a wide range of opinion makers who see both in AIPAC and prominent Jewish neoconservatives a conspiracy of sorts, which has pushed America into the war in Iraq against America's better interests. To be fair, Mearsheimer and Walt themselves maintain that AIPAC is doing what a lobby should do in a democratic society. However, they are somewhat like arsonists who torch a building and run outside crying, "Fire! Fire!" For those now in college and for parents and grandparents of college students, it will be important to listen to the debate about Israel on American college campuses this school year.

The new Mearsheimer-Walt book raises two important issues for us. How powerful are Israel's friends in America? And is the support of Israel in America's best strategic interests? To me, the questions are tied together. We know that American support of Israel has changed over time. At the moment of statehood, it was positive. The United States then backed away and did not really return to Israel's side until after the 1967 War. America's own involvement in the Middle East, petro-politics, the War on Terror, and more have made its relationship with Israel more complex.

I support the so-called Organski Thesis, which maintains that Israel is of high strategic value to the United States. It was first offered by Professor Organski of the University of Michigan in his book *The $36 Billion Bargain* (1990). Israel's strategic value to the United States, he argues, not the Israel lobby, is the determining factor in U.S. support of Israel, even though Israel occasionally strikes out on its own, as in its military contracts with China. I also believe the two countries, the United States and Israel, share a common set of democratic values.

This "double-value argument" is under heavy assault today among American academics, in stark contrast to the sustained grassroots support for Israel in the United States.

Finally, a broad range of scholarly opinions has developed about the relationship of historical anti-Semitism to modern anti-Zionism. Many critics of Israel insist that anti-Zionist is not anti-Semitism. By contrast, most scholars of the history of anti-Semitism maintain that anti-Zionism is a new expression of a very old hatred of the Jewish people. What was once religious anti-Semitism and then racial anti-Semitism is now political anti-Semitism. It claims that Jews, uniquely among the peoples of the earth, are not entitled to sovereignty, and it focuses myopically on the sins and so-called sins of the State of Israel, whether large or small and is either soft or uninterested in other nations' sins. Thus, British academics are quick to condemn Israeli universities but have little or nothing to say about problems of academic freedom and freedom of expression in North Korea and China. The Jew is different, sinister, and conspiratorial. As one French historian recently put it, the old Judenhass, hatred of the Jew, which once permeated European society, has now morphed into an obsessive hatred of the State of Israel. The Far Left, the Far Right, and Islamic extremists can only agree on one thing: they hate Israel and want to see it destroyed.

Thus, on the ground in the Golan and along the Gaza border, in the sweep of raging extremist Islam, in the halls of power in Damascus and Teheran, and in the hallowed faculty studies of Oxford and Harvard, an ever more virulent new strain of anti-Israelism has found a new set of voices during the last twelve months. Israel, on the other hand, on the eve of its sixtieth anniversary as a state, is more resilient and more self-reliant than ever.

What is our role in all this? We are tied to Israel by history and by destiny. Some of us have strong family ties in Israel. Most of all, we are connected to Israel because we want to be because we should be, and because the world simply won't have it any other way. The old hatred of Jews and Judaism—which plagued Europe, in particular—has found a new home in the world of anti-Zionism. Luckily, we don't feel the heat of that anti-Semitism and anti-Zionism every day the way that Jews outside the United States do.

Despite vestiges of domestic anti-Semitism, American Jews are blessed with a higher degree of acceptance and legal protection than any other Jewish community in that world. Our advantageous position does not absolve us of responsibility to the larger Jewish world; it increases our importance as partners in the defense of the Jewish state. We have numerous legitimate political, financial, cultural, and spiritual ways of supporting Israel.

Sadly, support for Israel among American Jews is loosening. Yes, Israel has problems. Yes, there are controversies. Yes, there have been some bad actions and decisions along the way. But there can be no question about Israel's right to exist, no question about the ultimate sources of hatred and violence in the Middle East, and no question that we are part of that struggle. To be a bystander is to aid the numerous and powerful enemies of Israel. Go to the AIPAC conference, write your senator, come with Liz and me to Israel this December. Every little show of support helps. There are hundreds of millions of people who support the idea of dismantling the Jewish state in the world today. There are no more than fourteen million Jews. On Rosh HaShanah, stand up, be counted, contribute to the strength of the Jewish state, but do not be silent. Do not bare the neck like a quiescent Isaac to the sharp, murderous knife of contemporary anti-Zionism.

Perhaps one day, the ambassador of the State of Israel to the United Nations will speak to the General Assembly, and no one will get up and leave. No one will step outside the building and join an anti-Zionist demonstration. Perhaps one day Israel's ambassador will move a resolution on education, technology, medicine, or aid to children; and the world will respond, "Yes, my brothers and sisters in Israel, lead the way. We will join you. You will visit our homes and we, yours. We will learn from each other. We will teach each other new ways to plant crops and design cell phones. Our children will sit in exchange programs. Our educators will join common seminars on inclusive teaching. There will be no more bombs, no more martyrs, no more mass funerals."

Until that day comes true, there is much work to be done. Let it begin with us—today—at the beginning of the new year.

Justice, Justice You Shall Pursue

Shabbat *Shof'tim* Deuteronomy 16:18
August 16, 2007

In many ways, ancient Judaism's passion for justice was among the most important contributions our ancestors bequeathed to humanity. Prince, judge, priest, the drawer of water, and the hewer of wood—every person and institution in biblical Israel was included in our people's covenant with God, which demanded not only compliance with the law but also a spirit of fairness. So, too, it urged kindness in all our encounters with fellow humans, animals, and even nature. In instructions to the judges, this week's Torah says emphatically and tersely, "Justice, justice [you shall] pursue!" (Deut. 16:20).

The prophetic passion for justice was and still is a defining feature of Reform Judaism. From the earlier efforts to secure Jewish emancipation in Europe to the breaking of the yoke of slavery in this country to the rights of child laborers at the beginning of the twentieth century, Reform Judaism has been there with a loud, clear voice challenging power, privilege, guarded silence, and indifference with the words of Amos, Isaiah, and Jeremiah.

Currently, I am working on a documentary with my friend and colleague Dr. Gary Zola, Director of the American Jewish Archives in Cincinnati, entitled *Voices for Justice*, which will document in sound and image some of the most important moments of modern prophetic Judaism as spoken by Reform rabbis and captured by movie cameras and audio recorders: the Holocaust, our role in the creation of the State of Israel, and the courageous actions of some of our colleagues during the Civil Rights struggle. The footage I have been reviewing is both rare and moving. I have learned a great deal about moral courage and the power of the pulpit from watching (now digitalized) tapes from the 1930s, '40s, '50s, and '60s.

For many years, I read about the work of Rabbi Stephen Wise, founder of the Jewish Institute of Religion and radio voice of American Jewry particularly during the Depression years. Now I've seen "with my own eyes and heard with my own ears" his thunderous voice, his rolling *r*'s, and his impassioned spirit railing against the likes of Father Coughlin and Adolf Hitler from the speaker's podium at Carnegie Hall. Wise's voice is deep and sonorous, drenched with emotion. His heart is full in his pleading with American Jews and the American government to take up the cause of Europe's doomed Jews. He screamed from the mountaintop. Few listened.

This week, via the miracle of email, I was also finally able to locate footage of Rabbi Abba Hillel Silver, Wise's successor, making the case for the creation of the State of Israel before the United Nations in May 1947. This is very rare footage and an incredibly important moment in the history of the Jewish people. Ten months later, the UN voted in favor of partition; and sixty years ago, in smoke and fire, Israel became the Jewish State. Silver called on the world to respond justly to the plight of the survivors of the Holocaust and give them a home of their own. Miraculously, most of the world heard him. Today, I am afraid, Rabbi Silver's plea would mostly fall on deaf ears.

Finally, I also have been watching a video of select Reform rabbis during the Civil Rights era as well as listening to tapes of Martin Luther King speaking at Reform synagogues around the country. One of my favorite recordings is of Rabbi Joachim Prinz speaking at the great 1963 March in Washington in front of the Lincoln Memorial. Prinz identified himself as a former rabbi of the Jewish community of Berlin under Hitler. Anticipating King himself, Rabbi Prinz spoke of the American dream of equality under the law and of the prophetic quest for justice. Most powerfully of all, he spoke of the greatest obstacle in the fight against injustice: silence. Indifference in the face of racism, Prinz declared, is humanity's greatest moral challenge.

Next time you sit in our beautiful Korn sanctuary, look at our Prophetic Windows, and reflect on the verses they display, think about modern voices for justice and the issues closest to your heart. Then, ask yourself, "Am I listening? Am I responding? Or am I still silent?"

"Justice, justice," this week's Torah portion urges us, "you shall pursue!" Shabbat Shalom!

Sin

September 21, 2007, Yom Kippur Evening 5768

A couple of years ago, I read a great article in *Sports Illustrated* that continues to resonate with me. The writer explained that he learned a great deal from baseball cards when he was a boy. He learned about record keeping, chronology, how to figure out percentages, statistical trends, and more.

Today, sports data is only second to financial information in the daily newspaper. If you watch a game on TV, the statistics the announcers pull up are incredible: "This pitcher throws an average of 23 pitches an inning." "This batter has hit 87 singles after the third inning against right-handed pitchers." "In three-and-two counts in the seventh inning during away games, the hitter has a .272 batting average." "The runner has stolen third base eight times in nine years in home games before the third inning. I think he's going to run."

Every pitch, every swing, every defensive move is recorded, analyzed, and projected ad infinitum.

By analogy, the High Holy Day liturgy depicts God as a kind of cosmic scorekeeper of the game of life who writes down everything in the Book of Life. Who knows what the entries look like? "Sussman made an error at the beginning of the seventh month. He had the same problem the year before and two years before that, and his RBIs [real brachah index] has been off too. It's not looking good for Sussman." "Rigler hit a double and two singles with his sermons during the High Holy Days last year in five swings at the bimah. He could be in a position to get the MVP this year,

Most Valued Preacher." "And the cantor had perfect pitch since the All-Star break, leaving her with an excellent ERA [earned repentance average] as we move into the World Series of Jewish holidays this September."

In our tradition, at least in the holiday liturgy, we paint an image of God as a kind of moral and spiritual scorekeeper, except, instead of fielding errors, we talk about moral mistakes. Instead of strike-outs, we talk about remembering failed ethical intentions. Instead of sacrifice flies, we talk about selflessness and putting others in front of ourselves. The idea on Yom Kippur is that the great statistician in the sky is looking over our stats for the last year, asking us to do the same, and then waiting to hear from us how we plan to improve our performance and our attitude toward the game of life.

In most sports, the most valued statistics tend to define the "offensive game": points scored, touchdowns, home runs, offensive rebounds, and on and on.

By contrast, on Yom Kippur, the stats are all about "offenses": misdeeds, mistakes, sins. It's meant to be a tough critique of our failures, our human strike-outs, our dropped balls of personal responsibility, our missed shots of opportunity, our failure to pass the ball of love, our reluctance to jump higher as people to stop our backhandedness, to be good sports, to win with dignity and to lose without losing respect.

The number one stat from a religious point of view on Yom Kippur is the state of sin, of failures to do the right thing at the right time. In Hebrew, this statistical method is called *Heshbon HaNefesh*, "an accounting of the soul." "Many times this year," some might say to themselves, "I could have been a better husband and wasn't." "Many times this year," others might say in their hearts, "I could have been a better daughter, and I wasn't." "Many times," still others might whisper in their inner being, "I could have dropped an old grudge, but I didn't."

The Book of Life, our tradition suggests, is like a huge database with certified numbers, comparative information from previous years, and perhaps even projections for the future.

Although both sports data and religious data, so to speak, in the Book of Life are about human behavior, my sense is that most of us would have trouble defining what a "religious error," or sin, is. Even more challenging is the question of whether or not we even believe there is something objectively identifiable as a sin. For most of us, sin is mainly a theme for Yom Kippur, not something we confront existentially on a daily basis.

Indeed, many people I talk to in the congregation and in the Jewish community are not even sure that sin is a Jewish concept.

Does Judaism believe that "in Adam's fall, we sinned all"? Does Judaism teach that in Eve's indiscretion, death and the pain of childbearing were introduced into the world, and snakes were condemned to crawl on their bellies and to be loathed by humans and beasts?

When most of us think about sin, we think more in terms of eating a double-fudge brownie with whipped cream and not in terms of our essential nature and fate as human beings.

Mortal sins, cardinal sins, original sins—they're not Jewish, are they? We have misdeeds. We make mistakes. They sin.

Jimmy Swaggart sins and then gets up and cries and begs and cries again.

Rabbis make mistakes and lose their contracts.

The great colonial preacher Jonathan Edwards could rail about "sinners in the hand of an angry god."

Rabbis talk about anger management.

And the great Christian hymn "Amazing Grace" can plead the cause of a hopeless, sinful "wretch like me" and then help carry the true believer from religious blindness to spiritual sightedness on the wings of a melody.

Do we have an amazing song of sin and forgiveness in our tradition?

Is there a Jewish parallel? Are we "wretched" before God in the Jewish tradition?

Think about the text of the *machzor*, the holiday prayer book. During the next twenty-four hours or so, we are going to read about three hundred pages, and on almost every page is a discussion about sin. The fact of the matter is that in the Yom Kippur liturgy, the human being is depicted as a pretty bad player in the game of life with lousy stats in almost every category.

The words of the familiar and beloved holiday prayer *Avinu Malkeinu*, actually among the most controversial in our whole tradition, say it straight out, "Our Father, our King, be gracious to us and answer us because we have no good deeds"—that is, we are wretches.

Then in the Confession of Sin, we state that we cannot claim to be righteous. Rather, we have sinned, we have transgressed, we have gone astray.

Then, on page after page in *Al Cheit*, we confess to a thousand different sins and misdeeds and throw ourselves on the mercy of the court, asking

God not to judge us based on the criteria of justice because even in the Jewish tradition, only a merciful God would even bother listening to the pleas of a "wretch like me."

That's what the tradition says. But what happens when we sit down and are confronted with these damning, negative, painful depictions of our moral lives? We tend to read the list of sins as an exercise of exclusion, not inclusion:

Arrogance—nope, not me.
Bigotry—not me. I accept everybody.
Cynicism—couldn't be. I'm no cynic.
Deceit—absolutely not. I'm an honest person.
Egotism—a bit.
Flattery—OK, a little more.
Greed—I like good things but greed? That's unfair.

The list goes on, and so do our pleas . . . of innocence. Not guilty. Not sinful.

If Yom Kippur was a trial of our lives, we probably would ask for the case to be dismissed, even before entering a plea. It's almost as if the idea of sin is a kind of sin itself from a modern Jewish perspective. The idea of sin, and especially the idea of deep sinfulness as a fundamental characteristic of the human being, is utterly foreign to most modern Jews today.

Yet it is a fact that the Hebrew language has over two dozen different terms for *sin*.

Cheit—failure to carry out an obligation
Zadon—intentional misdeed
Shegagah—unintentional misdeed
Avon, Peshah, Aveirah—the list goes on. Our liturgy includes an entire list of terms for the idea of sin from *A* to *Z* and *alef* to *tav*.

And still more. The Torah is filled with numerous etiological tales about the origin of sin in the Garden of Eden, the origins of the sins of violence in the stories of Cain and Abel, and again in the Noah story, the sin of idolatry in the Golden Calf story, the sins of lust in the episode of Baal Peor. There is no end to sin in the Torah, in the Talmud, and in our prayer book. Looking at the classical texts of our tradition, we are clearly a sin-centered tradition; and our most important holiday, Yom Kippur, is, above all, about sin and the forgiveness of sin.

How, then, are we supposed to understand the meaning of sin, of *aveirah* and *avon* and *peshah*, today as modern Jews?

The answer is not in books but in life. Sometimes, even among nonbelievers, the idea of sin can bring out very strong emotions. Ten years ago, one of our kids was very sick. In the hospital, being sustained by a feeding tube, he blurted, "I'll be good. I won't do anything bad again. I'll go to synagogue every week." It was painful to hear a child bargaining for a future. It was painful to hear a kind of forced confession that he was sinful and is now remorseful enough to earn a modicum of divine mercy. At the moment, when it looked like the doctors couldn't help, the appeal was made above—"Let me live. I'll be good. Please!"

We were lucky. Our child got better, and he went back to all the normal sins of adolescence, to our great relief. Like a kind of moral-spiritual gag reflex, many of us react to adversity by blaming ourselves. We may not always be able to offer a proper theological definition of sin, but some of us seem to know how to use sin's psychological corollary, guilt, with great skill for both masochistic and sadistic purposes.

Sometimes, however, some of us are not so lucky. About fifteen years ago, a woman asked to speak to me in my office at Temple Concord in Binghamton. Yael (not her real name) was an Israeli, a kibbutznik married to an American Jew who was a professor at the university. Yael came to tell me that she would not be coming to the synagogue for Yom Kippur. She was filled with rage and with tears. "I will not sit in the synagogue for a whole day and say that I sinned. I did not sin," she told me and then burst into tears. After a while, the truth came out. She had two children, beautiful girls, but she lost her third pregnancy during delivery. Ostensibly an atheist, she was angry at God and would not participate in any activity in which somehow she admitted that some misdeed, impure thought, or sin on her part led to her tragedy. I assured her she was right to be angry, that no one was accusing her of anything, and that I would like to find a way to be helpful and supportive.

At the historical level, the rejection of the sin-punishment continuum is a hallmark of modern Jewish thought. It represents the great dividing line between all the modern branches of Judaism, including Modern Orthodox and fervently Orthodox Judaism. In some corners of the Jewish world today, there are people who believe that the Holocaust was divine punishment for the sin of assimilation, the sin of Zionism, and the sin of Reform Judaism. For the rest of us, however, it is impossible to excuse the

SS, the Gestapo, and all the other workers of evil and murder who had no justification for their behavior in the so-called sins of the victims. What sin could have been great enough to have brought down on the house of Israel a punishment as calamitous as the Holocaust?

What then is sin to the modern Jewish person? When are feelings of guilt and culpability valid? When are they disingenuous? And most of all, on this night of Kol Nidrei and the Day of Atonement, why do we come to the synagogue to ask, at least in a mechanical fashion, for forgiveness for our sins? Is it simply a habit or a pattern to come to the synagogue on the one day of the year when we focus most fully on our sins? Or is there something about the idea of sin that is so basic, so human, so real, so impervious to the challenges of modernization and secularization that we must attend Yom Kippur services to meet a genuine religious need? Put in a different way, do we sing *Avinu Malkeinu* together because we like the tune or because we resonate with the meaning of its words and want to know that God will forgive wretches like us?

I think it is both, and I think that deep down, we believe that sin is more than just eating double chocolate cake with whipped cream and sprinkles on top.

In my opinion, in the Jewish tradition, sin is primarily about who we are as human beings, our nature, and our inherent condition as creatures. In fact, it is human to sin, and to sin is human. Cats, dogs, fish—all the creatures—live by their instincts. We alone have the ability to choose who we are and what we do. Sin, in my opinion, is as much a part of Judaism's anthropology as it is a function of our tradition's formal theology.

The ancient rabbis, reflecting on the meaning of the Torah, came to understand that human beings have two basic inclinations: an inclination to do good and an inclination not to do good. We have the capacity to imprint human footsteps on the surface of the moon and to destroy the earth's landscape with violence, greed, and negligence. We have learned to harness fire to warm our homes, and we have learned to burn our neighbors' houses to the ground with flames and torches.

However, to the rabbis, the struggle between the inclination toward good and toward evil is not simple. It's actually a paradox. They maintained that the evil inclination is just as necessary to human survival as the good inclination. If it weren't for a bit of lust and a bit of envy, we probably wouldn't marry, build a house, have kids, and strive to be destructive.

Torah and all its commandments, they maintained, were given to tutor both inclinations.

In this scenario, sin becomes our failure to use our good inclination for the good and to redirect our evil inclination to the good. To the rabbis, evil is inherent but it is not inevitable. Evil, sin—they are choices; and on Yom Kippur, we remind ourselves that at every turn of the clock, we have to decide: *mitzvah* or *aveirah*, good deed or bad?

How is the struggle going? What's the score in the Book of Life? What do the stats look like at the top of the new year we've just begun?

The rabbis were hardly optimistic about the human condition. One legend reports that the scholars of Israel debated for a very long time if it would have been better had God not created human beings in the first place. The rabbis' bottom line is twofold. As a species, the world would probably have been better if we had never been created at all. But we are here, they taught, so let us look into ourselves and look over the stats and do what we can to improve our game.

And that is why we come to synagogue on Yom Kippur. We know that we are not perfect as people. We know that we are complex and that we have contradictory tendencies as human beings. Some of us simply need to ask to stay the course and not be led astray, not such an easy task in a world of temptations and deceit. Others feel lost or angry or punished and need to relocate their spiritual center. Others need to be purged of feelings of inadequacy and hopelessness.

On Yom Kippur, we place our souls on the altar of existence and say, "I'm only me. I'm only human. I recognize that in the vastness of the universe, it is only my capacity to love that really makes me important. Sometimes I know that I'm a living contradiction. Help me. Forgive me. Guide me. Give me hope. Give me strength."

After Moses saw the Golden Calf and broke the original tablets, the Torah tells us, God revealed the inner nature of all that is divine to the prophet. We repeat these words on the High Holy Days before taking the Torah from the ark, "God is merciful, gracious, endlessly patient, loving, true, showing mercy to thousands; forgiving of iniquity, transgression, and sin; and granting pardon."

This is the message of Yom Kippur—to muster every resource we have to be good, decent human beings and, when we fall short, to be understanding and compassionate.

Think about the challenge of Yom Kippur when you drive your car, when you are stuck in a long checkout line, when you are angry at your kids, when you are fighting with your spouse, when you are asked to be helpful, when you are asked to step away, when you are at school, and when you are at work. The choice is always there: the high road and the low road, the mitzvah, and the sin, the good and the bad.

Perhaps an unseen statistician is keeping score. Maybe you have your own score sheet. It's always your choice. Choose well.

May you be blessed with a year of health, happiness, and not too many errors.

Amen.

Shabbat Shalom.

An easy fast.

Rabbis and Imams

November 17, 2007

This week's Torah portion is called *Vayetze* ("And he went out"). It begins with the story of Jacob leaving the Land of Israel and how, during his last night in Eretz Yisrael, he dreamed of a great ladder stretching from heaven to earth with "angels going up and down." It is a powerful and memorable image that has inspired generations of the Jewish people.

The idea of "going on a journey" and dreaming of new vistas became a reality for me last week at a remarkable series of meetings in New York City. The first National Summit of Imams and Rabbis brought together approximately twenty Muslim and twenty Jewish religious leaders from across the United States and across the theological and ethnic spectrums of both traditions. Among the imams were Sunnis and Shiites, Pakistanis, Arabs, Indonesians, and African Americans. The rabbi of the largest Modern Orthodox synagogue in the United States was there as was the rabbi of the Conservative Sutton Place Synagogue in New York. Of course, there were Reform rabbis too from Boston, San Diego, and Texas.

Our meeting was sponsored by the Foundation for Ethnic Understanding. The great Jewish philanthropist Ron Lauder came to speak to us, as did Russell Simmons of hip-hop fame. Russell is also the founder of Phat clothes. Our hosts were Rabbi Marc Schneier, leader of two Orthodox synagogues (Hamptons and Manhattan), and Sheikh Omar Abu Namous, the Senior Imam of the massive Islamic Center of New York, which attracts four thousand worshippers every Friday for prayer. We listened to speakers from both sides of the religious divide, we studied texts from the Quran and the Torah, we heard reports of case studies in Muslim-Jewish cooperation, and we ate together. In the end, we made one simple resolution: create one day a year when across the United States mosques and synagogues would "twin" with one another and reestablish some human ties between the families of Ishmael and Isaac.

One of the most important and interesting sessions we had together sought ways to strengthen the voice of moderate American Muslims in the American press. It is not an easy task, as the press tends not to run stories on "moderates" of any flavor. There are six to eight million Muslims in the United States and spread among their 1,200-some mosques are voices of moderation. I have heard some of them. We do not agree on everything. We did agree that we need to learn to talk to one another on issues of common interest. We need to create enough of a dialogue that one day we can begin to talk about the great issues of our day and "go out from there," to dream about a new tomorrow for all the children of Abraham.

Shabbat Shalom!

I Believe in Prayer

September 29, 2008, Rosh HaShanah Evening 5769

Many years ago, during one of our many national debates about whether or not there should be prayer in public school, it was remarked that "so long as there are algebra tests in school, there will be prayer in school." Certainly, from a metaphorical point of view, there will always be sweaty-palmed, semi-nauseated students praying, one way or another, before math tests. And what is true about math tests is doubly true of a stock market that drops nearly eight hundred points in one day. Praying is not easy for some people. For others, it is as natural as breathing.

My guess is that in the Reform movement in Judaism, prayer is not so easy. Yes, we can say a *b'rachah* real quick over the Shabbat or Hanukkah candles, but really deep prayer—prayer with God on the other end of the 1-800-Heaven direct line—that's not so easy for many, perhaps the majority, of Reform Jews. In part, our PQR, our Prayer Quota Rating, is so poor because the general culture around us does not jive with Jewish-style prayer. We don't bow our heads. We don't peak our hands or interlock our fingers. We don't have images of medieval knights down on one knee after battle, being blessed by their clergy. If you think about it, have you ever even heard of Judah Maccabee praying before or after liberating the Temple of Jerusalem on the eve of the first Hanukkah?

Jewish prayer is somehow different. In traditional Judaism, devotees sway back and forth. In Classical Reform, we stand for the *Sh'ma*, Judaism's pledge of allegiance, which we pronounce but don't really "pray." The most problematic moment comes with the silent prayer. Some people clearly are praying. Some are reading the suggested text. Others close their eyes and take a break from the official litany, kind of thankful that there's a break in all that praying; and still, others just kind of sit there, clocking how long the clergy will give the congregation to pray silently. By contrast, if we were Quakers or Buddhists, we could just stick with the silent prayer and skip the rest of the routine.

Prayer is also difficult for many Reform Jews because of their uncertainty about God. Why pray if I don't believe? It's a fair question. If you don't believe that there is a God or that prayer has any real power to effect change, why pray? We are realists. We are scientists. We are empiricists. We have a bad PQR. And why pray in a language you don't understand? The only thing worse than praying when you don't believe in prayer is praying when you don't believe in prayer in a language you don't understand!

Among many other factors, the feeling that prayer is questionable or at least not efficacious has to impact synagogue attendance. Why go to a dance if you can't dance or don't like to dance or won't dance? Ironically, the only distinguishable group in the United States that attends worship services less often than American Jews is atheists.

Prayer is a problem for most American Jews. Even for those who pray privately, there is the additional challenge of connecting their personal petitions with official Judaism. In short, we have a "prayer disconnect" in Jewish life today. But Judaism is resourceful and has multiple plans. If you are not a Shabbat regular and are not looking to rack up your "frequent prayer miles," you can still sign up for the "two-day-a-year super special" and pack in the most important prayers to cover your bases with God or at least recharge your Jewish batteries.

But the very essence, the building block of the High Holy Day experience is prayer—lots of prayers that cover the whole spectrum from prayers of praise and thanksgiving to prayers of petition and request, to prayers of confession. They are all packed in there, and if we are lucky and enjoy the music and the architecture of the building, we can find a line or two that actually resonates with something inside us, even if we have not sinned and even if we do not really believe that God is the One who listens to prayer.

Personally, I struggled with prayer for most of my life. My theology had no room for a God who not only listened but also had the power to intervene in nature and change circumstances for my benefit. When the

Reform movement first reintroduced the Mi Shebeirach Prayer, the prayer for healing and comfort, I cringed. Doctors healed, not God. "Science heals, not prayer," was my reflexive response to the idea of a prayer of comfort and healing. Nonsense. Superstition. Delusion.

All that has changed for me. I've come to see prayer in a very different way. I've learned that prayer begins in the heart, not in the head. No matter how correct the empirical, rational critique of prayer is, prayer persists anyway in the human heart because there are algebra tests, because there is sickness, because there is loss, because there are real moments of transcendence and beauty and thankfulness and grace in life to which the heart responds and overrules the head, moistens the eyes, and calms the soul. I have come to believe that the need to welcome a new baby into the world with prayer is irrepressible. The miracle of life is too great not to recognize that we are much more than mere biology.

I have come to recognize that every time a parent gets up to speak at his or her child's bar or bat mitzvah, there are such deep feelings of love and gratitude that mere thank-you speeches are not enough. You would think that after twenty-eight years of participating in *b'nai mitzvah* services I would be bored with the routine. But guess what? Each new attempt by a young person to connect to tradition and each parental response is refreshing and reaffirming and restorative.

I also have the privilege of meeting on a regular basis with couples preparing for their weddings. Sometimes I ask, why don't you just go to a Justice of the Peace? You will be just as married. The answer is consistent: we want something religious, something spiritual; we want our union to be consecrated. Is this just an extension of the romance? Is it a cultural convention, a soap-opera ending, or a genuine need to verify that love is a transcendent blessing, that a promise is truly sacred, that a home is a sanctuary and not just a place?

There are still moments that are hard for me. When I go to a hospital and a family asks for a blessing for the sick or the dying, sometimes I feel like a fraud. I know I have no power. But I also now know that they are hurting or scared or both, and they need some symbolic support from me. It's not about me. It's about the deep, genuine, unfiltered need to find help, support, unconditional love, and strength. The desire to help is there, and slowly, I have found enough words to share my empathy for them without intellectual, rational hesitation.

Learning how to pray is not easy for some of us. As a rabbinic student and a young rabbi, I learned the texts of the prayers and the rules of when and how to say them. Most of all, I learned that prayer is not homogeneous. There are all types of prayers and all types of styles. When you go to an art museum and you have a trained eye, it is relatively easy to distinguish between Greek art and Chinese art and between medieval art and modern abstract art. The same is true with prayers: they come in all flavors and all styles, even within the Jewish tradition.

Prayer in the Jewish tradition is broken down into two major categories: *keva* and *kavanah*. *Keva* prayers are fixed prayers. Their language is stable, and there are certain times to offer them. These prayers are often the script of our lives as Jews. The Shabbat prayers. The Hanukkah prayers. The readings from the Passover Haggadah. We say them at their appointed times, and they help define those moments as authentically Jewish. Sometimes they are focused on God. More often, they are ways of expressing our Jewishness, with or without great religious feelings.

Kavanah, on the other hand, means "intentionality." When you pray with *kavanah*, you pray with intensity and passion, investing the words with huge meaning and singing at full throttle. By definition, it is very difficult to sustain *kavanah* for long, but without *kavanah*, *keva* becomes mere rote. It is analogous to exercise. *Keva* keeps it regular. *Kavanah* is when you really are into it. It's not smart to try to run a marathon if you don't run regularly. *Keva* is training. Sometimes *kavanah* happens; sometimes it doesn't. But when a *kavanah* moment occurs in the context of regular keva, it is always more profound and more meaningful.

Two prayers from outside the tradition helped me make the *keva-kavanah* connection when I was growing up. The first was the Sabbath Prayer from *Fiddler on the Roof*. Back in the late Sixties, we sang it at camp before our Shabbat dinner. It was powerful and moving despite its secular origins on Broadway. "May you be like Ruth and like Esther. May you be deserving of praise. May you come to be in Israel a shining star." Somehow these words and the powerful melody that carried them also carried me and my soul. Sometimes I still hear it sung at a *bar mitzvah* reception. I try to listen to it and not the voices of its cultural despisers. There is something there that works for most of us. "Oh, hear our Sabbath prayer," it ends, "amen."

Another text that was not a Jewish prayer but worked as a prayer for me growing up was the pop song "Bridge over Troubled Waters" by Simon and Garfunkel. The words still move me: "When you're weary, feeling small, when tears are in your eyes, I will dry them all. I'm on your side when times get rough and friends just can't be found, like a bridge over troubled waters." For so many of us, if we could pray with heart and mind, prayer would be "a bridge over troubled waters." In fact, this song is a form of a *bakasha*, a prayer of petition in times of trouble, stress, and hopelessness.

During the course of the last year, a new prayer book, *Mishkan T'filah*, has been adopted by the Reform movement in Judaism. I have been deeply involved in the process of producing this new book and continue to serve as the national chair of the Press of the Central Conference of American Rabbis, which is publishing it. We have printed and distributed over 150,000 copies and have orders for double that number. Here at KI, our Religious Practices Committee will be recommending the adoption of this book at our next full board meeting. The new prayer book is comprehensive and replaces not the little gray Shabbat book but the big blue *Gates of Prayer for Daily, Shabbat, and Festival Worship*. Work on a new Reform High Holy Day book will commence at a think-tank meeting in New York this December under the sponsorship of the press group I chair.

What is most important about our new liturgy is not the layout of the book or even its theological range but its attempt to capture first-person prayers of *kavanah* to give voice, like never before in the Reform movement, to the individual's search for faith and for ways of reporting on that journey. It offers affirmations, praises, and questions. It speaks in the voice of women and men. It is respectful of tradition and shaped by modernity. It gives voice to our longings, our doubts, and our hopes. I believe it will be a valuable tool in closing the gap between public and private worship. As a society, we are living in a very difficult moment. The financial order that has sustained our lives since the recovery following the Great Depression is under tremendous stress, and so are we. It is a scary moment. We are also threatened by vicious enemies. The reality today is that there is a country called Iran that does sponsor terrorism, and there are organizations like al-Qaeda and the Taliban who are the foot soldiers in radical Islam's war against the West.

As Jews, we are also existentially tied to the State of Israel. Israel's enemies are dangerous and relentless. The Hezbollah, Iran's proxy army in Lebanon, presents a grave threat to Israel. Hezbollah is not only rearmed but has also greatly increased its capacity and now has forty thousand rockets, which can hit anywhere in Israel.

As Jews and Americans, we live in anxious times. Together, in a few weeks, we will be called upon to make choices of a lifetime, and we will do so with seriousness and resolve. But the financial and security dangers facing us and the world will not go away just because we have elections. The structural problems will remain, and we will have a great deal of work to do.

In these trying times, I believe that prayer can give us strength, steady our course, and fortify our convictions. Not brazen or strident prayers but quiet prayers in search of a measure of confidence and more wisdom, prayers asking for the ability to pursue justice and to do the right thing while being judicious at the same time. We live in a time of great anxiety and danger. We live at a time when we need to learn to be comfortable with prayer as an ally of rational analysis and principled beliefs.

On these High Holy Days, we come to synagogue to pray or to hear the prayers or to pray that we will find the capacity to pray. This evening, I want to affirm a few things about prayer and faith and what they have come to mean to me, and what, perhaps, they can also mean to you:

I believe in prayer.
I believe that prayer is the basic building block of religious life.
I believe that one can pray even if one does not believe.
I believe that prayer is irrepressible.
I believe that prayer is universal and not just Jewish or Christian or Muslim or Hindu.
I believe that a huge gap currently exists between personal prayer and public worship in our way of doing public prayer.
I believe that the only way to close that gap is through the cultivation of personal prayer.
I believe that prayer begins in the heart and is amplified by music and refracted by words and by art and by architecture.
I believe prayer is its own answer.
I believe prayer is beneficial to us both as people and indispensable to us as Jews trying to maintain our historic faith in unprecedented times.
What is prayer?
Prayer is the longing of the heart.
Prayer is pain in search of relief.
Prayer is fear in search of hope.
Prayer is hope in search of itself.
Prayer is thankfulness overflowing from the heart.

Prayer is need in search of an answer.
Prayer is a silent scream for help.
Prayer is in every tear.
Prayer is in every smile.
Prayer is in a comforting hug.
Prayer is in a demand for justice.
Prayer is in every act of kindness.

Can prayer really be of any help in this time of trouble and multi-faced danger?

This summer I was invited to an interfaith conference in Dallas, Texas. Seated around the table were scholars of Hinduism from India, professors of theology from an Egyptian university, a learned monk from Austria, a peace activist from Northern Ireland, an Episcopal priest from Oxford, and many others. Our job was to discuss and analyze the concept of thanksgiving from the perspective of our different faiths and to recommend a plan to the United Nations to create a unified approach to "world days of thanksgiving"—in other words, to take a category of prayer and use it as a foundation for expressing our common humanity. All people of every persuasion have reason to give thanks and have their own ways to express gratitude. Perhaps, then, prayer can contribute something to the improvement of this world, both in the inner recesses of our hearts and in the common actions of the family of nations.

In a world of nuclear bombs and trillion-dollar financial bailouts, I know this seems insignificant. But perhaps the power of prayer is like the power of the tiny atom, and within it is sufficient power to help us help ourselves to a better, safer tomorrow for all.

Judaism's profoundest vision for humanity is expressed in the form of a prayer. It is familiar to all of us. It is my prayer for this Rosh HaShanah, this New Year, which begins with such dark shadows cast over our lives. It reads, "O, may all, created in Your image, become one in spirit and one in friendship, forever united in Your service. Then shall Your kingdom be established on earth, and the word of Your prophet fulfilled: The Lord will reign for ever and ever."

Shana Tova, a good year, a year of peace and prosperity, a year of answered prayers for the good of all. Amen.

Abraham's Other Son: Jewish-Muslim Relations Today

September 30, 2008, Rosh HaShanah Morning 5769

About two years ago, I agreed to participate in a project whose goal was to create a documentary in DVD format entitled *Voices for Justice: Reform Rabbis and Moral Leadership*. It was a great project. Last March, our video premiered in Cincinnati before a convention of over four hundred rabbis. Subsequently, I showed the movie here at KI. The movie has been further edited and improved and is almost ready for national distribution.

One of the main scenes in our documentary has to do with pulpit-based efforts to counter the radio message of Father Charles Coughlin. Father Coughlin was a Canadian-born Catholic priest who, late in the 1920s, began to broadcast on the radio. Working from the National Shrine of the Little Flower in Royal Oak, Michigan, he became increasingly shrill and virulently anti-Semitic throughout the 1930s. By 1936, he was raising his arm in a Nazi-style salute in public programs. As many as one-third of the American public tuned in to his program, and his National Union for Social Justice gained a vast following.

If you would have asked an American Jew during the 1930s about the prospect of Jewish-Catholic reconciliation or even dialogue, my sense is that they would have dismissed you with a short semi-sarcastic laugh and said, "Yeah, right, and Father Coughlin will be at the table!" Jews and Catholics, the common wisdom had it, were implacable enemies. No one in the years prior to World War II could have imagined the level of interfaith dialogue that developed both during and following Vatican II. Convened by Pope John XXIII, Vatican II was attended by thousands of church leaders and, among many other things, led to a reversal of the prevailing view in the church that the Jews were culpable for the death of Christ.

In more recent times, the foundation built by John XXIII was further fortified by John Paul II, who visited Israel and Auschwitz and who became the first pope in history to visit a synagogue. On April 13, 1986, John Paul II, the Polish Pope, greeted the rabbi of the great synagogue of Rome with the timeless biblical words, "I am Joseph, your brother."

While all differences have not been resolved, in the seventy years since Father Coughlin was silenced, relations have vastly improved between Jews and Christians, specifically between Jews and Catholics. For years at KI, we have hosted annual Holocaust teach-ins organized by the local archdiocese. More recently, I was invited to speak at St. Joseph's University to dialogue with a visiting Jesuit scholar in a public forum. It was a wonderful, comfortable evening with open exchanges of ideas and a willingness to embrace both commonalities and differences.

Today, Jewish-Christian dialogue in the United States is accepted and encouraged as a normative part of American culture. The reality is that sometimes it is easier to talk to the clergy. However, there is one glaring exception to interfaith dialogue in America: the Muslim community. Is Jewish-Muslim cooperation possible? Who is available on their side? Can they be trusted? What are their real goals? What is the true nature of Islam? On this Rosh HaShanah, which coincides with the end of Ramadan, it is important that we explore these issues together. The paradigm for Jewish-Muslim relations, in part, can already be found in the biblical story of Ishmael. In traditional synagogues where two days of Rosh HaShanah are celebrated, the Torah portion for the first day of the holiday reports on the story of the birth of Isaac. In most Reform synagogues, we only observe one day of Rosh HaShanah and do not read that story but rather, to preserve our tie to tradition, read the *haftarah* from the first day on the birth of Samuel. In a few weeks, we will read in the Torah about the birth of Ishmael, the older brother of Isaac and the son of the Egyptian maid Hagar, who is sent away by Abraham.

According to Islamic tradition, it was Ishmael, not Isaac, who was almost offered by Abraham on Mount Moriah for a sacrifice. Ishmael, according to Islamic scholars, not only settled in Mecca but, along with his father, Abraham, the first Muslim, also helped establish the Kaaba, the great shrine of Mecca. In the Jewish tradition, some sources believe that Ishmael had two wives who had the same names as the wives of Mohammed, Aisha, and Fatima. In turn, the Jewish tradition views Ishmael as the father of both the Turkish and Arab peoples. In Islam, Mohammed is viewed as a descendant of Ishmael. The Jews, the Arabs, the Turks, and the Muslims are thus all tied together by family and by tradition and destiny. Jews, Arabs, and Muslims, according to all three traditions, view themselves as having linked ancestry and a common religious heritage. The history of Jewish-Muslim relations, in particular, is long and complex. At first, significant tension existed between the Jewish tribes in the Arabian Peninsula and emergent Islam. Subsequently, Jews were accorded, as monotheists, a favored status under Islamic law and were classified as "People of the Book."

Although not the legal equals of Muslims, Jews and Judaism in Islamic lands flourished in Iraq, Iran, and Spain. It eventually became a scholarly convention to speak about the golden age of Jews and Judaism in Muslim Spain. Beginning in the eighth century, Spain, the theory goes, saw a host of Jewish scholars, poets, and leaders including Hasdai ibn Shaprut, Solomon ibn Gabirol, Abraham and Moses ibn Ezra, and Shmuel HaNagid. Throughout this period, there was considerable scholarly exchange with the Muslims, and Jews became conversant in everyday and literary Arabic. By the time of Moses Maimonides, the greatest Jewish philosopher of the Middle Ages, Islamic Spain had become inhospitable to Jews. Maimonides then found safe refuge among the Muslims of Egypt for the rest of his life.

Two centuries later, following the Christian Reconquista of Spain and the expulsion of its Jewish population, another Islamic empire, the Ottomans, invited the Jews to settle in their midst. Not only did Jewish communities thrive in Turkey and Greece, but also, in the land of Israel, Jews settled in the holy cities of Jerusalem, Tiberius, Hebron, and, most of all, Safed, which in the sixteenth century became the world center of Jewish mysticism. To this day, we sing songs written in Islamic Safed, such as *"Shalom Aleichem"* and *"L'cha Dodi,"* on Friday nights. In fact, from the presidency of Thomas Jefferson until the time of Woodrow Wilson, the American government appointed Jews to diplomatic posts in the Ottoman Empire on the premise that Jews, not historically related to the Crusades, would be better received as American diplomats in the Middle East than Christians.

A dramatic change in Jewish-Arab-Muslim relations took place with the rise of Zionism in the twentieth century. By the 1920s, cycles of

Arab riots against the Jews of British Palestine took place with increasing frequency. With the rise of Nazism, the situation worsened again and the Grand Mufti of Jerusalem aligned himself with Hitler. The Arab League was founded in 1945, and in 1964, the League spawned the creation of the PLO, the first organization to give a political definition to the Palestinians, with the destruction of the State of Israel as its primary goal. In response to the establishment of the State of Israel, the Arab states expelled the majority of their Jewish citizens, most of whom settled in Israel, while a large minority gravitated toward France.

By the end of the twentieth century, the Arab-Israeli conflict had largely been recast as the Israeli-Palestinian conflict until the rise of radical Islam hijacked the conflict and added the ugly accelerant of religion to the flames engulfing the region. In the late 1970s, radical Shiite clerics overthrew the Shah of Iran and established a theocratic Islamic state, which included the destruction of Israel as one of its primary goals. In the same region, but among rival Sunni, the Taliban drove the Soviet Union from Afghanistan. In 1996, the Taliban were joined by Osama bin Laden and the al-Qaeda movement, also radical Sunni, a historical offshoot of the Saudi Arabian Islamic school of Wahhabism. While the Saudi government is Wahabi in its religious orientation, a major goal of al-Qaeda is the overthrow of the Saudi regime and the establishment of a Sunni theocracy in Mecca. Al-Qaeda, like its Shia counterpart, is fiercely anti-Zionist.

Today, the successors of the PLO prevail in the West Bank. The Hezbollah, founded in 1982 and made up of Lebanese Arab Shiites, is closely aligned with Iran and controls territory to the north of Israel. Hezbollah is in possession of a huge arsenal of rockets with increased trajectories and firepower. Hamas, founded in 1987, is broadly part of the Wahabi Sunni wing of Islam. In short, it is now more accurate today to talk about the Israeli-Palestinian-Islamic conflict and not just Arab-Israeli conflict, a smaller model from thirty years ago. Today, more than ever, on purely religious grounds, it seems that the descendants of Ishmael and the descendants of Isaac, both children of Abraham, are locked in an unsolvable conflict. Moreover, it seems that there is no limit as to what tactics or weapons Islamic extremists, both Sunni and Shiite, will use against their Abrahamic cousins in Israel. Thus, in the long history between the children of Ishmael and the children of Isaac, there are sources both of some hope and a great deal of despair. For sure, the scales of history are tipped away from any positive resolution in the short term. But is there any hope at all? Is there anything in the past and in our two traditions we can build on to begin a process of reconciliation?

My own current interest has to do with the possibilities of Jewish-Islamic dialogue—first, in the United States and, secondly, in the United Nations—to explore whether or not there are any domestic or UN-based possibilities for genuine exchange between our two faiths. The American context holds particular promise. The United States has a long history of religious disestablishment as well as interfaith cooperation. The Parliament of World Religions first held in Chicago in 1893 as part of the Columbian Exposition was one of the first paradigms of global multifaith exchange. In England, a parallel organization, the World Congress of Faiths, was founded in 1939. There are at least a dozen other like-minded organizations, many of which have NGO status at the United Nations. In each setting on a limited basis, there was and has been some Jewish-Muslim cooperation.

For most American Jews, the big question is whether or not there are partners in the Islamic community. At first blush, the picture does not look very promising. When I attended the AIPAC policy conference in Washington, DC last spring, I purposely went to the session on "Moderate Muslims." None of the speakers could identify a moderate Muslim constituency and therefore dismissed the whole line of thought. For sure, there is nothing to be done with the Nation of Islam who are followers of Louis Farrakhan. They are radical, anti-Semitic, and anti-Israel. And the press, in general, does not find the topic of moderate Muslims worthy of coverage, although strong examples do exist.

During the last few years, I have learned that the immigrant Muslim community in America sponsors a number of organizations that have expressed interest in talking with American Jews, the largest of which is the Islamic Society of North America. A smaller group, the American Islamic Council, has taken even bolder and more pluralistic stands. The Council on American-Islamic Relations also seeks to partner but is repeatedly charged with connections with terrorist organizations. In recent years, all three of these groups have shown a willingness to cooperate with American Jews at the domestic level. Assessing these groups is not easy. Many of the loudest voices in the American Jewish community, such as Daniel Pipes, are mostly associated with the struggle against Islamic extremism and do not provide a footpath to the Muslim community. For opposite reasons, pro Israel Islamic writers, particularly women, who are often showcased in the Jewish community in the United States, have no traction in the Islamic communities. Although there are only a few bridges connecting Jews and Muslims in the United States, I have become increasingly convinced that we need to travel down that shaky road. No one ever thought Jews and Catholics could talk, but look where we are now. Perhaps now is the time to start dialoguing with Muslims in the United States.

First, their numbers are growing; and at some point, they will be greater in population than Jews are in the United States.

Second, most of the American Muslim population wants to be "Americanistic." We now have a phenomenon in this country called the Islamic Sunday School. It is almost as absurd a concept as the Jewish Sunday School.

Third, the danger of radicalization is always present in the Islamic community; and creating ties now, when they are possible, is worth the effort because later there may be no possibility of connecting with one another at all.

My first connection with a Muslim community was in Binghamton, New York, where there was a small mosque in the city's historic First Ward. The imam was Turkish and a graduate of an Egyptian seminary. He was studying for a PhD in Ottoman studies at the university, and I was his minor adviser in religious history. We were easily able to bring our two congregations together. One of his leading members, a Pakistani neurosurgeon, was my doctor.

When I moved here eight years ago, I lost connection with the Muslim community. Although I organized the Cheltenham Area Multifaith Council, we had no Muslim clergymen; and the one meeting I went to, sponsored by the JCRC, turned into an unpleasant evening of pro- and anti-Israel exchanges. Philadelphia—unlike New York, LA, and a few other places—has not yet developed a framework for Jewish-Muslim dialogue.

That's why I was delighted last fall to receive an invitation from the Foundation for Ethnic Understanding, founded in New York City in 1989, to participate in the first-ever American Rabbi-Imam conference. The conference took place in November 2007. Several dozen rabbis and imams spent a morning together in an Orthodox synagogue and the afternoon at the Islamic Cultural Center at Ninety-Sixth and Third on New York's Upper East Side. It was a productive day of personal exchanges. The Foundation then invited twelve of us back to New York to make a public service announcement to be aired on CNN, advocating increased cooperation among all the children of Abraham. It will show this Fall just prior to America's great ecumenical celebration of Thanksgiving. At that time, hopefully, KI will also twin with a mosque I recently visited in Palmyra, New Jersey, whose leaders are interested in pursuing interfaith activities with us at KI. I hope you will join me in that pursuit.

I also had an opportunity to return to the Islamic Center in New York this summer with a busload of fifty KI members. We were warmly welcome by the senior imam of the mosque, Shamsi Ali. Imam Ali, originally from Indonesia, has distinguished himself by his interfaith work in New York City in the wake of 9/11. He is now running a soup kitchen in cooperation with the Jewish Theological Seminary. The soup kitchen is housed in a church in New York.

Finally, I was invited by a UN NGO to help work on creating an International Day of Thanksgiving. The first person I met with was a professor emeritus of Hindu studies at the University of Virginia. In turn, Dr. Rao and I traveled to New York to meet with a past Assistant Secretary of the United Nations, Ambassador Chaudhry of Bangladesh. There we were—a Jew, a Hindu, and a Muslim—sitting in the Delegates Dining Room overlooking the East River and talking about how to make the United Nations more "united" and less separate "nations," using the concept of gratitude as our "hook." In July, the three of us traveled to Dallas to be at the international conference of scholars sponsored by the Thanksgiving Square Foundation, which is heading the Gratitude Project at the UN.

The Reform movement in Judaism—through its leader Rabbi Eric Yoffie, President of the Union for Reform Judaism—has also broadly called on Reform Jews to join in forging a Jewish-Muslim dialogue in America. To that end, we will be hosting Walter Ruby, a leading New York Jewish journalist, to speak to us on December 12 on his view of the future of Jewish-Muslim dialogue.

Walter attended a large interfaith gathering in Madrid this summer sponsored by King Abdullah of Saudi Arabia and co-hosted by the King of Spain. Although the meeting met with mixed reviews, it was a remarkable departure from the hardline Wahabi Islamic theology, which has broadly characterized the Saudi monarchy heretofore.

Is it all a chasing after windmills? Is Islam fundamentally anti-Semitic, triumphalist, and bent on world domination? Are there any truly moderate Muslims, or are they all just jihadists lying in wait? My sense is that there are moderate Muslims out there, average people living regular lives, as well as imams and scholars who deeply believe that terror is not the way of Islam and not the road to redemption.

I believe that there is an opening today for scholarly religious organizations, ecumenical institutes, NGOs at the UN, and Jewish-Muslim dialogue groups to explore terms of peaceful coexistence. Muslim societies, like all societies, have their own internal challenges that they need to attend to, Iran being first among them, where domestic services are declining and inflation is rising. For moderate Muslims, cooperation, not confrontation, is the first order of business.

When I met with the imams in New York last fall, I found it took several hours of dialogue before we relaxed with one another. When we visited the mosque this summer, the imam greeted us with such joy and kindness that it was hard to imagine it was a show or a deception or a trap.

Is it possible that one day the children of Abraham, Isaac, and Ishmael will behave like brothers again? Is it possible that one day we will be able to go up to the Temple Mount of Jerusalem and offer our prayers to the One God over all of us, standing side by side, without guns or bombs or guard dogs?

Religion can do a lot of good in this world, and it can also do a lot of harm. Much of that harm today is within the family of Abraham. It is a tragedy and a betrayal of what is ultimately required of us as people and the children of Abraham. We need to stand firm. We need to be vigilant, but we also need to hold out a hand in peace with the hope that some will do the same from the other side of the monotheistic divide. We did it with Catholics twenty years too late, twenty years after the Nazis invaded Poland.

We cannot be twenty years too late this time.

The stakes are even higher.
May God bless us with strength.
May God bless us with wisdom.

May God bless us with peace.

JUDAISM AND THE DIFFICULT QUESTION OF RACE

October 8, 2008, Yom Kippur Evening 5769

Every four years, the United States votes for a new president. Campaigns are expensive and exhausting for the candidates and the country and yet essential to our well-being as a nation. This year's presidential campaign has not only been expensive and exhausting but has also been extraordinary in the number of the major themes of our American democracy it has compelled us to explore together. Some, but not all, of these themes include free market versus government regulation, America's internal kulturkampf, the nature of the War on Terror, the power and limits of the executive branch of government, and the role of race in American society.

They are all big topics and all topics worthy of deep exploration. An election is more than a choice of a candidate or candidates. An election, ultimately, is about setting the compass of the Ship of State and how to steer the boat, especially in troubled times.

Tonight, I want to explore just one of those themes with you, not only because it is close to my heart but also because it is central to who we are, both as Americans and as Jews. It is an issue I believe that Judaism speaks to directly and passionately. It is an issue that ultimately is not only a question of policy but also a deep philosophical and moral question about who we really are as human beings, and that is the issue of race.

Two moments in this exhausting presidential campaign stick out in my mind with respect to race. The first is Senator Obama's powerful statement here in Philadelphia this past March. In it, he gave a real-life example of his view on race, not only by telling his own life story but also by relating the story of a young white woman in distressed financial circumstances who had to take a time-out in her life to help her elderly parents get through a crisis in their lives and work for the Obama campaign. He then asked an elderly black man why he was working for the Obama campaign, and he replied because of what the white woman was doing.

The second occurred at the podium of the Republican convention when Governor Mike Huckabee spoke. Here are his exact words: "I grew up at a time and in a place where the Civil Rights movement was fought. I witnessed firsthand the shameful evils of racism. I saw how ignorance and prejudice caused people to do the unthinkable to people of color not so many years ago. So I say with sincerity that I have great respect for Senator Obama's historic achievement to become his party's nominee, not because of his color but with indifference to it. Party or politics aside, we celebrate this milestone because it elevates our country."

Tonight I call on you too to elevate your country, your faith, and yourself by thinking together about the state of race in our society, in Judaism, and in your hearts and to affirm both with Senator Obama and Governor Huckabee that you yourself—no matter whether you are a Democrat, a Republican, or an independent—can fully embrace the post-racial philosophy that both of these leaders, in very different ways, affirm.

I know that this is risky ground and that the mere mention of a candidate's name can be misconstrued as a pulpit endorsement. It is not. Rather, it is an attempt, on this most sacred night of the year in our tradition, to challenge you to think about your own views, your own beliefs, and your own track record on one of the oldest, most complex, and most soiled of all human discussions: the question of race. My question to all of us tonight is, are we truly post-racial in our worldviews?

Let me put it another way. Last year on July 9, 2007, the NAACP staged a funeral for the *N* word. It was a symbolic act directed as much against black rappers and their obscene use of the *N* word as it was against white racists. My sense is that no one in this room would disagree with the substance of this one-act play, even if you did not care for the political theater used to make the point.

Pushing this a little further, what would our reaction be to a leading Jewish civil rights group having a mock funeral for the *S* word in Jewish life? The *S* word, for those who do not know, means *black* in Yiddish,

German, and cognate languages. It is a word most of us have heard, some of us have used, and all of us need to abandon.

I once heard a professor of Yiddish say to his students, "If you don't have something nice to say about someone, say it in Yiddish." I know he wasn't thinking about the *S* word at that moment, but it is true that the *S* word is often used to give cultural cover to racial prejudice as if, somehow, Jewish racial prejudice is acceptable, whereas "white gentile" prejudice is not. The *S* word surely does not bring with it a history of the Klan and lynchings, but the bottom line is that racial prejudice is unacceptable and wrong, no matter in what language it is conveyed.

Race is a complex and emotional topic. I believe there are three salient issues we need to put on the table tonight: (1) the definition of the term *race*, (2) Judaism's view of race, and (3) the American Jewish experience of race. I believe all three point to a powerful conclusion that both Senator Obama and Governor Huckabee are right: we need to get ourselves to a post-racial view of race and thereby elevate ourselves, our faith, and our country and thus help heal the world of one of its deepest hurts.

It is important to note that the biological sciences today are distinctly "post-racial" in their thinking. All the old theories about "human types" based on skin color, type of hair, skull structure, and alike are in the wastebasket. As one scientist recently said to me, if you were at a crime scene where the perpetrator had fled but was wounded and there were blood samples available, you could not positively identify the color of the alleged criminal's skin by his or her blood. Yes, there are certain clusters of genetic information within highly defined subgroups or communities but nowhere near-enough data to scientifically delineate a racial group. Thus, about one-sixteenth of an inch beneath the surface of our dermis, we are all pretty much the same; and human blood, brains, and everything else on the inside is the same.

But when it comes to the social sciences and to law, the issue of race is not so clear-cut. Certainly, historians use the concept of race as a tool to study the past. However, historians do not need to determine whether or not race is a biological reality. Anthropologists, on the other hand, do, and like their colleagues in the "hard" sciences, broadly agree that "race" is a "social construct" and not a biological fact. The same is true in American law. The U.S. government, despite its broad use of post-racial disclaimers, actually defines race as a social construction and not as a scientific fact. In America, with the exception of our native peoples, we rely on "self-identification" and biological criteria to determine race, a process muddied by recent definitional changes enacted by the government, which only allow a person to define him or herself in terms of one, and not two, races. With respect to Native Americans, the current system involves both individual documentation of ancestry and government recognition of tribal status. Indeed, it is a perplexing and unsettled business. More broadly, the legal construction of race in the United States does little to advance a global definition of race, as different countries like Canada, Brazil, and others all have their own criteria.

Closely related to the social construction of race is the idea of "ethnicity," which removes the burden of biological and genetic proof and is almost entirely cultural in its orientation. However, ethnicity, which at a common-sense level seems to work as a sociocultural norm, also tends to dissolve upon close analysis. For example, we have created a macro-ethnicity in America called Hispanic, which is made up of nearly 35 million people of diverse backgrounds representing over 10 percent of the 322 million Spanish-speaking people in the world. Although some Hispanics could easily self-identify as White in the United States, Latino is legally considered a non-Caucasian ethno-racial classification in this country.

The most complicated use of race and ethnicity in the United States actually occurs in the area of law. On the one hand, we talk about the law being "color blind." On the other hand, suspected criminals are routinely announced to the community in terms of their gender, age, height, weight, and race—at least race as a social construct. It is also true that racial hate crimes can be prosecuted with vigor in the United States and that various legal instruments and government policies such as affirmative action and equal opportunity have played an important role in shaping American social policy.

The complexities of race and law in the United States can be seen in the reversal of the 1866 Equal Protection Clause of the Nineteenth Amendment in the Supreme Court's 1896 infamous decision in *Plessy v. Ferguson*, which legitimized racial segregation by twisting the meaning of "separate but equal." In the second half of the twentieth century, separate but equal was challenged in *Brown v. Board of Education*, and subsequent social policy was built on President Kennedy's 1961 Executive Order 10925, which helped launch the idea of affirmative action. For many American Jews, however, affirmative action came perilously close to being a quota system, as witnessed by the strong reaction in the American Jewish community to the Bakke case in California in 1978.

Thus, while race may not be a valid category of analysis both for the hard and social sciences, race and ethnicity continue to play a very real and very problematic role in our lives as Americans and as Jews. It is important then, also, to understand what Judaism itself actually teaches about race as well as the Jewish community's historical encounter with race and racism.

The Torah begins with a dramatic statement about the ultimate biological unity of humanity. In Genesis 1:27, we read, *"Va'yeev-ra Ehloheem et HaAdam B'itzal mo* [And God created man in His own image, in the image of God, He created him; male and female He created them]." In a non-literal way, this ideological view squares with the widely held view among anthropologists that human beings are of singular biological origin and adds that people, unique in all of creation, enjoy a special status in the eyes of God.

The unity of humanity is complemented by the diversity of human expression. The sons of Noah, Ham, Yaphet, and Shem are portrayed broadly as the founders of the African, European, and Semitic branches of the human family whose linguistic diversity is understood to have been a punishment, in the story of the Tower of Babel, for human hubris. Jews in this worldview are Shemites or Semites, and their worst enemies, Amalek, are viewed as being of the same sub-stock in the human tree.

Of all the nations, however, Israel is singled out for the special distinction of being "God's treasured people." For some Jews, the call of chosenness led to claims of superiority and favoritism, although many of the early family stories in the Book of Genesis are parables depicting the horrible consequences of favoritism.

A widespread feeling of superiority among ancient Israelites led the prophet Amos to declare, "Are you, Israel, not as the children of Ethiopians to me?" And then asks rhetorically in the name of God, "Have I not brought up Israel from Egypt and the Philistines from Caphtor and Aram from Kir?" (Amos 9:7).

The tension between ideas of Jewish superiority and universal equality was openly discussed by the rabbis. In trying to find a single verse that epitomizes all of Judaism, the rabbis rejected "Love your neighbor as yourself" as their main principle because the word *neighbor* in Hebrew could be construed to mean "fellow Jew" and not "fellow human being." Instead, the rabbis settled on the verse "These are the generations of

Adam" as the core teaching of Judaism because it affirms the ultimate unity of humanity.

To drive home their universal, nonhierarchical view of the human being, the rabbis selected the teaching of the prophet Amos on the equality of the Ethiopian and the Jew as the *haftarah* for the Torah portion containing the Golden Rule, thereby assuring Judaism's inclusive, universal understanding of the word *neighbor* as a moral term and not a limited ethnic relationship. Moreover, to ensure Judaism's nonracial character, our tradition has always affirmed, although rarely sought, the conversion to Judaism of people of any background.

Of course, there were racial tensions in Ancient Israel. Both Moses's brother and sister, Aaron and Miriam, objected to him marrying a Cushite or African woman. In the Song of Songs, Solomon's admirer is also a black woman. "Do not gaze at me," she pleads with the daughters of Jerusalem, "because I am dark." By contrast, Ethiopian legend traces the lineage of its people's royal household back to the union of Solomon and the Queen of Sheba.

In modern times, radically different views of "Jewish chosenness" developed. Rabbi David Einhorn, the first senior rabbi of KI and a staunch abolitionist, argued against mixed marriage on the grounds that Jews needed to preserve their group's unique genius for religion through strict endogamy. By contrast, Rabbi Mordecai Kaplan, the founder of the Reconstructionist Movement, argued against the doctrine of the Chosen People on the grounds that it suggested Jewish racial superiority. At the height of the outreach movement twenty-plus years ago, the Reform movement found a middle position, referring to Jews not as the chosen people or a race but as a "choosing people" of all ethnicities and races rooted in a covenant with God and not in their biology of origin. The racialization of Jewishness in modern times has resulted in the greatest tragedy ever to befall the Jewish people, if not in the history of all humanity. Nazi racial theory already had roots in the work of the seventeenth-century writings of François Bernier, who was among the first to speculate that there was not one human race but a variety of human races. That same line of thinking was reframed two hundred years later by the racialist Count Gobineau. The Nazis systematized a hierarchy of races and cast their relationship into a historical struggle between the German Herrenvolk (master race) and inferior people as well as nefarious racial enemies, most importantly, the Jews. In the end, Hitler and his followers concluded that the annihilation of the Jewish race would guarantee the German people their racially defined destiny as rulers of the world.

The idea of the Jews as a nefarious group again found expression just thirty years after the end of the Holocaust with the passage of the UN's resolution on "Zionism as Racism." This ideological perversion of Jewish nationalism stood for sixteen years until it was overturned by the General Assembly.

Within the Jewish community, the historical self-loathing that was yet another consequence of anti-Jewish racism also found a mirror image in Jewish self-aggrandizement as a defense against constant racial attacks on Jewishness. The most familiar racialized pro-Jewish arguments focus on inherent Jewish intelligence. In Yiddish, the expression *yiddishe kopf*, or a "Jewish head," is meant to stand in contrast to a *goyishe kopf*, or a "gentile head." Most of us have seen e-mails documenting the fact that 23 percent of all Nobel Prize winners and 37 percent of all American Nobel Prize winners have been Jews. The huge numbers are made possible by the inclusion of people of "half-Jewish descent," the implication being that Jewish genes are more likely to have the seeds of genius than non-Jewish genes.

On many counts, the Jewish experience of race in America has been equally complex and contradictory. While scholars initially focused on the place of Jews in America in the great debate over slavery in this country as well as the role of American Jews in the Civil Rights movement, research today has shifted to the subtler topic of "Jewish whiteness" in the United States. Two books, in particular, have shaped this debate. First, Karen Brodkin's 1998 anthropological study, *How Jews Became White Folks and What That Says about Race in America*, and Eric L. Goldstein's acclaimed 2006 work, *The Price of Whiteness: Jews, Race, and American Identity*.

While it is reassuring to know that a handful of American Jews, such as Rabbi Einhorn, stood up against slavery, the majority of American Jews were not abolitionists. Nearly all Southern Jews and some Northern Jews openly supported slavery and did so on racist grounds. The first and most famous (or infamous) rabbinic talk on slavery in America was delivered by the leading Jewish preacher of the period, Rabbi Morris J. Raphall of New York City, on January 4, 1861. In a speech entitled "The Bible View of Slavery," Raphall argued that the Bible sanctioned slavery, that the slavery of the American South was much crueler than biblical slavery, and that the enslavement of Africans was biologically justified.

Jews in the antebellum South broadly defended slavery. Aaron Hirsch, who arrived in the United States in 1847 and settled in the South, wrote after the Civil War that "the institution of slavery as it existed in the South was not so great a wrong as people believe . . . here, they were instructed to work, were civilized and got religion and were perfectly happy." In 1866, Eleanor H. Cohen wrote in a letter later discovered by Rabbi Korn of KI that "I, who believe in the institution of slavery, regret deeply its being abolished. I am accustomed much to have them wait on me, and I dislike white servants very much."

The racial antipathy between Blacks and Jews in America has gone through a number of different phases. In the 1920s and 1930s, when the American Jewish community was defending itself against the Klan, Henry Ford, and Father Charles Coughlin, it did not seek broad common cause with American Blacks, who also labored under the whip of discrimination in this country. It was only after World War II that Jews and Blacks began to make common cause in the Civil Rights movement. As one historian put it, "Things were never as good as some Jewish liberals would have had it; and never as bad as Black nationalists saw it."

For me personally, one experience growing up demonstrated the historical alignment of Jews and Blacks in America in the 1960s. One morning, our housekeeper, a heavy-set Black woman originally from southern Virginia, was making my breakfast. She was slamming pots and pans around. I asked her what was wrong. She looked at me and said with intensity, "No one likes you, and no one likes me because you are a Jew, and I am a [you fill in the word]."

Tensions between the two communities began to erupt by the mid-1960s. Economic conflict, riots, Black Nationalism, community control of schools, affirmative action, Zionism, and many other issues complicated Black-Jewish boundaries in this country. Jewish-Black tensions combined with America's ubiquitous anti-Black racism combined to push many American Jews culturally into what scholars increasingly call Whiteness.

Ironically, for many American Jews, the long-term process that increasingly identified Jews as part of white society in America has been highly ambivalent. Not only did it accelerate the acceptance of Jews into America, but it also proved to be an accelerant in Jewish assimilation. Jews, the saying goes, want to be like everybody else in society but different. In white society, however, it is very difficult to be different and still be white.

Today, this complex picture has moved on to yet another stage in its history. Scientific post-racial thinking, Judaism's nonracial view of humanity, the scars of racist anti-Semitism, the complexities and contradictions of American law, and the history of relations of Blacks and Jews—in particular, for good and for bad in America—all temper how we, in the Jewish community, view issues of race and racism in America today.

The reality of America today is that in an increasingly diverse society and in the foreseeable future, we will no longer have a white majority. Will Jews continue to identify with American Whiteness; or will we seek out a new unique American cultural Pale of Settlement among the Asian, Latino, and African American subcommunities? Or will we move on to a truly post-racial America, and, if we do so, in what way will we preserve our Jewishness?

These are not easy questions. Indeed, they are not even comfortable questions, but they are important questions that cut to the core of who we are as Jews, Americans, and human beings. They are questions posed to us by both sides of the current political debate in this most political of all seasons.

On these High Holy Days, we confess our personal and communal sins: *"Al cheit sh'cha-ta-nu l' fa-necha."* We all have committed offenses, and together, we confess these human sins: The sins of arrogance, bigotry, and cynicism [of] weakness of will and xenophobia."

The overcoming of racism has always been a messianic goal of the Jewish tradition. Judaism's highest vision of humanity is, indeed, post-racial. In the words of our old *Union Prayer Book*, "O, may all, created in Thine image, recognize that they are brethren so that, one in spirit and one in fellowship, they move be forever united before Thee."

So may it be God's will.

So may it be our will. Amen. An easy fast.

My Synagogue

September 27, 2009, Yom Kippur Evening 5770

"My synagogue."

What does it mean when a person refers to his or her synagogue as "my synagogue"?

What does it mean to be a member of a synagogue?

What makes a synagogue my synagogue?

What's so important about synagogues in the first place?

Take a moment and think about all the synagogues you have called my synagogue. Maybe the only synagogue on your list is KI.

Maybe your list begins in South Philly or Oxford Circle or somewhere in Israel or Europe. Maybe you don't have an answer to this question right now.

Personally, I am a synagogue person. I have always been part of a synagogue.

My decision many years ago to become a rabbi clearly grew out of my deep involvement in the synagogue of my youth.

My family was deeply rooted in our synagogue in Baltimore.

I knew, from when I was very young, that the synagogue my mother had attended as a child in Germany had been burned to the ground by the Nazis.

I later learned that the leading Jewish businessman of her community was beaten to death that night on the steps of his synagogue while trying to save a Torah scroll.

He was probably not even an observant Jew.

He just knew his community needed at least one scroll to survive.

My mother's mother was a quiet woman.

She did much more than she said.

One day, I learned she kept the Torah covers in the Ark in our synagogue in good repair. She never said a word about that to me. Because my grandmother's threads held our Torah covers together, those Torah became my Torahs.

My mother was always active in our synagogue.

First, there was Sisterhood and purple Uniongrams.

Our kitchen table disappeared under all those Uniongrams.

Later, I went to rabbinic school in Cincinnati and lived in the Sisterhood dorm. My dorm had been built with the sales of all those Uniongrams.

My father likes the music of the synagogue, the classical music of organ, choir, and tenor cantors who made it plausible that Verdi, Mozart, and Puccini must have been at least a little Jewish. The music of my synagogue made my synagogue my synagogue for me too.

I had some very good teachers in Sunday School when I was young.

In second grade, I had Mrs. Hortense Klotzman. She was the old-fashioned, classical Reform type of Sunday school teacher. I can't recall much about her except her name and that she had some kind of impact on me.

I had some very good rabbis growing up too. My senior rabbi was Rabbi Abraham Shaw. He had an FM voice. It was beautiful. It was almost the voice of heaven on earth. I remember him mostly as an older man. He had a saintly face. He had very old hands. When he blessed me for my Confirmation, his hands seemed to be the hands of our ancient tradition reaching out to me. I was seriously struggling with the idea of God at that time in my life, but something about his hands seemed like a genuine blessing to me.

My junior youth group adviser was a very nice lady. Her name was Mrs. Roz Keane. She lived in a beautiful house and invited us over to meet there. We met in the synagogue library too and had a pretty good time.

The synagogue of my youth had ushers—very formal ushers who wore white lapel flowers. I kind of laughed at them, but they were part of my synagogue too.

As kids, we used to work in the coat room on Friday nights.

The *Oneg Shabbat* was very good. One of the cookies looked like a wheel with a huge swirl of chocolate in the middle. Those cookies made my synagogue my synagogue.

We had a giant *sukkah* on the *bimah* when I was a kid. We had to bring cans of nonperishable food up on the altar while the organ played. It was scary and a little mystical too.

I spent a lot of time in synagogue as a kid. It was part of the flow of my life. My cousins had their synagogue, and I had mine. It was part of my home as a child and beyond.

When I went away to college, I didn't have a synagogue for a while. I tried Hillel. I went to the Orthodox shul near the campus. The rabbi was very nice. He gave me a pair of *tefillin* to wear while I was at school.

I taught Sunday School at the local Reform synagogue. It was a very old building from the Civil War.

At first, the rabbi didn't like me. My students wouldn't sing Jewish synagogues at the weekly assembly, so we had them sing "Feeling Groovy" to loosen them up.

The rabbi was very angry and fired me. Later, he served as my reference for rabbinic school.

I studied in Jerusalem and attended many synagogues there. My school had a synagogue. For music, I had a harpsichord and flute. It was beautiful in the Shabbat morning light of the Eternal City. I went to a Yemenite synagogue and an Afghan synagogue and the synagogue of the Chief Rabbi. Each had a flavor and a feeling of its own.

My first pulpit was in Harlingen, Texas. Flying out of the Cincinnati airport to Dallas proved to be an emotional moment for me. I was going to be an almost rabbi. But it was their synagogue.

My student pulpit was in Richmond, Indiana. It only had thirty families. I called them my Hebrew Hoosiers. Liz and I served that congregation for three years.

I served two pulpits in Binghamton: one Reconstructionist, the other Reform. Both were my synagogue. They were warm, inviting places. They were small town and big spirit. They were the synagogues of my own children's youth.

You know a synagogue is your synagogue when it is hard to leave it.

KI is now my synagogue. I have been in this pulpit for eight years. At first, I hardly knew anyone here. It took time. It is a big and complicated place.

Who knew that the switch for the air conditioner for the chapel is in the auditorium and that there is a secret light switch in my office that can shut the whole room down, but no one knew where it was when it went off?

During my eight years here, it has become clearer and clearer to me how much KI is "my synagogue" to so many of the people here.

I watched kids in second grade grow into KIFTY officers.

I met members whose families have been here for eight, nine generations, and more. I had never heard of such a family before I came to KI. Not only was KI their synagogue, but it is also their families' synagogue, including cousins and ancestors alike.

There are many people here at KI who say "my KI" all the time. Volunteers, officers, Friday-night regulars. Members who come to almost nothing but feel fiercely that this is their synagogue.

This is my synagogue, they tell me, and I listen. And I smile. And I think about how much responsibility I have and all the leaders have to maintain that relationship.

Every baby naming, every consecration, every bar and bat mitzvah, every confirmation, every *aufruf* and wedding, every anniversary prayer, every funeral, and every very long KI list of yahrzeits make this place my synagogue every day.

The associations and memories become infinite. Traveling together, learning together, visiting together in Florida or at the shore.

They are all pieces of what it means to call a synagogue my synagogue.

Sometimes synagogues have problems and become highly fractured places. There are meetings and protests and letters and votes. And hot emotions. People get supercharged when their synagogue no longer feels like their synagogue.

Sometimes the problems are ridiculous, and it is hard to imagine how things can get so bent. Sometimes they are very real and very legal and very moral.

When someone's synagogue is in turmoil, its members are often in turmoil too. Belonging to a synagogue is like having a family, and leaving a conflicted synagogue is almost like having a divorce.

Sometimes one doesn't understand how important their synagogue is to them until they are in a conflict in their synagogue.

Sometimes it is too late.

Sometimes we have to settle with the words "my former synagogue." They are rarely said without a touch of genuine grief or a sense of loss.

I have seen this from afar many times.

I've learned that the claim that "this synagogue is my synagogue" is very powerful, both in good times and in bad.

What makes a synagogue my synagogue? Memory is clearly the biggest part of it. A feeling of engagement and welcome is another. The belief that your synagogue embodies your beliefs about Judaism and Jewish living counts too. People make a synagogue a spiritual home. So does the art and the architecture.

Synagogues should be beautiful places—if possible, in stone and glass—but always in spirit.

The spirit of a synagogue is what makes a synagogue become a personal commitment. Its warmth, its inclusiveness, its pride in Jewishness, and its commitment to a broader humanity. Its ability to teach and inspire, its capacity to help us celebrate the peaks of youth and navigate the valleys of sickness and loss.

My synagogue is where I go to meet my Jewish communal and religious responsibilities. It is not just a place. It is a sacred place. A place that represents my highest aspirations as a Jew and as a person. It is where I am accepted for who I am and what I believe in and what I want for my family and for my community.

A rabbi once wrote that the synagogue is the sanctuary of Israel. The rabbi was not just talking about the actual sanctuary. He meant that the synagogue is the place of spiritual refuge and renewal in Jewish life. It is our shrine and our hideaway and our rampart in our lives as Jews.

Too many synagogues today are in steep decline. Fewer and fewer people are moved to say the words "my synagogue." The synagogue is viewed as a kind of trap: expensive, self-perpetuating, ineffective, and sometimes even hypocritical.

People talk about "that synagogue."

At KI, we can talk about our synagogue, and not everyone, but many of us, can honestly say that this place is my synagogue, and that is no small claim.

On this Yom Kippur, we can need to stock of ourselves, as always, as people and as Jews. To look inward, to ask the tough questions. To identify what we have done wrong and how we plan to do better.

On this Yom Kippur, I would also ask all our members and friends to ask themselves if they can say that this congregation is my synagogue.

If the answer is yes, try to figure out what makes this synagogue your synagogue. If the answer is no or not sure, again, try to think it through. It is an important and necessary spiritual exercise.

KI is not Judaism. It is not all things to all people. But it is home for many of us. I have been blessed to have had a number of spiritual homes along the path of life.

Today, this is my shul, not because I am the senior rabbi of this congregation but because consistent with my previous synagogue experiences, I can say "this is my synagogue."

On this Yom Kippur, it is my fervent prayer that each and every one of you be blessed with all that brings blessing and goodness and light into your lives.

I pray that you are surrounded with love that you seek, in your ways, paths to serve and bless others, that you experience a modicum of happiness, and even if you can't find the joy you want, you feel you have enough to say you are thankful for your life.

I pray that you find in this place a connection to your religious heritage and the whole of Israel—that you can say with some pride and even more satisfaction "this is my synagogue." By affirming that this is our synagogue, we will, I am confident, find true ways to bless one another as people and as Jews until we meet again in this same sacred place for Yom Kippur next year.

May it be a year of happiness. A year of good health. A year of peace. Amen.

On the Road Again: Maryland Jewish Heritage Tour

October 8, 2009, eKI

On Wednesday, October 7, a group of KI members, friends and I took a full-day bus trip to Baltimore and Annapolis. The weather was great, the camaraderie was wonderful, the food was OK and the tour was fantastic. We went to three sites: the Museum of the Maryland Jewish Historical Society and the adjacent restored synagogues, Fort McHenry, and the new Jewish Center at the United States Naval Academy. All three stops were not only worthwhile, they were inspiring.

The Maryland Jewish Museum is well known as the best Jewish regional museum in the United States. Now that I've been there, I can tell you that its reputation is on target. The museum has a lovely exhibition of East European Jewish life in Baltimore from one hundred years ago. Row homes, sweat shops and delis, they are all there. The fact that the menu from my grandfather's deli on Baltimore Street is on display didn't hurt either. On either side of the museum are restored synagogues. The older one is known as the Lloyd Street Synagogue. Built in 1845, it is the third oldest synagogue building in the United States today. On the other side is a Moorish building, the original home of Chizuk Amuno congregation. Both buildings are in fine shape and illustrate the early religious life of American Jewry in a pleasing fashion.

Next, it was off to Fort McHenry. OK, so there were only four Jews involved in the Battle of Baltimore on September 13–14, 1814 (two Cohens and two Ettings), but it is still a site every American should see. After watching the intro movie, the curtains to our right opened and there was the flag pole and flag flying over the fort. It was very moving. Then we walked into the fort, climbed the ramparts and took a group picture next to the largest cannon I've ever seen.

Finally, we went to the United States Naval Academy in Annapolis to visit the new Uriah P. Levy Jewish Center there. It is a beautiful, elegant building in the middle of the campus. The front looks like Monticello in white. The interior is in Jerusalem stone. Our guide was the Jewish Chaplain of the Academy, Rabbi Seth Phillips, an old school friend of mine. In the Social Hall we saw our Rabbi Korn's Admiral flag on display. All of us, especially his sister, Jean Korn, swelled with pride. Our faith is, indeed, well represented at one of America's most prestigious military schools.

Because it was Sukkot and the Yeshivas in Baltimore were closed, there were also many Orthodox Jewish families on tour as well. It was very gratifying that every segment of our community was there to see and support.

Every day something happened to make me feel proud to be an American Jew. This Wednesday, that pride was truly soaring.

Chag Sameach and Shabbat Shalom!

My Munich Report: The German Jewish Heritage and American Judaism

2009

I am at gate H3 at the Munich airport waiting for my flight back to Philadelphia. I came to Germany at the beginning of this week to participate in a small international academic conference sponsored by the University of Munich and the Berlin branch of the Leo Baeck Institute. The conference was held at the Akademie für Politische Bildung in Tutzing, an elegant lakeside community located in the foothills of the Alps (which are beautiful beyond description) about thirty miles south of Munich.

I was one of twenty-three presenters at the Conference. Entitled "The German Rabbinate Abroad: Transferring German-Jewish Modernity Into the World," the conference examined how rabbis from Germany broadly exported a new model of the rabbinate from Germany between 1781 and 1945 to countries all around the world. A new type of rabbinic seminary developed in Germany in the early nineteenth century, which was then copied in other places such as the United States (e.g., HUC-JIR). In addition, they established a tradition of the doctor-rabbi—that is, a rabbi with a PhD from a secular university whose broad cultural agenda was to bring a sophisticated intellectual approach to the study and practice of Judaism in conjunction with a broad appreciation for world culture. Indeed, one of the projects we heard about was a two-volume *Handbook of German Rabbis, 1791–1945*, which traced the lives and careers of several thousand German doctor-rabbis.

I have long seen myself a part of this cohort of doctor-rabbis who seek to combine the best of academic study with culture and synagogue life. Since the appointment of Rabbi Dr. David Einhorn in 1862, KI has had a long unbroken history of doctor-rabbis. With the recent release of our congregational program book, *Torah and Tarbut* (*Torah and Culture*), I hope we are taking this modality of Judaism to a new level. It not only defines us as a unique institution in the Philadelphia community but also gives us a deep and rich programmatic foundation to complement our many other fundamental endeavors as a synagogue community.

At the heart of this enterprise is the German language concept of Bildung. Literally translated as "education," *bildung* more precisely means something like "spiritual development." Bildung is a path that combines deep learning with a deep appreciation of the arts, history, and literature. It rejects the all-too-common and always-painful American town-gown polarity, which sadly places real (Jewish) learning beyond the pale of the synagogue. Jewish *bildung*—particularly the type that came out of the Lehrhaus in Frankfurt in the 1920s, combining "scientific study" with "personal existence"—is at the very heart of what I hope to continue to develop at KI.

At services and in other forums, I will give a more complete report on my trip, the conference, and my visit to the new Jewish center in Munich. Meanwhile, it is always exciting and important to travel but even better to come home.

Shabbat Shalom!

HUC-JIR Founders' Day Talk

2010 eKI

On Thursday, March 18, I had the great honor of giving the Annual Founders' Day talk at HUC-JIR in New York City. The Dean of the College invited me to talk, as part of morning services at the College, about the founding of the original Jewish Institute of Religion in 1922. The service was led beautifully by a group of rabbinic, cantorial and education students. The Dean read the Yahrzeit list of the deceased Presidents and Professors of the College-Institute. It was a beautiful and moving event. Students, administrators, faculty members, fellow academicians from the New York area and a few rabbinic colleagues in addition to Trustees of the College were all there in the beautiful well-lit chapel.

In my talk, I focused on the life and career of Stephen S. Wise, the founder of the Jewish Institute of Religion. I explained how he has become part of a historical controversy concerning the efforts, or lack thereof, by American Jewish leaders during the Holocaust, comparing accusations against Wise to those in this week's Torah portion, *Vayikra*, concerning those who fail to report catastrophic news. I then launched into the body of my talk.

Basically, Rabbi Wise, the leading Reform rabbi of the 20th century, believed that it was necessary to create a progressive, pro-Zionist rabbinic school in New York City. New York at the time was home to half of all American Jews and ten per cent of the total world Jewish population. He felt that HUC in Cincinnati was a stale, overly academic, anti-Zionist institution and that JTS, the Conservative seminary, was insufficiently Zionist and progressive itself.

Wise had the backing of his Board at the Free Synagogue in the Upper West Side of New York to create his school. He went to England, Germany and British Palestine in search of faculty. He created a remarkable visiting scholars' program at the Jewish Institute of Religion, the name he gave his school. By the time the school merged with HUC in 1949 creating HUC-JIR, it had graduated nearly 200 rabbis. In many ways, I believe, the JIR model became the standard for the Reform seminary system to this day.

Little has been written on the Jewish Institute of Religion, its innovative program and its work in fostering modern Hebrew literature and launching the careers of many of America's greatest Jewish historians. Perhaps a scholar or two will pick up the story from here and create a full history of New York's former Jewish Institute of Religion. Meanwhile, it was a splendid experience to have a chance to speak to the HUC-JIR community in New York, an experience I will long cherish and am delighted to share with all of you!

Shabbat Shalom.

JEWISH DANCE?

2010 eKI

Everybody dances. Dance exists in every human society. Children dance. Athletes dance when they win a game or a competition. Dance is part of courtship. Dance is central to celebration. Dance is a performance art. Leaves dance in the wind. Grasses dance in the breeze along the shore. Everyone and everything dances.

In this week's Torah portion, *Beshalach*, we encounter Miriam dancing with the Israelite women on the east bank of the Red Sea. Freed from slavery and safe from the walls of the sea and their Egyptian pursuers, "Miriam and women danced!" (Exodus 15:20).

Last semester, I had a student at Princeton who studied dance. In my "America in Judaism" class she researched how Jewish dance was created for three different movies: the original "The Jazz Singer" (1927), "Fiddler on the Roof" (1971) and "Dirty Dancing" (1987). In "The Jazz Singer," the young Al Jolson is shown dancing then-contemporary American dances to illustrate his distance from the Jewish tradition. In "Fiddler," the producer combines bottle dancing and ballet to create Jewish dance. In "Dirty Dancing," the cha-cha is "Jewish dancing" but "dancing dirty" is not.

My student repeatedly asked me the question, "What is Jewish Dance?" On close examination, we learned that the Hora is part of the larger dance culture of East Europe and the Balkans. It was brought to Israel by Rumanian Jews. The most famous Hora, *"Hava Nagilah,"* is of unknown origin. One theory suggests it was created by a Jewish musicologist, Abraham Z. Idelsohn, to celebrate the victories of the Allies over the Axis at the end of World War I. Today, non-Jewish entertainers use it as their central Jewish piece at *b'nai* Mitzvah and weddings. Other than the Jewish set of songs, one would be hard pressed to call dancing at most of our simchas "Jewish dance."

Dance is universal. It is fun. It is necessary. It is art. It is an essential part of life.

Is there enough dance in the Jewish world today? Do we need more dance to express our sense of community? To celebrate together? To express ourselves in motion? Can dance be used as part of worship? Our Torah portion today suggests that dance is more than possible; it is an authentic expression of self, Jewish and human!

Shabbat Shalom.

The Statute of Liberty and the New York Mosque Controversy

2010 eKI

The New York Harbor is graced with one of America's most powerful iconic images: the Statue of Liberty. The golden lamp, the beautiful sonnet by Emma Lazarus, the backgrounds of lower Manhattan to the north and Ellis Island to the east, all broadcast America's welcome to people of every possible stripe. "Come here," Ms. Liberty says, "You have a place in this broad land."

The Statue of Liberty is not only built on a pedestal of stone; it is also built on something much more important: a Statute of Liberty or, as it is mostly commonly known, the First Amendment of the American Constitution. From my viewpoint, the American way of freedom of religion, both free exercise and disestablishment, is legally uniquely and uniquely wonderful. It is the Statute of Liberty which allows in our country, like nowhere else in the world, people of every background to live together and worship separately. The issue of the New York mosque is first and foremost a question of our most fundamental rights in this country. They constitute a bundle of values which define us as a nation.

Personally, I was disappointed, deeply disappointed, in ADL and Abe Foxman, for abandoning their organizational mandate, for failing to make sure that New York and America have "no room to hate," for pandering to xenophobia and the Muslim bashers in this society. The proposed mosque and Islamic Center will not stand on Ground Zero. The building is nearby.

Perhaps, the German Consulate is too close to a New York synagogue? Perhaps an Armenian Church is too close to a Turkish restaurant?

Last week, Liz and I were on vacation in New York. Standing in Times Square at 11:00 p.m. after the show was the usual throng of people, thousands and thousands of people, including women in traditional Muslim clothing. They were simply part of the crowd, smiling, taking pictures of one another, being a little silly as tourists often do. No one singled them out or spat on them or even paid attention to them. They were part of an endless mix of humanity.

New York, America, is an endless mix. New York has mosques. I have been to mosques in New York. I am friends with the Imam of the Mosque of the Upper East Side. There are Muslim soldiers in our military. My doctor in Binghamton, NY was a practicing Muslim from Pakistan. His son was my student at the University. Aren't we different from the rest of the world? Don't we have a different, better context in which we can relate to one another?

"Rabbi," I hear some of you saying, "what about the Imam of the proposed mosque? Rabbi, where does his funding come from?" These are legitimate questions subject to investigation. My sense of the New York Muslim community, however, is that the "house is in order." The proposed Center will have an interfaith board, purposely including Jews and Christians.

In my view, if the attempt to build the New York mosque fails due to political pressure, we all lose and the murderers who attacked this country on 9/11 win, in that they will have divided us and caused us to diminish our sense of justice and liberty for all," not for a select few. This week's Torah portion urges us to pursue "justice." Justice and Liberty begin and end with freedom of worship, speech and assembly. Let's do the right thing as a nation and learn to live together in peace, at least here, at least beside "the Golden Door." Shabbat Shalom.

SHAMANG ISRAEL: ISRAEL'S RECENT CONVERSION CRISIS

July 22, 2010 eKI

It went down to the wire, but Israel's most recent conversion crisis finally went off the rails and the Israeli Knesset did not take up a vote on the administration of religious conversion in the Jewish State. As has happened before, an ill-conceived legislative proposal would have invalidated all unapproved, non-Orthodox conversions in Israel. In short, Orthodoxy's monopoly over Jewish identity would not only have been strengthened, but the unity of the world Jewish community would have been torn asunder to the detriment of Israel, the Diaspora and Israel-Diaspora relations. Luckily, thanks to a massive worldwide campaign, this disastrous scenario was averted. Indeed, we will need to remail eternally vigilant in order to prevent this ugly issue from gaining ground in the future.

The deeper issue at play here is the relationship of "Church and State," or should we say "synagogue and State," in Israel. Unlike the United States, Israel has neither a Constitution nor a doctrine of "separation." While the American doctrine of "separation" is both complex and uneven, the vast majority of people in this country seem to believe that we need some kind of separation between government and faith. How to do this is a matter of law and judicial interpretation. In the end, however, we do have the First Amendment. From my perspective, "disestablishment" is fundamental to Jewish well-being in the United States and to the general well-being of our society.

In Israel, the situation is very different. Not only is there no Constitution, but Israel was founded as a Jewish State, which means the State itself has some role in promoting and determining Jewishness. Because of the political equation in Israel, the Orthodox are in a good position to shape a number of governmental issues, such as the funding of religious schools and issues of personal identity. On the other hand, other religious communities also need to be granted powers of regulation and definition.

What can be done? Structurally, it is unlikely for Israel to reorganize its government along American lines. Perhaps more than one form of Judaism could be embraced by the State, or perhaps they could develop an unregulated but registered area of religious life in Israel based on the value of tolerance. It's a minimal solution. For Reform to be merely "tolerated" would be less than ideal, but it would be a lot better than being fully disenfranchised. There are other problems with this approach as well (what to do with messianic Judaism, for example) but at least it is a beginning toward a more inclusive approach.

Perhaps this week's Torah portion, *Va-et'chanan*, could inspire a solution. It includes the *Sh'ma* and, as we know every translation of the *Sh'ma* is different. In the oldest American prayer books even the word *Sh'ma* comes out as "*Shemang*" (based on a linguistic understanding of the letter Ayin). More importantly in this regard is the word "Israel," which is meant to serve as an umbrella term for all Jews. In the biblical sense of the word, it probably meant "Israelite," but for us it means all Jews, regardless. The bottom line is that Israel needs to remain inclusive of the majority faith of the large American Jewish community. As our ancestors proclaimed, "*Shemang* Israel: all Jews are one." Now "deal with it!!!!!"

No Place Like Home

September 8, 2010, Rosh HaShanah Evening 5771

As a kid, I went to summer camp
As a teenager, I worked at a summer camp
As a young rabbi, I led services at a camp
As a midcareer rabbi, I served as a camp rabbi
But I didn't always love camp

Like a lot of kids,
When I went to camp for the first time and my parents drove
Away and I was left sitting on a tightly made bunk bed in Boys 3
I had a lump in my throat
And praying that none of the other boys would see a tear roll down
    From my eyes.

That year, 1964, was the same year the world's greatest camp song
    Won the Grammy Award
Allan Sherman's "Hello Muddah, Hello Faddah."

I loved that song because it told the story of my first experience
    With homesickness . . .
    "Hello Muddah, Hello Faddah,
    Here I am at Camp Granada
Camp is very entertaining
And they say we'll have fun if it stops raining."

You know the lyrics,
They continue like this:
"I went hiking with Joe Spivy
He developed poison ivy.
You remember Leonard Skinner
He got ptomaine poisoning last night after dinner."

It all led up to the main point of the song:
"Take me home, oh mudda, faddah
I hate Grenada
Don't leave me out in the forest
Where I might be eaten by a bear."

Homesickness is not just a problem for little kids at camp and their parents at home. Jewish homesickness is a problem the majority of American Jews face today. In short, the majority of American Jews do not have a place in Judaism they can truly call home.

Only a minority belong to a synagogue, and the reality is that many people who belong to synagogues do so for reasons other than truly feeling "at home" in their shuls.

What makes a place a home?

> Memories
> Rootedness
> Safe
> Comfortable
> Familiar
> Cocoon, womblike
> Nest
> A den
> Home is your place on the planet from where
> You can view all of reality
> With a true sense of security of self.

The idea of place, *makom* (one's place in the world), is central to Judaism. Over the holidays, we will explore *makom* and talk about finding your place in Judaism.

The idea of finding one's place in Judaism goes back to our beginning as a people.

Abraham and Isaac. Temple of Jericho. After the Temple fell, synagogues were the primary Jewish place. The synagogue has been home of Jewish people for two hundred years.

This synagogue, this sanctuary, is our Jewish place. We broke ground in 1954, placed the cornerstone in 1956, and moved in 1957, fifty-five years ago. Our windows were added in the Seventies; and this summer, there was a comprehensive refurbishment including seats, carpet, organ screen, lower bimah, handicap ramp, dozens of new lights, screens, and projectors, an HD camera, a hearing-aid loop, new furniture, and a new sound system, praise God, hallelujah!

We are now soft on the tush, easy on the eye, still glorious, but also much more heimish.

Our goal: to be more comfortable, more intimate. The changes in this sanctuary reflect a broad change in Jewish religious life today from majestic to intimate, from public to private, from transcendent to immanent theology, and from a distant, formal commanding god to a comforting voice on the inside.

I love the changes in this room,
>   My fifty-year wish list was completed in three months.
>   People worked very hard to make this happen,
>   Wonderfully generous congregants helped pay the way
>   And an incredible group of architects, engineers, artists, designers,
>   Technicians, carpenters, electricians, carpet installers, and more.

A lot of people doubted we would be anywhere near ready. This place was a construction site with scaffolding up to the ceiling with boarded-up windows, and now there is electricity. But we are home again, home for the holiday, in an enriched, refurbished sanctuary, the sacred place we call home at KI. Rebuilding a synagogue sanctuary is a big job. If it works, a congregation should feel even more at home, but this is only the beginning of what we need to do.

The greatest sanctuary of Jewish life was not the Temple of Jerusalem or a three-thousand-year old Moorish-style synagogue in Berlin or Budapest or Warsaw. The most important sanctuary in our tradition is our homes. It doesn't matter how great or grand or impressive or *heimish* our sanctuaries are on Old York Road or Fifth Avenue or the Champs-Élysées if the sanctuaries we call our own homes lack Jewish light, Jewish sounds, Jewish memories.

The real sanctuary we need to rebuild is the sanctuary of our homes. How can we refurbish our Jewish homes? Do we need scaffolds and sound engineers? Hardly! It's little things:

Mezuzah, hang or rehang
Shabbat and/or *yahrzeit* candles
Locate, polish old Kiddush cup
Host a Shabbat meal for family/friends
Host a KI Shabbat dinner and invite me and four members

of the synagogue (The president said I could skip services and go to your house.)

Display Jewish art by children or grandchildren. Don't have any? We will have a student make it for you.

Get a t*zedakah* box, give change to the homeless, to the hungry.
You can take a tiny part of the blessing of your home and
Provide some comfort to those without any home at all.

And there is still a deeper level, a nonarchitectural home so to speak. It is us. It is our soul. It is our heart, our inner Jewish self. Refurbishing our Jewish selves is more difficult than rebuilding a synagogue or hanging a new *mezuzah*.

Most Jews love being Jewish but don't know what to do about Judaism. Answer this question: I am a Jew because . . .

Born that way?
Like bagels?
Believe in its ethical principles
Love its customs and practices
Because my connection with God is a Jewish connection?

My answer: I love being Jewish because Judaism is my spiritual home.

It is where I stand and from where I can see the whole world.
It is my anchor.
My resting place
My springboard
It is where I go to celebrate the happiest and saddest days of my life.
Judaism is my home.
It has no walls.
It is my atmosphere.
Everywhere I go, it goes with me.

It is my rock, my garden, my mountaintop, my rainbow.
My sunrise, my sunset
Judaism is my home. It provides the walls of love and meaning, which shelter my family
And nurture my grandchildren.

I know that my home is no better than my neighbor's home.
A Catholic home
A Hindu home
A Muslim home
They can all be the cradles of caring which make us good people.

The only real difference is that my home is mine. And that's why I love it. And why I respect others people's homes as well.

Maybe if we go find our way to our inner Jewish place
If we reboot the Jewish dimension of our homes
If we reroot ourselves in this sanctuary,
We will no longer be among the spiritually homeless and the homesick
In the Jewish community.
In ancient days, the prophet Balaam was hired to curse the Jewish people
Instead, he was compelled to declare, "*Mah tovu ohaleecha, Yaacov.*"
Book of Numbers
For Jewish life to really work, has to be lived at home
And practiced together in the community, synagogue.

In this new year, may we continue to win the praise of our neighbors and friends for our homes and their spirit.
In this year, may we enjoy our refurbished sanctuary even
As we endeavor to spiritually refurbish ourselves in more complete authentic ways.
In the coming year, may all God's children be blessed with
The peace, safety, and warmth of a real home.

And with Alan Sherman, let us hope that any personal feeling
Of displacement from Judaism and the synagogue has been resolved,
that the rain of alienation and discontent and has stopped,

that the sun of faith is shining
and, at last, we feel at home with ourselves in this sanctuary
and with our God.

May you be blessed with a year of health, happiness, and peace
Amen.
Shana Tova.

I LOVE ISRAEL

September 9, 2010, Rosh HaShanah Morning 5771

Several years ago, KI developed a strategic plan to create a path for us as a congregation for the foreseeable future. An important part of that process was the identification of and definition of our core values as a congregation.

Beginning with these High Holidays and continuing into the year ahead, each of these values will be discussed and analyzed in sermons, programs, and some amazing artwork to be displayed in our synagogue's lobby in a few weeks.

Today, I want to focus on one of those values, *ahavat Yisrael*, or the love of Israel and the Jewish people. This discussion, typical of synagogues and Jewish educational curricula around the world, is particularly important for our congregation. We have a history at KI of both anti-Zionism and non-Zionism from the pre-state period sixty-three years ago. This past has long been officially repudiated by the congregation, but it is not entirely erased in the collective memory of our community.

More importantly, there is a critical need to be publicly pro-Israel today because Israel both warrants and needs our support. To accomplish that goal, we need to educate ourselves as a congregation about Israel. Today, *ahavat Yisrael* is a value and emphasis strongly endorsed both by the lay and professional leadership of this congregation. *Ahavat Yisrael* (love of Israel) has become, in my opinion, a living, heartfelt reality at KI. During the course of the last few years, we have taken a number of practical and symbolic steps as an expression of *ahavat Yisrael* at KI.

In the Spring of my second year here, the Board voted overwhelmingly to place an Israeli flag on this bimah. As one board member stated, "I grew up here in an incomplete fashion. I now want my child to see the blue-and-white flag of Israel in our congregation." There is also a new emphasis on Israel in our school's curriculum both on Sundays and during Confirmation Academy on Tuesdays.

Several years ago, an Israel Committee was established at KI in the wake of a trip I took to Israel with the Jewish Agency. Next, KI is now the favored location for our Kehillah's annual Israel Independence Day celebration.

As a congregation, we are increasingly well-represented at American Israel Public Affairs Committee's (AIPAC's) annual policy conference. This last Spring, I was delighted when our members and long-term AIPAC supporters, Harriet and Larry Weiss, spoke about their commitment to Israel and AIPAC from this bimah. AIPAC, it is important to point out, works both sides of the aisle in Congress to maintain and grow support for Israel on the Hill and beyond. We also invest as a congregation in Israel Bonds.

This last year, KI officially entered into a relationship with the reform congregation in Zikhron Ya'akov near Caesarea on Israel's coast, just south of Haifa. We have many exchanges planned between us. I hope to visit our twin congregation Sulam Yaakov, or Jacob's Ladder, in December. One of our members, Bill Dodies, while on a family trip to Israel, has already done so!

Travel to Israel is an indispensable part of our commitment to *ahavat Yisrael*. I have led one congregational trip thus far and will travel with a member family this December for a bar mitzvah on Masada.

Next summer, August 2011, I'm planning another KI family trip to experience and bond with Israel with, hopefully, forty-plus members of this congregation. More information will be coming out shortly.

Of course, Israel is not perfect. It is a complicated place with many dimensions to it. Recently, the deep ethnic tensions between orthodox Ashkenazi and Sephardic Jews were made manifest in street demonstrations. Moreover, despite an unfortunate article in this week's *Time* magazine about affluence in Israel, a third of the country's population lives in poverty.

As Reform Jews, we are compelled to acknowledge our own problems in Israel as well. The rights of women to pray as equals to men in Israel, particularly at the Western Wall, are currently compromised. Indeed, it is a felony in Israel for a woman to wear a *tallit* at the *Kotel*.

We also witnessed an international Jewish crisis this year about conversion rights in Israel and the withdrawal of a bill before the Knesset that would have further strengthened Orthodoxy's position as the established form of Judaism in the Jewish state.

These problems pale in comparison to Israel's security problems. Israel's number one existential threat comes from the radical Shiite government in Iran, which sponsors world terrorism, advocates Holocaust denial, and persists in building up its nuclear program. Iran is a problem for everyone. India certainly doesn't need another Muslim country with the bomb. Turkey itself seems to be sinking into radical Islamic politics and would also be threatened by a nuclear Iran as would central Europe. The Russians, not surprisingly, are deluding themselves by playing ball with Iran's President Ahmadinejad.

A major part of Israel's foreign policy is the attempt to alert the world to the dangers of a nuclear Iran. At the same time, in a strategic alliance with German submarine builders, Israel is building a military defense against Iranian aggression.

Israel faces its most immediate existential threat form Hezbollah, Iran's proxy Shia terrorist force in Lebanon. Today, Hezbollah has anywhere from fifteen to forty thousand missiles and rockets, which have enough range to hit not only Tel Aviv and Jerusalem but also Beersheba and even Eilat in the distant south. Israel is actively building an Iron-Dome security system.

In the north, Israel remains at odds with Syria over the permanent status over the Golan. Syria has long been a front-line anti-Israel Arab state. It is a ruthless dictatorship and maintains a strategic alliance with Russia as well.

In the south, Israel continues to face the threat of Hamas rockets and Hamas-sponsored terrorism. Hamas is also officially at war with the Palestine Authority and is involved in numerous internecine Palestinian conflicts. It is a dangerous and radical enemy.

On the wider stage of world diplomacy, Israel faces enormous problems and challenges and is widely viewed with disdain by much of the world. In this regard, American support is paramount, and that is why I personally support and applaud the work of AIPAC. Even the UK is not a truly reliable partner for Israel today, given its own huge domestic Muslim population.

The United States is Israel's most important partner in the world today, but the United States also has its own self-interests to consider and is almost always involved in a difficult balancing act.

The fact of the matter is that the United States has allies on all sides of the Arab-Israeli-Muslim conflict. Among this country's most important allies, in addition to Israel, are Saudi Arabia, Kuwait, the United Arab Emirates, Egypt, and Jordan, to mention a few. We have geo-petrol concerns that are immense and historically go back to President Franklin Delano Roosevelt and postwar planning in the mid-1940s.

While I do not agree that the Arab-Israeli-Muslim conflict is the single most important issue in the Middle East, it is, nevertheless, a major issue and serves as an accelerant to the area's multiple problems. In that context, the United States clearly has strategic interests in finding structural solutions to the core Israel-Palestinian conflict, not to mention ideological and humanitarian concerns.

From my perspective, the United States has two major diplomatic objectives in sponsoring a peace process at this time: (1) the long-term security of the State of Israel and (2) the creation of a Palestinian state. The two biggest challenges to this process are (1) instilling confidence in the partners' peace and (2) containing the anti-peace extremists on both sides.

There are so many questions:

1. Does the so-called Arab Street among Palestinians want peace?
2. Are Egypt and Jordan real partners?
3. Is there sufficient political support for the peace process in the United States?
4. On the ground in the West Bank, can the Palestinian Authority contain Hamas and Islamic Jihad?
5. On the ground in the West Bank, can Israel contain the more extreme elements among the settlers who defy both the Israeli government and the army on a daily basis?
6. What can be done for stateless Palestinian refugees outside of Palestine?

Given all these factors, can anything positive be done?

- In my opinion, nothing will be easy, some things are possible.
- On other hand, long-term consequences of failure are greater than short-term setbacks, risks, or inactions.

Israel's reality today and tomorrow is that it has a demographic challenge. To remain a Jewish state, it needs to have borders that will guarantee a Jewish majority. That is why even Ariel Sharon decided to leave Gaza. Retention of all territories currently under Israel's control will, in the not-too-distant future, result in an Arab majority in Israel, which will undercut both the Jewish and democratic nature of the Jewish state.

What are the options? Here are ten options for starters:

1. One-state solution with an Arab majority
2. One-state solution with the removal of the Arab population
3. The so-called Allon Plan with the annexation of the West Bank by Jordan
4. A binational/federated Arab-Jewish state
5. A confederation of Israel, Palestine, and Jordan
6. A two-state solution with Israel-imposed borders and historical Jerusalem in Israeli hands
7. A two-state solution with the expansion of Gaza into the Sinai
8. A two-state solution with border adjustments, which would cede some Arab majority areas in the north of Israel to Palestine in return for retention of the major settlements in the West Bank
9. The old United Nations partition/Vatican plan with a two-state solution and the internationalization of Jerusalem
10. A two-state/two-Jerusalem option with border adjustments

There is one more dimension to this discussion, from my perspective, that is critical but rarely gets enough play in the press, and that is economic development. Last year, my personal high point at AIPAC came at the very end of the conference when former British Prime Minister Tony Blair gave his talk about his efforts on behalf of the Quartet to spark economic development in the West Bank and Israel. His principal partners are Shimon Peres and the Prime Minister of Palestine Salam Fayyad, who favors Palestinian state-building over confrontation with Israel.

The reality is that peace cannot root without prosperity on both sides of the security fence and that long-term peace is not viable without intraregional economic cooperation. There is more to this story than meets the eye. Much of it is based on Peres's vision of a "Valley of Peace"—that is, the *aravah*—connecting the Dead Sea and the Red Sea. It envisions broad Israeli, Palestinian, and Jordanian cooperation: a Dead-Red canal, an international airport, an expanded harbor in Eilat/Aqaba, and train service from Israel to Amman, Jordan.

Toyota and Renault are both interested in locating car factories in the area. Japan is interested in agricultural development around Jericho. In the north, both Turkey and Germany have expressed interest in projects in Jenin and Afula. For sure, the United States is cultivating the idea of a massive infusion of investment into the West Bank as part of the current peace process, as much as $50 billion.

Is this the stuff of dreams or fools? In part, it is a continuation of a Herzlian approach to Zionism using world politics as a major tool in Jewish state-building. Like Herzl, it has a dreamlike quality; but without vision, there is no hope for anything other than the current cycle of violence.

Other intractable conflicts in history have been solved or calmed down: the Balkans, Northern Ireland, and the Cold War. For that matter, the British once burned the White House.

On the other hand, there have also been colossal failures: northern Israel was destroyed in 722 BCE. Judah fell in 586 BCE and again in 70 CE.

Today, there are those who say the status quo is acceptable, and that Israel can tough it out. But the status quo is not static. Israel's enemies are mindful of the example of the Crusades.

"It is a matter of time," they say, "until we overwhelm by sheer force of our numbers." Masada, like the Crusader forts, they believe, will fall again.

Today, Israel is a small but strong country. It has incredible military and high-technological capacity. It also has an incredible spirit and a deep desire for peace and normalcy.

Is this the moment for peace between Israel and the Palestinians? Probably not, but to fail to try is to allow failure to succeed.

Pray for the peace of Jerusalem, we have been taught.

And act for the strength of Israel is something we have learned.

No scenario in the Middle East is easy.

No scenario comes without losses or risks.

And at the end of the day, only one scenario is acceptable: a Jewish state, safe in its own land.

Shana Tova. A good year.

Reform Judaism

September 17, 2010, Yom Kippur Evening 5771

I have been a Reform Jew my entire life. As a child, I attended a synagogue in Baltimore, Oheb Shalom, very similar to KI. Our congregation was started by a small group of German Jewish businessmen in the 1850s. It eventually built a grand temple modeled on the great synagogue of Florence, Italy, in a fine neighborhood, Eutaw Place, just north of downtown Baltimore.

In the 1950s, Oheb Shalom moved to the suburbs, the northwest corner of Baltimore. Like other area synagogues, it located itself on Park Heights Avenue, one synagogue after another. I called it Rue de La Shul. On the High Holy Days in the 1960s, Rue de La Shul was a sea of humanity. From the bimah to the back of the auditorium and even up on the stage, it was totally full and very impressive to me as a youngster.

Oheb's building was designed by Bauhaus architect Walter Gropius. Our clergy wore robes year-round and pill-box hats during services. Our prayer book, the *Union Prayer Book*, was compact and written in the original Elizabethan English God himself had used when he spoke to Moses 3,200 years ago on Mount Sinai. We were escorted to our seats for every service by ushers with boutonnieres in their lapels. We always rose and stood at attention when the clergy entered the sanctuary at the beginning of services. My childhood rabbi, Abraham Shaw, had the voice of an FM radio announcer: smooth, deep, and God-like.

My *bar mitzvah* was in June 1967. At that time, only boys had b*ar mitzvahs* at our synagogue. Three years later, exactly forty years ago this past Shavuot, I was confirmed. I was President of my Confirmation Class of 120 kids. By the year of my Confirmation, 1970, with the Vietnam War raging and a youth culture transforming the look and sound of America, we, the youth of Oheb Shalom, no longer felt at home with the *Union Prayer Book*. So we wrote our own service. Most of the music was either from the Civil Rights movement or Peter, Paul and Mary. I'm not sure Debbie Friedman had been born yet. Our text mostly came from Kahlil Gibran, a Lebanese poet. "Forget not that the earth delights to feel your bare feet," the bard of Beirut taught us, "and the winds long to play with your hair." However, the rabbi insisted that we had to wear shoes in the synagogue.

Confirmation in Baltimore forty years ago still attracted a large population to services. Our class was so big it covered our entire massive bimah, similar in scale to this one here at KI. It was a huge display of the growing might of the Reform movement in American Judaism. Today, if even the largest Reform synagogue can graduate thirty confirmands, it feels like it has done a good job. Something is going wrong with the Reform movement today, and it is not just the size of our Confirmation classes.

In my opinion, the Reform movement, which rocketed from the smallest institutional expression of American Judaism before WWII to the largest by the end of the twentieth century, is currently in decline. Unfortunately, none of our national leaders acknowledge the profound losses our movement has incurred in the last ten years in particular. They prefer to use peak numbers from 1990 or so and not deal with the realities of 2010.

According to Professor Steven M. Cohen of the Hebrew Union College and personal adviser to the College's President David Ellenson, the Reform movement is now made up of 850,000 people, which Cohen suggests is an 18.5 percent loss. My math suggests something more profound. Twenty years ago, the Reform movement began to talk about itself in terms of 1.5 million people. If that was true ten years ago, the drop is closer to 30 percent.

There are other indications on the ground of a deteriorating situation. We know that the Union for Reform Judaism—the former Union of American Hebrew Congregations, the parent body of the Reform movement—greatly contracted its regional operations during the course of the last few years. We know that the Hebrew Union College is struggling to keep all four of its campuses, where rabbis and others are trained, open, and running. We know that only half of graduating classes of Reform rabbis are getting synagogue placements after ordination. We know that very few new Reform synagogues are being formed today and that a greater number are either closing or merging.

The Reform movement in America is in trouble; and unlike the Conservative movement, which has acknowledged that it is rapidly shrinking, our movement prefers collective denial.

On this Yom Kippur, when we are supposed to come clean about ourselves, I challenge the Reform movement in America to look at itself and where it really is today and what the likely trends are to be in the next ten or twenty years. I make this challenge in the spirit of prophetic Judaism, the ancient form of Judaism so admired by previous generations of Reform Jews for its boldness and its capacity to speak truth courageously. I make this challenge in the spirit of Yom Kippur, which has served our people for centuries as a means of self-understanding and a way to self-improvement. I make this challenge for the well-being of our own congregation, which has served the local Jewish community well since 1847 but is now facing historic challenges, which it can and must meet in the years ahead.

As a movement and individuals, we need to cast away illusion. We need to shed the sin of denial. We need to look at ourselves in the mirror and say, "We have sinned, we have gone astray, and we have transgressed." We cannot allow ourselves to become the proverbial emperor without clothing. We need to begin by re-embracing the ideology of Reform Judaism in a serious fashion and not just as a trendy expression of contemporary Judaism or some expression of Judaism-light for the lightly affiliated.

During the course of our strategic planning process at KI, our congregation adopted *Yahadut Mitkademet* (Reform Judaism) as one of its core values. That decision was not redundant. Our official congregational name is Reform Congregation Keneseth Israel, and without a specific commitment to Reform Judaism, we run the risk of being a general agent of Jewishness but not of Judaism specifically; a script for a purely ethnic expression of being Jewish, ethnicity with perhaps a splash of ritual but not a path to embracing a living faith; a Jewish service station on the road of life like a rest stop on the turnpike or the expressway to Atlantic City where you get in and out of as fast as possible on the way to the real destination.

Tonight, I want to look at the Reform movement; and I want to look at it right in the eye and try to figure out what is going wrong, why we are sputtering, and what can be done to turn things around. I want to do this because, in my opinion, there is a historic need for Reform Judaism, and Reform Judaism is an authentic expression of Judaism. If done right, I absolutely believe that Reform Judaism can be a source of strength, joy, and comfort for the majority of Jewish people today around the world. Unfortunately, at the present moment, there is very little wind in our sail.

Our story began in Germany or, more accurately, the Holy Roman Empire—which was neither holy, Roman, nor an empire—two hundred years ago. On July 17, 1810, in the town of Seesen in the northwest province of Westphalia, the first full-fledged confirmation service was held. The class only had boys; but by the following year, girls participated too, breaking with thousands of years of tradition, a virtual revolution in Jewish history. An organ was played, and the students had reading parts in their vernacular language. In this fashion, Reform Judaism had begun and defined itself for sixteen decades.

Fourteen years later, the seed of Reform traveled to and rooted in Charleston, South Carolina. In 1824, a small group of mostly native-born American Jews of Sephardic origin learned about the existence of Reform Judaism in Germany from a newspaper account. "We want that too," they said. "We want to learn about Judaism in a rational fashion. We want to say our prayers in a language we understand. We would even prefer annual dues to the auctioning of honors on the High Holy Days." The board of their synagogue, correctly self-labeled as a junta, took their petition and threw it in the garbage.

Fortunately, Reform was irrepressible. By the time of the Civil War, six congregations were Reform or Reform-leaning, and KI was one of the six. By 1873, almost a hundred. By 1973, over seven hundred. By the beginning of the twenty-first century, nine-hundred-plus congregations.

Reform Judaism was born in the early decades of the nineteenth century to enable modern Jews to remain Jews and to be modern at the same time. It was started as an alternative to assimilation and not, as its detractors alleged, a path *to* assimilation.

Reform also created a new style of Jewish music, which synthesized Jewish prayer with European music. On Rosh HaShanah this year, the *New York Times* ran an op-ed piece about High Holy Day music and what it isn't. It was a shameful article, uninformed by knowledge of the music of early Reform, which sought to synthesize the grand musical traditions of Europe with the traditional sounds of Judaism. Sulzer, Lewandowski,

Janowski, and Steinberg have created a remarkable repertoire of liturgical music for our reform synagogues.

By the middle decades of the nineteenth century, Reform congregations built grand synagogues in Moorish, Romanesque, and Neoclassical styles to symbolize the ancient and enduring place of Judaism in society.

Reform valued decorum and good manners during services. It created a new type of modern, intellectual, university-educated rabbi who could speak in the vernacular. It created credos based on rationality, progress, and philosophical truth. It grappled with deep theological issues such as the nature of God, the possibility of revelation, the historicity of the biblical text, the relationship of religion and science, the relationship of personal ethics to public policy, and the challenges of Jewish nationalism and what it meant for Diaspora Jewish communities. Reform rejected biblical literalism, a belief in a personal messiah, and the physical resurrection of the dead. On the other hand, it wrapped itself in faith in progress, reason, and truth.

Early Reform Judaism made the *chutzpahdic* claim that a person could be both Jewish and modern at the same time. It saved tens of thousands of Jews from total assimilation and taught its non-Jewish neighbors that Jews and Judaism were good citizens, ethical, cultured, and law-abiding *and* still proud of their ancient heritage and bound together in a community of faith. Reform Judaism taught the world that the word Jew is not a dirty verb and that Judaism is one of humanity's classic religious traditions belonging on Main Street in every town and not in an alley or a basement.

For almost two hundred years, the Reform movement steadily grew and built institutions and met the religious needs of its adherents. It earned a place of honor both in the general and the Jewish communities. Many of the most distinguished and accomplished Jewish families of their day joined Reform temples. Reform rabbis liked Stephen Wise, Maurice Eisendrath, and Alexander Schindler served as national spokesmen for the American Jewish community. The president of the Hebrew Union College, Nelson Glueck, was featured on the front cover of *Time* magazine. Rabbi Abba Hillel Silver spoke before the United Nations calling for the establishment of a Jewish state in Palestine. A reform rabbi, Joshua Loth Liebman, wrote one of the all-time best-selling books in American history, *Peace of Mind*, in 1946.

Despite all the jokes and knocks and anti-Reform libels, which constantly pecked away at the movement and its legitimacy, Reform Judaism kept growing, kept building, kept asserting itself.

Until now. Today, Reform Judaism no longer seems irrepressible. Sometimes it barely seems confident. On the one hand, non-affiliation is growing. On the other hand, orthodoxy is growing. The center of the spectrum, it seems, is being hemmed in and whittled down. What are the structural factors that are challenging the Reform movement today, and what can we do to counter them?

In my opinion, the most corrosive element in Jewish life today is nonspiritual secularism. Religious secularism is pervasive in the Jewish community. It is a historic function of modernity. But without some core body of belief, compatible with science, reason, and modern ethics, Reform Judaism will be nothing more than an empty shell. Unless there is some aspect of a living God or sense of the sacred in our synagogues, then we have no reason to read the old prayers or write new ones. They are reduced to relics.

Second, Jewish adult illiteracy makes participation in Jewish life difficult if not impossible today. Jewish literacy, by any standard, is trending downward in the non-Orthodox world; and the reservoir of Jewish memories, so pervasive two or three generations ago, is becoming shallower and shallower as we move generationally further and further away from our immigrant roots.

Privatization is also sweeping the Jewish community today. Synagogues are communal institutions. If you feel you can rent a rabbi for a funeral or a bar mitzvah, that the service is the sole goal, that you do not need a community, or that you have no responsibility to sustain the community for others, then you can privatize your Judaism. It is a consumeristic, narcissistic approach to Jewish life. It is hard to resist and has all the logic of "fee for service." But it reduces Judaism to a series of disconnected ceremonies performed by unknown functionaries for a disengaged, uneducated Jewish population. It is the equivalent of limiting primary health care to the emergency room without the benefit of a family doctor or personal physician. It is Judaism on demand. It is a Judaism that also makes no demands or has any standards or transcendent purpose.

We also face technical and temporal challenges:

1. The Jewish birth rate among non-Orthodox Jews is down. There are fewer Jews to recruit. When I was born in 1954, there were 150 million Americans and 6 million American Jews. Today there are over 300 million Americans and 5.5 million American Jews, at most.

2. The meltdown in the Conservative movement is over. In the 1970s, Conservative Jews left their movement and joined either Orthodox or Reform synagogues. We no longer receive our share of that influx.
3. The aggregate mixed-marriage rate is now 50 percent. It is a fact that mixed-married households affiliate at a lower rate than Jewish-Jewish households. Inexplicably, the Reform movement rolled back its outreach movement several years ago.
4. Topographically, the Reform movement also has challenges. In the South and Midwest, where Reform was historically strongest, the Jewish population is down significantly. First-ring suburbs, which were built after WWII, are largely draining of their Jewish populations. On the other hand, outer-ring suburbs seem to attract less active Jews, and urban areas attract more traditional Jews.
5. In addition to topographic trends, we are gender challenged. Unlike in traditional Judaism, males in Reform Judaism tend to be largely passive about their religion; and as women took on greater and greater leadership roles, the more men receded into the background.
6. Finances have been a double burden in the Reform movement. On the hand, synagogue life can be expensive. On the other hand, synagogues, until now, have been less involved in development than Federations, Israel-based organizations, and, most recently, university-based Jewish programs.
7. A less tangible challenge is loss of prestige. In 1900, it was prestigious to belong to certain synagogues. Whole classes of merchants self-identified with given Jewish institutions. Synagogue today, for better or for worse, are less identified with class structures.
8. Rabbis. Rabbis have challenges too. Is a Reform rabbi as authentic a Rav as a Chabad rabbi? Is a Reform rabbi as learned as a scholar with a PhD in secular Jewish studies? Rabbis are less spokesmen than they are religious specialists today. Technicians instead of leaders. Voices of caution and tradition, not voices of ethical authority.
9. But probably the most difficult questions revolve around our religious program in the Reform synagogue.

This year I had the opportunity to write a book review for a new and leading Jewish journal of thought, the *Jewish Book Review*, in connection with my teaching at Princeton University. I was asked to comment on a new book assessing contemporary Judaism in America. In my review, I asked a very uncomfortable question: has the neo-traditional, spirituality movement in American Judaism succeeded or failed? In my opinion, it has succeeded with a very narrow part of the population: independent *chavurot*, some Reconstructionist congregations, JewBu/s or Jewish-Buddhist circles, and the renewal movement. I call it Voodstock Judaism. But for the other 90 percent of American Jews, answers need to come from the mainstream of culture, not from countercultural trends.

In short, we are facing huge challenges and massive problems in the Reform movement.

What can be done? What should be done? What must be done?

At the national and institutional level, our first order of business has to be membership.

We need to work on recruiting, integrating, and retaining our members. We need to work on this all the time, not just during synagogue shopping season. On a generational basis, the membership lifeline has grown shorter and shorter, and for many families today, it is only four years from the beginning of Hebrew school to the last line of *kaddish* at the *bar mitzvah* and then out the door. Everyone who belongs to a synagogue is a possible recruiter. Everyone who belongs to a synagogue is an actual SMP (synagogue maintenance person). We need to regularly remind each other about the importance of synagogue membership. We need national leadership in this area and marketing and local follow-up.

We need to reinvent outreach and in-reach in our synagogue. We have a massive mixed-married population. We need to reach out to them and make them comfortable here in this house. We need skill classes and support groups. And we need the same for our "just Jewish population" that does not have synagogue skills or an active Jewish vocabulary or a Jewish social network.

We need to put our synagogue on a sound financial basis. If synagogue leadership, lay and professional, devotes much or most of its time to development, then other basic things will go unattended. The pastoral work, the need for teaching and instruction, and community-building activities are where the action should be. If they are to be the focus, then the synagogue needs to have greater or, more precisely, adequate financial resources. That is why KI has launched Shelanu, our campaign to endow KI for the future. The work we do here is genuinely important, and the only way to get it done is to do it together, each one of us rowing his or her own oar spiritually, programmatically, and fiscally.

For sure, we need to stand for something. That is why we created a list of core congregational values. At the top of the list is the value of *kehillah*. We need to strive to be a genuine community. The key to community is kindness. One of the worst things you can say about a synagogue is that it is a cold place. We need to say hello to one another in the building when we sit down before services and when we park next to someone we don't know out in the parking lot.

In Hebrew, this is called *chesed*. *Chesed* is kindness. We teach it in our preschool and our school. We try to deliver our pastoral work. *Chesed* needs to permeate everything we do at KI.

Finally, we need to define and deepen the religious experience at KI. We do many things here at KI; but at the end of the day, we are a synagogue, a house of worship. The worship experience depends on many things: the liturgy; the leadership; the music; the amount of Hebrew; the length; the sense of community; and the possibility of actually praying, learning something new in one's heart and mind, feeling support or love, affirming one's Jewishness, leaving renewed and affirmed.

Traditionally, the object of prayer is God. We do not gather just to have a community assembly. Just to do a Jewish dance, a really long *hora*, or entertain one another. Our purpose here is to meet our individual and communal Jewish responsibilities, the mitzvot so to speak, and, whenever possible, to lift our spirits up, perhaps to God, perhaps to the universe, perhaps just to ourselves but beyond ourselves.

For Reform Judaism to survive in the coming years, for KI to thrive in the days ahead, we need to be a house of living Judaism: a place of Jewish purpose, of prayer and learning, of kindness and community, a sacred zone in an ever-less-sacred world, a place where we connect to Israel and immerse ourselves in the beauty and art of holiness.

If we can do all that, if we can infuse this house with a deep sense of purpose and peace, we will be more than OK. I don't think we are very far from our goals as a congregation.

But the race is long and hard, and those few laps can be very challenging.

In the year ahead, 5771, may we join together, strengthen one another, strengthen this house, and restore ourselves and our congregation.

G'mar Tov. May you be sealed for the good.
Amen.
Shabbat Shalom, Shana Tova.

Yizkor

September 18, 2010, Yom Kippur 5771

In ancient days when the Temple of Jerusalem stood, the most sacred moment of the most sacred day of the year is when the high priest entered into the holy of holiness and pronounced the ineffable name of God. We no longer have a temple or a high priest, but we still have that intensely sacred moment during the afternoon of Yom Kippur when we enter into the inner holy of holies of our hearts and utter the names of our departed. No other moment in our collective life as a synagogue is comparable. It stands alone in its sanctity and its intensity. At this service, we are as close as we can believe to those we have lost. We can behold them in our minds' eyes. We can embrace their memories with our love. We can allow the pain of loss to rise up in us for just a moment and then try to dry our tears. We remember. We long for more. We give thanks for every blessing, large and small, they have bequeathed to us.

On this afternoon of Yom Kippur, all of us stand together with those of you who have lost a loved one during the course of the last year. I have had the sad honor of standing with many of you during those difficult moments and know something of your pain. Sometimes a word or two may serve as a gentle compress on your wound. Sometimes a kind act helps mend a hurt. I am moved by how families and friends together encircle the mourners with hugs and food and even a little laughter. It all helps a little but never completely. Today, we acknowledge that there is still that horrible gap between life and death. Today, we hope and pray that prayers of comfort and songs of remembrance can span the abyss and give us a modicum of renewed hope and a greater sense of completeness.

Some of us die in the fullness of time and still the pain of loss is still terribly sharp. Some of us die too young, leaving behind a wake of pain that radiated throughout our lives. It is my prayer that these prayers and these songs do something, however minutely, to dull the hurt deep in your hearts. We will remember, we will be kind, we will continue to be there.

Almost all are here to remember those who have gone before us in years but continue to play living roles in our lives. The club of all mourners in the most inclusive club in human life. We are all part of it. Hopefully, it will remind us of our common humanity with all our neighbors.

Each of us has a list of names to contemplate this afternoon. For me, it is two grandmothers, two uncles, my in-laws, a brother-in-law, a cousin, my daughter-in-law's father, former congregants, and several dear teachers. They are all with me at this moment.

My mind wanders back to a different time in life when our family circle was so different than it is today. So many are gone, and yet, there are also new faces and new people who do not so much take their place as they continue the story of family and life.

I once read a parable from a distant land about how water can cross a desert. No one believed the water and said it would dry up and disappear. But the water knew better. "I will evaporate and then become a cloud and cross the desert. On the other side, I will rain and reform as little streams and then rivers and oceans."

The life force goes on. Its embodiment changes. It creates enduring memories and new life. Sometimes we flow with it, sometimes we are swept away, but it goes on and on. May the fresh waters of memory fall on our tears like raindrops. May they wash away the pain, refresh the plants of memory, and enable us to move ahead into the new year—hurt, even broken, but not defeated. "Yea though I walk through the valley of the shadow of death." That shadow is from a passing cloud, and on the other side of the narrow valley of grief is a trail that leads back to life and into the year ahead.

May your prayers of remembrance be heard on high, and the souls of your lost loved ones rest peacefully in their places in eternity.

Transcending an "Artless Tradition": The Birth of a Modern Jewish Art Movement

Winter 2010 Reform Judaism Magazine

Standing before the delegates of the World Zionist Congress in Basel, Switzerland in 1901, Martin Buber urged them to embrace art as a force to normalize the Jewish people. For the twenty-three-year-old Jewish philosopher, Zionism was not just about land and politics; it was also about culture. Jewish art was was a "beautiful possibility," he instead, which could play a key role in a national Jewish renaissance.

Failing to win the delegates' support, Buber turned directly to his artist friends, who staged an exhibition of forty-eight works at the Congress. It was now their task to create a national Jewish art movement.

For centuries, Judaism had been largely perceived as an "artless tradition" for both internal reasons—the Torah's prohibition against "graven images"—and because of antisemitic barriers- such as the exclusion of Jews from artists' guilds. While the German philosopher Immanuel Kant (1774–1804) praised Judaism for valuing "the moral law" more than the visual representation of truth, antisemites, such as the German composer Richard Wagner (1813–1863), belittled Jews as being incapable of creating true art. Even the German Jewish philosopher and Emancipation movement leader Moses Mendelssohn (1729–1786), who himself embraced representational art as "a perfection" of form, order, and harmony—true beauty—never challenged Kant's view that Judaism was an artless tradition.

What were Jewish artists of that era to do? Mendelssohn's grandson, the painter Philipp Veit (1793–1877), like many other Jewish artists, converted to Christianity as the only way to make it in 19th-century German society. Veit joined the Nazarenes, a group of Christian artists, in their quest "to contribute a new and original style to European art."

With the exceptions of religious crafts and synagogue architecture, Jewish art seemed destined to remain marginalized at best.

It wasn't until the middle decades of the 19th century, as Jewish artists started to explore Jewish themes in their paintings, that the first glimmer of a modern Jewish art movement emerged in Central Europe. Ironically, the most prominent of these painters, Moritz Daniel Oppenheim (1800–1882), an observant Jew, had been influenced by the art of the Nazarene movement after visiting Philipp Veit in Rome. Oppenheim received numerous portrait commissions from bourgeois Jewish families and patronage from the Rothschilds (beginning with Baron Carl Mayer von Rothschild of Frankfurt and, later, from the London and Paris branches of the family). Indeed, Oppenheim declared himself "the painter of the Rothschilds and the Rothschild of painters."

Oppenheim created a body of "Jewish history paintings" intended, in part, to make a visual argument for a genuine German Jewish aesthetic at a time when Central European Jews were struggling to achieve political emancipation. His *The Return of a Jewish Volunteer from the Wars of Liberation to His Family* (1833) testified to German Jewry's patriotism in its depiction of a Jewish soldier in uniform embraced by his loving family in a traditional Jewish home setting. More boldly, his *Lavater and Lessing Visit Mendelssohn* (1856) symbolized the Jews' struggle for emancipation in Europe. The painting depicted Moses Mendelssohn at home in his parlor (complete with a traditional Sabbath lamp) engaged in dialogue with Johann Kaspar Lavater (1741–1801), a Christian theologian who challenged Mendelssohn to abandon Judaism and convert to Christianity. Standing behind them is Mendelssohn's friend and advocate, Gotthold Ephraim Lessing (1729–1781), the literary leader of the German Enlightenment who believed in the compatibility of Judaism and reason. The Enlightenment itself was represented by a chess set, presumably used in friendly matches between Mendelssohn and Lessing.

Oppenheim is best known for his 1865 illustrated collections, *Scenes from Traditional Jewish Life*, which portray a harmonious vision of a German-Jewish cultural synthesis and would become "the most popular

Jewish book ever published in Germany," according to historian Ismar Schorsch.

Oppenheim's Jewish artistic heirs emerged farther to the east in the Galician districts of the Austro-Hungarian Empire. Among them was Maurycy Gottlieb (1856–1879), one of the most talented painters of the time. The leading German published Friedrich Bruckmann commissioned Gottlieb to create twelve illustrations for a special edition of *Nathan the Wise*, Gotthold Lessing's famous play about tolerance, featuring a protagonist based on Moses Mendelssohn. Gottlieb had completed seven of the works when, in 1877, yielding to antisemitic pressure, Bruckmann cancelled the contract. Gottlieb was devastated by this reversal of fortune.

Shortly before his untimely death at the age of twenty-three, Gottlieb, inspired by Heinrich Graetz's monumental *History of the Jews*, painted his psychological masterpiece, *Jews Praying on the Day of Atonement* (1878). Departing from Oppenheim's earlier, more formal, and politically motivated work, Gottlieb here infused the subjects with emotion, draped in traditional *tallitot*, their eyes turned downward into the pages of holy books or upward toward a distant deity. In the middle of the canvas was a self-portrait of the artist filled with the angst of an unsettled and exhausted young man—but giving the hint of promise, too, his colorful *kittel* (robe) reminiscent of the biblical Joseph's special coat.

In contrast to Gottlieb's intense, psychological work, the Hungarian-born Isidor Kaufmann (1853–1921), one of the Fifth World Zionist Congress exhibitors, depicted the more celebratory aspects of traditional Jewish life. "My intention," Kaufmann wrote, "has always been to praise and glorify Jewish culture . . . I want to reveal all its beauties and all its nobility . . . [make its] fervor accessible to gentiles as well." Traveling extensively in Galicia and the Ukraine to find his subjects, Kaufmann created a body of Jewish ethnographic portraits, often of bearded rabbis draped in traditional caftans. One of his paintings, *Rabbi's Visit* (1886), portraying a proud father watching his bashful son standing before a prominent rabbi, was presented by Emperor Franz Joseph to Vienna's prestigious Museum of Art.

At the end of the 19th century, the center of the Jewish art movement shifted eastward again, this time to Russia, where Jewish life was a churning sea full of cultural crosscurrents from Chasidism to Zionism to Bundism, all competing for Jewish hearts and minds within the Pale of Settlement and beyond. At the same time, the czarist government was keeping Jews impoverished and instigating violent pogroms against the Jewish community.

Against this background, Vladimir Stasov (1824–1906), a leading figure on the Russian art scene (who was not Jewish), began advocating the creation of a national Russian art, of which Jewish art (which he understood to be a mixture of Moorish and folk elements) would constitute an important part. Responding to Stasov's call, a number of Jewish artists, including the highly regard sculptor Mark Antokolsky (1843–1902), sought ways to introduce Jewish old elements into new art idioms, producing such works as *Jewish Tailor* (1864) and *Spinoza* (1881), as well as the complex yet unfinished compositions *Talmud Dispute* (1868) and *Inquisition Attacks the Jews* (1869). Many of these young Russian Jewish artists made their way to Paris, where, in 1912, several founded the first Jewish art group and journal, *Makhmadim* (Precious Ones). Located in the French capital's famed artist colony, La Ruche ("Beehive"), the building and its many studios attracted dozens of expatriate Jewish artists, among them Marc Chagall (1887–1985).

Perhaps more than any other Jewish artist to date, Chagall was a pioneer in presenting traditional Jewish images in modern art idioms. In *I and the Village* (1911), for example, Chagall combined Jewish subject matter while experimenting with Fauvism (the use of vivid, unnatural colors) and Cubism (the pronounced geometrical division of space).

After the outbreak of World War I, Chagall returned to his native Vitebsk, a shtetl in eastern Belarus, and joined the Russian army. He went on to direct Vitebsk's Free Academy of Art until he moved to Moscow, where he worked as a set designer in both Jewish and general theaters, creating many images for the new Soviet stage. Eventually, government interference prompted him to resign and return to Paris in 1923. He became a French citizen fourteen years later but fled after the Nazi occupation, living in the United States, Mexico, Italy, and other places until he could return safely to France.

Although Chagall had left the world of the shtetl as a young man, the shtetl never entirely left him. Much of his vast body of work drew on his experience of growing up in a world rich in Jewish culture, even as the Jews struggled with poverty and persecution. Brides, lovers, fiddlers, barnyard animals, flowers, and Jewish symbols all danced together on Chagall's canvases, murals, and ceramics. For Chagall, the visual details of Jewish life in his work were just as illustrative of the universal human experience as they were representative of his specifically Jewish memories. For this reason, perhaps, Chagall's works are among the very few pieces of art with explicitly Jewish themes displayed today in world-class museums.

In the early 20th century, three-dimensional art was still generally perceived by the traditional Jewish community as a violation of the second commandment ("You shall not make for yourself an idol.") Nonetheless, the Russian-born sculptor Jacques Lipchitz (1891–1973), who settled in France and became associated with Paris' avant-garde art circles, built on the precedent establish by Mark Antokolsky and took his own Jewish-infused sculpture in Cubist and neo-Baroque directions. In *The Prayer* (1943), for example, he showed in a sculpture rich in Baroque-like detail an elderly man swinging a rooster in the *kapparot* ritual (in which a person's sins are symbolically transferred to a fowl). *The Miracle* (1948), inspired by the newly created Jewish State, depicted an exultant figure with raised arms facing the Tablets of the Laws, out of which a seven-branched candelabrum grows. (One of the seven *Miracle* sculptures he created is on display at Congregation Ohabai Sholom in Nashville, Tennessee).

The careers of Jewish artists who remained within the Soviet orbit followed a much different trajectory from those of Chagall and Lipchitz. The Marxist El Lissitzky (1890–1941), who illustrated Yiddish books, for example, aided the Bolshevik Revolution by creating, among other works, the classic Soviet propaganda poster, *Beat the Whites with the Red Wedge* (1919), which used an anti-pogrom theme to rally Jewish support of the Communists. Soon his style became synonymous with Soviet Realism. Within a few years, however Lissitzky became disillusioned both with the Soviet Union and the subversion of art in the service of propaganda. "Art," he declared, "is created today by those who are strangers to it." The government retaliated by limiting his commissions, which, along with his poor health, greatly reduced his influence in the final decade of his life.

By the late 1920s, with the Russian homeland largely closed to Jewish artistic activity under Stalin, Jewish artists who had immigrated to Palestine and the United States from Eastern Europe became the cutting edge in the campaign Buber launched to create a national Jewish art movement. Palestine would develop along two distinct tracks, both growing out of the Bezalel Academy in Jerusalem. The first, promoting crafts for both artistic and commercial purposes as part of the national renaissance in the Jewish homeland, was spearheaded by Boris Schatz, the painter and sculptor who founded the Bezalel Academy in 1906. Initially Schatz attracted broad support among Zionist artists ranging from the Polish-born Jewish history painter Samuel Hirzenberg (1865–1908) to the Galician-born modernist Ephraim Moses Lilien (1874–1975), a pioneer in photography best known for his iconic portrait of Theodor Herzl gazing prophetically into the distance from the Rhine Bridge in Basel.

Within a generation, however, the modernist camp at the Bezalel Academy was in full revolt, seeking to overthow what they perceived as Schatz's anachronistic approach. They organized the first Association of Jewish Artists in 1920 and then, in 1923, staged the first major exhibition of modern Jewish art in Palestine, held at Jerusalem's Tower of David. By 1926 the center of art had shifted from Jerusalem to the modern "Hebrew" city of Tel Aviv.

In search of a national Jewish art, these second-generation Zionist artists rejected Diaspora images and drew inspiration from the landscapes of Israel, its local Arab population, and ancient New East cultures such as the Canaanites and Mesopotamians. At the forefront of this trend was the Romanian-born artist Reuven Rubin (1893–1974), who settled in Turkish-controlled Palestine in 1912 and enrolled in the Bezalel Academy. "From my childhood," he wrote in his 1970 autobiography, "I had dreamed of going to Palestine. It seems to me now that I always knew instinctively that there was the country where I would develop as a "Jewish artist." By "Jewish Artist," Rubin explained, "I don't mean a painter of Jewish subjects, but one whose roots are embedded in the soil of his own homeland, Zion, where the Bible lives naturally for him and where he feels his rightful place and is spiritually at ease." In *The Beginning of Tel Aviv* (1912), he offered a naïve view of a new town with simple buildings on sand dunes along the Mediterranean coast. His 1923 work, *First Fruits*, strongly influenced by the work of Gauguin, depicted actual fruit harvested form the soil of *Eretz Yisrael*.

With the expansion of the Jewish population in Palestine in the 1920s and the founding of the state in 1948, the stage was set for Zionist sculptors to create Jewish national art in public spaces for the first time since the Roman conquest. For centuries, Jewish visual art, with the exception of synagogue architecture, had been confined largely to interiors. Now, beginning with Abraham Melnikov's Assyrian-style nine-foot-tall *Roaring Lion* (1926) at Tel Chai (commemorating Joseph Trumpledor's last stand in the 1920 battle for control of the Huleh Valley), three-dimensional public art on Jewish and Zionist themes became a reality. In the aftermath of Israeli independence, even larger projects were undertaken, including Benno Elkan's *Menorah* (1956), a gift from the British Parliament to the State of Israel, which stands on the Knesset grounds; and Dani Karavan's massive, modern, abstract *Monument to the Negev Brigade* (1965), perched dramatically on Israel's southern desert terrain. In time, monumental public installations would come to stand as testimony to the Jewish art movement's success in normalizing art in modern Jewish life, at least in Israel.

In the U.S., the Jewish art scene was meager until masses of Eastern European Jewish immigrants arrived at the end of the 19th century. As Buber ascended the podium at the Fifth Zionist Congress in 1901, a nascent Jewish art movement was emerging in New York City with support from the Educational Alliance, a settlement house designed to accelerate the immigrants' Americanization. By 1917 Abbo Ostrowsky's new Educational Alliance Art School was attracting, as both instructors and students, stellar young Jewish artists, including Leonard Baskin, Barnett Newman, Isaac and Moses Soyer, and Louise Nevelson.

These artists were primarily concerned with developing their own techniques and styles, but on occasion they did so employing Jewish themes. Thus, the Soyers, who as Social Realists concentrated on social injustice, often featured images of working-class people, including Jews. Abstract expressionist Nevelson (1899–1988) became best known for large three-dimensional "assemblages," including artistic interpretations of the Holocaust. Another abstract expressionist, Newman (1905–1970) who helped develop the "color field" genre of paintings (characterized by areas of color separated by thin vertical lines or "zips," as he called them), also produced Jewish-themed paintings such as *Uriel* (1954) and *Abraham* (1949). Baskin (1922–2000) created sculptures such as the bronze *Isaac* (1973), seated with his hand on the killed ram in an interpretation of the *Akedah* story, as well as watercolor illustrations for *A Passover Haggadah* (CCAR Press, 1982).

By the middle of the 20th century, Martin Buber's dream of normalizing art within Jewish life had become a reality, evidenced in distinctive modes of Jewish visual representation from academic history paintings to monumental public sculptures in Israel. The defining historical events and significant new trends in Jewish life—the Holocaust, Israeli independence, feminism, Kabbalah, and the "return to tradition" in recent years- were also being captured through artistic expression, becoming part of our people's cultural legacy.

Today, Jewish art is found not only in Jewish homes and in synagogues but also in Jewish museums- which have increased exponentially in recent years to approximately 250, mostly in the U.S. and Israel. However, only a few of these museums are devoted solely to art; most focus on showcasing historical events or celebrating local Jewish communities.

Still lacking today is an appreciation of Jewish art as a genre of its own. Perhaps this is because the international art world has yet to recognize Jewish art in its own right. New York's Metropolitan Museum of Art, for example, has departments of Islamic, Asian and Egyptian art, but none for Jewish art (although the Museum does occasionally display Judaica).

Why have so many of the world's great museums not found Jewish art fit for inclusion? Maybe the answer lies in the persistent, deeply ingrained, and now clearly false notion that Judaism is an "artless tradition."

Generations: My Dad, Charles Sussman, z"l

2010

This week's Torah portion is called *Toledot* in Hebrew, which means "generations." It tells part of the story of the generation of Isaac and Rebecca and their sons, Jacob and Esau. As most of you know, the theme of generations is weighing heavily on me because of the passing of my father, Charles Sussman, on Wednesday, October 27. Although some of you have already heard his story directly from me, I thought it appropriate to memorialize my father one more time in this message.

My dad was one of three sons of Jacob and Anna Sussman. My grandfather immigrated to America as a boy from Minsk in czarist Russia. My grandmother was born in the United States shortly after her family moved here from Lithuania. They settled in Baltimore and ran a famous downtown deli called Sussman and Lev on East Baltimore Street. My father was extremely proud of his father's accomplishments and his ability to maintain the family during the worst of the Depression.

My dad loved to learn and believed deeply in education. Professionally, he was a teacher, guidance counselor, countywide supervisor of guidance (Baltimore County), and an instructor in guidance and counseling at Johns Hopkins University. He attended Baltimore's honor high school and City College and received his Bachelor's and Master's degrees plus additional certificates in advanced educational training from Hopkins. My dad taught me how to read (one page at a time with a gold star on top of each completed page) and literally surrounded me with books from that moment to today.

My dad loved music. He loved opera, classical music, and, above all, Mozart. He had a vast 33, CD, and tape collection of fine music. He regularly quizzed me on music history and provided a lifelong course in music appreciation. Our dinners were always accompanied by quartets playing the muse of Salzburg. Music provided my dad with a true sense of transcendence in his life.

My dad was a soldier in World War II and fought in France, Belgium, and Germany. He fought in the Battle of the Bulge. His division, the Ninety-Fifth, suffered terrible causalities. In Germany, my father's unit was cut off and took heavy fire. A communications sergeant, he carried a "300 radio" half a mile "with little regard for his own personal safety" until he could call in relief. It was a miracle he survived that and many other actions. For his bravery, he was awarded the Bronze Star. My father did not like to talk about his war experience. However, his medal is my most prized and proud possession.

After the war, my father and mother, Freda (nee Sacki) married. They were married for sixty-four years. It is difficult for me not to think of Mom and Dad as a single unit. They had an excellent marriage, one that I deeply admire. It was based on love, friendship, and respect. I have one younger sister, Marcelle, who lives in New York. She shares the same memories and same deep sense of loss and gratitude I am experiencing at present.

My father was a very good father. He gave me a lot of time growing up. He took me places and introduced me to the various genres of culture I enjoy so much today. He also took me to Civil War battlefields and other historic sites. My dad lived to be a grandfather and a great-grandfather. He was also a much-beloved uncle. My cousins all lived nearby in my growing-up years and loved my father as well.

My dad died peacefully at Sinai Hospital in Baltimore. My mother, sister, Liz, and I were present. I now have a different and deeper appreciation of the meaning of the biblical generations. My dad was always a blessing in my life. Now, he will remain so forever.

Shabbat Shalom.

Part 3

A Night of Watching
2012–2016

A Night of Watching, 2012-2016

British Rabbi Lionel Blue (1930–2016), a well-known broadcaster and journalist, once remarked that "Jews are like everybody else but more so." The same could be said about my third quinquennial at KI. The years 2012–2016 were, in most respects, like the decade that preceded them "but more so." In particular, these years were characterized by intense debate over the future of the synagogue as anxiety over long-term trends in congregational membership. During this time, synagogue leadership courageously focused much of their energy on possibilities of partnering and even merging with other congregations and Jewish organizations. In many ways, it was a "night of watching" (Exod. 12:42).

The main questions that emerged during this period were anchored in the issue of congregational identity and autonomy. What was more important: the continuation of KI as a historic organization or the maintenance of its functions as a religious organization. For example, was it necessary for us to have our own religious school even if enrollment fell below critical mass, or would it be better to have a communal school with more children but no longer part of KI? Both our internal discussions and our conversations with other area synagogues revealed that no congregation "on our street" was willing to give up its identity, and even more, they were unsure of how much congregational autonomy they could give up. For me as Rabbi of KI, I found myself in the delicate position of having to support the debate and, at the same time, take a stand in favor of maintaining KI's historic identity as the congregation approached the 170th anniversary of its founding in 1847.

In the end, various attempts at merging and partnering failed. On the other hand, a small Conservative synagogue, Melrose B'nai Israel

Emanu-El, sold their building and leased space at KI while maintaining their identity and autonomy. Eight years later in 2020, Philadelphia's Holocaust Awareness Museum and Education Center (HAMEC) also "moved into" KI, again preserving their identity and autonomy. We had discovered a "middle path" that greatly benefited all three organizations and perhaps created a model for others to follow.

If the primary internal reality of KI between 2012 and 2016 was a continuation of the previous five years, so too was the greatest external factor shaping our congregation's continuation with the immediate past "but more so"! The hard-fought presidential campaign of 2016 not only was passionate but also resulted in the surprise election of Donald J. Trump as the forty-fifth president of the United States. The great fissures in American life that had been developing under Barack Obama were now open wounds, and the challenge of speaking about the great headlines of the day, foreign and domestic, became greater than ever before. The desire to retreat to safe topics was always present. Then again, as an heir of the prophets and mindful of the lessons of bystanderism during the Holocaust, silence was not an option.

The headlines of the five years from 2012 to 2016 were dramatic and painful. The death of Osama bin Laden; the Boston bombing; the Sandy Hook massacre of little children; shootings in Charleston, South Carolina, Paris, and the Pulse nightclub; the 2014 Russian invasion of Ukrainian territory; and the civil war in Syria all cried out for elucidation from the perspective of Reform Judaism. At the same time, the need for reassuring messages about the blessings of daily life and the value of tradition needed to be presented. It was a night of watching filled with anxiety and the search for hints of hope and redemption.

Parallel to my rabbinic work, I also remained committed to the academic dimension of my career that continued undiminished during these years. I published a number of articles on Jewish history in various journals on the history of Reform Judaism, Jews and World War I, art, theology, Jewish leadership, Philadelphia Jewish history, and the Holocaust. However, the capstone of the period was the invitation to teach several undergraduate seminars at Princeton, present a paper on KI's Rabbi Joseph Krauskopf (1858–1923) to members of the university's faculty and graduate students, and offer programs at the school's Center for Jewish Life. As I approached the final period of my time at KI, I felt a bit like the biblical Jacob who had struggled through a long night and, as the Torah stated, "prevailed."

Passover Report: Seeing Oneself Going Forth from Egypt

April 21, 2011, e-KI

It's officially the middle of Passover, so I thought I would offer a "Passover Report 2011" for this week's column. Passover this year has been wonderful. Our preschool kicked things off with its own celebrations. I personally ran four seders: Rydal Park Retirement Home, my home, the KI congregational seder, and the Hillel seder at Delaware Valley College. Each was very special: all were a great deal of fun. As has been the practice for the last few years, we also had a combined Passover morning service at Beth Am, which I led with Cantor Zarkh and enjoyed a great deal.

Seders have always been a mixture of tradition and innovation. This year was no different. In addition to all the familiar prayers, symbols, and Passover songs, there was also something very new: a Visual Haggadah, which I made with my daughter Chana, with some final stage help from Ross M. Levy. Our PowerPoint Visual Haggadah made it possible to follow a central dictum of the Passover seder, namely, "to see oneself as if we personally had gone forth from Egypt." Next year, after a little more editing, I am planning to have a corresponding printed Haggadah, as well as a digitalized version for those of you who want to run a "techie" seder of your own.

The highlight of our home seder came quite unexpectedly. Our two-year-old granddaughter, Sophie, decided on her own to lift her Kiddush cup and shout out, "L'chaim!" We howled, and she laughed and then continued to punctuate the rest of our seder with her happy rendition of "to life!"

Another Passover surprise came the other day when our KI member Eve Mennies stopped by the office and presented me with a copy of an heirloom Haggadah her family had brought to America from Germany. Printed in 1913, it features illustrations from a 1738 German Haggadah depicting various seder and biblical scenes. Most striking to me is the cover of Eve's Haggadah, which is exactly the same as the design of the Haggadah my family used in Germany many, many decades ago.

Seder, as we know, is the most observed Jewish ritual in America. Reports vary, but it is clear that the vast majority of American Jews (and many non-Jews) celebrate at least one seder. It's fun. It's at home. It's child-oriented, and it successfully helps us tie our own family story to the story of our people. Passover is all about connecting with the Jewish people and affirming our tradition's most cherished values: family, freedom, and faith. I hope you are enjoying a pleasant Passover. I know I am!

Shabbat Shalom and Chag Sameach!

You Can't Go Home Again?
President Obama's Peace Proposal

2011

Today President Obama delivered an update on his view of the current realities in the Middle East as well as a suggestion as to how to reinvigorate the Israel-Palestine peace process. The basic principle of the proposal is to return to pre-1967 borders and allow for practical adjustments. The President also emphasized his view that Hamas is not a legitimate partner for peace at this time and needs to renounce its goal of destroying the State of Israel. Furthermore, he called on the Palestinians to halt their efforts to de-legitimatize Israel in the United Nations. While an earlier part of the speech focused on the current situation in Syria, the President did not specify if he included the Golan in his understanding of pre-1967 borders. He did, however, raise the complex issue of the Palestinian refugees and the need to read them into an overall peace agreement. Tough issues like Jerusalem, the President remarked, need to be addressed at a later stage.

Reactions to the proposal were predictable. The Israeli right as well as Israel's prime minister quickly rejected the proposal. The head of the PA thanked the president of the United States for taking the initiative. The head of Hamas denounced the plan as just more pro-Israel bunk from the United States. However, one Israeli leader, Tzipi Livni, a Right-center politician, applauded the president's remarks.

From my perspective, starting the discussion with the model of the 1967 borders in mind is fine, but what is really important are the future adjustments to that border. The old Green Line itself is not viable. A modified border, however, is probably the best path to peace. For sure a one-state solution is not viable, as it would doom Israel's Jewish population to minority status. On the other hand, a modified '67 border with strong security arrangements is probably the best path Israel and the Palestinians can hope to take together.

Sadly, I am less than hopeful that a just and lasting peace can be achieved at this moment. The Israeli Right still harbors a belief in a Greater Israel, and the Arab rejectionists really do not want to coexist with Israel. They want Israel destroyed.

Meanwhile, some incremental progress can be made. If some compromises are worked out, it will be necessary to be prepared for extremist efforts to undermine a peace arrangement, and that is when the real work will begin. For now, as always, Israel will need to remain strong, vigilant, and prepared to defend herself.

Shabbat shalom.

Taking Syria Seriously

May 20, 2011

My first encounter with Syria occurred in December 1969. I was fifteen and on tour in Israel with Camp Harlam's Winter Travel Program under the direction of Arie Gluck. Unlike today, the signs of the Six-Day War were apparent everywhere. The hills of the Golan were still raw with the remnants of war. Captured Syrian military equipment was visibly impounded in Al Quneitra. Israeli armored equipment was even more in evidence with makeshift camps and convoys everywhere you turned. It was "glorious" to my naive eyes.

Four years and a lifetime later, the Yom Kippur War broke out, and the Syrian border became the scene of murderous fighting again. This time, I had a little skin in the game. My best friend was in the Israeli reserves. I had just spent the summer of 1973 learning Hebrew in Jerusalem. The word reached me that Amos's helicopter had been shot down. He survived but was subsequently shot by Syrian troops doing a "cleanup" operation. It was his birthday, and he was gravely wounded. It was a bad moment.

If you want to get a sense of what Amos Gitai went through, watch his movie *Kippur*. It tells the story in graphic detail. When I returned to Israel in 1975, Amos was still recovering. He forced me to visit wounded and disfigured soldiers in far worse shape than he was. It was ugly. Not one young person in Israel would party. All notions of glory had become fleeting.

I tried to understand. I focused one of my two senior undergraduate projects on Syria and its ruling political party, the Ba'athists. As in Iraq, the Ba'ath party was in control. Secular, brutal, and militaristic, it was thoroughly revolting and still is little more than a concocted ideological program that cannot hide the hideous reality of a military dictatorship.

The Syrian Ba'ath party, now in power for decades, represents the desperate interests of a religious-ethnic minority. If they lose, they will be slaughtered, and they know it. They are totally ruthless in their attempt to stay in power. They continue to hide behind their anti-Israel rhetoric. They continue to support Hezbollah, and they continue to harbor dangerous weapons of terrible capacity.

Israel needs to take Syria seriously. If that means destroying missile warehouses and supply lines to Hezbollah in Lebanon, so be it. Assad has been weakened. Now is the time to make him and his allies still weaker without strengthening the Islamist presence among his Arab opponents. A post-Assad Syria will probably be a dangerous place. How Israel and the United States act today will help determine Syria's future character. Now is the time to be strong, resolute, and smart. Ba'athism is bad. Jihadism is worse.

I am confident Israel's strategists at every level will figure out what to do. They have no choice, and we are well advised to support them.

Rabbi's Journal:
The Feminine Mystique at 50

2012

The last time I wrote to you in this column, I talked about some of my pastoral duties. Your responses were amazing. I received e-mails, phone calls and real letters all expressing a sense of personal identification with the mitzvah of "comforting the mourner" and of being of service to others in general. We are, indeed, a community of mutual concern and love of one's neighbor.

Today, I want to report on a different aspect of my work: the life of the mind. I take great pride and experience great pleasure as rabbi *qua* teacher. I regularly experience the truth of the old saying that "when one teaches, two learn." This week I was given two assignments: to speak in honor of the upcoming 50th anniversary of the publication of Betty Friedan's *The Feminine Mystique* and to give a talk on Judaism's view of the afterlife. Both were welcome assignments, and both were good learning and sharing experiences.

On Wednesday night, May 9, I gave my annual book review for Sisterhood. This year we decided on something different: not to review a new work of fiction but to give a retrospective view of one of the most important books ever written about women, and more specifically a book written by a Jewish woman about women in America in 1963.

Basically, Friedan argued in her book that the non-wager earning, suburban wife of the 1950s was trapped by a "feminine mystique" which unsatisfactorily defined her in terms of a Freudian-derived construct of womanhood and Freud's belief that "biology" was destiny. Friedan further argued that unhappy mothers would lead not only to bad mental health for women, but to unhappiness in their children as well.

The publication of *The Feminine Mystique* proved to be a landmark in the evolution of feminism in the 1960s. Thereafter, the women's movement generated significant legislation at all levels of government, women's studies programs were created and the place of women in American society changed dramatically. How this has impacted Jewish women is of tremendous importance to all of us in the context of a Reform synagogue. Even more specifically, new questions about women, Sisterhood and the culture of the Reform synagogue remain challenging and, to a large extent, unresolved.

My second assignment was to talk about "Jewish Views of the Afterlife" to the Cultural Council. Using a traditional lecture format (no PowerPoint on this one yet!), I explored both different views of the soul and ancient Judaism's belief in the physical resurrection of the dead. Where is *Gan Eden*? What Judaism means by the next world, angels and dybbuks were all explored. Reform views of the immortality of the soul, memory and enduring love were all discussed as well. At the end of the talk, I simply asked, "Are there any answers?" Judaism's response, "to life," works for me!

So, not only am I given the opportunity to serve but I am also given the opportunity to teach. I am grateful for having a community which accepts both services from me. Together, we have much to do. Together, we have much to learn! How lucky we are to be part of such an ancient, venerable and inspiring tradition!

Shabbat Shalom.

Rabbi's Journal III: My Cup Overfloweth

2012 eKI

For this week's column, I want to continue sharing aspects of my work as a congregational rabbi with you. I have already shared a little bit about my pastoral and educational work. Today, I want to talk about *"Bimah"* work and, in particular, Bar and Bat Mitzvahs.

I've done a lot of *b'nai mitzvah* services. My guess is that number exceeds 1,000 and may even be closer to 1,500. With very rare exceptions, they are wonderful experiences. Each child, each family is different, so it's not ever boring. The power of the *bar* or *bat mitzvah* in summoning families and friends from far-flung places never ceases to amaze me. People will stop their lives, and suspend business and fly across oceans just to come to a *bar* or *bat mitzvah*.

This week's story begins in my office with the usual parent-child *"D'var Torah"* meeting, the purpose of which is to help the student write his or her *bar/bat mitzvah* speech. It's a good opportunity to get to know one another, check on the student's progress, ascertain family dynamics and, most importantly, keep parental anxiety in check. For many of the families it is also the first visit to my office. I have a rather big office with lots of books and all types of religious objects I use to illustrate talks on comparative religion.

When Alyssa G came to see me with her mom, she happened to notice a miniature version of the large "Family" statue in the circle at the main entrance to the synagogue. Alyssa asked where it was from and I explained how an eighty-something-year-old member of the congregation once walked into the office with it in hand. She explained that she was very inspired by the original piece out front and decided to make her own version of it to be placed in the rabbi's office as a gift. Little did I know that Alyssa instantly took this story to heart.

At her *bat mitzvah*, a couple of weeks later, Alyssa began her "thank you" speech in the usual way. Then, all of a sudden, she stopped and said she had something to give to the clergy. She went over to a box she had placed near the Ark and preceded to take out beautiful, colorful glazed clay cups she had made for each of us and complete with Jewish symbols and Hebrew letters. She explained the replica in my office was the product of someone else being inspired, which in turn inspired her, the *bat mitzvah*, to do something similar. Today, my *bat mitzvah* cup and its rainbow of colors is on my desk at KI. When I look at it, I smile, and think to myself how wonderful it is to have an appreciative student.

Alyssa's cup reminds me that I, indeed all of us, have a tremendous responsibility. We only get to grow up once and if our parents entrust our Jewish education to a synagogue and its clergy team then we get one swing of the bat. My job is to help people remember where they came from, engage in the present and prepare for the Jewish future. Alyssa's cup reminded me of how heavy and joyful that responsibility is. She gave me/us a true gift of the heart. I feel I have to do the same for all of you every day. When we connect, as did happen at Alyssa's Bat Mitzvah, "my cup overflows."

May we all have our moments of giving and receiving gifts of the heart. They are the sacred moments which give life its purpose, depth and sweetness.

Shabbat Shalom.

Why Hanukkah?

2012 eKI

Years ago, friends of ours in Binghamton recorded a startling message on their phone.

"You have called our house," the message began and abruptly ended with a simple "Why?" Not surprisingly, most people did not leave a message or an explanation.

Interestingly, the Talmud begins its discussion in the same terse manner. It simply asks the question, "Why Hanukkah?" Let me suggest eight plus one reasons corresponding to the eight candles on the Hanukkah Menorah and the *Shamash*, the helper candle:

My eight reasons we should celebrate Hanukkah:

1. "Remember Jerusalem." The main story takes place in the eternal capital of the Jewish people. We are taught to "remember Jerusalem above our highest joys" and even invoke an image of it as a true city of peace at the end of the Jewish wedding ceremony.
2. "Be Aware of the Miraculous." We can easily debate whether or not there really are events called miracles. Some say yes. Some say no. In my opinion, that is very different from seeing life itself as "miraculous." Hanukkah teaches us to look harder to find the miraculous in life.
3. "Courage." My favorite line from the Wizard of Oz is "Who put the ape in apricot . . . Courage!" Judah and the Maccabees had courage. We all need courage to face the everyday events of life

and the extraordinary challenges that come our way. Hanukkah summons us to find our courage!
4. "Freedom of Religion." As Jews and Americans, we will not be denied freedom of religion. It is the keystone of our civil rights in this country. The Maccabees fought to establish it; we need to fight to preserve it!
5. "Jewish Sovereignty." We live in a very special time in Jewish history. We live with the blessing of a sovereign Jewish State. The Maccabees understood the value of Jewish autonomy and so should we.
6. "Jewish Pride." One important lesson Hanukkah can teach us is to be proud of our tradition. Resistance to assimilation and the determination to learn about one's heritage begins with pride. Let us be like the Maccabees; let us be proud of who we are as Jews and children of an ancient and worthy tradition.
7. "Jewish survival." Much of Jewish life today is focused on the issue of Jewish survival. In Israel, the fight is physical. In America, the battle is spiritual and cultural. We have inherited much and it is our responsibility to maintain our tradition in our time and present it to future generations with hope for its long-term viability.
8. "Dedication." The word Hanukkah means "dedication." Jewish life cannot endure without personal dedication to our tradition. Only we can maintain our heritage. On Hanukkah, let us rededicate ourselves to that duty and privilege.

Finally, there is the *Shamash*, the helper candle. Who is the helper candle? We are. You are. In our tradition, only we can light the menorah. We are the *Shamash* and we keep the flame of our tradition alive.

May you have a light filled, joyous and dedicated Hanukkah and a happy, healthy New Year!

Shabbat Shalom and Chag Hanukkah Sameach.

Zimmerman Trial

July 19, 2013 eKI

My wife, Liz, and I were leading a group in Israel during most of the Zimmerman trial. We could not access it directly while there. However, since the trial was not over by the time we arrived home, I was able to pick up the thread and certainly understood the intensity of the event. Every once in a while, the attention of our country is riveted on an extraordinary event because of its importance, its capacity to indicate something essential, something central, about our lives as Americans and, from our perspective, I would also say, as American Jews.

Personally, and speaking only for myself, I was both mystified and horrified by the Zimmerman verdict. I did not expect such a verdict to be delivered in such a short time, about fifteen/sixteen hours of deliberation without the jury actually getting all tied up in knots over some of the fine points of law that are involved here. I am not a lawyer. I did not read the twenty-six pages of jury instruction but, in my opinion, something went terribly wrong here. Either the jury didn't do it right or state law wasn't right or the prosecution simply failed to make its case.

In any event, from my point of view as a citizen, from the point of view of religious leadership and from the point of view of somebody who studies American history in a rather serious fashion, I think I can make that claim that this was all wrong and as a result, it lingers in the national consciousness. There is a heaviness that goes with this particular trial and although we have very short news cycles in this country, my sense is this one is going to linger a bit longer and perhaps lead to broader discussion, as well it should. Whatever the verdict could have been at this level, we don't know if there will be subsequent trials.

For sure, the Simpson case comes to mind where state civil law functioned in very different ways. Florida is different than California. The Federal government has been indicating through the Attorney General that federal prosecution is pretty iffy and there are dangers as I understand it for the Martin family if they file suit against George Zimmerman, which could place them in bankruptcy and with a verdict that again does not go their way. So it's very much in limbo right now. What we do have and can work with and think about is the fact as it stands that a six-person, a six-woman jury, came up with a not-guilty verdict.

What's wrong here? From my point of view there are several things that are extremely wrong. The first is the person who was killed in this event was a minor and there was really nothing in the judicial procedure that spoke to the fact that a seventeen- year-old, not an eighteen-year-old, not a twenty-five-year old, but a person who is considered by law in any of the fifty states to be a child, to be a dependent, a tax deduction, whatever you want to call them, a person who has to abide by education law, a person not old enough yet to serve in the United States military, not old enough to vote, a person who is still growing up, was killed. There was never a question that he was killed. There's a body. The person who pulled the trigger said he pulled the trigger. A young person, a minor, a child, somebody's child was shot just a few hundred feet from his father's home and for whatever technical reason in the law, that was not considered. A society that does not take cognizance of the rights of its children is a society that is off track.

No child should have to be put in a position where they can be shot by a non-official person and then that person is fully exonerated. A child's life was taken, one who was not involved at that particular moment in any mischief whatsoever, who hadn't just mugged somebody, who hadn't just beaten somebody up, who hadn't had a fight. He was simply walking. He had been to a store. We all know these facts. There was no behavior reported on the part of Trayvon Martin prior to the confrontation that should have elicited a police-like response and questioning. Whatever he did prior in his life, and it seemed he was not an angel, should not have warranted the kind of lethal response on the part of George Zimmerman. The fact that the person charged was not charged with the death of a minor bothers me tremendously.

The second thing I think that went terribly wrong is the time frame that the trial considered. The time frame in play in court was apparently a very small portion of the entire incident. This was an incident that played out with a man in a car, then following someone in the car, then on foot and then a face-to-face confrontation. In this particular trial, the only question that was being asked was whether or not the minor who was killed was involved in aggressive behavior that was homicidal, a completely subjective call under any circumstances, just in the last few minutes, shall we say last 300 seconds of his life.

The record shows Zimmerman had not done his job very well before either, as he had contacted the police a hundred times before, and a hundred times before the police had told him to buzz off and told him again on this particular evening that his work was done, that he had made the call, that they would now take over and that they were the police.

In my opinion, the court should have focused in the trial at the point where a grown man with a loaded weapon purposely, consciously, wittingly, defied police orders. If you and I were involved in something on the street and there was some sort of altercation and we intervened, and a policeman said to us, "Please back away. We have this under control" and we insisted that no, I don't think you have it under control officer, I think I have to get this under control, and then go across that police line and intervene and do anything, just talk to a person involved with whom the police are talking. . . a person could get arrested for interfering with police business. In this case, a person who was trained and had a lousy experience as a community volunteer, defied police orders. So far as I am personally concerned, that's where the clock should have started.

Moreover, no person who suspects another person of being truly dangerous would risk getting out of the car, and somehow creating the confrontation, unless they felt they had the upper hand. Now George Zimmerman did not know whether or not Trayvon Martin was armed but George Zimmerman knew that he was armed and that gave him the power, not the right, the power to intervene. He was told not to intervene. He defied police orders and it defies my moral consciousness as to how a court of law simply does not look at that.

I don't question the idea of community watch organizations, I don't question the right of citizens to bear arms, even concealed weapons if they are trained. That's not the issue here. The issue is the police said, "Go away" and my experience with police is if they tell you go away, you should go away. That's their job and they risk everything every day for their work. Let's give them some credit here. They said the right thing to Mr. Zimmerman.

The third thing that surprised me here was the jury. I was surprised about the jury even before some of the jurors started talking on the radio and the television. At that point, I was no longer surprised. I was mortified as to the nonsensical logic or lack of logic that was going through some of their heads. The whole basis of trial by jury is a jury of peers. This was not a jury of peers for George Zimmerman by any stretch of the imagination.

This was a strange jury to say the least. How odd it is that it used to be that all male juries were considered unfair. Now it's an all-female jury that is unfair. But the fact of the matter is both in gender, race or ethnicity, it was not a balanced jury. The quality of the jurors was really up to the prosecution and the defense. How they decided on these six people is something I have not studied that but it seems to me after having listened to their logic, the prosecution really was without any clue as to how to talk to them, without any clue whatsoever as to what was on their minds. They misjudged the jury. They did not know which buttons to push, which strings to pull, and the result was that the jury heard twenty-six pages of instruction on technical issues that focused on a four- or five-minute part of the entire episode in which they made the determination without any corroborated evidence that Trayvon Martin, a minor, was intent on murder and that George Zimmerman fired at close range, that he had no other option, that his life was in danger. They know that he killed Trayvon Martin but they don't know definitively as to how George Zimmerman came to the decision that his life was completely in danger.

I wasn't in many fights in high school. Luckily nature or God endowed me with a big frame and that scared off most people. I would really have had no ability to defend myself but I was witness to a number of after school fights. It seems that every once in a while, fifteen-, sixteen-, seventeen-year-old boys schedule fights and they are usually between the better fighters so that they could be real gladiator matches. And as a bookish, Jewish kid growing up in Baltimore, I was in awe of people who could fight. The fights that I did see, which were always on the grounds of the elementary school (because if they were on the high school grounds, I guess they could have gotten in more trouble), were vicious affairs and punches were really flying. I never saw a fight with a weapon.

And in this case, other than certain claims about the use of concrete, there was no blade, there were no brass knuckles, there was no hammer, screwdriver, or pistol involved. I don't know the statistics but I think if we did a search across police records in which police intervened in high school fights among sixteen- and seventeen-year-olds that were fistfights, that the mortality rate is not very high. People generally don't get killed in fistfights. And so the jury somehow made the determination that Trayvon Martin was a homicidal criminal and that George Zimmerman only had a single remedy and that was to shoot him through the heart at point blank range. Maybe that was the only good thing here. I truly hope the kid didn't feel too much pain before his eyes closed forever.

All these points bother me tremendously about this case. The jury was not a jury of peers but this is the law and this is what has to be lived with at this point in time There are other legal avenues to have this thing explored, but for me personally justice has not yet been served.

On the other hand, what was not surprising, and this is from the context of American history, is that the person who died here was a young Black male. We all know the statistics when we are looking at crime within the Black community, which needs much more airing, when it has to do with incarceration rates, when it has to do with unemployment rates - the highest in the country is that cohort, nineteen percent unemployment, is among Black males. At that rate, crime can't be far away.

If we go back in American Jewish history to the Lower East Side, it was not the Mrs. Goldberg show. There was a great deal of crime in the Jewish slums, especially when unemployment rates were very, very high. There was also genuine tension between the Jewish community, uptown and downtown and the NYC police department who in 1910 openly blamed NY's Jews for half the crime in the city. Anti-Semitism among New York's Irish and German was the rule, not the exception, and the old line Dutch and English were no different. In other words, for much of American history racial and ethnic animus are sadly never far from the surface in daily life, politics and the courts.

Luckily, race did not enter the trial directly in the Zimmerman case. The Martin family has done a good job of tamping down that card. It's not clear whether that will prevail or not, but for the time being it has not factored in directly or legally. If the federal government goes for a hate crime, then that will be raised again, but we all know the profile, we all know the differentials in rates of execution between White prisoners and

Black prisoners, the rate of arrests for drug crimes between young Black men and young White men. There's no way around it so that's the part that didn't surprise me. It's a sad fact of American history that issues of race and racism have been a rather consistent factor.

We are better than we have been. This is not WWI and Woodrow Wilson officially declaring the segregation of the American army. This is not the 1890s and the Supreme Court coming up with *Plessy v Ferguson*. We're on this side of 1954. We are on this side of 1964 but we're not there yet. As one person said, there's still a crack in the Liberty Bell. It's not all liberty. It's not all freedom yet.

And finally, from a Jewish point of view and this is what I shared with the broader congregation in my E-KI column, what does Judaism have to say about this very difficult situation? What came to mind actually occurred to me while we were in Israel. We did things a little backwards on this point in our trip. We saw the grave of Itzhak Rabin first and then we passed in our bus by Rabin Square where Israelis have marked off the place where Rabin was assassinated. Rabin's death continues to traumatize Israel just as the memories of Lincoln and JFK's murders haunt Americans.

Rabin's assassin was an Orthodox Jewish student at Bar Elan University who was well versed in Jewish law. He had taken it into his head that Itzhak Rabin was a *Rodef*. We all know the word Rodef in Philadelphia because of our sister congregation Rodeph Shalom, which means pursuer of peace, but the word Rodef in Hebrew by itself and is a legal term in Jewish Halacha—and remember that until the emancipation and Jews becoming citizens of the United States, Jews always had their own courts - so there is a whole corpus of Jewish law that is called *Halacha*.

There is a category in Jewish Law called *Rodef*. *Rodef* is a person who is intent on a crime that rises to the level of capital punishment and needs to be intercepted immediately. With respect to a person intent on murder, or a person intent on rape, Jewish law theoretically allows for a bystander, in extrajudicial fashion, to intercept a *Rodef* and kill them. Yigal Amir made the assumption that Yitzhak Rabin, because he was willing to trade land for peace, was a *Rodef* and therefore Amir was authorized by Judaism to kill, murder/assassinate the Prime Minister of the state of Israel. In short, it is a form of vigilantism. There were some rabbis that said absolutely that this was a *Rodef* situation. The majority said no. Obviously the state said no and Amir went to jail.

To me, "Stand your ground" and the decision that George Zimmerman made, from a Judaic point of view, are misappropriations of the idea of *Rodef*. The whole concept of *Rodef*, or even more importantly how to intercept the *Rodef*, how to go beyond the law, is a big question. We are entitled to self-defense. We are allowed to protect our homes. But how far can you go in taking the life of another to preserve society, to preserve yourself, to preserve another person is at best blurry.

The Zimmerman verdict, unfortunately, seems to give some sanction to the idea that killing the *Rodef* is a discretionary call that can be easily defended. In my view, there is great danger in this—that it is nihilistic and threatens the general security of society. If I don't like you, I don't like the way you talk to me, and I determine that you might threaten me, can I shoot you? We don't need to get into that as a society. We already have enough problems.

So we are faced with a moral dilemma in this country. We have laws that need to be assessed, and we have a national consciousness that needs to be assessed, all questions raised by the death of a minor and the exoneration of the man who took his life. It is a painful moment. I am glad that up to the present, civil disobedience has mostly been quiet, and I hope it continues that way. I certainly hope that in the weeks ahead we will not have a short news cycle but that we will dig a little deeper and try to understand the relationship between law and justice both in the United States and in our own Jewish tradition.

A Blessing for Everything

September 4, 2013, Erev Rosh HaShanah 5774

Sometime in the 1970s, Americans started to use the phrase "Have a nice day."
    Or "have a good day."
The phrase spread like a brush fire.
    The Acme cashier ended her transaction with "Have a nice day."
    At the bank, "Have a nice day."
    News broadcasters at 9:00 a.m. would sign, "Have a nice day."
    At the dry cleaner's, "Have a nice day."
    Your bill at a restaurant, "Have a nice day."
    The scheduler at the end of a doctor's appointment as you hobble out on your broken ankle, "Have a nice day."
    By 1980, everywhere you went, it was "Have a nice day, have a nice day, have a nice day."
Of course, we weren't the only country in the world:
France: "Bon journee" almost sounds like "Have a good day."
Germany: "Gutentag"—didn't quite feel sincere
Spanish-speaking countries settle on "Tenga un good day."
And in Israel, the literal version "Yom Tov" leaves one unsure
    If you were wished a good day or with a gnawing uncertainty that
    Today was a major Jewish holiday and you didn't know about it.

Cynics, grumps, and other malcontents found ways of saying "Have a good day" in their own special way. For example, at the end of sentencing, a

judge might say, "You are hereby sentenced to twenty years. Have a good day!" Polite bank robbers grabbed their loot and said to the nervous clerk, "Have a nice day." The scariest spin was offered by Clint Eastwood, "Make my day." Then. of course, George Carlin once did a whole routine on "I don't want to have a nice day."
Every once in a while, usually at a discount department store, a cashier will finish up
With "Have a blessed day."
Sometimes, I really like that
Confident in their faith
A lot higher in octane than a mere "Have a good day"
And as for "Have a nice day," almost childish in comparison.
Now, if we compare "Have a good day" with "Have a blessed day" philosophically
A huge gap opens up between the two valedictions.
"Have a good day" is something an Aristotle or a Plato might have said.
    It posits the idea of the good
    A secular, rational proposition
By contrast, "Have a blessed day" or its variant "blessed" day
    Is loaded with theological implications.
    Who blessed the day?
    Who singled you out to be blessed?
    Did you earn your blessing, or is it random?

Now, I realize every time we sneeze, and someone says, "God bless you,"
    they are not evangelizing or challenging someone's agnosticism.
    It's something you say, like "gesundheit."
    Then again, I never heard an atheist with hay fever tell a
        Well-wisher to retract a "God bless you."
Is there really a difference between "Have a good day" and "Have a blessed day"?
    What makes for a good day?
    You feel good
    An old friend calls
    The price of gas drops 20 cents
    Your least favorite coworker takes the day off
    Is it clear skies for a pilot?
    Calm waters for a ship's captain?

200 points up for the Dow Industrials by 9:42
Perhaps an A in Algebra
They all make a day good.
What about a blessed day? What makes a day blessed?
A ray of light?
A perfectly formed rainbow?
A sudden feeling of inner peace?
Accidentally finding a photo of a long-deceased loved one you miss terribly?

Is good always random?
Is blessed always intended?
Is the sense of experiencing a blessing in life delusional, the suspicious Stuff of the "true believer"
Is it the reward of faith?
Can an atheist have a sense of blessedness?
In Judaism, we are taught to say one hundred blessings a day
So even if we don't have a blessed day, we can have a day of blessings.
The first ninety-five are all required, embedded in our daily services and minyans.
Five more, we are taught, are "user's choice."
It's just like in *Fiddler on the Roof*,
The old rabbi tells his followers, "There is a blessing for everything."
He is then challenged, "Is there a blessing for the czar?"
You know the answer: "God bless the czar and . . . keep him from us!"
If you open a traditional prayer book, you will actually find blessings for everything.
A blessing for eating a potato
seeing a tree with blossoms on it
seeing a scholar
seeing a secular ruler
smelling a fine perfume
washing one's hands
hanging a mezuzah
rainbows, thunder, and lightning
earthquakes
seeing the ocean (particularly appropriate for this Rosh HaShanah)
seeing a destroyed synagogue

seeing a rebuilt synagogue
bad news or good news
getting a new suit or dress
seeing six hundred thousand Jews together in one place
or, in our case, seventy-five members at the annual meeting of the congregation
In fact, there are really two different kinds of blessings

1) a benediction, a *b'rachah*, a formulaic expression of thanks and praise
2) a gift, a very special gift, a gift from God

B'rachah/b'rachot come in two forms: long and short
Long ones, *Baruch atah Adonai Eloheinu Melech haolam* either stand alone
    Like *Shehecheyanu* or begin a paragraph long prayer like a full
    Friday night Kiddush
Short *b'rachot* are used to end those long paragraphs.
These formula blessings keep us in good spiritual shape.
Constant reminders of all the things that enrich life and give it
    Meaning and purpose.
Our tradition of saying lots of little blessings, hopefully, keeps us ready to see the
Other types of blessings in our lives, the big blessings, the gifts in life that seem to define our essence as good people
The blessing of new life
The blessing of finding love and a partner
The blessing of peace
    Who remembers VE Day or VJ Day?
    Or Israel's victory in '67
The blessing of having a true friend
The blessing of a good teacher
A good doctor,
A good rabbi,
The blessing of a short sermon?
Rabbi Abraham J. Heschel, one of the outstanding rabbis of the twentieth century, was
    A rabbi who walked with Martin Luther King
    A scholar whose philosophical treatises are written like poetry

Talked about Judaism as the experience of "radical amazement"
A feeling that just being alive and experiencing the world is
Amazing
My religious studies teacher in college described Heschel as
The kind of person who would walk around a corner
And say wow.

During the course of the last year, we have experimented with the use of Visual *t'filot* or visual prayer at KI.

The cantor has done the lion's share of the work, but so have dozens of our *b'nai mitzvah* students.

Two things are very clear from this experience: most of us see the blessings in life either in natural beauty or in the beauty of acts of loving kindness. Rosh HaShanah is a similar annual religious exercise
Not just a chance to say some of our favorite blessings from the liturgy
But to hit the refresh button of life with the hope of seeing life and family and faith as gifts for which we should be deeply grateful.

The Torah begins not only with an account of creation but also with the message that
Existence is inherently good, that life is a blessing and love a gift.
The Talmud, the great classic work of the rabbis, begins with a tractate on blessings, a training manual on how to see the blessings in our lives and how to respond to them.
The blessing of life and the benedictions of faith are Judaism's eternal dance with radical amazement and sacred living.

But what happens when life is cruel? When our blessings turn into pain, when life is too hard to allow us to thank you for clouds and rainbows and perfumes?
What do we do then?
Are we to go into denial or become bitter or disconnect ourselves and drown in the deep waters of depression?
What if life has become a curse and not a blessing?
Then what, then what do we do?
I find a great deal of wisdom in one of Judaism's mourning rituals.
It is called *k'riah*.
Just before the funeral service begins, we gather and stand in a family circle.
Then, we attach a black ribbon to our outer garment.

A blessing is then recited acknowledging our lack of ability to always understand
> Life's crazy twists and turns.

We are asked to bless at the moment life seems devoid of blessing.
We are challenged to affirm what is true and abiding in our lives;
> Family love, undying memories, the strength provided by
>> Enduring friendships.

The ribbon is then cut to symbolize the torn heart beating inside our chests.
Those who see the ribbon know to be kind and gentle in our presence.
Life is fleeting, our tradition teaches us.
Learn to recognize our blessings as they occur.
Accept the blessings of care and comfort
Don't pretend your heart isn't torn.
It's OK to display your pain on the outside, until it subsides, even a little,
On the inside.

If we are really lucky, we will have many opportunities to experience the
> Blessings we yearn for, as children, young adults, middle aged
> And seniors. Each phase of life has its blessings.

If we are mindful of our tradition or moved by our own inner sensibility,
> We will also find ways to state the blessings which define birth,
> Growth, marriage, the seasons, our history, and all of creation.

In Judaism, there is a blessing for everything.
There is also the realization that everything is a blessing, a gift from some transcendent, eternal source, way bigger than us.

On this Rosh HaShanah, let us join together in saying the blessings of our faith and let us affirm together that life itself, the universe we inhabit, and our tradition of Torah and mitzvot are all blessings.

May you be inscribed for a year of peace and many blessings.

Amen.

The Blessing of Peace

September 5, 2013, Rosh HaShanah Morning 5774

I led a group to Israel this July. When we returned, the big question everybody asked was "Did Egypt impact you? How about Syria? Did you see anything?" Well, it's as if you visited Washington and there was a problem in Boston, you wouldn't really be confronted by what was happening, except as events unfolded on TV. Despite the turmoil in the Middle East, it was almost as if we were in a bubble—a steel bubble but a bubble nonetheless.

In Jerusalem, we were wowed by the supermodern surface train system that has changed the whole city. The Israel Museum is completely refurbished. Sometimes a well-spent $150 million can really show in a good way.

In Tel Aviv, they are building like crazy. The city council just approved plans for an eighty-story building. Whole new upscale neighborhoods have popped up overnight. Our guide bragged that the construction crane is the national bird of Israel.

In Ashkelon, the world's largest desalinization plant is now operational. Israel now can meet all its water needs and more. Israel's coastal Silicon Valley, second in the world to California's Silicon Valley, is now known as Silicon Wadi. Over sixty Israeli companies are now listed with NASDAQ, the most of any country outside of the United States.

Israel, of course, has its share of problems. There is too much poverty. Housing is too expensive. And Western Wall controversies are unending. But all in all, things are going pretty well in Israel.

Short term, even some security situations are improving. The return of the Egyptian military has led to some improvement in Sinai. Hamas, patronized by Egypt's Muslim Brotherhood, is deeply weakened in the West Bank, especially Gaza. The head of the Palestinian Authority is publicly calling for a revolt. For reasons I can't understand, the United States launched a peace initiative that seems to have been buried under other heavier headlines from the region.

To the north, Hezbollah seems diverted by the Syrian civil war, its supply lines endangered, its sponsor compromised. Farther North, Turkey has announced its willingness to participate in a coalition against Syria. Of course, Turkey is always ready to confront Syria. There are territorial, demographic, and other conflicts. The prime minister of Turkey even had to stop his nauseating tirades against Israel because he had to deal with the tens of thousands of Arab and Kurdish refugees streaming into his country.

And while the UK temporarily stepped out, France has stepped up, ready to join in an anti-Assad coalition. It has had long-term interests in Syria and Lebanon and wants to curry favor with the Arab League, which is mildly anti-Assad with the Saudis and Qatar taking the lead.

On the other side of the equation are Russia and Iran. Iran has close ties with Syria's Alawite Shiite rulers and with the proxy Syrian-Iranian militia Hezbollah. In the good old days, Iran used Syria to outflank Saddam Hussein in Iraq. Now Teheran dreams of a Shiite homeland from Iran to Iraq to Syria to Lebanon to the sea.

The Russians are in this mess too. Russia was the patron of a socialist Arab republic back in the Sixties. Egypt and Syria coalesced into the United Arab Republic and took a beating from Israel in 1967. However, Russians never left Syria. They have an important naval presence and have moved additional warships into the Eastern Mediterranean. It's unclear if Russians would seek to intercept a U.S. missile launch and thereby greatly broaden the conflict. No question, Russians will protect Syria in the UN. With President Obama visiting Russia this week, it will be interesting to see if statesmanship is morphed into brinksmanship. For their part, Putin and the Russians dream of their own Moscow-Tehran with big militaries and mutually beneficial psychoses.

So what is going on in Syria, and what does it have to do with the United States and with Israel?

Remember the 1962 David Lean supermovie, *Lawrence of Arabia*, starring Peter O'Toole? During WWI, the British advanced north out of Egypt against the Ottomans. In 1917, they took Jerusalem and pushed on to Damascus. Led by Lawrence of Arabia, they took the Syrian capital and convened an Arab congress, which quickly descended into total chaos. Lawrence then slipped away, and the movie ended.

Syria, like Iraq, was formed by European powers and has been an ungovernable country. Only an iron fist can hold the Syrian state together. After the Turks, an independent monarchy ruled briefly, then the British, followed by the French; and when mainland France divided with the rise of Hitler, Syria came under the control of the pro-Nazi Vichy regime.

Unstable after World War II, Syria was ultimately dominated by the pro-Soviet Ba'ath party. The ruling Ba'ath party, in turn, was controlled by a Shia subethnicity, the Alawites who—under Bashar al-Assad and his father, Hafez al-Assad—dominate the Syrian military. Hafez and Bashar have both proven to be ruthless dictators in league with both Tehran and Moscow.

In 1979, the United States declared Syria to be a terrorist state. Today, Syria is embroiled in a civil war, which has already cost over one hundred thousand lives and resulted in the largest refugee crisis in the world today. Two million Syrians have fled their country; another four million are displaced internally. It is a humanitarian crisis of the highest order and a political nightmare for the whole world.

The question is whether or not the United States should launch a limited tactical missile attack to punish Assad, degrade his delivery capacity, and deter future actions. Or if the same question would be asked in a theological idiom: Should Abraham wield the knife or put it back in the sheath?

Is it time to concur with Isaiah and beat swords into plowshares or follow the prophet Joel and beat plowshares into swords?

For sure, the response of the United States is more complicated to determine than the response of Israel. Israel must and has acted in a number of ways:

The Iron Dome missile defense is up.
Other missile systems are being tested.
Tanks and infantry are being assembled on the northern border.
Gas masks are being distributed.
Gas tanks are being emptied.
The country is on alert.
For the United States, it is different. We do not have a Syrian-Iranian

proxy army on our borders. We do not have an enemy armed with chemical weapons one hundred miles north of our major population centers. We do not have other armed enemies on our borders and a massive enemy population in our midst. We do not have a deranged regime in Iran within missile striking distance making existential threats to us. Israel has to be ready for the worst and, given an opportunity to knock out a major weapon delivery system, will do so and has done so.

What about the United States? First, what are our vital interests? For sure, there are international treaties going back to 1925 prohibiting the use of chemical weapons. Treaties were signed by the United States under President Nixon, and the United States took significant steps to destroy its own stockpile of biological weapons and reduce its chemical weapon capacity.

Second, our enemies, Iran and Syria, are clearly testing our resolve and will continue to do so with the most lethal of results.

Third, our front-line allies—Turkey and Israel and our strategic partner, Saudi Arabia—all favor U.S. action against Syria.

Fourth, the United States has recognized the main council of the anti-Assad forces as the legitimate voice of the Syrian people.

Fifth, Syrians hackers and/or their surrogates have been infiltrating American websites. Failure to act will only embolden Syria to use its chemical weapons again and perhaps not only on its own people but on Israel as well. Failure to act will signal the North Koreans they have options with their huge inventory of chemical weapons. Failure to act will signal Teheran to plow ahead with impunity with its nuclear arms program.

In the world of Holocaust studies, a new term was coined to help explain why the Nazis were able to get away with their program of genocide. That term is *bystanderism*. "Bystanderism" is when good people who have the capacity to do something do nothing in the face of evil.

The United States is not just another county. We claim to be a beacon of light in a darkened world. We have the greatest military in history. Around the world, both good people and evil people look at us. We have a unique responsibility.

How to conduct ourselves, when to intervene, how to intervene, and how much to intervene are all among the deepest questions we are compelled to ask of ourselves.

Burned by WWI, America was slow to respond to Hitler. Today, on the other side of Vietnam, Iraq, and Afghanistan, we are understandably uneasy about any intervention.

Does Syria rise to the level of intervention? Our signature on international treaties, the wishes of some of our closest allies, and some of our worst enemies, all suggest some action is necessary. Our need to contain, degrade, and deter the use of chemical weapons by terrorist states suggests we take action.

In the short term, even a regime change in Syria will not guarantee peace for that country. The Arab Spring unleashed all types of forces in the Middle East. It will take time for a new order to emerge there, as it did in Europe and even this continent.

We now have the military and technological ability to take effective action at a distance without boots on the ground. A well-placed charge at the bottom of the largest dam is all it takes for the structure to lose its integrity and self-destruct.

In a world of asymmetrical warfare and sleeper-cell terrorism, there are always risks. There are even greater risks in doing nothing.

I find myself in a strange place. I am a child of the Sixties who has become pro-military. I am a child of the Vietnam era who rejected the domino theory and did not believe the North Vietnamese posed a threat to the United States. I was uneasy about Iraq and less than enthusiastic about Afghanistan. I have repeatedly thought that it is much easier to get into a war than to get out of one. I am a person who believes that aggressive war is collective psychosis. But I am also the son of a WWII combat vet and a Jew who has lived in Israel, and I know what it takes for that nation to defend itself. A failure to act at this time will put Tel Aviv at risk, as well as Istanbul and Seoul Korea and perhaps even Tokyo. This time, there is real evidence in plain sight.

In the Jewish tradition, the greatest of all God's gifts is the blessing of peace.

Jerusalem means "city of peace." In Hebrew, you don't just say hello. You say, "Peace to you." Global peace was a vision and a goal given to the world by our prophets. They were to teach that the lion and the lamb could live together. Maybe in God's time, that will come true. But for now, the lion is sick and rabid, and the lambs are endangered.

May we be blessed with wisdom.

May we be blessed with strength.

May we never abandon the vision, the hope, of a world in which there is no war and hatred is banished.

May we be blessed with prosperity, justice, and peace in the year ahead. Amen.

The Blessing of Love

September 13, 2013, Yom Kippur Evening 5774

The theme of the High Holy Days this year is Blessings.

Tonight, my topic is the blessing of love. I personally discovered love, or at least, the love of love in 1968—fourteen years old, at the height of my bout with acne, terrified of girls. Then Franco Zeffirelli's *Romeo and Juliet* came out. Laurence Olivier narrated. The theme song "What Is a Youth?" gave the movie wings. And Olivia Hussey, who played Juliet, created a hormonal imbalance in me that took years to overcome. With the help of a few like-minded, lovestruck friends, we began memorizing and acting out the play over and over again.

The best Yom Kippur–related quote from that story belongs to Romeo after he kisses Juliet for the first time, "Sin from my lips? O, trespass sweetly urged! Give me my sin again!"

Love is the most universal of all themes. Teenagers, musicians, writers, philosophers, even theologians all love love. If love itself is not everywhere in this broken world of ours, then the love of love is. You cannot escape a report on love. Even if you fled with Jonah, even there, even in the belly of the whale, is love.

Let's take a love test. What are your favorite songs about love?
"I Wanna Dance with Somebody"
"I Will always Love You"
"She Loves You, Yeah, Yeah"
"In My Life"
"Stop in the Name of Love"

"What the World Needs Now"
"To Sir with Love"
"Baby Love"
"First Time I Ever Saw Your Face"
"My Heart Will Go On"
The list is endless.
How about love in the movies?
Dr. Zhivago
Gone with the Wind
Beauty and the Beast
Bridges of Madison County
Brokeback Mountain
Annie Hall
Sleepless in Seattle

There is no end to cultural representations of love.

Can you imagine opera without love (*La Boheme*, *Tosca*, and *Madame Butterfly*) or Broadway (*West Side Story* or *Les Mis*)? I think the only love story I really don't like is Lancelot and Guinevere.

But what happens when we turn to Judaism? Where's the love? Is love part of our faith? Isn't religious love a Christian idea?

Well, we have all types of love stories too in our tradition. You can thank Adam and Eve for the institution of marriage. Abraham and Sarah for home hospitality. Jacob and Rachel for a paradigm of love's sacrifices. David and Bathsheba for passion. Ruth and Naomi for loyalty.

Solomon and Sheba for courtship. Hosea and Gomer for love's capacity to forgive and reset itself.

There are postbiblical Jewish love stories as well. Golde and Tevye—the unspoken bond. Yentl illustrated irrepressible and forbidden love. Fanny Brice and Nicky Arnstein—love's limits. *Dirty Dancing*—the reality of loving someone beyond our community's borders.

Love is more than a universal theme in the Jewish tradition. It is the heart of the matter. There are three commandments in the Torah "to love":

To love God, as in *v'ahavta*, the most challenging of these mitzvot

To love one's neighbor as oneself (the Golden Rule).

To love the stranger, for you were strangers in the Land of Egypt (from the Book of Exodus).

Love is the basis of all theology and all ethics in the Jewish tradition. Judaism's ethical core is a compound of immanent and transcendent love. Judaism also recognizes the tensions and contradictions in the realm of love. On the one hand, a bride and groom are often referred to as *bashert*. Destined ones, an idea almost approaching the Pauline idea that "what God brings together, no man can render asunder." On the other hand, we allow for divorce and a *get*. I always tell couples who meet with me that the Jewish wedding service does not include the phrase "till death do us part," but that is still the goal.

What is love? Scholars usually divide love into four parts:

1. Love of family
2. Love of friends
3. Romantic love
4. Transcendent love as in love of country, love of freedom, love of God

Some people say the opposite of love is hate; others say love's opposite is apathy and indifference. Some people believe in Virgil's great teaching *amor vincit omnia* or "love conquers all."

Evolutionary biologists see love as a mechanism for survival and a "need" like hunger or thirst. Others see it as a cultural construct that, when properly regulated, promotes loyalty and diminishes the risk of STDs. Freud views it as a neurotic response to separation anxiety. Legal historians view it as a social necessity to limit questions of paternity, parental responsibility, and even inheritance. In all such cases, love is essentially utilitarian and not really of transcendent origin and metaphysical value.

Along those lines, some take tremendous exception to the Crosby, Stills, Nash and Young song, which made it to #14 on the charts in 1970's "Love the One You Are With." Love, they teach, is companionate, not fatuous. Some serious scholars even believe in the Beatles' 1967 #1 song's message, "All You Need Is Love," including its unlikely British nod to the French national anthem. In Chinese, Japanese, Turkish, Turkish, and South Asian cultures are innumerable views and teachings on love as well.

The American psychologist Abraham Maslow believed that family, friendship, and romantic love were essential building blocks in human development and that transcendent love or self-actualization was the highest human need. In his 1956 book *The Art of Loving*, social philosopher

Eric Fromm rooted his controversial theory of love in his earlier Talmudic studies. Love, Fromm taught, is "not a sentiment easily indulged in." He believed that higher love was disintegrating in modern society. "Falling in love," he taught, was more fantasy than reality. True self-love, he said, reminiscent of Leviticus, was necessary to go beyond mere self-centeredness and conceit and begin to see all of humanity in terms of a transcendent love.

For Fromm, love ultimately has four components: care, responsibility, respect, and knowledge. Others argue that love does not have a single essence.

I see love all the time. I also see the consequences of the lack of love. I have stood under the *chuppah* hundreds of times as an officiant, delighted to see the anticipation and hope unique to young love. I have torn divorce gets and heard the cry of abandonment and betrayal.

I believe that the bond of love in the nuclear family has latent nuclear power. The joy of watching a child learn to walk and then talk is incomparable. When a child is kidnapped or molested or killed, no one is immune to the overwhelming feelings which are released. The death of a young person. A life cut short at any age leaves us empty and unsure of how we can love again.

I experienced the love of family in my childhood as a kind of cosmic womb. My base in life is pure love. Like many of you, I have known courtship and early marriage and parenthood: a new universe of meaning and new relationships of my own making that has become my place in the universe. There are billions of people, only a handful are my family and my friends. Yet I know that all those people need their own set of key people to ground them in life.

Now, I can see the world as a grandparent and have experienced the cycle of life with more joy and happiness than I thought possible. I have seen the care of the elderly that approaches the angelic. Sometimes family, sometimes an aide. The power of love is powerful.

But what does it mean to die alone? What does it mean to be homeless and to live unloved on the streets?

What does it mean to become so depressed that you can no longer feel the love for self or others in your heart? To seek escape in addictions and in death. I have seen what it means when love fails to heal only to come back to the conclusion that to love and to be loved is as necessary to life as oxygen and water. The tragedy of losing one's ability to absorb the life-giving properties of love is shattering to family and friends. But it does not diminish the continuing need for life and love.

All of us have learned that love entails sacrifice. Parents sacrifice for kids in little and big ways every day. Married couples have to sacrifice all the time. Whose education is primary? Whose career comes first? Whose dream vacation is delayed or lost or given as a gift or sacrifice of one's own dream?

Military personnel, police, and firefighters are asked to sacrifice for the common good. What does it mean to go on a dangerous mission?

Listen to the words of a young woman, Hannah Szenes, who joined the Haganah and knew she would be called upon to sacrifice her life to try to save her own family: "Blessed is the heart," she wrote on the beach at Caesarea. "Blessed is the heart with the strength to stop its beating for honor's sake."

Two thousand years earlier, Rabbi Akiba faced his own death at that spot, executed by the Romans. Before he died the death of a religious martyr, he explained that in his whole life, he did not understand the meaning of the *v'ahavta* (to love God with all his heart). Only at the point of losing his life for his faith did he understand how big a love he had for his people and his Maker.

May all of us be spared any future need to test our willingness to make an ultimate sacrifice for love. And yet we know that a certain way out there on the emotional horizon, life and love converge into one.

And that is why Yom Kippur is so important. It is our annual chance to atone for any offense against those we love the most, the chance to weigh the consequences of our decisions, to compare personal gains and private hurts, to seek forgiveness in the name of love and with the promise of love renewed. It is our chance to test the proposition that at the heart of life, there is love and that love requires forgiveness.

Love cannot exist without forgiveness. Life cannot endure without love. The blessing of love is a wonderful blessing. It makes life sacred beyond the tests of science and reason. It is as necessary as the air we breathe. It is our hope in death as it is in life.

On this Yom Kippur, let us do our best to atone, to forgive, and to recommit to love with all our hearts, with all our might, and with our souls.

May you be blessed with health, life, and love in the year ahead.

Amen.

The Blessing of Memory

September 14, 2013, Yom Kippur Yizkor 5774

Our theme for these High Holy Days has been Blessings. We started with the concept of blessings in Judaism; studied basic texts about them; and spoke about the blessings of peace, love, and work. Now, in this service of remembrance, let us take a moment or two to consider a final blessing: the blessing of memory.

Zichronom livrachah, we say of our departed loved ones—"May their memories be a blessing."

In King Solomon's beautiful love song, The Song of Songs in the Hebrew Bible, we learn of the relationship of love, death, and memory:

> Let me be a seal upon your heart,
> Like the seal upon your hand.
> For love is as strong as death . . .
> Vast floods cannot quench love,
> Nor rivers drown it.

From these ancient words, an ever-new message can be learned.
Death is not stronger than love.
Death can only claim the body, the physical, the perishable.
Love itself does not die.
Loyalty does not die and

presence does not die.

Our souls, our essence, our inner spirit
Which puts life in life, vitality in life, and meaning in life
Does not die.
It goes on in memory, in the heart, and in the soul.

I was once sternly reprimanded in a patient's room at a local hospital
By an angry physician who said I was encouraging denial,
That dead is dead, and that any other advice was ill-informed and unhealthy.

Perhaps from a purely scientific view, a view focused on the body,
The good doctor was right.
But he wasn't right enough.
Because there is an aspect of life that cannot be reduced to the laws of nature.
Our nature as human beings includes the rational, the intuitive, the spiritual, and the metaphysical.

We are more than flowers that fade.
We live in the land of life
And the realm of memories,
Which never die.

Faith in Art: Visual Culture and the Future of Judaism

Winter 2013 CCAR Journal: The Reform Jewish Quarterly

In December 1969 I went to Israel for the first time. Everything about that trip was transformative. Traveling with my summer friends from Camp Harlem (UAHC), flying on a "Jewish airplane," and seeing the coastline of the Jewish state for the first time were powerful experiences for me. But perhaps the most surprising experience during those magical two weeks was my encounter with public art in Israel. By age fifteen, I had already visited numerous leading art museums with my family. My childhood synagogue, Oheb Shalom in Baltimore, Maryland, itself was an important architectural statement created by Walter Gropius, a leader in the Bauhaus movement. But nothing fully prepared me for coming face to face with powerful, dramatic, public art portraying Jewish and Israeli themes with boldness and a uniquely modern beauty. After arriving at the old Ben Gurion airport with its open metal hangers, cracked sunflower seed-covered sidewalks, and pungent cigarette smoke, we were whisked off toward Haifa. Because it was already night and I was exhausted, I did not really "see" Israel until morning. Stepping out of the old guest house, I was immediately confronted with David Polus's little-known sculpture *Israel Saba*, a two-figure metal statute, which could have worked perfectly as the cover for Amos Elon's iconoclastic 1971 book, *The Israelis: Founders and Sons*.

For me, Polus's work provided the perfect Zionist framework for my first journey to Israel: a biblical grandfather walking with his arm around a farmer-soldier *kibbutznik*. Much more than my first encounter with the Western Wall, Polus's sculpture, the Billy Rose Art Garden in Jerusalem, and the white modernism of Tel Aviv connected me visually with Israel and instilled a sense of excitement in me about the possibilities of a modem Jewish culture.

Although art and architecture remained a private interest for many years, my decision to study to be rabbi eventually took priority and other interests prevailed. In recent years, however, I found myself increasingly returning to images as a source of religious inspiration and Judaic knowledge. Quite unexpectedly, my vision was threatened by premature cataracts and a retina that detached twice. Surgery, eye patches, and double- and triple-vision all made sight much more important to me. I started to look at the world differently. I discovered a universe of discourse among the visually impaired. The Macular Degeneration group, which met at the far end of our synagogue, were no longer exotic guests, but "my people." My sight improved and ultimately was fully restored; however, my thinking about the importance of the visual in life and in the dynamic of the synagogue will never recover.

The New Union Haggadah:
Exodus as a Theme in American
History and Culture

2014

Few biblical themes are as ubiquitous in American history as that of the Exodus. From the Puritans to the Black church to the Mormons to the Civil Rghts movement and more, the escape of the ancient Hebrews from Egypt and their long journey to the Promised Land has served as a paradigm for freedom and redemption for Americans of every faith, race, and nationality since colonial times. Conversely, the Exodus has also served as a moral measure by which expulsions, population transfers, and forced migrations have been evaluated by many Americans as antithetical to their national ethos.

America's topography, a subcontinent framed by two oceans, provides a physical basis for New World adaptations of the Exodus story. First, Native Americans leave their places of Asian origin and cross a sea on "dry ground" before beginning their wanderings in an unknown land. On the Atlantic side, particularly among pious English colonists, America was viewed as a promised land reachable only after a near-miraculous and often horrifically dangerous passage across the sea. For many Jewish immigrants to America, the North Atlantic Passage to their new Zion was deeply symbolic. Pacific immigrants also adopted the same redemptive metaphor in their journey to America.

The depth of the identification with the Exodus narrative in the newly independent United States is symbolized by proposals both by Benjamin Franklin and Thomas Jefferson for the first Great Seal of the United States in 1776. Franklin envisioned a dramatic picture of Moses with his hand over the sea opposite a defiant Pharaoh, with signs of God's support for the Hebrews in the background. Franklin's motto on his design for the seal declared, "Rebellion to Tyrants is Obedience to God." Similarly, Jefferson envisioned a picture of the Children of Israel being led through the wilderness by a pillar of fire. Remarkably, both Franklin and Jefferson were deists whose personal philosophies maintained that God created the universe and then withdrew from it. However, American independence must have struck both of them as providential, thereby allowing them to embrace a God of history, at least for that moment.

Nowhere in American history is the Exodus story more central than in the African American experience. Already early in the history of the Black church, the stories of Jesus and Moses were fused, and the story of the Exodus was made inseparable from the passion of Christ. White abolitionists too seized upon the Exodus story for inspiration and proof of their cause, as did everyone involved in the Underground Railroad, from those "going through the sea" to those splitting the waters. Subsequently, internal migrations of American Blacks such as the exodus of 1879 also specifically referenced the biblical story in name and spirit. In post–World War II America, Martin Luther King Jr. was seen by his supporters as a kind of modern Moses who led his Exodus but, like his biblical predecessor, tragically did not make it to his Promised Land.

Indeed, little in American history and culture was untouched by the story of the Exodus of the Hebrews through the Sinai. Images of Daniel Boone leading pioneers into the wilderness have a biblical feel about them. Internal explorers such as Lewis and Clark, as well as John C. Fremont (accompanied by a Jewish artist and photographer Solomon Nunes Carvalho), were perceived as American incarnations of Moses's famed scouts. More explicitly, the prophetic career of the founder of the Mormon Church and the dramatic journey of the members of the Church of Latter-Day Saints is perfectly synchronized with the biblical Exodus.

Popular culture in the United States is also infused with Exodus themes. Best known is the 1956 classic film *The Ten Commandments*. Four years later, the dramatic story of modern Israel's birth, complete with emotionally compelling music, was captured in the film *Exodus*. With its explicit biblical themes, the movie played a significant role in deepening support for the Jewish state in the United States. More recently, the animated 1998 film *The Prince of Egypt* helped introduce the Exodus theme to millions of young and largely secular Americans.

The biblical story of the Exodus also casts a moral shadow across darker episodes in American history. The Trail of Tears removal of Native people under President Jackson, the shortlived 1862 expulsion of American Jews by General Grant from areas under his command in the South, and the internment of Japanese Americans during World War II all have qualities of being an anti-Exodus unworthy of either the biblical Exodus or the American promise of freedom. Increasingly problematic among American Jews was the American failure to lead a redemptive Exodus of Jews from Europe during the final years of the Holocaust.

For American Jews, the Passover story found its most dramatic expression in the Soviet Jewry movement. "Let my people go" found a new meaning among American Jews as they worked for the exodus of Jews from the Soviet Union. Beginning in 1964, American Jews increasingly rallied in support of "refuseniks" and prospective Russian Jewish immigrants, culminating in the 1987 March on Washington, DC, which attracted 250,000 supporters, the largest gathering in the history of the American Jewish community.

In the final analysis, for most American Jews, the Haggadah combines the American belief in freedom with Judaism's ancient hope for redemption. The story of our ancestors' flight from Egypt becomes one with our own ancestors' decision to leave Germany, Poland, and Russia and come to the American promised land. It has also served as the foundation of our communal ethos that so often equates deliverance in our own time with social justice and Jewish activism. Lastly, for American Reform Jews, the inherent Zionism of the traditional call for a return to Jerusalem is no longer viewed in terms of a potential conflict of dueling nationalities but as a uniquely comfortable synthesis of the deepest universal and particular aspects of our ever-redemptive Jewish tradition. Indeed, for most American Jews, it remains existentially possible to see ourselves as if we personally had gone forth from Egypt over and over again!

Second Isaiah: "A Light to the Nations" and the Mission of Reform Judaism

September 24, 2014, Rosh HaShanah Evening 5775

I have always been a Reform Jew
I grew up Reform
My childhood home was Reform
and our synagogue, Oheb Shalom, in Baltimore, is Reform.

As a congregation, Oheb is an exact parallel to KI
Established by traditional German Jews before the Civil War
Quickly turned toward Reform
Then radicalized.

The synagogue grew by leaps and bounds in late nineteenth century
Built a magnificent cathedral like structure in
The emerging German Jewish uptown of 1890s
On Eutaw Street in Baltimore
    modeled after great synagogue of Florence, Italy.

During the 1950s, the congregation started moving assets toward the suburbs
Built a supermodern new cathedral structure, designed by Walter Gropius, a Bauhaus architect, and thrived.

The synagogue-based Reform Judaism of my youth was formal, impressive and transcendent
We had a large usher corps
Complete with vested suits and white flower boutonnieres;
All holiday seats were ticketed, front and back
Decorum was perfect.

Our clergy wore flowing robes
On their heads, pillbox hats, equal at
Least to cardinals in the Vatican.
When they entered the sanctuary
The congregation rose
As if the Supreme Court had just been convened.

Our Rabbis spoke in deep FM voices
Directly from Sinai, so it seemed.
For the benediction,
They raised their hands above us
Like Moses at the sea
And sent us forward like the ancient Hebrews
Traveling under divine protection.

Our prayer book, the little but well-written *Union Prayer Book*,
Fit in the palm of our hands
It was small, elegant, Shakespearian in tone
And reformed, not just Reform, in theology.

The *Union Prayer Book* was filled with memorable passages.
"May the time not be distant" the concluding prayers began
And with that, I knew the end of the service was very near
About seven minutes
And also that my favorite chocolate button cookies were waiting
    in the auditorium to be my Sabbath delight at the Friday night *Oneg*
      As well as . . . experimenting with my first cups of coffee
        Actually, I only added a little coffee to my sugar
          And couldn't wait to get to the sweet sandy bottom of the cup.

Sunday school was good too
Even though many of the teachers were strict
The school was so big we needed a safety patrol
I rose to the rank of captain, blue badge.

We also always collected *Keren Ami* every Sunday
Everyone brought pennies
The change was counted
using the gold standard of 1960s accounting
and taken to the lady in the glass both
In front of the school office
She looked like a tollbooth collector on I-95
    Or the outside ticket person in a movie theater
Her son became a rabbi and then gave up the pulpit
    To become a stand-up comedian.

In my childhood home
Friday night was temple night
We made the blessings at home, ate dinner, and went to temple.
The kitchen table was covered with purple uniongrams
A magnet eventually was attached to the fridge
"Friday night is Temple night"
and that wasn't a reference to Owls' basketball.

On Sukkot, the synagogue was packed with kids for the evening family service
we wrapped canned food in tin foil
And would bring them up to the altar to be placed
Under our designer indoor sukkah
With its massive indoor cornucopia
Ties and jackets and skirts were required
Even for six- and seven-year-olds.

It was all normal, natural, and authentically Jewish to me
It was my habitat
It was totally comfortable
I was a young Jewish nestling and
Reform Judaism was my religious habitat.

Of course, I knew there were other types of Judaism
My paternal cousins who lived on the same street were Conservative Jews
But we went to temple more than they did
And their cousins who lived one block away
were Modern Orthodox and they were always at synagogue.
Their dad was president of their synagogue.
The corner shul was always packed.
Boys in half tucked-in white shirts
from the Yeshiva turned the three number dials on the wall
      so the congregation knew what page the prayer leader was on.
The women were packed in the back on the sides and the lobby was
jammed with baby strollers
like a busy street in Tel Aviv.

I admit I liked going to shul as well as temple
But shul was exotic.
My Judaism, my Reform Judaism,
on the other hand
fit me like a tailor-made bar mitzvah suit.

It wasn't until my college years that I learned how big and divided
The Jewish religious spectrum really is.
To my surprise, I learned that not everybody in the Jewish community
Liked Reform Judaism.
My cousins teased me a little
but those early taunts didn't make a dent
and were mostly about our ancient cantor
who sounded like a car on a freezing morning
with insufficient cranking power.

Around fifteen years old, I decided to wear a yarmulke at services
No one knew the word *kippah* then.
You had to supply your own yarmulke too
and tallit were completely out of the question
      at Oheb Shalom

I also decided we needed a more intense Passover Seder at home
So I did a lot of research

That started early in my life and
Wrote out notes on a whole pack of 3x5 index cards.
Basically I took my family captive
For what must have felt like forty years in the desert
for several years during Passover.

Summer camp, camp Harlam,
Introduced me to Jewish guitar music
This was long before Debbie Friedman
    She actually showed up at Camp Harlam
    at age sixteen
    very whiny and always overly-dramatic
We mostly sang civil rights, songs from the Black Church and
Peace songs
Khalil Gibran replaced Moses as our main prophet.

My 1950s Ozzie and Harriet Judaism started going hippie.
One of my uncles told me, with total disapproval
that my confirmation service was pacifist, probably Hindu
    and was, furthermore, Jewishly inauthentic.
But I thought the "Great Mandala" by Peter, Paul and Mary was Jewish
in spirit
    and at least one of them was Jewish.
    I wasn't sure who.
    Of course, their names didn't help.

In college, I taught in the local Reform Sunday School
starting in my sophomore year
My roommate was the music teacher
The kids wouldn't sing any of the songs included in the curriculum, they were terrible!
So we started the assembly with Simon and Garfunkel's
"Feeling Groovy."
They sang and danced and acted silly until the old rabbi stormed
in and screamed at who was responsible for defiling his temple with
libertine music.
We raised our hands and were fired on the spot.
Reform Judaism wasn't groovy yet.

So initially I tried going to Orthodox services on my own
There was a little shul near my campus
in Lancaster, PA.
By then I could read, even translate, a little Hebrew
But I couldn't get my huge tent-like Tallit to stay on
It kept sliding off my shoulders
and my cousins weren't around to help.
I also didn't know how to daven!
Were they really reading all those prayers that fast?
Why were some words called out?
Why were other parts mumbled?
Sometimes congregants were making sounds like I did in a swimming pool
Playing motorboat as a kid.

However, I kind of liked the rocking back and forth part at services
but I couldn't figure out
When to do the Jewish "cha-cha" or go up on my toes, or turn
Side by side
Sometimes people weren't even using the same book
And at this shul, almost nobody was on the same page.

Eventually, I realized I was not on the same page as Orthodoxy either!
I didn't believe in most of Orthodoxy's key concepts including the coming of the Messiah, the rebuilding of the Temple of Jerusalem and the physical resurrection of the dead
Things like looking for kosher certification on bottles of water seemed
Overboard to me.
Separate seating of men and women now seemed wrong, almost a civil rights issue and the
idea of women not being allowed to sing in front of men was ridiculous.
An Orthodox Passover seder seemed more like slavery than redemption to me
And a strict observed Sabbath was liked being chained…
Only the sense of community and the use of Hebrew made any sense to me during those years.

What I really needed to learn was the deep religious basis of my own Reform Judaism.

Embracing traditional Judaism had become impossible for me,
It wasn't mine,
But Reform was still not fully restored as authentic in my mind either. It was Judaism-like.

It was no longer a question of how much Hebrew or how long services were.
I needed to know the ideas behind Reform,
the guiding principles.
What it really stood for.

So I began to study the matter
I studied both the history of Reform and the history of anti-Reform Judaism.
Ultimately what I discovered was more than satisfactory, it was truly grounding!
I discovered that Reform Judaism is principled, dynamic, and adaptive.
That in theory, it really worked for me, with or without Simon and Garfunkel.

So what did I learn about "my Reform Judaism?"
Basically, Reform has experienced several distinct phases.
Today, we are living through
the latest internal battle to determine the character of Reform Judaism.

For its first 120 years, Classical Reform Judaism was basically grounded in three major principles:

1. Ethical monotheism
2. Progressive revelation
3. The Mission of Israel

Its only purpose was to modernize Jews and Judaism.

Ethical monotheism taught that there is one God and that God wants us to be good people. Ethical monotheism also had the effect of denationalizing and de-ethnicizing early Reform Jews who wanted to become Jewish Germans, Jewish Englishmen, and Jewish Americans and did not want to remain as outsiders in their host societies. Jews wanted to act like Episcopalians and pray like Episcopalians but still wanted to be Jews or at least Jewishopalians.

Idea 2, Progressive Revelation combined ideas from the Torah, social Darwinism, and nineteenth-century optimism. Progressive Revelation meant that Judaism not only changes over time but also gets better as time goes on, especially in modern times. In this view, modern Judaism is better than medieval Judaism and is successfully recapturing our tradition's original religious insights blocked by centuries of Talmudic obscurantism. It meant that organ music and decorum were better than the cacophony of the Orthodox shul and eventually that Joan Baez and Pete Seger were more Jewish than Bach or Haydn.

The final original Reform doctrine was the mission of Israel. The mission of Israel, or the reason to be Jewish, was to bring the idea of ethical monotheism to the world. It was a defense against assimilation and missionary activity. We needed to stay Jewish because we had a global mission, a specifically Jewishopalian mission.

The mission of Israel doctrine is highlighted in the middle stained-glass window in our sanctuary to my left and to your right. It explores the teaching of Second Isaiah as understood by the window's amazing artist, Jacob Landau. "I have chosen you," said the Isaiah of the Exile over 2,500 years ago, "to be my servant, to be a light to the nations [or *la-goyim*]!" During the course of the holidays, we will look at our windows during every service as we celebrate the fortieth anniversary of their installation.

Without question, the mission of Israel doctrine animated the teachings of KI rabbis from David Einhorn in 1865 to Bertram Korn in 1965. It urged us to take the lead in interfaith work and establish a common ground in the idea of one God among all our neighbors. It made Reform Judaism the public face of Judaism in the larger community and reassured its followers that Judaism was not a liability but a source of empowering pride.

But it was not until this summer that I fully appreciated how important the mission of Israel doctrine has been in Reform Judaism. I finally had the opportunity and privilege of visiting the birthplace of Reform Judaism in Seesen, Germany. Seesen is a little town with mostly half-timber houses in northern Germany, midway between Berlin and Amsterdam, the two main places we visited. The local high school is named after the founder of Reform Judaism, Israel Jacobson. The footprint of the synagogue building, destroyed on Kristallnacht in November 1938, is now a memorial, and several monuments include inscriptions from Jacobson's inaugural 1810 address.

Jacobson's text was from Malachi, the final Hebrew prophet who is represented in the window closest to the bimah on your right. "Have we not all one Father? Has not one God created us?" Jacobson piously quoted the last of our prophets.

In the school Jacobson founded in Seesen along with his Temple, forty Jewish and twenty Christian students learned together, a near-miraculous event for Westphalia in 1810. Reform, Jacobson, believed, was the beacon of light that Germany and the world desperately needed. He still may be right.

One hundred twenty years later, during the 1930s, the rise of global anti-Semitism resulted in Reform Judaism tempering its universal vision of ethical monotheism. Ethical monotheism now morphed into a more particularistic monotheistic ethnicity and the particularistic mission of Israel became the general idea of social justice, now called *tikkun olam*. The survival of the Jewish people, not the redemption of the world, became our new mission.

At the heart of neo-Reform was the idea of Jewish peoplehood, the central idea of Zionism and American Judaism's most recent addition, Reconstructionism. Jewish peoplehood, once entirely dismissed by the Reform movement, now became its main pillar. Zionism, Jewish ethnicity, and Yiddishkeit turned the lofty notion of ethical monotheism on its head. In 1900, one went to a Reform Temple to hear Zionism denounced. By 1940, Reform Jews were going to shul to get an update on Zionist efforts in British Palestine. Unlike Classical Reform, the purpose of neo-reform was to Judaize, not to Americanize.

But nothing stays the same for long, and by the end of the twentieth century, Reform Judaism underwent a third metamorphosis. This set of changes was a direct result of the cultural revolutions of the 1960s and early 1970s. The time for "feeling groovy" finally arrived.

Monotheistic ethnicity and peoplehood largely remained in place, as did Social Justice. But Progressive Revelation, once used to de-ritualize Reform, now came to be a justification for restoring discarded ritual practices, like the wearing of kippot, and the basis for the radical expansion of Reform's sociological borders including the acceptance of mixed religious households and same-sex marriage. By the end of the twentieth century, the riptides in the sea of Reform Judaism were both pulling our movement to new and unknown beaches and back out to the sea of traditionalism, both with tremendous power.

At the core of the new Reform Judaism of the 1970s was the idea of personal autonomy. This idea allowed for maximum personal choice in the practice of Judaism. You did your own thing. You could choose never to go to shul or daven wearing a multicolored poncho-like mega-tallit in a classical Reform temple. It also shepherded women into roles of leadership from congregational president to rabbi to cantor.

To hold the ever more complex movement together, a corollary of personal autonomy was proposed and generously called unity in diversity. Reform Judaism, it was now believed, would be the ultimate religious greenhouse in the history of the Jewish people.

However, in 1998, the Central Conference of American Rabbis decided to turn the tide and limit the twin doctrines of autonomy and diversity by writing a new set of Principles for the movement. "We need limits, we need borders, we need rules," we were told. Supporters of the platform cheered the idea of Reform returning to tradition. Its opponents warned that inclusion and personal autonomy were central to the reform experiment in Judaism and that traditionalism alone would not carry the day among the majority of Reform Jews. One speaker even compared Classical Reform to the original sin in the Garden of Eden.

Two major economic downturns early in the twenty-first century, the aging of the baby-boomer generation, the rise of new millennial generations, the unprecedented reemergence of Jewish religious orthodoxy, and the diminishing affiliation trends all combined to confront the Reform movement. After two hundred years of institutional success, Reform Judaism was now at a dangerous crossroads.

Today, Reform Judaism is still the largest movement in American Judaism. But nationally, our numbers, both in terms of the numbers of synagogues and the number of individual members, are down. We lack a consistent ideology and are losing ground to Chabad, the "rent a rabbi" phenomenon, and secularism.

We need a new beacon of light, good navigational tools, and enough confidence to start singing "Feeling Groovy" or "Let It Go" or "Don't Be a Shmoe" or whatever will get the kids, their parents, and grandparents going.

I believe that here at KI we have a winning formula for Reform Judaism. After a four-decade decline, we are growing.

As of this Rosh HaShanah (2014), we are finally back up over one thousand families,

A huge wonderful recovery!

Why? The are several parts to the answer. First and foremost, we are inclusive and open-minded. Jew and gentile both have a seat in this house. A Christian grandmother and a Jewish uncle both can have an *aliyah* here for a family *simcha*.

In this house, love and respect are the founding principles of all our families, straight or gay.

We are thoroughly modern in our thinking and proudly Jewish in our actions. We respect tradition for tradition's sake but also seek innovation to make tradition come alive.

We cherish intellectual and artistic excellence as ways of expressing our views of Judaism.

We love Israel fiercely, and we love humanity passionately. We pursue social justice and *tikkun olam* daily. We delight in lifelong learning. We use technology to amplify our message. We teach c*hesed* or kindness as our first order of business. We are energetic in our efforts to make a modern Reform Judaism live in the hearts of all our members.

Fourteen years ago, when my family moved to Cheltenham, my kids would come home from school and report to us that other kids on the bus said that KI was a church and not a real synagogue. Unbelievably, I heard the same attack again this last week. Two things. First, what's wrong with a church? How can you be incensed by anti-Semitism but say that anti-*goyism* is OK? And who says we are not a real synagogue? That old prejudice has run its course and was never valid in the first place.

This is a house of fifty *b'nai mitzvah* a year.

This is a place for mourners to come and grieve in the safety of their own spiritual homes.

This is a giant Jewish learning center with a big school and an incredible adult ed program.

This is a synagogue with a world-class art museum, which is now challenging us to rethink the prophetic in Jewish life.

This is a synagogue that can boast a strong pulpit, capable lay leadership, and a growing, loyal membership.

I am not sure where the national Reform movement is headed today. But I do know we are ready to do our share in maintaining the integrity and vitality of Reform Judaism.

Inside this house, I know the lights of Judaism are lit. The burners are burning, and we have a hundred more families than last year and continue to grow.

We are strong as a congregation because of our energy, our quality, and our commitment to one another. The name Keneseth Israel means a place for all Jews and all who seek to support our mission. We strive to be a light to our members, our community, and the world.

In the year ahead, let each of us work to make that light brighter and stronger than ever before and may the light of transcendent, eternal source of light help guide us on our way.

Amen.
Shana Tova.

Ahavat Yisrael: Love of Israel

September 25, 2014, Rosh HaShanah Morning 5775

I have been to Israel approximately thirty times.
The first time was December 1969,
I was fifteen. I went with a group of friends from Camp Harlam
    It was the trip of a lifetime.

Taking off in an El Al jet from JFK was an incredible thrill
Seeing the coastline for the first time was ridiculously emotional for me
Like everybody else, I clapped and cheered when we landed in the
    dusty, frontier-like Ben Gurion Airport
    Their palm trees
    Skeletal remains of old aircraft
    Chaos and cigarette smoke everywhere.
    It was amazing.

By the time we got to the *kibbutz* where we stayed our first night
Bet Oren, House of Pine Trees, on the eastern slope of the Carmel
    just below Haifa, it was already night
    the air was crisp and clean
    pine trees gave off their scent willingly in the breeze.
When I awoke in the morning, I walked to the dining hall
Along the way I encountered a piece of art
A statute of an ancient Hebrew prophet with his arm
    around a young strong Jewish pioneer

This was Israel, I thought to myself,
Ancient, modern, courageous, strong, Jewish home.

For a long time, the politics and wars of the Middle East since that
incredible clear morning have made it hard to recapture
that moment.

My earliest relationship with Israel was shaped
By the fact that we had family in Haifa
And by the miracle victory of the 1967 Six-Day War.
Stunned by the Yom Kippur surprise attack in 1973
I became resolute in my support of Israel
And went to live and work in the Huleh Valley
in 1975 right next to Fatah land on the Lebanon border,
complete with nightly rocket attacks
fired by Palestinian guerillas from the other side of the border

Horrified by PLO hijackings and the Munich massacre
I was also confused by the early intifadas
And wrongly felt Israel was too harsh
And was increasingly uncertain about settlement policies in the West Bank.
I was even attracted to Peace Now,
especially after I learned a cousin and army
commander in the IDF supported it

I was also a little defensive about the role Israel was playing in Lebanon
And both hopeful and uneasy about Camp David

I remember Rabin's arm looked like overcooked spaghetti
when he shook hands with Arafat.
His body language suggested the risk was too gray

Like millions of other Jews, I was devastated by Rabin's murder
By another Jew and concerned that civil war
In Israel was no longer unthinkable
Especially as tempers flared over Israel's
"who is a Jew" debate.

Most recently, my thinking on Israel has again been redefined by the
emergence of Hezbollah and Hamas.
With the Islamification of the conflict, it increasingly seems that
    Only hanging tough—real tough—was the only real option.

Where was the Israel of my youth?
That Spartan-like, socialist utopian state?
Where was the spirit of Bet Oren, the crisp newness
    of that kibbutz on a hill overlooking the Mediterranean Sea.

After many trips during the last few years,
I finally happened upon a spot
the SW corner of the Kineret
a grove of pine trees along the beach
which housed the cemetery of Israel's first pioneers.
I was traveling with a group of American Jewish educators
Under the aegis of the Jewish Agency.
Our task was to rethink and reposition Israel more toward
The Center of American Jewish schools' curricula.

In this little cemetery
One of the graves belonged to Rachel
She was the poetess laureate of the *chalutzim*, the early pioneers.
Russian Jewish youth intent on creating a Zionist utopia
    At the eastern of the Mediterranean.

Rachel wrote in terse, precise Hebrew.
Her texts were among the first I studied in *ulpan*.
Now I was standing by her simple grave,
Worn copies of her poems were stuffed into a nearby basket and read
by all who loved her simplicity, her devotion to the land of Israel
and the Zionist dream.
She was afflicted with tuberculosis and died young, banished from her
beloved *kibbutz*,
    The first kibbutz, Degania, by the sea of Galilee.

The spirt of her poetry is still young but
tinged with sorrow, suffering, and love for Zion.

She sang of that place, its landscape, the trees and the stones which would forever define the love affair between the Jewish people and its ancestral homeland.

"Perhaps it was never so,"
The dying poet wrote,
"Perhaps I never woke early and went to the fields
To labour in the sweat of my brow . . .
Nor bathed myself in the calm blue water
Of my Kinneret;
O, my Kinneret,
Were you really there
Or did I only dream of you?"

This summer, decades after my own roller-coaster ride with Israel began, the depth of my tie to Israel was again made manifest.

It began with a triple murder of Jewish teens,
then a revenge killing of an Arab youth,
then rockets and more rockets, hundreds of rockets, thousands of rockets.

Life in Israel lost its carefree nature.
Tourists started slipping away and staying home
Massive bloodthirsty demonstrations against Israel rocked the streets
      of Paris, London, and Berlin.

Israel started to fight back.
An air war was launched.
Skilled IDF spokesmen, native English speakers, vainly
tried to explain to a skeptical press corps and an even more distrustful world
that all precautions were being taken,
that Israel telephoned Gazans and told them to leave their homes in advance of air and artillery strikes;
leaflets were dropped from the sky as well.
All to no avail.

The Iron Dome system went up and performed remarkably well
On-target Hamas rockets were blown from the sky
Off-target rockets were allowed to fall into fields.

Even before the IDF infantry went in
Arab civilian casualties started to mount.

Much of Gaza is densely urban and Hamas terrorists purposefully fired from schools, hospitals, and mosques, sucker punches, which drew Israeli fire from across the border.
If Israel called its operation Protective Edge, I think Hamas should have Called their strategy Operation Human Shield.

Reservists were called up
It seemed to take forever
Limited objectives were announced by Jerusalem.
The vast Hamas tunnel network,
its main project and the core of the Hamas economy were
to be located and destroyed.

In the end, three dozen massive tunnels were rendered inoperable,
hellish maze of underground channels of death.

Today, Rosh HaShanah 5775, was Hamas's planned D-Day,
Thousands of Hamas terrorists would charge through the tunnels as
      Israelis prayed in their synagogues or relaxed at home with family
Tens of thousands were to be slaughtered.
Israel was to be stabbed in the heart, in the stomach, in the eye, with maximum bleeding and pain.

Even if every terrorist was to get killed, it was worth it to Hamas!
Even if women, children, the elderly, hospital patients, and foreign aid workers were to be killed in Gaza when Israel's return fire hit human shields
deliberately set up to be martyrs and PR props,
it was worth it to them

Disproportionally the world screamed
Israeli recklessness,
Genocide!
The invectives flowed like the rockets of Gaza.
No amount of Arab loss of life or destruction of property in Gaza
Gave Hamas pause to think—enough!
Indeed, the greater their losses, the greater their sense of accomplishment!

How, I ask, how do you fight the mass psychosis called Hamas
that loves death and martyrdom above the lives of their own children?

And from the rest of the world, especially the Arab and Muslim world,
not one word about the two hundred thousand dead civilians just one
hundred miles north in Syria
    Butchered in Arab internecine warfare,
not one word about the millions of refugees throughout Mesopotamia,
not one word about ISIS and the suffering of the Yazidis and the Kurds
in Iraq.

    Indeed, in one news report, a Kurdish man was interviewed in front of his former home, totally destroyed by ISIS forces. "No one cares about us," he lamented. "If only my home had been bombed by Israel, then, at least, we would get some sympathy."
    You didn't have to be a genius to understand that if Israel had wanted to kill tens of thousands of Gazans, they have the power to do so. You didn't have to be a genius to understand that Hamas refused or violated one cease-fire after another to rack up civilian casualties and then had the chutzpah to proclaim it had won the war because it had survived as an organization, despite having lost many of its top leaders, 2,100 civilian lives and about a third of the infrastructure of Gaza, a place whose infrastructure previously didn't even rise to third-world standards.
    Did Hamas build schools, hospitals, water, and sanitation systems during the last eight years it has ruled by the gun in Gaza? No, they built terrorist tunnels and acquired rockets.
    Can you imagine the response of the United States if Mexican drug gangs began firing rockets into Brownsville and El Paso, Texas, and built tunnels not only to smuggle illegals but to launch terrorist attacks in San Antonio and Austin? Does anyone think the United States would match

ordnance with these bandits? That it wouldn't use the full might of the American military to achieve major military victories and restore peace and quiet to the Lone Star State? Well, then, think again.

A retired air force ordnance officer personally told me Israel never got close to using the firepower he saw employed by the Americans in recent years in Afghanistan. No sovereign state will sit idly by the blood of its preschoolers who are the intended victims of its enemies. Right now, the cease-fire is mostly holding. Experts claim Hamas will need five years to rebuild militarily and in their civilian sector.

Meanwhile, the Palestine Authority did not rush in to give Hamas on-the-ground support. Nor did any Arab country.

Egypt—already opposed to Hamas and its sponsor, the Muslim Brotherhood—also commenced operations against the tunnels linking Gaza and Israel, the last pipeline to Hamas. Some Gazans told the press they hated Egypt more than they hated Israel this summer.

So where does all this leave us?

First, the deep tensions between Hamas and the Palestine Authority have become manifest. The PA wants to return to Gaza and administer the territory. Hamas is not interested in returning the power they have gained by slaughtering PA forces in Gaza. It is likely that Gaza actually picked a fight with Israel to try to win favor among Palestinians in the West Bank dissatisfied with Abbas and the PA.

Second, Hamas has not renounced its goals of destroying Israel and annihilating the Jewish people. Only rogue states like Iran and North Korea support Hamas. To the rest of the world, they are terrorists and murderers.

Next, Israel remains politically and militarily resolute. A new generation of soldiers, unfortunately, have proven themselves. When you fight fifty miles from the home where you grew up, you don't have second thoughts. Moreover, Israel's technological superiority was also tested and passed, and new technologies will be developed for the early detection of tunnels.

Fourth, the meteoric rise of ISIS in Iraq and Syria has demonstrated what out-of-control Sunni terrorists are capable of. Our own country is now taking military action against ISIS. And what is the difference between ISIS and Hamas? Not much. Both groups are jihadist and genocidal. Both groups want to establish radical Muslim theocracies. Both groups easily resort to terror and murder to achieve their goals.

ISIS has even motivated select Arab monarchies to take military action. Is the enemy of my enemy my friend? Sometimes, I guess. Perhaps the Saudis, the Jordanians, and some of the Persian Gulf states will further soften their views of Israel.

Fifth, Europe is in play. The mobs protesting against Israel on the continent are a strange mix of Muslims and European socialists. Center, nationalist, and even right-wing parties are reevaluating their opinions of Jews and Israel. A backlash is certainly possible in some countries. Most remarkable is the change among the younger members of the National Front in France, long dominated by the Le Pen family. European anti-Semitism has reawakened and is dangerous. But I am convinced the situation in Europe is complicated, dynamic, and perhaps unpredictable.

Sixth, in the United States, support for Israel has held on both sides of the aisle.

Yes, there are Republican isolationist and Democratic pro-Palestinian types. But overwhelmingly, political and military support for Israel remains intact in the halls of power. On campuses and in the media, the situation is less sanguine, and much needs to be done with the youngest cohort of voters. But overall, America and Americans remain pro-Israel.

Finally, there is the question of American Jewish opinion. Are American Jews abandoning Israel? Do American Jews believe Israel has lost the moral high ground in this conflict? I don't think so. I think the vast majority of American Jews understand that Israel is caught between a rock and a hard place, that Israel has horrible enemies, and that self-defense is necessary even in the face of political opposition from all the usual places. Few people I have talked with in the last few weeks are at ease with the heavy loss of life in Gaza but, on the other hand, believe Israel has had to do what it had to do. American Jews also believe that the Israeli military will review accusations of improper behavior and that the rule of law will prevail in Israel and the IDF.

Israel is locked in an existential fight for its life.
Israel is committed to being self-reliant and will protect itself as necessary.
Israel has extreme enemies from Hamas to Hezbollah to Iran.
The Middle East is not a nice place, and Israel will not fall on the sword of public opinion to gain a few PR points.

Above the din and smoke of battle,
My mind takes me back to the shores of the Kinneret
To the grove of pine trees where Rachel and early *kibbutzniks* are

Buried.
My mind takes me back to that quiet place and the dreams that were planted there
Long ago.

Just a few feet away from Rachel's grave is the grave of another woman poet.
Naomi Shemer, Israel's greatest songwriter, also grew up at Degania on the shores of the Kinneret and asked to be buried near Rachel, not in Jerusalem, not on Mount Herzl, but quietly by the sea among the trees.

Naomi Shemer's songs helped sustain Israel during the Six-Day War, the Yom Kippur War. The most famous is, of course, *"Jerusalem of Gold."*

It begins like Rachel sitting by the Kinneret:
"The mountain air is clear as wine
And the scent of pines
Is carried on the breeze of twilight."

"I come to sing to you today
To tell of your praise
I am the smallest of the youngest of your children
And of all the poets born."

"Behold," Shemer, and Rachel before her, concludes,
"I am a violin for all of your songs."

The Israel of Rachel and Naomi Shemer still lives
Their songs are still heard in the land
Despite the conflicts, the wars, the tragedies, and the criticisms,

Despite all that Jewish people
Still yearn to dwell quietly in their own land
Singing their own songs
Whispering their own prayers.

In 5775, let us join them in spirit and more
Let us sing songs of Zion, Jerusalem, and the Kinneret with them

Let us be strong and unwavering in our support
And together let us maintain the hope, the promise,
Of a day when every man, woman, and child in Israel
Will dwell under their own vine and fig tree
At peace and unafraid. Amen. Shana Tova.

Malachi: Healing, Comfort, and the Hearts of the Children

October 3, 2014, Yom Kippur Evening 5775

As best as I can recall, the worst class I had in college, or at least the class I enjoyed the least and got the worst grade in, was anthropology, the Fall semester of my freshman year. I think the class mostly was about family structures and kinship systems.

So what was the problem? The vocabulary of anthropology was totally foreign to me:

- neolocality—the kids marry and move away to their own place.
- bilocalism—kids marry, relocate, return, and relocate.
- affinial uncle—a nice older guy who is really not your uncle but you wish he was.
- avuncular—your real uncle who is a little too close.
- serial monogamy—marry, divorce, marry, divorce (repeat three times).
- totemism—never criticize your ancestors because their spirits live in giant wooden poles, and they don't like to be disturbed.

I soon realized that there are places and societies where what we call weird or illegal is normal, and that what we called normal about family life is actually culturally and geographically specific.

Of course, by the tender age of eighteen, I already knew that families were both wonderful and complex, nurturing and stifling, empowering and repressive, loving and conflicted, colorful and boring, and, finally, necessary social units from which you worked hard to liberate yourself from and then remain completely loyal.

Marriage, I learned in a subsequent class, was the decision to merge two families and become one of them, the supreme act of loyalty or treason depending on where Thanksgiving dinner is going to be this year.

Some theoreticians of family truly admire family life. "The family," George Santayana remarked, "is one of nature's masterpieces." "Little children are the symbol of the eternal marriage between love and duty," said English author George Elliot.

Others are much more negative: "The bourgeois sees his wife a mere instrument of production" (Karl Marx). Freud, of course, blamed everything on mothers in the family system.

Early *kibbutzniks* took little children away from their parents to socialize them into their peer group only to discover that they had created people unable to have close relationships with those peers—good for the army, less good for a family. Mark Twain defined happiness as having a big family in a different city. Sam Levinson said, "Insanity is hereditary. You get it from your children."

During our child-rearing years in the Sussman household, we had various pearls of wisdom about family life posted on our refrigerator: "Let's put the fun back in dysfunctional" was my favorite. "Families are like fudge; mostly sweet with a few nuts" is the most recent.

Family life is not literally part of the Declaration of Independence, the Constitution, or the Gettysburg Address, but familialism is as American as is the separation of powers, an independent judiciary, bicameral legislative bodies, baseball, and apple pie. We even invented the ultimate American family holiday: Thanksgiving, purposefully designed to celebrate New England–style food and family life—in Hawaii and New Mexico. Originating right here in Philadelphia, it combines domesticity with consumerism and football, exactly as imagined by John Winthrop and Miles Standish in seventeenth-century Massachusetts. Somehow the Fourth of July, which predates the invention of the hamburger, is now deeply anchored in the great American family barbecue.

American familialism also reigns supreme on TV, especially early-evening TV or, you might say, family TV time. America is a nation of families that spends a fourth of its time watching other American families on TV. I cannot imagine how many hours I have spent watching television shows built on the theme of the family. Thinking back on my viewing choices over the last fifty years, it is now clear that my favorite family TV shows provided me with a running family history of American society.

Now my list of TV shows is idiosyncratic. So in the spirit of Yom Kippur, I ask your forgiveness in advance if your favorites are not mentioned. My TV viewing began with *Leave It to Beaver* and other family shows all about the benevolent patriarchal family of the 1950s and early 1960s. I mostly watched on a black-and-white Philco, which was 95 percent furniture and 5 percent screen. There was no question about it, the Beaver, Tony, and even Eddie would all grow up to be benevolent patriarchs.

The same was true for the *Dick Van Dyke Show* and the benevolent patriarchal widower in *My Three Sons* as well as in the *Andy Griffith Show*. Ironically, perhaps the most emasculated of the benevolent husbands of this generation was a hot-blooded Cuban Ricky Ricardo on the *I Love Lucy* show.

Subconsciously, my generation of Jewish suburban kids was introduced to the possibility of viable mixed marriage by shows like *Bewitched*, which clearly demonstrated that even a non-Protestant witch with blonde hair and a cute little nose could make a great partner for life for a squeaky-clean WASPy husband who, despite his apparent lack of intelligence, worked as a NASA astronaut.

With the cultural revolutions of the Sixties and early Seventies fading away, TV began validating the new non-family family: *Mary Tyler Moore*, *Seinfeld*, *Cheers*, *Frazier*, and many more showed how nonmarried or lightly married people could bond and form their own surrogate families. *The Golden Girls* showed how mature widowed and divorced women could do the same.

Archie Bunker and *Roseanne*, among others, were "class" specific and particularly powerful in addressing the issues in the lives of America's vast so-called silent majority, including racism and the diminishing economic power of the middle class. *Family Ties* helped us understand the rise of neoconservatism in the post-Seventies world of Dayton, Ohio, pitting the preppy Michael Fox against his graying hippie parents. *The Cosby Show* demonstrated that affluent black families were just like affluent white families and that a black man could be an ob-gyn and sexually moral at the same time.

Jewish characters would creep into the picture too. I was too young for the original *Goldbergs* but watched many episodes of *The Nanny* without becoming anti-Semitic despite Fran Drescher's remarkable capacity to be really annoying. *The Nanny* also demonstrated how blue-collar Jews could become blue-blood Englishmen and remain Jewish at the same time.

Will & Grace helped present gay men as members of a new type of family, and the current comedy *Modern Family* is a dizzying collage of a May-December Hispanic American marriage, a squeaky-clean suburban Ken-Barbie couple with full-throttle adolescent girls, and a same-sex gay household with an adopted Asian girl.

I can't imagine what the next step might be in the evolution of the American TV family, but one thing is for sure: the family unit, however defined, will continue to dominate the fifty-inch flat screens in American homes for the foreseeable future and our internal lives forever.

Now what about the Jewish family? How has it evolved over time? Jewish history begins with a family, Abraham and Sarah. Thirty-seven centuries ago. They occupied a completely different cultural planet than us. Their household was polygynous, including both multiple wives and concubines. Abraham's separation from wife number two, Hagar, was never amicably resolved. Child support was not provided or visiting rights established. On the other hand, there seems to have been genuine tenderness between Abraham and Sarah; and Abraham decided not to kill their son even though he was forty years old, not working, and still living at home.

Polygyny was officially banned among Ashkenazic Jews in the year 1000. The ban was for one thousand years but was actually not renewed in 2000 by Ashkenazic rabbis. Technically, the ban was never lifted among Sephardic Jews. However, bigamy is illegal everywhere Jews live today; and in the Jewish tradition, the legal principle of *dina de-Malkhuta dina* (the law of the land) is always the law. So please do not get any ideas.

Interestingly, some modern biblical scholars as well as archeologists today challenge the biblical story of Joshua conquering the Land of Israel. Instead, they propose that the Jews were already there and that Jewish control of the land was a function of population growth—that is, a changing model of Jewish family life. In historical terms, that represents a switch from the settlement-conquest model to the traditional, biblical conquest-settlement sequence.

Some demographers today are suggesting that population studies in Israel indicate that Jews, especially settlers and the Orthodox, have higher fertility rates than Arabs. Thus, minus Gaza, it is possible that Israel could absorb the West Bank and not lose the Jewish majority in Israel itself.

This family factor is clearly fueling right-wing politics in Israel, which openly advocate a settlement-conquest strategy of the West Bank through increased fertility.

In the Jewish tradition, from Abraham and Sarah to the beginning of the nineteenth century, most marriages were arranged for financial and social reasons. A matchmaker was called a *shadchan*. Today, *shadchanim* work from computer databases with files on their clients with everything from Dun & Bradstreet to DNA reports.

The beloved now-fifty-year-old *Fiddler on the Roof* is basically a eulogy for the death of the traditional Jewish family of the Russian Pale of Settlement although *shadchanut* is making a comeback today among the ultra-Orthodox.

Social scientists working on information made available after the collapse of the USSR have determined that by the end of the nineteenth century, the divorce rate among Russian Jews, including those who came to America, was close to 50 percent. There were also serious problems with abandonment and with chained women—that is, divorced women were prevented from remarrying by their ex-husbands.

Nostalgia about Jewish immigrants purposefully removes some of the worst plights in Jewish history. For example, the Lower East Side in New York City was not only the biggest Jewish neighborhood in the world in 1910 but was also the red-light district of the Big Apple.

Groups like the National Federation of Temple Sisterhoods, now WRJ, as well as organizations like the National Council of Jewish Women, maintained vigorous anti-prostitution programs in the American Jewish community of the Progressive Era. A false report that half the crimes in NYC in 1910 were committed by Jews helped stimulate the creation and expansion of the Federation system. Less than 10 percent of Jewish kids went to Hebrew school, and with Prohibition, Jewish men served not only as accountants but also hit men for organized crime. Immigration was hardly a cakewalk for the Jewish community and Jewish families.

Historical demographers have also demonstrated that Jewish immigrants from East Europe were generally part of very large families in the old country before coming to America. By contrast, Italian immigrants were anchored in smaller families. In America, Jewish families purposefully contracted for economic reasons and Italian families grew as soon as family finances improved. The result is clear. Americans eat more pizza than they eat bagels.

Around 1960, the rate of mixed marriage began to go up in the United States. Today, it is around 50 percent, statistically normal. The high rate of religious exogamous households—that's one of those anthropological terms—affiliating with the Jewish community has helped prevent significant population loss.

On the other hand, except for the Orthodox, American Jews generally marry late or not at all, have fewer children, and live longer lives. The demographic impact is immense. American Jews are also more likely to be neolocal in their settlement patterns after leaving their families of origin. Pursuing the American dream is so ingrained in the Jewish community that we have fewer and fewer three-generation households.

The single largest cohort today among American Jews are adults living in a single-person household. The second largest cohort is two adults living together without children. The third cohort, which made up 70 percent of the American Jewish population forty years ago, is made up of two adults and children in the same household. The fourth largest cohort is single adults with children. The divorce rate among American Jews today is the same as it is among other Americans or 50 percent based on the number of marriages—that's *serial monogamy* anthropologically speaking. However, fifty years ago, divorce was almost unheard of in the Jewish community. During my school-boy years, I only had one friend with divorced parents, and no one ever talked about it.

There are other changes as well in the face of the American Jewish family. One out of seven American Jews today was born in the Soviet Union. No one has more complex family systems of any subethnicity than Russians. One out of ten American Jews are Israeli, and a guess is 50 percent of our Hebrew schoolteachers are Israeli.

Finally, as in the TV show *Modern Family*, same-sex households are taking root in the general Jewish community today as well as in their own sub-communities.

The situation among Orthodox Jews is radically different. In those communities, both earlier marriage and superhuman, or superwoman, fertility rates prevail. It reads almost like the Midrash about the Hebrew slave women in Egypt. They were so vigorous, the rabbis later said, that they had their babies before the midwives could arrive and the Pharaonic decree of infanticide was not able to be enforced. In fact, the birth rate has become so high with so many babies being born to older mothers that the private schools Orthodox kids attend can no longer meet their needs.

In Monsey and Brooklyn and other centers of Orthodox life, tensions are rising over the use of community, tax-based resources.

The twenty-first-century American Jewish family, like families in general, is complex, dynamic, and highly adaptable. The immigrant Jewish family of the 1910s bore little resemblance to the Jewish Cleaver families of the 1950s or to the postmodern families early in the twenty-first century.

The rapidly changing Jewish family of today also presents numerous challenges to the American synagogue. For example, Reform synagogues historically count their membership in terms of households or families. KI has one thousand members today. That represents about 2,700 people. No one cohort dominates our population, from single-person households to two-person households, two-parent-two-kid households, single-parent households, mixed-religious households, nonreligious households, same-sex households, multiracial households, adoptive-parent households, legal guardian-custodial parents, paying households, and nonpaying households. We are all here, a microcosm of America and the American Jewish community.

At the end of the day, our highest hope as a synagogue is to be a congregational family of families, a safe place for those with little or no family of their own, a venue for large extended functional families, and a sanctuary for dysfunctional families and for individuals who struggle within their own families.

Sometimes a family is a wonderful place; sometimes it is a tough place. At KI, acceptance, inclusion, and kindness are carved into stone as our family values. It is a family place for everybody who seeks family here. We strive to raise the level of life for all our members, to make the good moments better and the tough moments softer, to have a place to share life's most important smiles and tears.

In the Torah portion for Yom Kippur in the Reform movement, we read from *haazinu* in Deuteronomy. It instructs the people to gather to renew their covenant with God. Everyone, the Torah says, from the "chopper of wood" to the "drawer of water" will be included. Who are these people?

The Talmud says the chopper of wood is Abraham when he went to sacrifice Isaac and chopped wood for the dreaded event. However, we then learned that the first order of family life is "Don't hurt each other," "Don't sacrifice others on the altar of your ego," "Bind up each other's wounds," and "Don't handcuff each other to their hurts and worries."

Who is the drawer of water? It is Elijah, the Tishbi, the prophet we sing about at *havdalah* and welcome to our Passover seders. It was Elijah who soaked the altars of the pagan god Baal on the slopes of Mount Carmel with water and then lit them without assistance to win the ancient people away from Baal and back to the God of Israel.

Who is Elijah? Elijah is also the last prophet referenced in the last book of prophecy in the Hebrew Bible, the Book of Malachi, the final window in our sanctuary, the one to my immediate left.

What is the last prophecy our people heard out loud and in public according to the Hebrew Bible? It was Elijah exhorting parents to turn to their children in love and then exhorting the children to turn to their parents with love and forgiveness.

Judaism begins with the clarion call to form loving families and make our homes sanctuaries of acceptance, nurture, support, and love.

What is Judaism's ultimate goal? Why is it necessary for us to perpetuate our heritage? Because Judaism deeply believes that the ultimate goal of history—of humanity—is to create a time on earth when there will be universal peace: peace at home, peace within our families, peace among the nations and among the peoples.

That is *aleph-tav*, the alpha omega of Judaism: the creation, maintenance, and perpetuation of loving families.

On Yom Kippur, we are urged to be careful about what vows we make and then to keep the vows we utter in our hearts. Each one of us is part of some kind of family: neolocal, matrifocal, serial, dysfunctional, endogamous, and pretty good! Take stock of your family on this Yom Kippur, your place in it, and vow to keep it good or make it better.

One day, when each of us gets it right or right enough, then Kol Nidrei, all our vows will be met; and Elijah will announce the dawning of an age of peace for every child, every man, every woman under heaven.

Ken y'hei ratzon! So may it be God's will. Amen.

Ezekiel: Renewal and Awakening

October 4, 2014, Yom Kippur Yizkor 5775

After the *Sh'ma*, perhaps the most revered of all Jewish prayers is the Kaddish. The Kaddish appears in multiple forms, all of which begin the same way: *Yitgadal v'yitkadash.*

These two words, which actually mean "May God be magnified and sanctified," have become the ultimate sound of mourning in the Jewish tradition. For the vast majority of Jews the world over, they are both among the most feared and the most cherished of all words.

Yitgadal v'yitkadash are based on a passage from Ezekiel 38. Ezekiel is the prophet depicted in the second to the last window on your right, toward the back of the sanctuary. Although he is depicted as standing on the graves of the slain of Jerusalem, Ezekiel is actually a prophet of hope, rebuilding, and restoration. Ezekiel is the first prophet to proclaim that the grave is not the end. That we do endure, that something remains, and that there is something that will yet be restored.

Yitgadal v'yikadash—these are the words of the prophet of hope.

Yitgadal v'yitkadash—we say them for the first time at graveside, the painful, comforting, definitive statement of acknowledgment.

Yitgadal v'yitkadash, I now relinquish the body of my loved one for eternity. Grandfather, grandmother, father, mother, sister, brother, aunt, uncle, cousin, friend—someone whose physical presence was a given in life, a fact of existence, is now gone.

Yitgadal v'yitkadash—I place my loved into the soft earth, the eternal cradle of the soul, the life-giving soil from which new life will come: new grass, new trees, and new flowers. Life will burst forth again, irrepressible and fresh and green.

Yitgadal v'yitkadash—the words stir memory like an old wooden cooking spoon stirs a pot of soup: aromatic and intoxicating to the soul.

Yitgadal v'yitkadash—these sounds punctuate time for ever more. Seven days of mourning. The thirty days. A year's time. Another year. Ten years and more. They reconnect us. They redress our old wounds. They hurt, and they refresh.

Yitgadal v'yitkadash—my friends and neighbors say these words too. They are like a cold compress on a hot day, a day of painful remembering. They ask us to enlarge our own spiritual capacity. They ask us to affirm, to continue, to move on.

The *Kaddish* is both personal and communal.

Everyone reads it for him or herself.

Yitgadal v'yitkadash—it is the most private and the most public thing we will ever say.

Death never discriminates. Death comes to all living things: rich and poor, young and old, strong and weak. It is the same for all.

Yitgadal v'yitkadash—my pain is so personal, so unique, so mine.

Yitgadal v'yitkadash—we all say the same thing, the same way.

Y'hei sh'mei raba m'varach l'alam ul'almei almaya—now help us to find continued purpose and meaning, something bigger than ourselves, something transcendent that preserves all that is good from destruction.

V'nomar. Amen—let this be true, let it be affirmed, let me be healed. Remember my loved ones. Keep their souls. Keep them in your heart. keep them close.

Kaddish is a powerful prayer.

It has a sacred cadence and holy sounds.

It is reassuring and empowering.

It is timely and timeless.

It comes from the depths.

It reaches to the height of human spiritual capacity.

It restores, and then it recedes.

V'nomar. Amen. *Kaddish* is now over. It is time to go. It is time to let it go. It is time, yet it is forever. Amen.

ACHAREI MOT K'DOSHIM: THE BATTLE OF BALTIMORE

April 1, 2015, eKI

As many of you know, I was born and grew up in Baltimore, the "Monument City" in the "Land of Pleasant Living." Sadly, there was little pleasant about life in Baltimore this week. My hometown was a city on edge, and watching live TV of the pitched street battles on the familiar streets of what was once Baltimore's core Jewish neighborhood was no fun. The hard, courageous work of city officials, law enforcement and thousands of citizen volunteers seems to have restored some order to Maryland's largest city.

This last week's "Battle" was not the first battle to be fought in Baltimore. The British shelling of Fort McHenry inspired the writing of the Star-Spangled Banner. The Pratt Street Riot of 1861, when pro-South Baltimoreans attacked Union troops en route to Washington, led to the first death of the American Civil War. In my own lifetime, I clearly recall the riots of 1968 which brought the entire city to a standstill for over a week. At the corner of the street where I lived, the Army positioned an Armored Personnel Carrier (APC) to block traffic into the city and all gas stations were closed to cut off the supply of fuel for Molotov cocktails.

The most recent Battle of Baltimore was smaller but still terribly painful. There is too much bad behavior. There is also too much poverty, too little quality public education and too many issues with the city police. I am totally pro-police and would not want to live anywhere for even five minutes without police. I understand that our police have to deal with too many horrible problems but there are issues with training, policy and occasionally, a bad cop. None of this excuses any form of criminality. But there are problems, all around, on all sides.

The biggest problem is indifference. This week's problems were in Baltimore. But Baltimore is not unique. Philadelphia is another Baltimore, God forbid, waiting to happen. So is New York and Boston and Cincinnati and Chicago and everywhere else in this country with deep urban challenges. We may live in the suburbs or retirement communities or in nice apartments in town. But the problem is right down the street. So let's not kid ourselves that indifference is an option.

This week's Torah portion from Leviticus (*Acharei Mot K'doshim*) says it best: "Don't stand idly by the blood of your brother" and even more succinctly, "Love your neighbor as yourself!" These are the principles which should inform our lives as individuals and as a sacred community.

I am not talking about government or politics here. I am talking about us at KI, you and me. What can we do as neighbors and a religious community to help and not to ignore, to heal and not to be hurtful by being indifferent. In my opinion, we can be of help by focusing our efforts in the area of education. At the urging of our congregational President, Dr. Arnold Meshkov, my colleagues and me, we need to put our heads together and determine what we can do to help with education at many levels in Philadelphia. Collect books, donate computers, tutor after school . . . the possibilities are endless. More importantly, the need is now and it is urgent.

Shortly, we will be rolling out some ideas and a schedule to start shaping KI's renewed devotion to Social Justice, this time through education. It's not a platitude to say that "if you are not a part of the solution, you are part of the problem." We will not be a part of the problem as a congregation. By embracing one of our core values, the value of education, we can do a lot of good. So, let the work begin and let it continue and may we be strong in efforts to treat our neighbors and our neighbors' children as ourselves.

Shabbat Shalom.

SEEING IS BELIEVING: VISUAL T'FILOT AND THE FUTURE OF JEWISH WORSHIP

2015 e-Jewish Philanthropy

Three years ago, my synagogue agreed to install large retractable screens on either side of the Ark and mounted projectors on the back wall of our nine hundred-seat sanctuary. With almost no resistance, we quickly transitioned from late 15th century technology to early twenty-first century modalities of communication.

It was a relatively easy process. In addition to her musical talents, our Cantor discovered she had an inherent talent for developing liturgical PowerPoint. What size font, which colors, Hebrew versus transliteration, translation versus epitomes of the text, iconic images versus new art and still life versus video instantly presented themselves as questions we needed to address. One by one, we worked our way through the various technological and philosophical issues.

We also had to decide whether to look for commercially made liturgical PowerPoints or develop our own. What we discovered was that we had ample talent to do our own thing from our staff to our lay people professionally involved in digital illustration to our *b'nai mitzvah* students eager to personalize their own services.

The results were phenomenal. Our religious school created liturgical PowerPoint classes. Students began debating among themselves how to illustrate the *Sh'ma*, the *Amidah* and their own special prayers of thanks. Regular worshippers and first-time visitors alike began to look up during services instead of down into their prayer books. The elderly shared that they were glad to be rid of heavy *siddurim* and quite happy to look up at the large-letter liturgical texts well within their visual capacity.

Of course, there was some resistance. One *bat mitzvah* told me she did not want to use *Visual T'filot* because "Moses did not have PowerPoint." Of course, Miriam did not have a *bat mitzvah* either, a point which impressed the student but did not cause her to change her mind. Others said they did not mind the visuals but wanted the option of using "real" books as well. No problem there. We never even discussed removing our *s'farim* and have learned to integrate the use of print and digital in worship. Today's reality is that if you go to a major league ball game, you still watch half the game or more on a screen. There are digital billboards on major highways and flat-screen menus in neighborhood greasy-spoon diners. The digital revolution has already won the day. It is high time for the modern synagogue to catch up with its host culture.

I also have members who come to services with app-based liturgy loaded into their iPhones, iPads and tablets. We are even considering switching from the weekly memorial plaques and their old fashioned orange light bulbs to a flat-screen with images of the same. Early modem Judaism transitioned from handwritten books to printed books; post-modem Judaism can go digital as well. In fact, on a cost-benefit basis, the move to digital makes a great deal of sense. It is much cheaper to install a screen and a projector than it is to buy a thousand new *machzorim* for the High Holy days. All the unselected material can be shifted to files, texts can be customized and "new" material from original poetry to Rashi commentaries can be inserted effortlessly. We have also learned how to use mixed media *Shabbat* announcements and what to display for the purpose of memorialization. My congregation finds comfort in the image of a lit *yahrzeit* candle before *Kaddish* but does like seeing "the list" up on the screens.

For nearly twenty centuries, rabbis and others have debated the value of visual representations of *hidur mitzvah* and the dangers of *Avodah Zara*. Today, art and illustration are widely used in Jewish life and universal visual *T'filot* is the next logical step in the adaptation of Judaism to the modem world.

We live in a visual world. It is time to visualize our prayers and "text" our sacred images. The polarity of service and party will lessen, behavior during services will improve, and Judaism will find a new place in the eyes, minds and hearts of the Jewish people.

Visual *t'filot* is fun, engaging and authentic. If you are not sure how to proceed, just ask any ten-year-old in your community what to do. They are ready. Are you?

The Confirmation Revolution: Then and Now

May 21, 2015

Today's North American Reform synagogues have increasingly begun to rethink and attempt to reinvigorate the contemporary practice of bar and bat mitzvah, a practice that may transform Reform Judaism in general. In many ways, these conversations are reminiscent of the emergence of confirmation at the beginning of the nineteenth century, a significant part of a broad effort to reenvision Judaism's well-known adolescent rites-de-passage in communities throughout Central Europe. In time, Confirmation largely became associated with Reform Judaism.

With respect to the practice of bar mitzvah, several issues confronted early Reformers and other Jewish modernizers in Europe. The bar mitzvah's popularity was waning, and educational questions arose regarding comprehension versus mastering prescribed ritual practices. There was also the issue of coeducation and whether or not girls, as well as boys, could be confirmed if the reading of Torah was eliminated.

With the dawn of the nineteenth century, ritual and educational change proved irrepressible in many Central European communities. Jewish communities broadly adopted a catechetical approach to Jewish learning, and a new type of educational textbook quickly appeared to meet the need of the day.

The first modern Jewish confirmation (for boys only) likely took place in Dessau, Germany, in 1803 in the town's school. Four years later, Leopold Zunz, considered the founder of modern Jewish scholarship, was confirmed in Wolfenbuttel, about one hundred miles away. Subsequently, the Jewish Consistory of Westphalia sought to root confirmation throughout the Napoleonic Kingdom it served, but the practice only took hold in a few towns.

In Germany, the most revolutionary aspect of confirmation was its embrace of the coeducation of boys and girls. The earliest report of boys and girls being confirmed together was in 1811; by 1831, Samuel Levin Egers, one of Germany's leading Orthodox rabbis, instituted coeducational Confirmation in Brunswick, later a site of one of the principal Reform rabbinic conferences of the nineteenth century. Jewish coeducation reached the United States in 1838 when Rebecca Gratz created the Hebrew Sunday School, which employed catechetical teaching methods and exclusively presented an "Orthodox" Jewish theology. Curiously, Gratz's school did not adopt Confirmation and instead had a public examination/graduation exercise in March.

In the United States, the Reformed Society of Israelites envisioned confirmation as early as the 1820s, but it was not until 1843 that we have a report from the Danish possession of St. Thomas in the Virgin Islands of a (coeducational) Confirmation taking place in the New World. Max Lilienthal, the "Chief Rabbi of New York," proposed in 1846 that the Hebrew Union School Society adopt Confirmation both for boys and girls; and later that year, a Confirmation service was held at a traditional synagogue, Anshe Chesed, on Shavuot. The *Occident*, an Orthodox newspaper, reported that 1,500 people attended and that "the Rabbi delivered an impressive sermon, which drew tears from all, and satisfied everyone, that far from being a destructive innovation, 'confirmation' was an earnest appeal to every Jew to rally heart and soul round the standard of our holy religion."

Although ultimately rejected by New York's traditional congregations, Confirmation was successfully rooted in U.S. Reform synagogues, often in lieu of *b'nai mitzvah*. Ultimately, the American Reform movement took ownership of confirmation and, toward the end of the nineteenth century, made Confirmation its hallmark event. The Confirmation itself often became a lavish affair, with incredible floral displays consistent with the cultural mores of the Gilded Age. Formal photographs of the confirmation class and its rabbinic instructor were placed on permanent display in nearly every American Reform synagogue; confirmation yearbooks were published, and confirmation class trips became integral. Despite the increased popularity of b'nai mitzvah during the course of the twentieth century, Reform families still typically kept their children enrolled in confirmation (generally until the end of tenth grade).

Still, concerns arose outside Reform Judaism about the educational value and quality of Confirmation, and questions persisted about its Jewish authenticity. In particular, the English name *confirmation* raised issues, as it was clearly borrowed from Christianity, where it is intimately connected to the practice of baptism. Today, some congregations use Hebrew substitute terms like *kabbalat Torah* or *b'rit Torah* in lieu of *Confirmation*. In some Reform congregations, the traditional counting of the Omer has been tied to the counting of days to confirmation. Early proponents of Confirmation pointed out both biblical and rabbinic proof texts for the public confession of faith in the Jewish tradition to strengthen claims of the Jewish authenticity of Confirmation.

During the twentieth century, though, the American Reform movement became increasingly ambivalent about Confirmation and unsure of its religious purpose. The 1940 *Union Prayer Book* spoke of bringing "our children unto Thine altar that they may renew the vow of their fathers," but 1975's *Gates of Prayer* speaks simply of "their children learn[ing] the joy of the mitzvot." The 2007 Reform prayer book *Mishkan T'filah* contains no reference to Confirmation at all.

Looking back, it is clear that this Confirmation revolution played a central role in the rise and spread of Reform Judaism, revolutionizing Jewish education and blazing educational and religious pathways for Jewish women. Today's Confirmation, however, is in need of redefinition. Just as confirmation once solved the problem of the bar mitzvah for West European and American Jews, perhaps today's conversations about *b'nai mitzvah*, including such initiatives as the Reform movement's *b'nai mitzvah* revolution, will now help reinvigorate Confirmation. It would be a shame to take down all those Confirmation class pictures in our Reform synagogues as relics of a lost past when it is more than possible that they also contain the seed of a reinvigorated twenty-first-century Reform movement in Judaism.

Back to Ohio: Revisiting My First Pulpit

2015

This week I went back to Middletown, Ohio, where I served Temple Beth Shalom from 1982 to 1986. Middletown is located halfway (hence the name) between Cincinnati and Dayton on the Miami River. The synagogue, in those days, had about seventy families and, very importantly, a lovely split-level house just two doors away from the synagogue.

Middletown was my first pulpit after ordination (I actually spent two years after ordination preparing for my comprehensive doctoral exams in Jewish and American history and my required languages) and the place where I wrote my PhD thesis. In many ways, my Middletown years were foundational to my work both as a rabbi and a historian.

My first day on the job was the hardest of my career. I was busy unpacking my books and files in my new office when the phone rang. It was one of the older members of the congregation, Manny Garlikov, who had personally helped orient me to the town and the congregation. He had bad news—horrible news. His grandsons had been playing behind their house. The older boy had a hatchet and was hitting a tree trunk when the tree snapped, fell on his little brother, and instantly killed the child.

I ran to their house. There are no words to describe the grief I saw and felt. It was a terrible initiation to pastoral work for a very green rabbi. Later that year, I learned my first bar mitzvah student from my student pulpit had perished in a frat fire at his college. Liz and I traveled to nearby

Richmond, Indiana. What hopefully never happens in a whole career had happened on my beat in less than one year—my first year. I didn't second-guess my career path, but its potential seriousness was, all of a sudden, a brutal reality. I learned that these scenarios are both the worst part of my chosen work and, perhaps, the most important.

The pulpit in Middletown came with an unusual requirement. The rabbi of Temple Beth Shalom was also the state-contracted Jewish chaplain at a medium-security prison, the Lebanon Correctional Institution, a sprawling 1,900-acre facility with over 2,500 inmates, many of them convicted murderers, all of them hardened criminals. I never adjusted to my work in the slammer. It was too threatening for me. I was scared when I went "in," drenched in sweat when I came out, and nervous I would be contacted to go back in.

Yet to this day, I make a special effort to support the work of jailhouse rabbis. Most recently, that has translated into helping the Minyan at Graterford Prison. One Rosh HaShanah, I received a letter from the president of the Jewish prisoners' group. He told me that unlike any other synagogue, "they were happy they had not grown during the last year!" Amen to that.

In the summer of 1986, having completed four years in Middletown and having completed my doctoral studies, we moved to Binghamton, New York. Our fourth child, Judah, had just been born (four for four at Cincinnati's Jewish Hospital). Liz couldn't travel to look for a house, and she told me to only rent because, alone, I would surely buy the wrong house. In the end, I rented the wrong house, and we had to move again. That's when Chana was born, our fifth child and first daughter, completing our young but big family. We ended up staying in the Binghamton area for fourteen years before moving to Elkins Park in 2001. Each step along the way provided new opportunities, new challenges, and endless memories.

Thirty-three years after starting my first pulpit in Middletown, I was honored to be asked to come back to Temple Beth Shalom to give the keynote for the sixtieth anniversary celebration of their building. There were only seventy families there in 1982, but I learned something about the rabbinate and life from my time with them and look back on those years with fondness. It was not easy being so far from our extended families on the East Coast for so long in such a remote place, but it was good to be so intimately involved in the life of a Jewish community with the paradigmatic

American name of Middletown. I am forever grateful to Temple Beth Shalom for having given me the opportunity to launch my rabbinate and my scholarly career in the heartland of America with "all my heart, my soul, and my might."

Rabbi, What Do You Believe?

June 4, 2015 eKI

For the last few weeks, it seems I have had more than the usual number of requests to share what it is about Judaism I actually believe. Here is a quick summary. What do you believe?

GOD
Different people and traditions understand and relate to God in different ways.
At different times and in different circumstances, sometimes the same person can hold different views of God and, at still other times, the same person can hold multiple and even contradictory views of God.
The rejection of inadequate concepts of God is intellectually and morally necessary.
The possibility of an uncreated God necessarily preexists the possibility of existence whether the universe is created or eternal.
The possibility of God anchors the existence of love, justice, and truth in reality and places them beyond mere utilitarian or constructed values.
Ethical living, personal kindness, and the call to work for a just society are the central expressions of faith derived from a belief in God.
Prayer is the heart in search of one's God.

TORAH
Torah (or "Judaism as Sacred Teaching") is an enduring dialogue with God as understood and experienced by the Jewish people.

Torah is an emergent process which created the "Five Books of Moses," the rabbinic tradition, and continues to inform contemporary expressions of Judaism.
Torah works in concert with modern science and reason and does not seek to ground itself in the supernatural.
Distinguishing between *Mitzvah* (commandment) and *Minhag* (custom) is an ongoing personal and collective process.

ISRAEL
The Jewish people or "Keneseth Israel" is the Jewish people in its historical and future totality from its ancient origins to the present to the unknown future.
Zionism and the State of Israel are authentic, democratic, and historical embodiments of a nationalist understanding of Jewish life.
Diaspora Jewish life is an authentic expression of Keneseth Israel anchored in respective host countries and cultures and tied to the State of Israel by enduring spiritual, cultural, historical and human bonds.
Judaism believes in the humanity of every individual and the necessity of peaceful, multi-faith cooperation with our friends and neighbors around the world.
Worship in the Jewish tradition provides spiritual depth to Jewish life and unity to the Jewish people.

The "Mission of Keneseth Israel" is to strive for world peace and to promote justice and among all people, nations and faiths.
I believe in an enduring spiritual, transcendent presence.
I hope this helps or at least gently provokes some good thinking. I realize some of my points are more philosophical than others. Let me know what it is that you believe.
Shabbat Shalom.

A Sacred Event: Social Justice, *Chesed*, and Reform Judaism

September 22, 2015, Yom Kippur Evening 5776

March 4, 1865, was a miserable, rainy day in Washington DC. Still, thousands gathered on the eastern face of the Capitol building. As Abraham Lincoln rose to speak, the sun burst through for the first time that day. What followed was a short, 703-word talk, Lincoln's second inaugural. Surprisingly, it was totally devoid of any reference to the North's impending military victory after four years of bloody civil war.

Instead, Lincoln offered a deeply religious talk, filled with biblical quotes and framed by a theology based heavily on the Hebrew prophets. God's justice is more a function of kindness and charity than the work of great armies, the President said.

"With malice toward none," Lincoln concluded, "with charity for all, with firmness in the right, as God gives us to see the right, let us strive on to finish the work we are in, to bind up the nation's wounds, to care for him who shall have borne the battle, and for his widow and orphan—*to do* all which may achieve and cherish a just and a lasting peace, among ourselves and with all nations."

The press yawned! John Wilkes Booth, who was present in the crowd that day and would soon murder the President at nearby Ford's theater, sneered; and Frederick Douglass, the great African American abolitionist, called the Second Inauguration oration "a sacred event."

Every time I read Lincoln's words from March 1865, whether in a book or online or as they are carved inside the Lincoln Memorial, I too experience a sacred event. For me, they perfectly encapsulate the merger of the spiritual and the ethical so passionately envisioned by the ancient prophets of Israel for the first time in all history.

From Abraham, the first Prophet, to Moses, the greatest of our Prophets, to Malachi, the final Prophet in our tradition, come the same basic set of ideas: there is a transcendent source of all existence who has given us the capacity to shape the kind of people and nation we want to be and consistently challenges us to follow the paths of justice, mercy, and peace.

In Judaism, above riches, power, and fame, there is *chesed*, our love for one another combined with our love for our God, the source of *chesed*. *Chesed*, the prophets taught us, is anchored in a cosmic source Who summons us not to be great for greatness' sake but to be good, for in seeking justice, there is life.

On Yom Kippur Day, we read from the prophet Isaiah, Chapter 58, that it is not our physical fasting and day-long prayers that truly matter to God. They are fine and acceptable, if offered with the right spirit, and, more importantly, accompanied by the right actions. What really counts, the prophet proclaims, is the fast from injustice, the fast from hypocrisy, and the active pursuit of a good life, a life filled with justice, love, and *chesed*.

In the Torah, we find Judaism's moral blueprint for humanity, literally, to care for the widow and the orphan and to leave the corners of the field unharvested so the poor can come and claim the wheat and other fresh products for themselves! We are commanded to pay the day laborer at sunset, not to take a poor person's blanket to secure a loan, treat prisoners of war with dignity, build safe homes for people to live in, return lost property to friends and enemy alike, not to abuse animals, give all things a Sabbath of rest from their work, honor our parents, be hospitable and kind to the stranger, tell the truth in court, not to slander or libel anyone, not to mock the deaf or trip the blind, not to engage in wars with wanton disregard for life, compensate those we injure, educate our children, not to stand idly by the blood of our neighbors, and love all of God's children as we would have them love us.

Judaism has always stood for justice and mercy, righteous and kindness, peace and peacefulness. Judaism has always stood for *chesed*.

In the ancient world, following the destruction of Jerusalem, the Jewish people were dispersed across the globe. Wherever we landed, we created new communities and immediately established funds for poor brides, the hungry, and the elderly with insufficient means to care for themselves.

The *pushke*, the little box with the big heart, was to be found in every Jewish community and every Jewish house—Ashkenazic and Sephardic, German and Russian, Italian and Iraqi. Wherever there was Jewish life, there was a concern for the other, a command to take up the cause of the widow and the orphans. With pennies from children, placed into the little blue Jewish National Fund (JNF) box, the Jewish people literally redeemed the Land of Israel one coin at a time.

When Jews first settled in North America in the seventeenth century, they created communal funds for the next wave of immigrants and the next to the next.

When Rebecca Gratz started the Hebrew Sunday School in Philadelphia, the country and the city were in the depths of an economic depression. She raised the funds necessary for the poorest students to attend her classes without paying tuition, so they could learn alongside their more fortunate coreligionists. She also made sure her indigent students had both winter coats and firewood in the winter. "A mind can't learn if a child is hungry or cold or both."

Here is the opening prayer the first Sunday school students recited here in Philadelphia on March 4, 1838: "O God, give unto us the help we need: give us bread to eat and raiment to put on and instruction to understand Thy mercies."

And what Rebecca Gratz did for the poor Jewish immigrant children, she also did for the Irish and the German kids through her work in local civic associations. And when as an older woman, the Civil War broke out, she worked tirelessly to care for the wounded of all faiths—to care for the soldier, the widow, and the orphan.

When Rabbi David Einhorn came to KI in 1862, his antislavery message was loud, clear, and undiminished, just as it had been in Baltimore. Slavery, he taught, is the ultimate perversion of ethics and economy. It is all greed and no heart. If we are commanded to help an overworked ox, in the Torah, what about a slave who is whipped, bound, and hanged for sport?

This is not the Jewish way, he taught. This is not the prophetic path. Slavery is wrong and must be stopped even if it splits the community. Justice, fairness, and kindness, Einhorn taught, are our principles: no false peace, no submission to evil in the name of communal unity.

How bad was slavery in the American South? I have a friend who is a legal historian of slavery. He has collected tens of thousands of cases documenting the brutality and utter depravity of America's peculiar Institution. Here is one report from St. Louis in 1844:

> *On Friday last, the coroner held an inquest at the house of Judge Dunica, a few miles south of the city, over the body of a negro girl, about 8 years of age, belonging to Mr. Cordell. The body exhibited evidence of the most cruel whipping and beating we have ever heard of. The flesh on the back and limbs was beaten to a jelly—one shoulder-bone was laid bare—there were several cuts, apparently from a club, on the head—and around the neck was the indentation of a cord, by which it is supposed she had been confined to a tree. She had been hired by a man by the name of Tanner, residing in the neighborhood, and was sent home in this condition. After coming home, her constant request, until her death, was for bread, by which it would seem that she had been starved, as well as unmercifully whipped. The jury returned a verdict that she came to her death by the blows inflicted by some persons unknown whilst she was in the employ of Mr. Tanner. Mrs. Tanner has been tried and acquitted.*

To this and tens of thousands of other documented cases, the rabbi of KI said *no more!*

In 1866, Rabbi Einhorn went to New York and was followed here by Rabbi Samuel Hirsch. Hirsch had been the Grand Rabbi of Luxembourg and was a widely respected Jewish philosopher. Hirsch too was passionate in his concern for the poor, for poor children, and, most of all, for the impoverished orphan. He created the KI Orphans Guardian Society. It became the signature activity of our congregation for generations.

Hirsch opposed faceless large institutional orphanages. Kids don't need institutions, they need homes, he taught. They don't need large wards, they need real families. The congregation responded; and an army of home visitors was raised from people who went into the slums with food, blankets, coal, and love to care for the widow and the orphan in Philadelphia in the 1860s, 1870s, and 1880s.

In 1881, Philadelphia finally dedicated a proper new Jewish orphanage. At the dedication ceremony in Germantown, the following words were shared by Edward I. Weil, having been introduced by Isidore Binswanger, a member of KI: "We [now] dedicate this Temple to the God of love and mercy. This Home, where the outcast little one will find shelter. This asylum where the fatherless child can be reared and protected. This religion teaches that the deed which is upmost acceptable to God is to break the yoke of the oppressed, to deal out the bread to the hungry, to bring the poor that are outcast to our home and to satisfy the afflicted soul."

In 1887, Rabbi Hirsch retired and joined his family in Chicago. He was followed by KI's longest-serving rabbi, Rabbi Joseph Krauskopf. Like Einhorn, Krauskopf spoke out against exploited labor. Like Hirsch, Krauskopf called on the congregation to care for orphans in their homes. But he did something else. Rabbi Krauskopf understood that city slums are not places for children to thrive, to be educated, to be healthy. So he started a farm school in Doylestown to take the kids out of the city, put them on the land and in fresh air. At first, he spent his own money to buy land. He then lobbied presidents and great philanthropists to support his school. They responded in kind.

A few weeks ago, Krauskopf's Farm School officially became the Delaware Valley University. Nearly every older building on that campus bears the name of a KI family to this very day. For decades, and maybe again in the future, it was one of this synagogue's many ways to care for the orphans of Philadelphia and beyond.

In 1920, a young man by the name of Lessing Rosenwald settled in Jenkintown to help expand his family's world-famous business, Sears, Roebuck and Co. He came to Philadelphia from Chicago. He immediately joined KI. His father, Julius Rosenwald, was one of the great philanthropists in all of American history and a congregant in the Chicago synagogue, headed by Samuel Hirsch's son, Rabbi Emil Hirsch. Julius Rosenwald was a Jewish Andrew Carnegie. In his lifetime (1862–1932), Rosenwald gave away seventy million dollars to promote education and fight racism in Chicago and across the Deep South. He took up the cause of the widow and the orphan with all his heart, with all his soul, and with all his might. He embodied the spirit of the prophets of ancient Israel and the spirit of KI where his rabbi had been reared as a child.

In many ways, prophetic social justice was the central message and principal method of the early Reform movement in the United States. Reform was not just an easy path to Jewish ritual observance. It was a gallant attempt to restore the prophetic passion to Jews and Judaism late in the nineteenth century. Slavery, unfair labor practices, poverty, inferior education, racial and religious discrimination, and unjust war were among its chief concerns.

On the one hand, classical Reform rejected anarchism and the call to destroy government and authority. On the other hand, it equally resisted the centralization of national economies by the left and the right, as well as government curtailment of human rights.

Reform sought a middle course: the prophetic way. It was closely aligned with American progressivism. Rabbi Krauskopf, for example, was a personal friend of Teddy Roosevelt. To this day, our lobby has a stained-glass window in memory of Roosevelt.

Rabbi Emil Hirsch in Chicago championed economic justice and had it added as the final plank of our movement's first great Platform, the Pittsburgh Platform of 1885, which addressed the great economic disparities of its day.

Perhaps the greatest Reform voice for justice was Rabbi Stephen Wise. He was a founder of the National Association for the Advancement of Colored People (NAACP) long before the rest of the Jewish community took up the cause of Civil Rights. He battled the anti-Semitic priest, Charles Coughlin, on the radio and, along with Louis Brandeis, championed the cause of Zionism for decades prior to World War II.

In 1959, the Reform movement voted to establish a real presence in Washington, DC to bring its prophetic message to the nation's capital on a permanent basis. The Religious Action Center quickly emerged as a central meeting place of the American Civil Rights movement. Federal legislation was prepared at the RAC despite tremendous resistance from within and beyond our movement. The RAC Director Rabbi David Saperstein became one of the nation's best-known voices for justice.

In 1970, our own congregation, Keneseth Israel, decided to immortalize the prophetic message of social justice by commissioning artist Jacob Landau to create our stained-glass windows. Our windows are not just ornaments. They are massive statements about justice, forgiveness, and peace. They are not art for art's sake, they are visual *midrashim* urging us to reach further in our own pursuit of justice.

So what are we doing today as a congregation? As individuals, hopefully, most, if not all of us, are doing something for the common good.

If anyone in this sanctuary tonight is personally involved in the work of social justice, as you yourself define it, whether through education, art, philanthropy, political activism, cultural programs, after-school programs, teaching, mentoring, sponsorships, health care, social work, employment, anti-hunger programs, or any other means of helping those less fortunate than ourselves, please stand for just a moment!

But how about us as a congregation, as a totality? Thanks to our third-term president Dr. Arnold Meshkov and the work of Rabbi Kevin Kleinman, social justice is fully reinvigorated at KI. We have many, many congregational projects. Among them are two major initiatives.

First, we have expanded our relationship with Lowell Elementary School in Philadelphia. In addition to school supplies and winter clothes, we are now organizing an extensive volunteer tutoring program to be held at the school. Education is a foundational value in Judaism. The Torah speaks of the priority of education. The kids at Lowell need our help, our extra concern, our capacity to help them secure the basics in math and reading so that they can excel later in life.

"Give a person a fish, they eat a meal. Teach a person to fish, they can feed themselves and their family in perpetuity." Literacy and math competency is something we can help them achieve. But we need volunteer tutors, congregants who are committed to social justice one child at a time. If we can create a team of forty tutors to help a hundred kids and if hundreds of other synagogues across the country do the same, we can begin to make a dent in the endless and devastating cycle of poverty in this country.

Second, we have our HaMotzi Campaign addressing food insecurity in Philadelphia and Montgomery County. We have our holiday food drive and mitzvah garden. This year, starting this November, we will be providing a cooked dinner on the third Sunday of each month at KI to anyone who is food insecure in our area. We will buy the food, cook the food, and serve the food in our auditorium. We will listen to the ancient words of our Passover Haggadah. "All who are hungry, come let them eat" at our table in this house. We have already received funds to pay for the November and December dinners from a devoted family of this congregation. We hope to make this program another signature activity at KI for years to come.

Every Hanukkah for the last few years, we have created a huge menorah in our lobby. Each class in JQuest is responsible for an arm of the menorah, an arm built with large clear plastic boxes to be filled with care products for the widow and the orphan. Our menorah literally becomes a giant *mitzvah* machine. KI should be a giant *mitzvah* machine, and we are well on our way to becoming one, again, as we were in the past.

But there needs to be more—much more—at KI. We need to do research on contemporary social justice issues, we need to test the feasibility of addressing those needs here at KI, and we need to marshal our resources, human and material. Even more than that, we need—and the Reform movement needs—a clear policy statement and philosophy on social justice, on caring for the widow and the orphan.

We also need to identify our blockers that keep us from pushing forward. What are these blockers? Indifference? Apathy? The false confidence that somebody else will do the work for us? Racism? We really don't want to help "them," some might say. Classism? The poor bring it upon themselves. They are lazy, wasteful, and cheaters! Inefficiency? Too many will cheat and steal from us. Defeatism? The problem is too big, and we are too little. Contempt? "Do-gooders" are fools. Perhaps it's the government's problem, and they have already messed things up so badly that we as a community have no chance of making a real contribution?

Perhaps the real blocker is me-ism? I need to take care of me and mine, not yours and theirs. The gauntlet of excuses, protests, and counterarguments are endless.

Perhaps the upcoming visit of Pope Francis to our area will help wake us up in this regard. A friend of interfaith cooperation, the new Pope is rooted in the work of a devoted priest in a hopelessly poor parish. It is not grandeur that makes the Catholic Church great, he teaches his flock. It is the use of its resources to do good for all people. We know we have many areas of official difference with the Catholic Church, but we also have areas of possible cooperation at the local level, at the level of social justice. Let us listen to Francis's message, reach across the aisle to our neighbors of every religious stripe, and get to work in pursuit of the prophetic quest.

KI has done it in the past! Jews have done it throughout the ages! The Jewish community of Philadelphia has a heritage of helping. Tomorrow, we will listen to Isaiah 58 for our haftarah reading for Yom Kippur. It will tell us, yet again, that our faith demands of us both to fast from inequity and to engage in the active pursuit of justice, kindness, and love of neighbor.

Social justice is in the DNA of our congregation! We can keep our congregation strong by making it a great mitzvah machine. Not by might and not by power, the prophet Zechariah taught, "but by *my* spirit" can we dedicate ourselves to greatness through goodness.

May we be filled with the spirit of prophetic justice, mercy, and kindness from this Yom Kippur to the next.

May we become living examples of "good neighbors and decent human beings" and take up the cause of the widow and the orphan and together *bind up the wounds* of our nation and the world.

Amen.

An easy fast!

Rabbi Joseph Krauskopf, Reform Triumphalism, and the 1885 Pittsburgh Platform

2015 ReformJudaism.org

In November, 1885, a small group of Reform rabbis met in Pittsburgh, Pennsylvania, to discuss the basic principles of the then-growing Reform Movement in Judaism in America. Their deliberations were summarized in what quickly became the foundational document of "Classical" American Reform Judaism. Bold and controversial, the Pittsburgh Platform continues to evoke powerful reactions and scholarly interest 130 years after its promulgation.

Scholars of the Pittsburgh Platform have primarily focused on the leading role Rabbi Kaufmann Kohler played in the convening of the conference, its writing and its contentious post-promulgation reception in the American Jewish community of the late 19th century. Similarly, historians have largely located the genesis of the platform as a specific reaction to the high-pitched public debate Rabbi Kohler was having in the summer of 1885 with Rabbi Alexander Kohut, an ardent proponent of "traditional" Judaism and leading critic of Reform theology and practice.

A critically important perspective was offered by Prof. Sefton Temkin in 1985 when he demonstrated that the final version of the platform was as much a reaction to the then-emerging Ethical Culture movement founded by Dr. Felix Adler and its criticism of Reform theism and the Reform Movement's continued attachment to Jewish ethnicity. Indeed, it seems that the best way of reading the Pittsburgh Platform as an historical document is to understand it as a dynamic "middle position" between the secularism of the Ethical Culture movement and traditionalism of the nascent Conservative Movement in American Judaism during the 1880s.

Given the great importance of the Pittsburgh Platform in the history of Reform Judaism in America, it would seem a bit strange then that the rabbi chosen to preside over the Conference that produced it was twenty-seven-year-old Joseph Krauskopf, who had been ordained only two years earlier, in 1883, a member of the first graduating class of the Hebrew Union College (HUC) in Cincinnati. An investigation of the role Krauskopf played in the process which led to the writing of the platform reveals not only his role as the person who first thought of the idea of a Reform platform, but also as an unrestrained champion of a long-forgotten triumphalism which once characterized American Reform Judaism.

Although the original correspondence between Krauskopf and Kohler seems to be lost at the current moment, a lengthy article published about Krauskopf immediately after he returned home from Pittsburgh clearly explains why such a young rabbi was chosen to head the Conference in Pittsburgh. In a recently obtained copy of an article from the *Kansas City Daily Journal* (November 21, 1885), it is clearly reported that it was Krauskopf who urged Kohler to consider convening a conference of Reform rabbis. At that time, Krauskopf was serving as the rabbi of Congregation B'nai Jehudah in Kansas City, Missouri, and was basking in the light of national media attention given to his popular lecture series on the Jews of Spain which quickly became a book, *The Jews and Moors in Spain* (1886).

In his groundbreaking book, Krauskopf waxes ecstatically about the intellectual achievement of Spain's rationalist Jewish philosophers and predicts the demise of non-rational approaches to Jewish life. Krauskopf was studying Iberian Jewish history as part of his post-ordination doctoral studies at HUC. From Krauskopf's perspective, America was the new Spain and Reform Judaism was the ultimate expression of a Maimonidean approach to Jewish life and thought which would move Judaism forward as the cutting edge of redemption, i.e., the "Mission of Israel," in modern times. Interestingly, Krauskopf's next blockbuster series of sermons lined him up clearly with Darwin and evolution, in sharp contrast to the views of HUC President Isaac M. Wise.

Krauskopf was an unrestrained religious modernist and Reform triumphalist whose growing fame later brought him to the attention of

Reform Congregation Keneseth Israel, Philadelphia, Pennsylvania, then one of the largest, wealthiest synagogues in the United States. Once settled in Philadelphia, the indefatigable Krauskopf went on to found the Jewish Publication Society and the National Farm School, now Delaware Valley University, located in Doylestown, PA. He also served as president of the Central Conference of American Rabbis.

Today, as we reconsider the Pittsburgh Platform on its 130th anniversary, it is important to understand both the spirit in which it was conceived and the dynamic context in which it was promulgated. In the end, the platform was more than a defense of Reform Judaism to its critics, it was a clarion call to its followers to move forward in its redemptive work with confidence. In a similar manner, we might also reconsider our own specific historical moment and the manner and spirit in which we practice and advocate Reform Judaism today.

Part 4

Crossroads, Conflicts, and Challenges
2017–2022

Crossroads, Conflicts, and Challenges 2017-2022

By 2017, at the age of sixty-three, I began thinking about retirement. In two years, I would turn sixty-five. At first, I felt that would be too young for me to step down from my pulpit. My goal was to work to seventy-two. Meanwhile, I started paying attention to the steady stream of communications from my pension plan, which regularly suggested to begin the planning process as early as possible. So I decided to go to a pension-planning seminar in Chicago on the suggestion of our synagogue administrator. Many if not most of the members of my class from HUC-JIR (1980) had already retired or begun a step-down process. So I saw no harm in getting things started. The Chicago seminar was excellent, and I learned about the steps I would have to take in the next few years and, most importantly, to retire *to* something and not simply to retire *from* congregational work.

My father retired at the age of fifty-seven for health reasons. My mother, who worked a combination of part-time jobs and was an active volunteer in our home synagogue, kept going full force and never formally retired. At first, my dad kept himself busy with his many cultural interests and joined a ROMEO (Retired Old Men Eating Out) group at a local McDonald's that regularly read and discussed books together. As his health declined, he was compelled to stay at home, read multiple newspapers, and listen to classical music and opera. I knew that was not going to work for me.

My emerging plan was to step down from the pulpit in as orderly and smoothly a manner as possible, return to academia full-time, and write several books, beginning with this collection of my sermons. I love to teach and write, and I began to look forward to a decade or more of "my time." For the most part, my plan to retire to the next phase of my life worked, but a number of unforeseen conflicts and challenges arose, changing the dynamics and timing of my retirement. More than I could have ever imagined, I was at a crossroads in my life but, like everyone else, could not see what was just around the bend of life.

Everything seemed to be on track. As I was always involved in multiple projects at once, my work at KI actually intensified at this point and my literary output increased. I wrote a five-part online series on the Book of Leviticus for the Reform movement and moved into governance at Gratz College, eventually becoming Chair of the Board of Governors of the oldest nondenominational coed Jewish school of higher learning in the United States. Running the Board at Gratz gave me a unique perspective on synagogue governance and administration, which are not as regulated by law as those of universities and colleges. I even had the opportunity to speak about synagogue Board-Rabbi relations at a Founders' Day ceremony at HUC-JIR (Cincinnati) during this period. In preparing for that talk, I learned that the critical study of this area of synagogue life is still in its infancy. Moreover, although the Reform movement had begun investigating new models of synagogue membership, little new was being proposed in the area of governance.

While life in the synagogue was proceeding in a relatively normal fashion, the outside world was becoming increasingly chaotic. In January 2017, Donald J. Trump was inaugurated as the forty-fifth president of the United States. In my estimation, KI is approximately 75 percent Democratic, and an unusual number of congregants expressed grave concerns about the future of the country to me, especially teenage girls who correctly were concerned about the future of reproductive rights in the United States. Eight months later, neo-Nazis carrying torches during a night march in Charlottesville, Virginia, chanted, "Jews will not replace us!" A new era of anti-Semitism in America had begun. Then, on October 27, 2018, a lone gunman attacked the Tree of Life Synagogue in Pittsburgh. Eleven people were killed at services on a Shabbat morning, and six others were wounded, including Holocaust survivors. The number of anti-Semitic incidents in the United States began to escalate rapidly. According to the Anti-Defamation League (ADL), Pennsylvania was at the epicenter of the new reality of American anti-Jewish animus. Later, President Trump's Abraham Accords

(2020), including naming Jerusalem as the capital of Israel, had little effect on calming the nerves of my congregation.

Although I had probably officiated at more than a thousand funerals over forty years in the rabbinate, the untimely death of USMC Captain Samuel A. Schultz (who had grown up locally) on April 3, 2018, on the California-Mexico border deeply affected me. I had officiated at many veterans' funerals but never for an active-service young soldier. Sam's grieving parents were referred to me, and I conducted his service. Over two hundred marines, mostly captains plus one Four-Star general, attended. Their demeanor and camaraderie were deeply impressive. Shortly thereafter, I published a memorial book, *How the Mighty Are Fallen* (2018), about the twenty-four soldiers and sailors from KI who had given their lives in the defense of the United States. In the Introduction, I wrote, "The purpose of this book is to know and remember more than just [the] names. Who were they? Where were they born? Where did they fall . . . and anything else we could learn from public and military records." Somehow, the project deepened my own sense of mission as a rabbi.

With the world seemingly spinning out of control on the outside, my inner life was also rocked by a series of serious problems that developed for several members of my family. It is not easy being victims, and the stress of the moment was intense, if not unbearable, for all of us. Others had seriously wronged us, and so, on the evening of Yom Kippur 2018, I gave a holiday-specific sermon with a twist and asked the question, "What if I cannot forgive you?" It was a question I had pondered about the aftermath of the Holocaust, but this time, it was personal. I cannot remember a more intense or timely Yom Kippur.

The following Spring, I enjoyed a brief respite. On April 12, 2019, the synagogue officially announced the establishment of the Lance J. Sussman Rabbinic Chair, an endowed fund that received one million dollars in my honor. Subsequently, I entered into negotiations for what proved to be my final contract with the synagogue, including the terms but not the date for my actual retirement. Other still-unknown factors would determine when that would happen.

The double helix of internal and external factors shaping my life at the beginning of the third decade of the twenty-first century continued to unfold with unprecedented intensity. In January 2020, COVID officially arrived in the United States. Not only were the numbers of cases and deaths staggering, but we also had to pivot our entire congregational operation to online programming and services. To its credit, the synagogue was keenly aware of the needs of our most isolated, least technologically capable population. My message became increasingly pastoral, and efforts to hold the congregation together, from the youngest to the oldest, were prioritized to the highest level.

On May 25, 2020, an African American man, George Floyd, was murdered by a police officer in Minneapolis, Minnesota. His dying words "I can't breathe" became a rallying call chanted across the country and around the world. Racism and police reform dominated conversations everywhere. It seemed as if the world was out of control. How, we asked ourselves, could we hold our synagogue community together as a place of civility and conscience while severely limited by necessary public health policies during the pandemic? It was not easy, but the social fabric of the congregation held, and slowly but surely "a new normal" began to emerge.

Perhaps it was all too much for me. Secret retirement planning, polarized national politics, COVID, family problems, racial injustice, and rising anti-Semitism all took a heavy toll on me. Early in November 2020, while at a regular doctor's appointment, my primary physician discovered that I had heart disease and needed emergency surgery. I was taken by ambulance to Abington-Jefferson and, after a few days, had a double bypass. Complications followed, and months would pass before I was back at work on a limited basis. I then suffered a setback and had a heart attack. My heretofore carefully planned retirement was now on a fast track. At the synagogue, our cantor Amy Levy doubled down on her efforts as the guiding spiritual light of the congregation while providing me with essential and loving pastoral care.

My family, doctors, and congregation were magnificent. Everyone rallied around me. I received excellent care and experienced, looking up from the bed in CCU, what empathy was all about. Deeply moved, I started writing poems about my experience. In January 2021, with the assistance of my daughter, Chana, I published a book of sixteen poems called *The Kindness Response*. "This slim book," I wrote in the preface, "mostly includes poems written in the wake of my brush with death at the age of sixty-six . . . I hope it adequately expresses my gratitude to those who took care of me in my hour of need and helps others see the need for kindness in everything we do in the hospital, on the street, and at home."

The world, of course, did not stop because I was sick. On January 6, 2022, just prior to the inauguration of Joe Biden as the forty-sixth president of the United States, the first full-scale attempt to overthrow the lawfully elected government of the United States took place in Washington DC. Thousands of demonstrators stormed the Capitol Building. Overwhelmed by the insurrectionists, the Capitol Police fought both outside and inside the House of the People and courageously prevented a coup from disrupting the orderly transfer of government at the executive level. As a nation, we still have not recovered from that moment, and a huge percentage of the American people continue to believe falsely that the 2021 election had been stolen. It is unclear how we as a nation will ever recover from this divide.

Five months later, on May 18, 2021, my own mother, Freda Sacki Sussman, a Holocaust survivor, died at the age of ninety-five. Because of my medical condition, I was unable to officiate at her funeral. Along with my sister, Marcelle, I was now officially an orphan. My mother and her family had been remarkably courageous in fleeing Germany and building a new life in America. The least I could do in her memory was to do the same: survive and remain future-oriented. Part of that effort involved working on a video documentary of a cantata commissioned by KI based on George Washington's 1790 "Letter to the Jews of Newport, Rhode Island," which premiered in June 2021.

I now had exactly one year to go to get to the last day of June 2022. Along the way, I was able to produce with the help of an artist friend Marlene Adler an original art *megillah* called *The Purim Story*. Looking back I realized how appropriate it was that I reformulated a story that teaches the need to laugh in the face of danger. The seasons passed quickly; and a parade of special events, services, and tributes took place. It was a grand send-off. I felt appreciated. I also felt the time had come to stand down.

My time at KI began literally just days before 9/11 in 2001 and ended following the 1/6 attack on the U.S. Capitol in the waning days of the COVID pandemic. During those twenty-one years, a ceaseless stream of external events shaped the life of Reform Congregation Keneseth Israel just as the decline in the Jewish population of Elkins Park challenged its internal operation. Literally, there was never a dull moment as I strove to provide pastoral and spiritual support, offer a wide array of educational and cultural programs, and provide relevant messages from the pulpit and in writing.

Jewish life is anchored in an ancient belief in a covenant between the Jewish people and the Eternal One of Israel. That faith, the steadfastness of the members of the congregation, their generosity of spirit, and the belief in a future envisioned by the prophets when "the lion will lie down with lamb" have kept all of us going in the darkest of hours in recent years. The first decades of the twenty-first century proved more challenging for KI, the Jewish people, and me than anyone could have predicted. But in the words of the Torah, I believe we "prevailed" (Gen. 32:29). I can only hope that the words I offered, written and oral, helped our generation bequeath a vibrant Judaism to our children, grandchildren, and great-grandchildren.

Strangers and Neighbors: The Golden Rule Today

October 2, 2016, Rosh HaShanah Evening 5777

In casual parlor discussions about religion, in general, these days, I often hear two basic opinions. One, all religion is bad. It is the root of evil in the world. Or two, all religions basically have the same basic ethical teaching: love your neighbor as yourself, the so-called golden rule. The two propositions do not work together very well. If number one is true, then number two can't be attributed to religion; and Moses, the Buddha, Lao Tzu, Confucius, Jesus, and a few others were misquoted. If number two is true and religion ultimately is about loving our neighbor, then number one has to be false and religion, at least in its essence, isn't so bad.

I will readily and sadly admit that religionists often make a mess out of their religion. I once bought a bumper sticker that exclaimed, "Lord, save me from Your followers!" I didn't think it was a good idea to put it on my car. On the other hand, murdering people in the name of God is not very religious. Nor is destroying cities a good thing. Blowing up one-thousand-year-old rock-carved statues of the Buddha is not being respectful of others either. The list goes on.

The fact of the matter is that if you drill down into scripture—all types of scripture, not just Jewish—chances are you are going to find the golden rule stated somewhere, in some form, positive or negative: love your neighbor or "don't do to others what you don't want them to do to you." Either way, it says the same thing. But basically, in addition to a spiritual paths, symbols, holidays, theological concepts, constructs of community, and alike, you are going to find somebody in a high place in almost every religious tradition saying, very simply, "Love your neighbor as yourself."

In our tradition, it is in the Book of Leviticus. KI likes the Golden Rule so much that we made the Golden Rule the motto of our congregation, recorded it in our charter of incorporation, carved it on the pillars on Old York Road, and, most recently, added it to the front of the lower *bimah* reading desk in Hebrew: *V'ahavta l'rayahcha comocha*, just three words in Hebrew, "to love your neighbor as yourself."

Probably the best-known illustration of this principle, at least to Americans, is Norman Rockwell's 1961 cover of the *Saturday Evening Post*. You know the picture. There's a rabbi with a tallis over his head. A German or Norwegian mother with a braid in her hair holding her blond child, an African boy holding a bowl, a Chinese child in a red coat, a Japanese lady in a kimono, and several dozen other people with the golden words "Do unto others as you would have them do unto you" neatly printed, Rockwell style, in the front.

Interestingly, Rockwell did not have to travel around the world to find models for the people in his picture. In a 1961 interview, indicating the man wearing a wide-brimmed hat in the upper-right corner, Rockwell said, "He's part Brazilian, part Hungarian, I think. Then there is Choi, a Korean. He's a student at Ohio State University. Here is a Japanese student at Bennington College, and here is a Jewish student. He was taking summer school courses at the Indian Hill Museum School." Pointing to the rabbi, he continued, "He's the retired postmaster of Stockbridge. He made a pretty good rabbi [but] in real life a devout Catholic. I got all my Middle East faces from Abdalla, who runs the Elm Street market, just one block from my house." Seems the whole world was just around the corner from his studio. They were all his neighbors, and he loved them all.

The Golden Rule was the subject of considerable debate among the ancient rabbis. Some pointed out that the word *neighbor* might mistakenly be understood too narrowly and mean somebody we already know or who lives next to us or maybe only other Jewish people. Maybe it means we should love other Jewish people more than we love other people and treat them Jews in a nicer fashion because they are Jewish. Well, to make sure that didn't happen, the haftarah the rabbis attached to that Torah portion was from The Book of Amos Chapter 9 and begins, "Are you not as the children of Ethiopians to me, O Children of Israel? says the Lord."

Make no mistake about it. *Neighbor* in the Golden Rule "Love your neighbor as yourself" means everybody—all our neighbors, the ones who are like us and the ones who are not like us, the ones we like and the ones we don't necessarily like. All of them are people, all are the children of God, all are entitled to our neighborly love and respect.

Like Einstein's famous equation $E=mc^2$, the Golden Rule is easy to say but not so easy to apply in real life when your neighbor is a nut or a louse or noisy or messy. And what happens when you don't love yourself? Am I entitled to not love my neighbor? And what about the narcissist? He loves himself so much there's no room left to love anybody anyway.

Hence, the variants in how to state the Golden Rule anticipate overinflated objections to what is the basic foundation of human society, which is "to love one's neighbor as oneself"!

To make the golden rule a living principle, there are many challenges:

We need to respect each other's rights and property.

We need to be mindful of each other's feelings, needs, shortcomings, and failings.

At times, we would need to go beyond ourselves and try to become aware of the reality of others.

We would need to assume some basic shared humanity with other people; and we need to act accordingly at least as a starting point before life gets messy, noisy, litigious, or, God forbid, violent.

We might even want to share our material wealth to help strangers just because they are, so to speak, neighbors.

In our society, perhaps no issue involving acceptance of "neighbor" has been more traumatized, over more time, than with the African American community. It is an old and deep issue in this country. America did not invent racism. America did not even invent slavery. But America found a way to institutionalize racism in its own image and to create and destroy its own system of slavery. In my mind, we as a society are actually getting better, and we have abrogated bad laws and instituted new paths to equality. There is a rising middle class in the black community, and we elected a black president—unthinkable as little as fifty years ago. But those paths to acceptance have not always been paved smoothly or directly or completely. We have many successes, as a nation, but we still have a way to go to achieve the scriptural goal of placing the "Ethiopian" on the same plane as the chosen.

At the height of this summer's tensions between the black community and various community police forces, the chief of police of Cheltenham

Township approached KI about us serving as the venue for an open community meeting. We were honored by the police's request and opened our building to them and the community at large. The local NAACP (National Association for the Advancement of Colored People) and area pastors joined us as well. Cheltenham residents—young and old, black and white, police and citizens—came and spoke and shared. People were honest and respectful. The police were patient and humble. Democracy was well served. Police community relations were well served. "Love of neighbor" was well served.

This summer, Liz and I also went to a place, at her suggestion, in Atlanta, Georgia, called the Center for Human and Civil Rights. It is on the same campus as the World of Coca-Cola and the Georgia Aquarium. It is family-friendly, but it is also profoundly moving and challenging. The main exhibit is a high-tech, interactive series of well-lit displays about the Civil Rights movement of the twentieth century. You can sit at a recreated segregated lunch counter in the South in the 1950s. The barstool under you shakes. The headphones around your ears relay the cursing and hot breathing of pro-segregation protesters with lifelike clarity. You feel the heat. You get to see the side of a freedom-burnt freedom rider bus. You get to sit in an "all sides," bigger-than-life theater as you listen to Dr. King share his dream. You get to feel the hate, the resistance, the wall of intolerance, as best as a museum can do.

Across town, we also went to the old Ebenezer Baptist Church and sat in a pew listening to a recording of Black gospel music and a eulogy for Dr. King. It's now a quiet National Historic site. But in that pew, and in those displays, we learned something deep about what it feels like when love of neighbor fails and how strong love of neighbor can be when it no longer allows itself to be denied by anybody, no matter how strong or how persistent.

We live in complicated times, and we have a complicated history. There are always shades of truth, and there are shining truths. Love of neighbor is a shining truth and an enduring challenge. It was a challenge in Ancient Israel. It was a challenge in 1954 in America, and it is a challenge today.

Earlier this summer, in the wee hours of June 12, a twenty-nine-year-old shooter by the name of Omar Mateen, an American of Afghan descent, entered the Pulse Nightclub in Orlando, Florida. At about 2:00 a.m., when the last call for drinks was announced, he opened fire with a semi-automatic assault rifle and a Glock handgun. Three hours later—after a wild binge of killing and mayhem, phone calls, texts, and Facebook postings—the security forces on the scene reported that the shooter was down. Forty-nine innocent people were dead, and even a greater number were wounded, many seriously. Mostly from the LGBTQ community. Many Hispanic. Some were just kids looking to have a night of dancing and fun.

Mateen's coworkers later reported he was filled with hatred and contempt. He hated gays, blacks, Hispanics, and Jews. The felonies he committed at the Pulse club were classified as hate crimes and acts of terrorism. Wrenching questions about gun control, immigrant screening, domestic terrorism, and even American foreign policy began swirling in the media and in society.

But it was the outpouring of love of neighbor from across the country and across the land that caught my attention and moved my heart. American flags, public and private, went to half-staff. The rainbow flag was unfurled everywhere. Blood drives were held, many sponsored by Muslim groups. Five days after the massacre, fifty thousand people gathered in a park in Orlando, the fun capitol of Florida and America, to mourn together and to reaffirm love of neighbor.

Here at KI, we served as the venue for a multi-faith memorial service for the killings in Orlando. We met in the Cook Courtyard in an open space, under our pillars with the words of the Golden Rule engraved directly above us. Christians, Jews, Muslims, straight, gay, clergy, lay, public officials, old, and young participated. We lit forty-nine candles. We prayed silently for forty-nine seconds. We listened to a proclamation against terrorism here, in France, in Israel by the Board of Rabbis. We posted our pictures on social media; and hundreds more added their prayers, their tears, and their concerns to ours.

In the Jewish tradition, the Torah supplies us with a rationale for our tradition's ethics. "Love the stranger," we are taught, "because you were once strangers in the land of Egypt." In the Jewish tradition, we have a collective memory of what it means to be the "other," "the outsider," "the marginalized," "the oppressed," and, too often, "the victim." Centuries of suffering have informed our ethics as a people not to oppress, not to hold the whip, but to be a good neighbor, to put down the whip, to respect the body, the person, and the soul of the other.

It is not surprising that in modern times, Jews were among the first to take up the cause of the other, first in Europe and then in America, combining ancient Jewish teachings with modern sensibilities about human rights for all people. The Reform movement in Judaism, in particular, found its social conscience during the years of the American Civil War and then again in the fight against the exploitation of child labor; the denial of black civil rights; and the political, social, and economic subjugation of women.

The 2016 June massacre in Orlando brought into focus three streams of animus, which challenge us as Americans and as Jews, including homophobia, xenophobia, and Islamophobia. In 1965, the Women of Reform Judaism passed a historic resolution calling for the decriminalization of homosexuality in the United States; and thirty-five years later, in March 2000, the reform rabbinate became the first clergy organization in the world to sanction same-gender officiating. Just one year ago, the Reform movement passed a resolution calling for equality, inclusion, and acceptance of all gender identities and expressions. Every one of these issues has a corollary, a household or two or three, in this congregation. We are serious about inclusion at KI in our philosophy and in our practice. Please look at our museum display on "Gay, Jewish, or Both" sometime during this holiday season.

I actually learned the word *xenophobia*, fear of foreigners, from our High Holy Day prayer book. It's one of the sins we seek to expiate from ourselves and our society on Yom Kippur. No one knows better than the Jew how hurtful xenophobia can be. In the wake of the Civil War, restrictive covenants were increasingly employed in the United States to block unwanted groups like Jews, Italians, and other immigrant groups from housing, social clubs, and recreation. Neighborhoods were closed. Beaches were closed. Country clubs were closed. Quotas were then used to limit Jewish enrollment in Ivy League schools and, ultimately, Jewish entrance to the United States with the passage of the National Origins Act of 1924 was effectively blocked.

Earlier this year, I had the pleasure and honor of speaking before the United States Capitol Historical Society in a Senate hearing room in Washington, DC. I was one of a dozen speakers on American immigration policy on the occasion of the fiftieth anniversary of the 1965 Immigration Act, cosponsored by a Jewish congressman from NYC Emanuel Celler. Celler was the only member of Congress present when the United States closed its doors to North Atlantic immigration in 1924 and then spent the rest of his life trying to reopen the gates. He was the only Congressman to universally receive good marks for consistent rescue efforts during the Holocaust and then was the driving force behind allowing Holocaust survivors to come here in the 1950s. Celler successfully fought for family reunification and special skills allowances in immigration law.

Today, much of his work is under scrutiny again although his legislation did not speak to the long-term, purposefully porous, and only recently militarized southern border of the United States. Why did so many Americans want to keep Jews out of this country prior to the 1950s? Well, obviously, Russian Jews, in particular, were known to be attracted to dangerous political ideologies; and they were easily radicalized and were often tied to violent, bomb-throwing groups, especially anarchists and, later, Bolsheviks. They also took jobs away from native-born Americans and then undercut wages by working off the books. Jews were also poor, prone to street crime, and had bad morals—working all sides of the nation's red-light districts. "Keep them out of the country, the neighborhood, and the country club" was the cry of the day in 1890, 1920, and 1935.

To this day, American Jews take a leadership role in immigration reform through HIAS (originally the Hebrew Immigration Aid Society) and other agencies and continue the work of the absorption, integration, and naturalization of new immigrants. When I was a child, my own father, a native-born American but the son of an immigrant father and the husband of an immigrant wife, spent his evenings teaching English as a second language. "Love your neighbor as yourself" was the unspoken motto of his community work.

For sure, the most challenging form of social animus for today's American Jewish community is Islamophobia. Both parts of our identity are in play here. As Americans, we know our country is under attack by Islamic terrorists and extremists looking for the next soft target to hurt us. As Jews, we know that Islamic terrorism includes a deep violent hatred of Jews, Judaism, and Israel. They hate us without reservation and will do anything to inflict pain on us and, given the opportunity, kill us—all of us. Jihadism is genocidal, and it has been since the days when the Mufti of Jerusalem met with Hitler. Whether Sunni or Shia, Hamas or Hezbollah, there is no question as to their intentions.

We are then left with a series of very difficult issues and challenges. Are all Muslims jihadists? Is Islam inherently jihadist? How do we balance our security interests with our democratic principles? How do respond to Abraham's impassioned challenge to God not to wipe out the wicked of

Sodom and Gomorrah along with the innocent? That question alone is significant enough that we display it in the very first of our own stained-glass windows in the sanctuary.

If you look around the Jewish world, you will find amazing responses to Islamophobia. IsraAID, a global Israeli rescue effort on whose North American Board I proudly sit, has operations in Jordan, Iraq, and Turkey, aiding Syrian refugees by the thousands as well as Yazidis and others. In Germany, despite the backlash, Reform synagogues with the help of the American Jewish Committee are working directly with Syrian refugees in Berlin and other German cities. In Los Angeles, the Hebrew Union College is spearheading Jewish-Muslim dialogue. And here at KI, for five years, we have been hosting a Turkish Muslim group for an annual breakfast for Ramadan.

I know there is tremendous skepticism about these efforts. But they are part of a larger whole that seeks to embrace love of neighbor as a guiding principle and a source of hope. The reality in America is that many of us have Muslim medical doctors. The reality in America is that there is Muslim military personnel deployed on the front lines serving and dying to defend us. The reality in Philadelphia is that there are already as many Muslims as there are Jews in this region. We can build moats and castles and increase our security systems, or we can find ways to break bread together. The growth of Islam in America, in Europe, and around the world is statistically inevitable. We cannot control it, but we can control our response and decide whether we are going to put all our efforts into sandbags or into bridge building. The question is, are we going to live by the Golden Rule and our higher selves, or are we going to become some kind of mirror image of everything our tradition has resisted for thirty-six centuries?

Loving one's neighbor as oneself is not easy. It means going beyond one's safe place. It means reaching out. It means meeting others on the shaky bridge of humanity, which spans the roaring waters of hatred and mistrust.

KI has always worked institutionally to enact its belief in the Golden Rule. First, in the struggle against slavery. Later, in its work on behalf of orphans and indigent children in nineteenth-century Philadelphia. Now, in its expanded HaMotzi dinner and Lowell School projects. We serve home-cooked meals to the food insecure once a month in this building. We have a small army of tutors who go to an elementary school in Logan where 100 percent of the children live below the poverty line. We plan to build a beautiful playground for those children along with their school and a church in North Philadelphia.

Thanks to our cantor, we now have a *tzedek* center for the collection of clothing, food, and books in our lobby. We are the founders and host site for the Cheltenham Area Multi-faith Council, and we continue our Muslim-Jewish dialogue. We are a giant mitzvah machine trying to achieve the challenge of our congregational motto and our tradition's fundamental principle: love your neighbor as yourself.

Precisely because we love our tradition, so too we love our neighbors: Jewish, Christian, Muslim, gay, straight, immigrant, native-born, Black, White, yellow, red, and brown.

Finally, if you want to see love of neighbor, come to a Tot Shabbat here at KI. We have a completely diverse community in our preschool—every hue, every faith, and no faith at all, together, here in this synagogue. Non-Jewish families trust us with their little ones because they know we will love them like our own and share, not impose, our faith. I see it every day at the ground level of this synagogue. In a world filled with hate, violence, mistrust, anger, and despair, it gives me hope that one day the same little kids who sing and dance and hug each other as children here will be able to do the same as adults wherever they live, however they will pray. *Kain y'hi ratzon*. So may this be God's will, and so may it be our mandate to love one another. Amen.

The Fight Against BDS: Israel's Battle for Legitimacy

October 3, 2016, Rosh HaShanah Morning 5777

Three days ago, on Friday, September 30, 2016, leaders from around the world assembled in Jerusalem to pay their last respects to Shimon Peres. Peres, born in 1923 in Poland, was the last link to the founding generation of the Jewish state and one of Israel's most respected statesmen. Peres was one of the major architects of Israel's military, the father of Israel's nuclear program, and the visionary of Israel as a "startup" state, a world leader in technology. He was also a visionary for peace and a man who believed that through strength, Israel could achieve peace with its neighbors. Peres believed in the two-state solution, helped negotiate the Oslo Accords, and was a leading figure in creating a peace treaty between Israel and the Hashemite Kingdom of Jordan. For his efforts, he was awarded the Nobel Peace Prize in 1994.

Because he was brilliant, handsome, and worldly, the top leaders of every major country on this planet—from China and Russia to France, the UK, and the United States—felt drawn to this man. It is less clear, however, that the respect they had for Peres is not matched by the respect they have for the State of Israel. Peres represented the mythic Israel to the world. He embodied the ideals of the founders of the State and truly believed in the prophetic purpose of the State of Israel as laid out in Israel's Declaration of Independence. That is transcendent Israel, the Israel of heaven.

The earthly Israel is another place. A place of stone and conflict. A place of competing nationalisms and, increasingly, a place of clashing religious ideologies. A place where it seems that the plough is beaten into the sword more often than swords are beaten into ploughshares. Israel was born in fire, and by might and by spirit, it has endured. It is an intense mixture of idealism and dreams and hard realities and bitter challenges. Peres helped remind the world of Israel's aspirations as a new nation. The world, however, has a tough time allowing those aspirations to become secure realities.

As a nation, Israel can send its delegation to the Olympics. But Israeli athletes are disrespected in Munich and in Rio, and the Olympic Committee does virtually nothing. Why? Because the world, the Olympic Committee, has not exorcized the demon of deep anti-Zionism and, therefore, anti-Semitism. It is this demon that whispers the old slander that Jews, Judaism, and their national aspirations are not fully legitimate but suspect in their basic humanity.

The reality is that Israel always has had to fight both for its security and its political legitimacy. In many ways, Israel has had more success in the area of security, as difficult as that has been, than it has in the fight for legitimacy and parity among the nations. This is not to say that the issue of Israel's national security is resolved. The recently concluded thirty-eight billion dollar deal with the United States helps as does increased military cooperation with the United States. Opinions are deeply divided as to whether or not the Iran nuclear deal helps or hurts. Those who favor it claim the treaty derailed Iran's nuclear program. Those who disapprove believe the Iranians, no matter what guarantees they may offer, cannot be trusted.

Then there are the very real issues of Hamas in Gaza and Hezbollah in Southern Lebanon and Syria. Hezbollah, in particular, although currently caught up in the Syrian civil war, now probably has two hundred thousand missiles, which can fall on Haifa, Jerusalem, and even Tel Aviv, a continuing existential threat. And there is the security threat of terrorism, while not existential, is significant nevertheless.

In each case, Israel has military responses ready. In each case, Israelis have the psychological armament to deal with the situation at hand.

But as much as Israel wants and fights for physical security, it also battles and craves political legitimacy, a less measurable but nevertheless very real national need. Zionism tried to solve the question of global anti-Semitism by offering oppressed Jews a Jewish place to live and offering hostile nations a way of emptying themselves of their Jewish population. But it wasn't enough. In the end, the establishment of Israel only repositioned anti-Semitism as anti-Zionism. Israel was to be the Jewish national home in the family of nations. However, much of the world has yet to accept the proposition that the Jews of Israel constitute a legitimate nation. Instead, Israel, with all its ideals, is called a pariah state, a European colonial enterprise, and, worst of all, inherently racist.

In my opinion, Israel continues to meet its burden of self-defense through military preparation, resiliency, and tactical and strategic superiority. By contrast, the battle for national legitimacy lags behind. What Israel's enemies can't do with bombs, they do with propaganda, diplomatic ploys, and other weapons of delegitimization.

Perhaps the best-known current campaign to de-legitimize Israel at the grassroots level, particularly in Europe and the United States, is BDS (Boycott, Divest, Sanction). BDS technically started in July 2005 and was convened by a BDS National Committee with 170 constituent groups. The failure of the Second Intifada and the beginning of the construction of the West Bank separation fence sparked the organizing of BDS. The first BDS conference was held in Ramallah in 2007 and has since grown into an organized worldwide operation.

BDS is actually an extension and expansion of the older Arab League economic boycott of all Israeli products and includes cultural and academic boycotts as well as material ones. In this regard, BDS builds on the work of groups like Students for Justice in Palestine, founded in 1993, which now has over eighty chapters on American college campuses. BDS also seeks support from the third-world trade unions, professional academic groups, and university-based student organizations.

Highly organized, BDS has three major objectives, which, in a coded way, call for the delegitimization and destruction of Israel as a Jewish State:

1. Ending the occupation and what BDS calls the colonization of all Arab lands including the dismantling of the security fence
2. Working for the full equality of Arab Palestinian citizens of Israel
3. The Right of Return of all Palestinian refugees to their homes and properties

To be clear, BDS is not just an anti-settler campaign, and it is not just a campaign against Israeli policies and practices in the territories. BDS is against everything Israeli without differentiation. It is this distinction and the attempt to isolate and quarantine everything Israeli, including all its scholars and artists, that makes BDS so nefarious and dangerous. And yet it is often confused with more limited protests, an objective its founders and operatives work toward. Therefore, clarity on the matter of BDS is particularly important. I personally was confronted with this blurring of the lines several times during the past year in conversations with sophisticated, educated friends and colleagues who insisted that BDS was a righteous struggle against Israel's activities in the territories. And while I agree that those policies need study and debate, they are not the sum total of Israel as a nation.

By analogy, it is one thing to say that the United States has deep problems. It is another thing to say that the whole country should be destroyed and its population dispersed or destroyed. We should be clear what BDS is really about, and that it is not a legitimate prosecutor of the sins of Israel.

In fact, on the global stage, BDS sees itself as the heir to the anticolonial struggle against apartheid in South Africa and characterizes Israel as an apartheid state despite the political realities of Arabs in Israel proper. To that effect, BDS sponsors an international Israeli Apartheid Week, which is usually held in February or March and is now observed in dozens of countries and on scores of college campuses around the world. It has attracted the support of celebrities like Pink Floyd musician Roger Waters, American novelist Alice Walker, Stephen Hawking, and Anglican Archbishop Desmond Tutu. Teachers' unions in England and Quebec have also voted to support BDS.

On the other side of the equation, celebrities like Gene Simmons of KISS are publicly opposed to BDS as are Jon Bon Jovi, Celine Dion, Jennifer Lopez, Justin Timberlake, and novelist Ian McEwan. I mention these names from popular culture for a specific reason. Whereas scholars differ as to the economic effectiveness of BDS, I worry about its cultural impact on students and young adults. Even when it cannot win over converts, BDS has the effect of making anti-Israel activity seem benign.

Millennials, in particular, both here and abroad, are susceptible to BDS influence. BDS is particularly active on college campuses and can have a Marrano effect on many Jewish students who shrink from controversy that might adversely affect them both socially and academically. We know from the Pew reports and other places that there is a significant drop in support for Israel among young American Jews. They did not live through the Holocaust or experience the traumas of the 1967 and 1973 Wars. To young

Americans and young American Jews, Israel, though tiny, is a military superpower, apparently invincible and often inappropriately heavy-handed in its military and police actions. It is, therefore, easily criticized and always suspected of being anti-third world.

BDS and its allies are working relentlessly on shaping the global narrative about Israel. They are arguing that in 1948 the Haganah was militarily superior to the Arab forces and that its commanders were responsible for the mass ethnic cleaning of Palestinian Arabs. They are arguing that the '67 war was a war of aggression and that the Israeli conquest of the territories was illegal. Most of all, they argue that the occupation of the West Bank is irredentist and seeks to suppress both the national and civil rights of its inhabitants. It claims that Zionism is ultimately a racist and colonialist enterprise and that whatever reactions the residents of the West Bank have, from bombs to knives, they are understandable and forgivable given their life situation. BDS is forgiving of terrorism and soft on the religious extremism of Israel's enemies and tough on Israel in every respect. Its goal is to destroy Israel's image and delegitimize it in every way possible.

As we know, these opinions are present, particularly on college campuses today. Sometimes they are expressed as a matter of free speech. Sometimes they are introduced in courses not as viewpoints in the conflict but as the opinion of the instructor who can take cover behind the veil of academic freedom. And sometimes they are the course itself, as is currently happening at UC Berkeley.

What can be done to fight BDS? First, here at KI, one-third of the Confirmation year in tenth grade is spent studying the Arab-Israeli conflict. We are explicit in telling our students and their families we seek to bolster our students so they will be ready to participate in the conversations that await them in college. Second, Birthright Israel is an excellent opportunity for Jewish college kids to go to Israel with their peers to learn about Israel and bond with Israel. Third, good information is critical. An online resource called JerusalemU.org is particularly effective for college students and young adults.

While BDS is waging an overt propaganda war against Israel and seeks to bring economic pressure on the Jewish State, Israel also faces other forms of delegitimization. To me, no issue is more important in this regard than the public perception of Israel's borders and what territory Israel can legitimately lay claim to.

While it is true that the United Nations did vote for the establishment of a Jewish State in 1947, a fact many of Israel's enemies conveniently forget, the borders of the actual State of Israel have never been fully defined by the United Nations and the nations of the world, including the United States of America.

Because of hard-fought wars in 1948, 1967, and 1973, Israel's borders have changed dramatically. Today, a few countries accept the so-called Green Line of 1967 but do not accept Israel's version of the map when it comes to the Golan Heights, Latrun (that is, the gateway to Jerusalem), and the municipal boundaries of the city of Jerusalem. Others accept the Green Line for Israel but not for Palestinians, who, it is argued, have unqualified rights of repatriation on the Israeli side of the Green Line in Israel proper.

In my opinion, with respect to the question of Israeli national legitimacy, the most important of these boundary disputes is Jerusalem. According to international law—the UN, the United States, the Vatican, and others—Jerusalem legally should be a *corpus separatum*, an international zone that is neither Israeli nor Palestinian. Hence, from an American perspective, Peres's funeral on Friday was in a stateless place called Jerusalem, not Jerusalem comma Israel.

Ultimately, the United States and others are saying that with a final settlement of the Arab-Israeli conflict, they will eventually support a two-Jerusalem solution—that is, an Israeli Jerusalem and an Arab East Jerusalem—although no one knows where the boundaries will be, and whether or not this "double Jerusalem of the future" will have a single or a double set of municipal services like the Cold War–divided city of Berlin.

By contrast, Israel and the Zionist movement before it have always viewed Jerusalem as the political capital of the Jewish State and the spiritual capital of the Jewish world. Already in 1877, when Naftali Herz Imber wrote *Hatikvah*, he assumed that Jerusalem would be the capital of the future Jewish State. In 1927, the Jewish Agency built its campus on King George Street in Jerusalem, and it served as the governmental center of the nascent Jewish State except for a brief period during the War of Independence.

Because of the fighting and siege in 1948, the State of Israel was proclaimed from a location in Tel Aviv; but already in February, 1949, when the Knesset convened for the first time, it did so at the Jewish Agency location in Jerusalem.

With the help of the Rothschild family, the current Knesset opened in Jerusalem in August, 1966.

From the earliest dreams about a Jewish State to the founding of the State of Israel, the Zionist movement always held that its capital was Jerusalem as generations of Jews had done before them in their dreams of returning to Zion. Even this morning's Torah portion, the binding of Isaac, is widely understood that the location of that story, Moriah, the mountain upon which the Temple was first built, indicates that Jerusalem would be the capital of the Jewish people. By comparison, would anybody still insist that Philadelphia is the capital of the United States because the Declaration of Independence was written here and Congress did not meet in Washington, DC until 1800?

Today, the situation with respect to Jerusalem is absurd. The government of Israel is in Jerusalem with the important exception of the Defense Ministry, which is in Tel Aviv. But then again, the Pentagon is not in Washington, DC either. On the other hand, all of the embassies in Israel are in Tel Aviv while the Ministry of Foreign Affairs, the State Department of Israel, is in Jerusalem.

From the perspective of the American diplomats, every time they meet with their counterparts in the Israeli government, they have to get in their cars, leave Israel, and go to Jerusalem. Moreover, when Anwar Sadat and King Hussein spoke in the Knesset years ago, they could technically claim they were not speaking in Israel or in Israel's capital city.

A fully legitimate State does not have its capital in disputed territory.

It is time for the U.S. Senate's Jerusalem Embassy Act of 1995, an act that would move the U.S. Embassy from Tel Aviv to Jerusalem, to be enforced; recognize Jerusalem as the capital of Israel; and still affirm our government's commitment to a two-state solution. You would think that a country that can pledge thirty-eight billion dollars to a military ally over a ten-year period could also respect that nation's self-understanding as to where its capital is located.

What is holding this up? The serious matters of the separation of constitutional authority in the United States and the wider politics of the city of Jerusalem both serve as blockers. There is also the question of Palestinian national rights and custodial rights over the city's sacred places.

The Palestinian side is complicated. Although the so-called two-state solution calls for a Palestinian capital to be in East Jerusalem, there is, in fact, no municipality called East Jerusalem. So, while there is no State of

Palestine and the provisional capital of that state is in nearby Ramallah, the world inherently accepts East Jerusalem as the capital of Palestine. By contrast, there is a Jewish State, and it has a self-designated and historically justified capital, but literally nobody recognizes Jerusalem as the capital of the State of Israel.

The question of the legitimacy of Jerusalem also includes the final status of the Old City of Jerusalem and its holy sites including the Islamic Dome of the Rock, Christianity's Church of the Holy Sepulcher, and the Western Wall. Unfortunately, the question of the guardianship of the Old City of Jerusalem, particularly the Temple Mount, functionally turns Jerusalem into a kind of cosmic hand grenade and makes the Al-Aqsa Mosque the pin in that dangerous, unstable explosive device.

The political status of the Old City is, in fact, used by the enemies of Israel to block any aspect of normalization with respect to Jerusalem and, by extension, to the whole Jewish State. In my opinion, the failure of the world to accept Jewish Jerusalem as the legitimate capital of the Jewish State deeply contributes to the delegitimization of Israel and the destabilization of the Middle East as a whole.

As Israel enters its post-Rabin, post-Peres era, it does so as a militarily strong country. But there are other battles to be fought for Israel and the Jewish people. Number one on that list is the struggle for political, cultural, and social legitimacy. That fight includes both counterefforts to neutralize BDS and diplomatic efforts to end the confusion over Jerusalem and make Israel a complete State with the capital of its choice and historic right as its true political center.

Let us resolve to join in these struggles. Israel has plenty of problems and many controversial policies. But deep down, it is a legitimate, sovereign State and a true peer in the family of nations. We are part of Israel's struggle for its existence and even its legitimacy whether we accept that challenge or not. So let us be strong and acknowledge that silence strengths delegitimization. By contrast, knowledge and informed participation will go a long way toward the defense of Israel and the well-being of our people around the world. Shana Tova.

Not by Might: Jews, Guns, and Violence

October 12, 2016, Yom Kippur Morning 5777

When I was a kid, I played with guns.
Water guns
Cap guns
Replica Civil War rifles
Plastic Tommy guns
And even blank guns.
At carnivals, I fired phony guns that barely looked like guns at bobbing ducks that never dropped
And fired simulated machine guns on old-fashioned video games at arcades.
And if I didn't have a plastic gun, then I picked up a stick and starting shooting my imaginary enemies with my high-powered pretend tree gun either as a charging marine or a high-power sniper. I was a mean, killing machine in chubby-size shorts who was afraid of stray dogs, all cats, and creepy bugs.

For a short while, my summer camp, Camp Harlam, had riflery.
We had single-shot 22-caliber carbines.
We fired at targets fifty feet away.
Although we were also taught the songs of the civil rights and peace movements of the 1960s, we did have real guns, and I loved it.
I loved the guns, the bullets, the smell of the spent shots; and I loved my

punctured targets, which indicated that I was on my way to being the next Davy Crockett,
King of the Wild Frontier just north of Route 209 in the Poconos.
In Israel, I stood real guard duty on several occasions.
I was issued a very big, very heavy WWII Czechy rifle.
I was also offered to hold and fire an M-16, but I turned it down
But I did accept an invitation to go to a firing range
And shot at indoor targets with a .38.
It was very powerful and very loud.

However, most of my experience with guns was really just watching them on TV and at the movies.
Lots of guns, lots of shooting, lots of single-shot kills.
Today, most American kids watch hundreds of thousands of acts of media violence by age eighteen and see about sixteen thousand stimulated fatal shootings by the time they graduate high school.

My late father, on the other hand, was a real combat soldier in WWII in Europe.
He had extensive training with firearms.
A few years ago, I even found his military-issued license to kill.
I know he was issued a rifle and
he operated a 300 radio in the Battle of Bulge.
He told me he admired his fellow soldiers' gun skills.
They were mostly farm boys from Arkansas and Oklahoma.
He said they could shoot a whisker off a cat at fifty yards.
But he was very afraid of hand grenades and said he taped his up
So they wouldn't accidentally detonate while he was running.
My dad told me he hated guns, his words,
But admired his officers and General Patton, in particular, for their and his Gallantry, courage, and fearlessness that were
Necessary to defeat the Nazi army.
We need people like Patton, my dad said to me, to win war but, soon as the war is over, lock them up like caged tigers.

In college, I was stunned to learn that critics of Judaism, both classical and modern, accused the ancient Hebrews, their God, and their Jewish descendants of being violent and mass murderers.

They had too many horrible examples to prove their point.
The Torah says to kill a people called Amalek—all of them, man, woman, child and beast.
The Bible sanctions revenge killing, they pointed out.
Rebellious sons are to be executed by stoning.
Elijah hacked the priests of Baal into chopped meat.
Haman's sons were publicly impaled.
And Mattathias, at the beginning of the Hanukkah story, killed a Jewish collaborator with a spear in a public square before his townsmen.

In rabbinic school, by way of contrast, I learned about the widespread pacifism of the Reform movement in the early decades of the twentieth century and its enduring rejection of right-wing Zionism, militant Orthodoxy, and, later, the settler movement.

By contrast, I was also taught to believe that Israel's right to self-defense, including preemptive strikes, was morally justified and that a strict adherence to the doctrine of the "purity of weapons" and limiting civilian causalities were deeply embedded in the Jewish State's military ethic. At one point, I even wanted to serve in the Israeli army, although at the time, I was against American military involvement in Vietnam.

As a newly minted rabbi, my very first pastoral hospital visit was to a young man who had accidentally shot himself down the leg while putting his gun into his holster and was in terrible pain. As a prison chaplain for four years, I met with prisoners, convicted of felonies both with and without guns, all of whom insisted they were totally innocent.

Today, I am a mix of feelings and memories about selective conscientious objection, an instinctive inability to fully embrace pacifism, a strong belief in nonviolent political dissent, overwhelming pride in my own father's military service, and a lifelong passion for war movies and visiting battlefields. All swirl around in my head, heart, and soul in unresolved, contradictory, and paradoxical ways.

One issue, however, is un-conflicted for me, and that is a belief in gun control in the United States. Maybe it was the assassinations of JFK, then Martin Luther King, and finally Robert F. Kennedy that did it. Each one of those leaders was a kind of Hollywood idol to me, and each one was cut down by a murderer. Each killing left me sick, angry, and, in a qualified way, anti-gun.

Maybe it was the incredible tide of violent crime sweeping over our cities. When I was a kid, one of my neighbors who owned a pharmacy was shot by a robber. He survived, but his guard dog didn't. My best friend's father, who owned a hardware store, was shot too and barely survived. My uncle, a pharmacist, was robbed at gunpoint. The robber even stuck the barrel of his pistol in my uncle's nose before fleeing the scene.

But long before Columbine and Sandy Hook, I already had a conviction that gun violence was out of control in this country—that efforts to limit the sale of assault weapons and high-capacity magazines were wrong, deplorable, and morally offensive. That efforts resisting and limiting background checks were excessive, that missing guns needed to be reported, and that statistical information on violence needed to be collected by national security agencies and by public health institutions.

There was no question in my mind that the Second Amendment was not endangered by the "slippery slope" of responsible gun legislation but rather that well-being of Americans was compromised by the steep success of anti-gun control forces.

Academic reports that in the big picture violent crime in America was actually decreasing did not offset the reality of actual shooting statistics in Baltimore, Chicago, and Philadelphia. Our cities are, without question, battlegrounds. Our suicide rates are staggering. In fact, self-killing is the leading cause of violent death in America today.

Our use of weapons against one another and on ourselves is unrelenting. And with all that, the successful use of arms for self-defense is statistically irrelevant: a myth, a legend, a projection, but not a real shield against crime. We are willing to take radical action against one form of terrorism, yet precious little against another also vicious from of domestic violence I would also call the terrorism of gun violence.

How many murdered schoolchildren will it take?

How many murdered people in a gay club will it take?

How many random bystanders mowed down by stray bullets will it take?

How many kids who accidentally put a bullet in their heads or their siblings' chests from a gun left unchecked at home will it take until we take some kind of reasonable common-sense action to protect ourselves from the arsenal of inappropriate and illegally owned guns in this country?

A few facts: In the United States, there are approximately three hundred million privately owned guns, one for almost every person in this country. Our total death rate per 100,000 is 10.2; in Australia, it is 1; in Japan, it is 0; in the UK, it's .2. Three countries in the world have a higher firearm homicide rate than United States: Afghanistan, Iraq, and the Congo.

In my view, the "gun status quo" in the United States today is unacceptable. We have too many oversized weapons and too many innocent lives lost and at risk.

What does our tradition have to say about weapons, violence, and self-defense? Judaism painfully recognizes that we are, as a species, fratricidal beings being with story of Cain killing Abel. Yet weapons, Judaism teaches, since we do not hunt in our tradition, are necessary but for extreme circumstances and need to be regulated. In Judaism, self-defense and wars of self-defense are permissible. On the other hand, a tradition that teaches that a flat roof must have a fence to prevent unnecessary injury or loss of life is going to be at least as strict with respect to lethal weapons under that roof.

The Talmud is explicit in urging that neither proven criminals nor known unstable people be allowed to own lethal weapons, and obviously, neither the Torah nor the Talmud can talk about guns per se. Thus, I think it is fair to say that Judaism is not anti-weapon but does not romanticize either weapons or violence.

Just as the prophetic goal of Judaism is to beat swords into ploughshares, there is also the admonition that there is a time to beat ploughshares into swords. So just as Judaism takes a realistic view of weapons and self-defense, it also clearly values peace and security over conflict and a warrior culture.

The Torah teaches that the original altars of the Jewish people were symbolically made of unhewn stone, "lest your sword come upon it and desecrate it." At the end of days, the prophet Isaiah looks toward a time "when the wolf shall live with the lamb . . . and war will cease and the land will be as full of knowledge of the Lord as the water that covers the sea" (1:6).

On Rosh HaShanah, we have prayers and readings that cry out against violence! When Abraham lifts the knife to slaughter his son, a voice thunders from heaven, "Do not hurt the child, do not cut him, do not slay him, do not harm in any fashion."

A ram is sacrificed instead, and the ram's horn, the shofar, is made the permanent reminder, the eternal voice against mindless slaughter and the shedding of innocent blood.

Tekiah—do not stand by when children are being slaughtered.

Shevarim—do not stand by when the peace of your cities is being shattered.

Teruah—do not stand by as rapid-fire automatic gun fire is sprayed across movie theaters and dance floors and schools.

And on both Rosh HaShanah and Yom Kippur, we have the words and warning of the great holiday prayer, *Un'taneh Tokef*, written with the blood of our own medieval martyrs:

On Rosh HaShanah it is written
On Yom Kippur it is sealed:
How many will pass away, and how many shall be born.
Who shall live and who shall die
Who shall live their allotted time and who shall not live their allotted time
Who by fire and who by water
Who by sword and who by wild beast
Who by hunger and who by thirst
Who by earthquake and who by pestilence . . .
Who shall be poor and who shall be rich
Who shall be humbled and who shall be exalted.

To these sacred words, let us add and:
Who by high-capacity magazines and who by semi-automatic fire
Who by indifference and who by fear
Who by political incapacity and who by moral numbness
Who by unenforced law and who by lack of legal sanity?

There is much we can do to improve our situation in our country today:
We can work toward limiting magazine capacity.
We can improve and universalize background checks.
We can insist that if you can't fly, you can't buy a gun.
We can insist on tracking every gun sale at gun shows and online, just as we track every car sale in this country.
We can do a much better job collecting and analyzing the data of gun-related violence both for the purpose of policy and public health.
We can rethink our policies of mass incarceration, which help create hard criminals out of offenders who are not necessarily homicidal in the first place.
And we can do a much better job of working with kids in all areas of

society to teach them that guns are not the answer and that good education and work are the ultimate solutions to our problems and are the true mandated paths of life.

We can do all this and maintain our Second Amendment rights for self-defense, recreation, and collecting.

We can and we must say no to Sandy Hook, Columbine, and Orlando and yes to life, liberty, and the pursuit of happiness.

In the year ahead, let us begin a fast from violence, a reduction in gun-based crime, and vow anew that we will not rest until every citizen in this great land can dwell beneath their own grapevine in peace and with security.

Amen.

Celebrating Hanukkah: To Decorate or Not to Decorate, That Is the Question!

December 2016

It is a well-known fact that Christmas in Western civilization was deeply transformed by the combination of nineteenth-century religious romanticism and (secular) commercialization. First came the romanticized German and English stories and treatises on Christmas at home with family and friends, celebrating with angelic warmth and favorite culinary delights. Then came Woolworths and mass-produced decorations, followed by a boatload of secular Christmas songs (many written by Jews), and bingo—the modern Christmas with lightbulb displays, model Victorian city scenes, and office Christmas parties and bonuses became the old-new way of celebrating the founding of Christianity.

It is also a well-known fact that as Christmas grew in America, Hanukkah also expanded. Expanded gift giving, Hanukkah parties, and competitive Jewish songs were just a few of the compensatory strategies designed to afford our kids "equal treatment." A generation or two ago, many Jewish families even had Christmas trees or "Hanukkah bushes" so as not to lose out on the spirit of the season. If you can't beat 'em, many believed, "join them!" at least for "the holidays." Fortunately, other strategies prevailed.

In my own childhood, we simply lit several menorahs and exchanged basic gifts—nothing fancy. There were no frills or extras, but it still felt good; and from my perspective in suburban Baltimore, the world of Christmas was like a foreign country. Clearly, during the last fifty years, a lot has changed. Christmas has become even more commercial. Also, more Jews work in the "general economy" and less in family businesses or mostly Jewish professional offices. Most of all, the cumulative rate of interfaith marriage has brought at least half the American Jewish community into direct (family) connections to Christmas. When I was a kid, Christmas was "over there," beyond my cultural zone. Today, it is part of shared family space.

Given the dramatic changes in holiday culture, what are we (modern American Jews) supposed to do? Ignore all the lights and carry on? Join in with the Christmas celebrations or further amplify our Hanukkah celebrations? I guess there is wisdom in all three, but I find option three, further amplification of Hanukkah, the best choice. To a certain degree, Chabad led the way with their controversial gigantic public-space Hanukkah menorahs. But I have also noticed an increase in interior home decorations: blue-and-gold pillows with menorahs printed on them, blue-and-silver streamers to decorate the family room and large printed dreidel cut-outs to put on interior doors. No trees, no Hanukkah bushes so to speak, but many more Hanukkah visuals scattered throughout the house.

One area where I only see limited experimentation is outdoor decorations. Chabad has its menorahs, some mounted on cars like Jewish reindeer antlers. Occasionally, I see a blow-up air dreidel, but for the most part, it's quiet outdoors. Should Jewish homes be trimmed with blue-and-white lights? Is there a Jewish version of a wreath for a door? Hey, we already have the modest little mezuzah out there. I am not sure, except that anything garish is too much for me!

So to decorate or not to decorate the outside of our homes on Hanukkah, that is the question! Luckily, tradition offers some guidance here. A menorah should be lit in a window so that we share the "miracle of Hanukkah" with the outside world. Perhaps the time has come to stylize our home *m'norot* so that they can be used meaningfully inside our homes for the blessings and also proclaim our pride in our tradition and our faith in the power, which has sustained us for centuries as a people! Design suggestions welcome!

Shabbat Shalom and Happy Hanukkah!

Neglect: The Hidden Crime

March 3, 2017

Liz and I went to the rally on Independence Mall on Thursday protesting the vandalism in Philadelphia's Mount Carmel Cemetery and the many other acts of animus against the American Jewish community in recent weeks. It was well attended and well run. The crowd was enthusiastic but polite. Muslim, gay activists, Christian clergy, and others were there too as was a student choir from the Barrack Academy. Speaker after speaker condemned hate and spoke out for love. It was a good event with a clear, positive message. Its organizers, particularly the Jewish Federation of Greater Philadelphia, deserve our collective thanks.

But thanks alone, echoing our *High Holy Day Prayer Book*, is not enough. There is another story here that is seeping out in the press about long-term problems with too many of our local Jewish cemeteries. The reality is that the condition of many of the area's older and increasingly forgotten Jewish cemeteries is deteriorating. Landscaping is minimal. Graves settle and stones pitch. Cemetery roads disappear under weeds. Inscriptions vanish.

Leaves pile up. Maintenance shacks rust. Broken shovels and wheelbarrows are only partly hidden away. In others, serious problems with water drainage is rampant. And in still others, repair work never seems to be completed, and there is no general sense of dignified rest. It is easy to rail against acts of hatred; it is harder to perpetuate acts of loving-kindness. Perhaps some of the spirit of volunteerism that stirred up the still-unknown criminals who attacked Mount Carmel could also be used to repair the many graves throughout our area forgotten by time and their management companies. Perhaps professional preservationists could be consulted. Perhaps databases could be constructed. Love, we are told, is stronger than death. Perhaps this would be a good time to prove that proposition.

And more. Yes, we have an obligation to honor our dead. We also have an obligation to nurture our living tradition. Synagogue membership is dropping in America. Enrollment of students in most Jewish education programs is dropping. If no one goes to synagogue, chances are no one is checking on our ancestors' graves either. Acts of hate are crimes and stir us to action, and action is praiseworthy, but it is incomplete if it does not extend to the living community.

In my opinion, the real action against the bomb threats and grave desecrators is involvement in daily Jewish life. The real perpetual care of our tradition is regular engagement in Jewish education, worship, and cultural programming. It is necessary to stand up to injustice. It is also crucial to stand up for tradition. The doors are open. The Eternal Light is still lit. Please keep it that way!

Between a Rock and a Hard Place: Navigating the Book of Leviticus

Vayikra, Leviticus 1:1–5:26
ReformJudaism.org
March 7, 2017

If we were to compare the Book of Exodus to a "rock" (as in Mt. Sinai) and the Book of Numbers to a "hard place" (as in the "wilderness"), then the Book of Leviticus would be somewhere "between a rock and a hard place." My sense is that for most Reform Jews, reading the third book of the Torah, Leviticus, is more a function of calendar than choice: a tough, unavoidable literary landscape with only a few rest stops or scenic overlooks. It's just a territory we must traverse in order to get to the next major site on our annual pilgrimage through the Five Books of Moses.

We are hardly alone in our relationship with the Book of Leviticus. In 1982, Reader's Digest published a condensed version of the Revised Standard Version of the Bible, edited by Bruce M. Metzger, a New Testament scholar at Princeton Theological Seminary. Not surprisingly, Hebrew Scripture in general was condensed by Reader's Digest more than the books of the New Testament, and the Book of Leviticus was compressed the most into just a few pages! Except for its key ethical passages, Leviticus was clearly a spiritual challenge to Professor Metzger and his editorial team. American religious modernists, it would seem, Jewish and non-Jewish, just do not gravitate toward the spirituality of an ancient priestly cult, its sacrifices, garments, and premodern medical practices.

For today's Reform Jews, the Book of Leviticus—including its first portion, *vayikra*—is a spiritual challenge, although we seem to prefer a select reading of the whole book to a condensed version. Our movement's massive and illuminating modern commentary (1981; rev., 2005) to the Torah treats Leviticus in a fashion completely equal to the other four books of the Pentateuch. Anecdotally, it seems that synagogue-based *parashat hashavuah* (weekly portion) groups do not change their curriculum or methodology when they encounter Leviticus on an annual basis. Our *b'nai mitzvah* also are regularly assigned portions from Leviticus in order and without substitution. Of course, some families dread the idea of their children having to study the diagnosis and treatment of leprosy for months on end before their *b'nai mitzvah*, but are still willing for them to learn to vocalize the Hebrew text and find an apt modern, medical metaphor for skin disease for their *divrei Torah*. On the afternoon of Yom Kippur, Reform Judaism has stayed with Leviticus although it did shift the Torah reading by one portion to Leviticus 19. And on the morning of Yom Kippur, we substitute the uplifting report of Moses' ceremony on covenantal renewal in *Nitzavim* (Deuteronomy 29:9–14) for the ancient ritual of the scapegoat (Leviticus 16). (However, the new Reform *machzor, Mishkan HaNefesh,* 2015, includes the option of reading a section of Leviticus 16 on Yom Kippur afternoon.)

Deep down, much of Leviticus remains a problem for most Reform Jews today. Given the history of Leviticus in Reform Judaism, our aversion to much of the Torah's third book should not be a surprise. First, early in its development Reform Judaism openly repudiated Ancient Israel's priestly tradition. In no uncertain terms, Reform Judaism rejected the idea of a dynastic priesthood, the practice of sacrifice, and the belief in the restoration of the Temple cult. Despite the various efforts of neo-Reformers to reclaim "tradition" for Reform Judaism, beginning with the 1937 Columbus Platform, the rejection of the Levitical tradition among Reform Jews has remained virtually complete. In this sense, we are truly "reformed," not Reform Jews.

At the first conference of Reform Rabbis in America held in Philadelphia in 1869, three of the meeting's seven resolutions focused specifically on the place of the Jerusalem Temple and its priesthood in Reform Judaism, relegated them to the distant past, and reinterpreted them as prelude to the enduring mission of the Reform Movement. The conference's original language is both dramatic and definitive:

1. We look upon the destruction of the second Jewish commonwealth not as a punishment for the sinfulness of Israel, but as a result of the divine purpose revealed to Abraham, which, as has become ever clearer in the course of the world's history, consists in the dispersion of the Jews to all parts of the earth, for the realization of their high-priestly mission, to lead the nations to the true knowledge and worship of God.
2. The Aaronic priesthood and the Mosaic sacrificial cult were preparatory steps to the real priesthood of the whole people, which began with the dispersion of the Jews, and to the sacrifices of sincere devotion and moral sanctification, which alone are pleasing and acceptable to the Most Holy. These institutions, preparatory to higher religiosity, were consigned to the past, once for all, with the destruction of the Second Temple, and only in this sense—as educational influences in the past—are they to be mentioned in our prayers.
3. Every distinction between Aaronides and non-Aaronides, as far as religious rites and duties are concerned, is consequently inadmissible, both in the religious cult and in social life.

Sixteen years later, in 1885, a second group of Reform rabbis met in Pittsburgh and again issued a statement of principles in which they reaffirmed their colleagues' earlier rejection of "a sacrificial worship under the sons of Aaron." They also explicitly rejected all forms of priestly purity, dress, and diet as "they fail to impress the modern Jew with a spirit of priestly holiness" consistent with the goals of Reform Judaism.

Sometimes, it seems that we may be softening on our commitment to a Reform Jewish version of "the priesthood of all believers." But, in fact, I believe we are holding the theological line. For sure, issues of diet and dress are now broadly viewed by the Reform Movement as being spiritually relevant in our own time. On the other hand, even in the current attempt to open the Western Wall Plaza to progressive forms of Jewish worship, is anyone calling for a Reform section in a rebuilt Third Temple or the establishment of an egalitarian Aaronide priesthood? The current demands for a pluralistic area at the *Kotel* are spiritual, political, and symbolic but not eschatological. For Reform Jews, the Book of Leviticus is part of our sacred heritage and proof of its evolutionary nature, but clearly not our blueprint for the future of Judaism and the Jewish people.

Unlike in Jewish religious Orthodoxy, Reform Jews today do not read the specifically levitical sections of the Book of Leviticus as a valid substitute for the sacrifices themselves given the absence of a Temple in Jerusalem nor as a training manual for a restored sacrificial mode of worship in the future. For sure, with the help of Midrash, particularly the third century Sifra and subsequent homiletical treatments, we can continue to find spiritual meaning in Leviticus. But in the last analysis, perhaps it was the great reformer and a participant in the 1869 conference, Rabbi David Einhorn, who got it right when he renamed his 1856 prayer book *Olat Tamid*, "The Eternal Sacrifice," using the vocabulary of Leviticus 1 and its description of the burnt sacrifices as his basic spiritual metaphor. The ancient sacrifices may have been appropriate centuries ago. But for us, Rabbi Einhorn, and other Reform Jews, prayer, study, and good deeds are the eternal spiritual sacrifices on the altars of our hearts.

IT ALL DEPENDS: FINDING THE MIDDLE OF THE TORAH

Tzav, Leviticus 6:1–8:36
ReformJudaism.org
March 13, 2017

"Dad, are we almost there?" "Mom, how much longer until we are there?" Anyone, who has taken a family driving trip is well acquainted with these questions from the back seat. Those of us familiar with these junior AAA inquiries also know that answering them exactly is no easy task. Do we simply say, "forty more miles" or do we say, "about an hour"? It all depends on the type of road, traffic, weather, driving style, and possible unplanned stops along the way. Figuring out how to answer "how much longer" or "are we halfway there" is not always an exact science.

Finding the midpoint in the Torah is also a matter of considerable debate. Logically, you might think you could simply unroll a Torah scroll, measure it, and divide that number in half. Basically, that should land you somewhere in the Book of Leviticus, the third of five books of the Torah, assuming that each book of the Torah is about the same length. In fact, they are not equal. Genesis is the longest book, Leviticus is the shortest, and Exodus is longer than Deuteronomy. With the Torah weighted toward the first two books, it makes sense that the midpoint should be somewhere toward the front of the middle book. But that is about all tradition can agree upon with respect to the Torah's centroid. Once you drill down into the details of counting the problem becomes increasingly complicated and finding the middle of the Torah, both mathematically and theologically, is no easy task. It all depends on what you mean exactly by "the middle of the Torah!"

While a tight statistical control of the text of the Torah has been part of Jewish tradition at least since the closing of the Babylonian Talmud over fifteen centuries ago, only with the invention of modern printing, and its mathematically informed computation of book size, did a limited consensus develop as to the middle of the Torah. A commentary to the Talmud, *Massoret ha-Shas* by an Italian Sephardi Rabbi, Joshua Boaz ben Simon Baruch (d. 1557) puts the midpoint of the Torah in this week's portion, *Parashat T'zav*, in a section that discusses the clothing of the High Priest (see Lev. 8:7–8). He observed that "in every *Chumash* and in the reliable *tikkunim* in *Parashat T'zav* [at the point where it says], 'And he put upon him the tunic' [Leviticus 8:7–8], it is printed in the margin 'half the Torah in verses,' which is still the practice to this day." Of course, not everyone was convinced. A second Italian rabbi from a subsequent generation, Yedidiah Solomon ben Abraham Norzi (d.1626), unable to reconcile earlier determinations of the Torah's center based not on verses, but on words and letters, essentially gave up and declared that we "must wait for the prophet Elijah to come to sort things out."

Perhaps the earliest discussion about determining the mathematical center of Torah can be found in the Babylonian Talmud in *Kiddushin* 30a. Here we read about a group of ancient scholars called the *sof'rim*. The Gemara explains that this particular group of *sof'rim*, professional ancestors of our current day Torah scribes, counted the letters of the Torah to ensure the accuracy of the text as it was hand-copied and there was a reasonable risk of error, or what might be called "quality control."

According to the *sof'rim*, the midpoint of the Torah could best be determined in two ways: either by counting by letters or by counting words. Counting by letters only, they determined that the middle letter of the Torah is the *vav* in the word *gachon*, "belly," in Leviticus 11:42. But by counting by words, they determined that the phrase *darosh darash*," diligently inquire" (Leviticus 10:16), is the exact center of the Torah. Finally, they determined that Leviticus 13:33 marked the middle of the Torah if one counted by verses, if there are 5,888 verses in the Torah. But then they immediately added that there are multiple traditions for versification even within the Jewish tradition, so the "middle by verse" could not be definitively determined. No wonder Rabbi Norzi gave up!

Of course, tradition was not willing simply to give up and wait for the Messiah to determine the center of the Torah. Thus, a second, essentialist approach to the question of the essential teaching of the Torah or *Lev HaTorah*, "heart of the Torah," was also explored by the Rabbis. In this case, however, the question is not a mathematical challenge but a philosophical one. The discussion is well known. The core passage is found in the Jerusalem

Talmud, *N'darim* 30b: "Rabbi Akiva [second century CE] taught: 'Love your neighbor as yourself'" (Leviticus 19:18). This is the most important rule in the Torah. But Ben Azzai says: "This is the Book of Chronologies of Adam" (Genesis 5:1).

Ben Azzai's challenge to Akiva's teaching is based on the meaning of the word "neighbor." In the context of the original passage in Leviticus, neighbor could be understood narrowly as "someone you already know" or "your Jewish neighbor." Seeking to universalize the commandment, Ben Azzai demonstrates that all people, Jewish and non-Jewish, are all descendants of Adam and, therefore, all neighbors. The (Ashkenazic) haftarah to Leviticus 19 from Amos 9:7 deflects Ben Azzai's comment by reminding the Jewish people that they, the Jews, and the Ethiopians are all equal in the eyes of God.

It is also possible to discover essentialist meaning in the mathematically determined "hearts" of the Torah. For example, following the word count of the *sof'rim*, the word, belly, suggesting gastronomical Judaism, is key for many people. Keeping kosher or eating traditional Jewish holiday food is, for a number of people today, their principal tie to the Jewish tradition. For others, *darosh darash*, diligently inquire, is the essential principle of Judaism. "The study of Torah," the ancient Rabbis assure us, leads us to the performance of other mitzvot. Today, we even have a widespread phenomenon in the Reform Movement of people who come regularly to Shabbat morning Torah study, delve deeply into the weekly portion, and then promptly leave before services begin. *Darosh darash* is their middle of the Torah.

What about "putting on the tunic"? Very often, particularly at occasions at *b'naii mitzvah* services, weddings, and funerals, people who neither keep kosher nor study Torah insist on wearing a *kippah* or a women's head covering. It makes them feel connected to the tradition, even authentic. For them, "putting on the tunic" is the middle of the Torah.

Finally, the classic middle or heart of the Torah for a large, if not majority of Jewish people today is to "love your neighbor as yourself." Particularly in its expanded, more universalistic meaning, this reflects the view that the essence of Judaism is ethics. In this view, the essence of *Yiddishkeit* is *menschlichkeit*, that is, the uber principle of Judaism is ethics. The principle seems to work equally well for believers and nonbelievers. And as for our super Jewish patriots or Jewish nationalists, the sociologically narrower view of "love your [Jewish] neighbor" works as the middle point for them as well.

Finding the middle of the Torah is no easy matter and the fact is that the lack of a widely agreed upon central teaching creates numerous challenges for the Jewish people. Very frequently, a sincere Christian will say to me that the heart of their faith is "love" and then ask, "What is the central teaching of Judaism?" How we answer that query says as much about us as it says about Judaism. Reform Judaism itself is not above this challenge. We have our principles and we have our practices, but what is the middle of our Torah? I guess it all depends on what you mean by middle and whether the concept of middle as an essentialist viewpoint is even the right way to conceptualize our tradition.

The 13 *Midot*: God is Ethical and So Are We

Chol HaMo-eid Pesach, Holidays Exodus 33:12–34:26
ReformJudaism.org
March 27, 2017

The special Torah reading for *Chol HaMo-eid Pesach*, the intermediate Sabbath of Passover, is Exodus 33:12–34:26, which includes the "13 *Midot*" (Exodus 34:6–7) or "Attributes of God." Maimonides, following the early midrashic work, *Sifrei*, argued that the section would be better known as the 13 "ways" of God: or, better still, ways that we can embrace to be godlike since "knowing" God is not really possible either from the perspective of Judaism's radical monotheism or, for that matter, from the perspective of most branches of philosophy. Thus, proponents both of positive and negative theology turn to Exodus 34:6–7 to ground themselves in a viable Jewish theology of God.

The place of the 13 Attributes in the text of the Torah is important. They appear just after the story of the Golden Calf. Seeing what the people have done in his absence, Moses smashes the first set of tablets. Punishment is then exacted upon the guilty Levites and a general plague serves as a further scourge among the people. Only then does Moses go back up Mount Sinai and cut a second set of tablets. The Eternal One, the Torah reports, passes before Moses and proclaims (according to the prayer book version of the passage): *"Adonai, Adonai,* a God compassionate and gracious, slow to anger, abounding in kindness and faithfulness, extending kindness to the thousandth generation, forgiving iniquity, transgression and sin, and granting pardon" (*Mishkan T'filah* [NY: CCAR, 2007], p. 496).

What is most remarkable about this passage is its emphasis on the ethical. God is not called holy or commanding or jealous. Instead, God self-describes as first and foremost an ethical being. In fact, it would be even more accurate to call God in this passage "the Ethical Being" or, perhaps, the ethical ground of all being. The God of the *Midot* is also a universal God, with a universal set of behavioral norms for all people. The God of the *Midot* does not self-describe as the God who took the Hebrew slaves out of Egypt but rather as a God for all people who need to strive to be like God in order to fulfill their nature as having been created in the image of the One and only God. Perhaps that is why in one midrash, the God of the second tablets is depicted as self-enclosed in a tallit "like a prayer leader" to maintain some Jewish specificity in this important passage.

Early in its development, the Reform Movement made the argument that the essence of Judaism was ethical. Ritual, ethnicity, mystical experience, and alike were downgraded. Judaism was an ethical monotheism that believed in the Golden Rule, the pursuit of justice and humility. The prophets were hailed as ethicists and social activists. Their nationalism was downgraded or ignored. Kabbalah was dismissed as irrational and superstitious. Judaism, to use the language of the day, was all about the "Fatherhood of God" and the "brotherhood of man."

To a large extent, the Reform Movement's reinterpretation of Judaism as ethical monotheism was based on a select reading of the German idealist philosopher, Immanuel Kant (1724–1804), who actually was highly critical of much of organized religion. Like Kant, leaders of the movement believed in ethics as a matter of duty. Unlike Kant, they remained, for the most part, fully theistic and convinced that the Jews remained the Chosen People to lead the world to salvation through morality. One dissident, Felix Adler, son of Reform Rabbi Samuel Adler, rejected both God and Jewish peoplehood, and seized on morality alone, founding the Ethical Culture Society in 1876.

Later in the 19th century, the study of Kant's philosophy was revitalized by Hermann Cohen (1842–1918). The son of a cantor, Cohen had studied at the Jewish Theological Seminary of Breslau to become a rabbi before shifting to the study of philosophy. Ultimately, he combined both interests and became of the one most important modern philosophers of Judaism.

In 1873, Cohen was invited to teach at the University of Marburg. Three years later he was promoted to full professor and remained there until 1912. A respected teacher and prolific author, Cohen transformed Marburg into the center of Neo-Kantian Studies. Like Moses Mendelssohn before him, Cohen quickly became involved in the intellectual defense of Judaism. First, in 1879, he responded to attacks by the historian and nationalist, Heinreich von Treitschke, who claimed that Jews refused to assimilate into Germans. He also denounced the immigration of East European Jews to Germany. For his part, Cohen believed deeply in the compatibility of Judaism and German culture.

Four years later, Cohen was called to testify in a lawsuit against an anti-Semitic teacher who claimed that Jews were bound by the Torah and the Talmud to treat other Jews in an ethical fashion but were permitted by Judaism to defraud other people. Cohen refuted the charge, and argued that God and the Jews "loved the stranger" and that the ultimate goal of Judaism was the unity of all humanity as a reflection of the unity of the one God. Judaism, Cohen taught, teaches that all human beings are co-workers in the work of Creation.

In 1912, Cohen moved to Berlin where he taught at the Reform rabbinic seminary or the Institute for the Scientific Study of Judaism. There he worked on one of his most important books, *Religion of Reason from the Sources of Judaism*, published in 1919, where he further demonstrated the interconnections of Judaism and Kantian moral philosophy. Cohen's work directly influenced the subsequent thinking of Leo Baeck, the leading German Reform Rabbi of the 20th century; Franz Rosenzweig, a leading figure in modern Jewish philosophy; and Martin Buber, the author of *I and Thou*, one of the most important religious texts of modern times. Like his teacher, Rosenzweig rejected Zionism as being contrary to Judaism's universalistic messianic hope for humanity, whereas both Baeck and Buber found ways to embrace Jewish nationalism. Joseph B. Soloveitchik (1903–1993), one of America's leading Orthodox rabbis of the 20th century and a leading professor of Talmud at Yeshiva University, was also profoundly influenced by Hermann Cohen.

Today, it is important to see Hermann Cohen as the intellectual bridge connecting the "ethical" and the "monotheistic" in contemporary Reform Judaism. This is true with respect not only to our personal ethics, but also to social ethics and the program that we call *tikkun olam*. Although that title is borrowed from mystical sources, it is very much rooted in Judaism's prophetic quest and reflects the ethical-religious teachings of Hermann Cohen.

Perhaps Cohen himself said it best when he declared that "I cannot love God without devoting my whole heart as living for the sake of my fellow-men, without devoting my entire soul as responsive to all the spiritual trends in the world around me, without devoting all my force to this God in His correlation with man" (Louis P. Pojman, Michael Rea, *Philosophy of Religion: An Anthology* [Stanford, CT: Cengage Learning, 2015], p. 58). How can we achieve this lofty goal? Perhaps by rereading the 13 *Midot* in this week's Torah portion and making them our path on earth as individuals and as part of the sacred, covenantal Jewish community.

You Are What You Eat: The New World of Kosher Food

Sh'mini Leviticus 9:1–11:47
ReformJudaism.org
April 5, 2017

Thousands of years before the 19th century saying, "you are what you eat" came into being, Judaism recognized the essential significance of food in the Jewish and human experience. Originally, without explaining "why" we should eat some, but not all types of different foods, the Torah in this week's portion, *Sh'mini* (Leviticus 11), laid down a lengthy list of culinary dos and don'ts, the textual foundation of *kashrut*, Jewish dietary practice and law. Subsequently, the laws of *kashrut* were greatly expanded by the Rabbis to include food preparation in general and, especially, on the Sabbath, the full separation of milk and meat products, methods of slaughter, and a whole range of food regulations during Passover.

Kashrut became more complex and even controversial in modern times. A number of factors contributed to the debate over kosher food during the last two centuries. Among those factors are massive acculturation, changes in food production including the industrialization of the making of foods, "new" foods from tofu to genetically modified products, changing views of hygiene, the application of scientific method to kosher food inspection, mass marketing, the health food movement, new understandings of Jewish spirituality, and the recent growth of Orthodox Judaism to mention a few.

Today, according to *Forbes*, sales in the kosher food business may exceed twelve billion dollars with 800,000 products under rabbinic supervision that are being produced in over 8,500 food processing plants and with sales markets in one hundred countries. At present, it is probable that Jews are neither the majority of kosher food consumers or producers. On the other hand, today it is possible both to shop in large, upscale kosher food stores in many Jewish communities in the United States and dine in five-star kosher restaurants on several continents.

Until the post–World War II era, the kosher food industry was widely afflicted by an endless array of problems involving fraud, price fixing, and even infiltration by organized crime. As early as 1771 there was a complaint against "*Shochet* Moshe" in colonial New York and in 1796, a New York kosher butcher had his business license revoked. The well-known American Jewish leader Mordecai Manuel Noah unsuccessfully tried in 1844 to develop a chemical test to detect lard in Jewish food products. And in 1888 Orthodox Jews in New York hired Jacob Joseph to be their chief rabbi and bring order to the city's kosher food industry. Although personally popular, Rabbi Joseph was unable to tame the Big Apple's unruly kosher food industry. Before World War I, a number of American Jewish communities even witnessed kosher food boycotts and riots protesting price fixing and other questionable practices.

Progressivism and its "quest for order," ultimately solved the problem. In 1911, Procter and Gamble, a large company, sought and received kosher certification for Crisco. Other corporations quickly followed suit. In 1915, New York State passed its first kosher fraud law. The New York law, as well as other laws enacted in New Jersey and Maryland, initially failed to meet the constitutional requirements of separating church and state, but subsequent rewrites, in some cases, helped impose the police power of the state on the supervision of kosher food in America. In other cases, the precedent of Sunday Blue Laws allowed the courts to uphold the legality of state standards in kosher food cases. In Postville, Iowa, complex issues of fraud and labor practices led to a series of trials involving a Chasidic meat slaughtering operation, which had been first established there in 1987.

Ultimately, however, it was self-regulation that righted the course of America's problematic kosher food industry. In 1918, Abraham Goldstein, a New York City chemist, began importing kosher food products. Goldstein was hired in 1924 by the Orthodox Union (est. 1898) to head up its newly founded kosher-certification program under the OU brand. One of his successors, Rabbi Alexander S. Rosenberg, greatly expanded the

OU operation from 1950 to 1972, laying the foundation for the huge expansion of kosher food certification in the last quarter of the 20th century. Thereafter, demographic growth in the Orthodox community and the rise of "foodie-ism" among other factors helped propel phenomenal growth of kosher food in America and elsewhere.

How did Reform Judaism fit into the picture of modern kosher food history? Within the Reform Movement, early radicals such as Rabbi David Einhorn taught that *kashrut* was largely part of the ancient Levitical religious system and was no longer binding on Reform Jews. Other reformers reversed traditional wisdom about Jewish dietary practice, which was understood to have the social consequence of isolating Jews in their diaspora communities and therefore contrary to the higher, even messianic purposes of the emerging Reform Movement. On the other hand, Reform moderates who organized the Union of American Hebrew Congregations in 1873 ruled that it was expected that all UAHC synagogues would maintain traditional *kashrut* in their quest to build an inclusive Jewish religious movement.

Within ten years, however, a more radical Reform prevailed, and at the ordination of the first class of rabbis at the Hebrew Union College in July 1883, a non-kosher meal later known as the *Trefa* banquet was served. In fact, the Cincinnati dinner was typical of American Jewish banquet practice at the time: similar food was served at the double wedding of two ordainees in the class, as well as at a national convention of B'nai B'rith, which met in Cincinnati that Fall. Two years later, an anti-*kashrut* position, influenced by Einhorn, was adopted at the Pittsburgh meeting of a group of leading Reform rabbis in 1885. The wisdom of a policy allowing food acculturation was reinforced by a 1918 Reform responsum granting Jewish soldiers an exemption from keeping kosher during World War I.

For approximately the next sixty years, Reform Jewish food policy was a settled matter until the great revolution in the kosher food industry began in the last quarter of the 20th century. In 1979, a lengthy historical Reform responsum on Reform Judaism and kashrut helped set the stage for a new approach to the issue of food in the Reform Movement. At the same, Rabbi Simeon J. Maslin's book, *The Gates of Mitzvah*, appeared, urging religious experimentation with "keeping kosher." Thereafter, Reform synagogues increasingly began defining their food policies in "Levitical" terms, prohibiting the consumption of pork and shellfish on the premises of the synagogue. The second Pittsburgh Platform (1999) also recognized the new openness to tradition in late 20th century Reform by stating: "We are committed to the ongoing study of the whole array of mitzvot and to the fulfillment of those that address us as individuals and as a community. Some of these mitzvot, sacred obligations, have long been observed by Reform Jews; others, both ancient and modern, demand renewed attention as the result of the unique context of our own times."

Most recently, the early years of the 21st century have witnessed a general broadening of the debate over kashrut both within and beyond the Reform Movement. Very importantly, in 2008 the Conservative rabbinate embraced the concept of *Magen Tzedek*, a certification of kosher food products based on a whole spectrum of food issues from labor practices to health concerns. In 2011, the Central Conference of American Rabbis published *The Sacred Table*, edited by Rabbi Mary L. Zamore, again widening and intensifying the Reform debate about the movement's food policy. The possibilities of an ethical, health-based, spiritual approach to culinary culture in the Progressive Jewish community are endless today, an increasingly important part of the flourishing of *kashrut* in our time.

WHAT WE CAN CONFIRM: THE PATH OF TORAH

Spring 2017 Bulletin

After taking a few years off, I decided to attend the annual national convention of the Central Conference of American Rabbis this year. The well-organized 2017 conference was held in Atlanta and included a number of visits to area museums, historical sites and "The Temple," where we saw a dramatic reading of "The Temple Bombing," a play about the Ku Klux Klan's (KKK) attack on the area's largest synagogue in the fall of 1958. In hindsight, the decision to go to the CCAR was a good one. The programs were excellent. The classes provided new insights and seeing classmates and school friends is always worthwhile. I also learned about new types of synagogue software, travel programs and even bought a copper Hamsa for Liz's collection.

A particularly interesting class I attended was on the question of "Who Gave the Torah." It was offered by HUC-JIR NY Bible Professor David Sperling, who has written widely on the question of Biblical authorship. As I had attended the Cincinnati School, studying with Rabbi Sperling was a new experience for me. S. David Sperling holds a Ph.D. from Columbia and is best known for his book *The Original Torah*. In his presentation, he made two major points. Most importantly, he argued that the Torah, as we know it, was created in and by the political and cultural context of the Persian Empire following the 6th century BCE Babylonian Exile of the Jews. Second, he demonstrated the existence of Persian anachronisms in the Pentateuch including the idea of an "Eternal Light" and, believe it or not, the ancient priests wearing "pants," a uniquely Persian outfit in the ancient world! The same view is widely held in much of academia today and also informs the Reform Torah commentary we have used at KI for over forty years. Simply put, the Torah of Moses probably did not appear in its final form for about seven centuries after the conventional date for Moses himself during the Persian Period.

In the wake of Dr. Sperling's talk, I found myself reviewing other questions about the Torah, especially how it formed over time and what is revelation, the key theological proposition behind the idea of Torah? Questions about the origin of Torah are central not only to understanding ancient Jewish history but in constructing a modern, contemporary theology of Torah. In my view, the development of Torah was complex, slow and has many components. Let me explain.

Personally, I believe some of the material in Torah grew out of extremely ancient oral traditions, especially the more mythic components of Torah. Let's call this class of literature "the wisdom of the ages." As with all myths, they do not have a single author but instead are presented as a national voice. Some of these myths are etiological and explain things like the origin of music, others are representative of universal themes, even a type of deep Jungian collective unconscious. Some of this ancient material also has parallels in the literature of other ancient Near Eastern people but has been reworked from an Israelite viewpoint.

Second, I believe some of the literature of the Torah is inspired. By inspired I mean something akin to artistic inspiration. However, in the ancient world inspiration was attributed to heavenly beings like Muses or even to God or the gods. From an ancient and maybe a modern perspective too, inspiration, literary, musical, or visual is somewhat miraculous. Who is to say where the melody or artistic vision really comes from? The human imagination? From an exterior source? True inspiration remains a mystery!

On the other hand, in the ancient world there were also professional oracles, diviners and prophets. True prophets in the ancient world were not viewed as psychotics who heard voices but rather as credible spokesmen of cosmic truth. In ancient Israel, there was a professional class of prophets although they were not a guild, dynastic or trained to prophesy.

Leaving the question of a historic Moses aside, it is clear from the Torah (and subsequently reinforced by others) that the revelation to Moses as depicted in the text was unique, face to face and during waking consciousness. All the other prophets hear God through dreams and visions, a different level of information than the supreme Prophet. So, if there was a Moses who heard God, did Moses hear words or, as the later prophet Elijah suggested, Moses heard God in silence? Even the mechanics of revelation remain a mystery. Perhaps when the rabbis later conceded, "Torah speaks in human language," they were referring both to the experience and dissemination of Torah.

It is also important to note that modern Biblical scholarship has long held that prophetic literature began as solely oral, later included the writing down of oracles and ultimately was created as written literature. Subsequently, a complex editorial process began in which aggregators brought together the many types of prophetic literature and created books of prophecy and Biblical wisdom. These books, in turn, were edited by final redactors who rendered them into the form we have today.

The great early 20th century Jewish existentialist philosopher, Franz Rosenzweig, referred to these redactors as Rabbeinu, "our teachers," the spiritual-literary genius who put sacred Scripture into its final form. According to Sperling and many others, much of that process took place in the Persian Period, 535–333 BCE. That process, by any standard, created some of the greatest literature in all of human history.

Revelation, both in classic and modern Judaism, does not really end once a text has been codified. Revelation in Judaism is an unfolding of meaning over time. Translators, commentators and jurists of every stripe have continued to unpack the meaning of Torah for centuries. In the language of Reform Jewish theology, revelation of the meaning of Torah is ongoing, progressive and dynamic. Sinai is not the end of revelation but its midpoint, a continuing trajectory of teaching and inspiration.

This year for Confirmation I can confirm with our students that Torah is an ancient and ongoing process. It begins in the deep mists of tradition's beginnings, it was amplified by ancient wisdom, it echoes the mysteries of century-old inspiration, it sanctifies and dignifies as it weaves through the generations, it grows progressively and from its mysterious origins above, below and within, it defines who we are as Jews and people. This year I can again affirm that Judaism is Torah and that Torah is our ongoing, sacred path in life.

Mazal Tov to our Confirmands and their families!

Happy *Shavuot* and Shabbat Shalom.

Judaism, Medical Science, and Spirituality: A Brief History

Tazria-M'Tzora, Leviticus 12:1–15:33
ReformJudaism.org
April 29, 2017

It rarely fails. *B'nai mitzvah* families come to me three, four, five years in advance. "Is it possible," they ask, "that our child not be assigned the portion in the Torah on leprosy? We're just not sure," they continue somewhat disingenuously, "it will be meaningful." So, we talk about leprosy as metaphor and explore questions like, "what is the leprosy of our era?" and the parental anxiety slowly relaxes. By contrast, only twice in thirty years families came to me and actually asked to be assigned the portion that discusses leprosy, *Tazria*. "Why?" I ask them. Both times either one or both parents were dermatologists eager to accept the portion, and equally ready to disprove the biblical diagnosis and suggest an alternate skin disease. This week, we read the double portion, *Tazria/M'tzora*.

If nothing else, *Tazria* demonstrates a positive relationship between Judaism and medicine. Long before Hippocrates and Galen began shaping the practice of Western medicine, the Torah depicted Moses as a healer (see Numbers 12:13, 21:9), a role later assigned to priests and prophets alike. However, there was also resistance to doctors and medical science in the Jewish tradition. In Exodus 15:26, the phrase, "I the Eternal am your healer" has been interpreted to mean God alone is the source of good health and recovery from illness. Subsequently, throughout Jewish history, a spectrum of attitudes toward doctors and the medical sciences have presented themselves.

At one level, it is fair to say that Judaism has been radically pro-doctor and pro-medical science for a very long time. For sure, we have had outstanding rabbi-doctors like Maimonides (1135–1204), who represent a synthesis of Judaism and science. In modern times, many, if not most Jews, have fully embraced scientific medicine and rejected most if not every aspect of spiritual healing. However, the spiritual aspects of healing never fully disappeared from the Jewish faith and today, at various levels, they are blended with scientific medical practice. In this regard, it is interesting to note that in a 2012 University of Chicago study, ninety per cent of America's 850,000 doctors report a religious affiliation and claim their religious views influence their practice.

On the other hand, there has been a now largely forgotten anti-medical treatment trend in Judaism. King Asa (late 19th century BCE king of Judah) is censured because, "in his illness he sought not God but rather physicians" (2 Chronicles 16:12). According to a rabbinic legend, King Hezekiah (seventh century BCE) is considered praiseworthy "for hiding away a medical book as a means of encouraging the people to turn to God, and not to physicians, for healing." The Mishnah, the first code of Jewish law, goes so far as to declare in *Kiddushin* 4:14 that "even the best physician is deserving of hell." Later, even rabbi-doctors like Ramban (1194–1270) felt a tension between medical and spiritual healing.

In modern times, a radical, singular spiritual path to healing was embraced by Rabbi A. G. Moses in Mobile, Alabama, and subsequently by Rabbi Morris Lichtenstein and his wife, Tehilla, who founded the Jewish Science movement in 1921 in New York. Although it did not become part of the mainstream of American Jewish life, Jewish Science served as a precedent for the expansion of Jewish pastoral care in the post-World War II era. In 1946, Rabbi Joshua L. Liebman published the best seller, *Peace of Mind*, in which he attempts to reconcile religion and psychiatry. Clinical pastoral education (CPE) remained largely outside of mainstream rabbinic training for nearly another fifty years. In 1987, song leader, composer, and ultimately, "spiritual healer" Debbie Friedman began working on a musical rendition and feminist rewrite of *Mi Shebeirach*. Friedman's song-prayer revolutionized Reform prayer and restored the idea of medical *bakashote*, "petitionary prayers," but without negating the value of scientific, medical treatment.

While faith and science work hand in hand in the Jewish community today, the value of science and medical treatment is overwhelmingly upheld in today's Jewish community. Although Jews make up two per cent of the American population, over fourteen per cent of American doctors are Jewish. More broadly, twenty-six per cent of Nobel Prize winners in medicine have been Jewish. In the United States, Israel, and Argentina, to name a few places, the Jewish community supports numerous outstanding hospitals and medical research centers. Even the most traditional sectors of the Jewish community broadly support the value of the Talmudic doctrine of *pikuach nefesh*, which maintains that the "saving of a life" takes precedence over ritual requirements including on Shabbat and even Yom Kippur.

From the commandment to circumcise to "Moses the healer" to Asaph ben Berechiah (Syria, sixth century), the first Jewish medical writer, Jews have made outstanding contributions to the world of medicine. Isaac Judaeus wrote a *Book of Urine* in the ninth century. A wounded 16th century French King, Francis I, insisted to his captors that he be treated by a Jewish doctor. Rembrandt painted Jewish doctors. George and Martha Washington called on a Jewish doctor, John de Sequeyra, to treat one of their children, Patsy, for epilepsy. A Jew, Phillip Moses Russell, although not medically trained, served as the American "surgeon" at Valley Forge. Walter Jonas Judah, was the first American Jew to enroll in a medical school. He died in 1798 treating yellow fever victims in Philadelphia. Dr. Isaac Hayes of Philadelphia pioneered treatment of the eye and helped found Wills Eye Hospital, also in Philadelphia.

Jewish communal hospitals were founded in the United States beginning in 1852, originally for the benefit of the Jewish poor. Abraham Lincoln used a Jewish doctor, Isachar Zacharie, to treat his feet and a Jewish doctor was among those who treated Lincoln when the president was fatally wounded. Simon Baruch, a surgeon in the Confederate Army, wrote the book on appendectomies as well as the treatment of bayonet wounds. Phoebe Yates Levy Pember, a pro-Confederate Jewish woman, was the administrator of a vast hospital in Richmond, Virginia where wounded Southern soldiers were treated. Several Jews served as doctors in the North's Navy. Following the war, Dr. Abraham Jacobi, a German Jewish immigrant, helped establish the field of pediatrics in the United States. A national tuberculosis hospital opened in Denver, Colorado in 1899 with significant funding from B'nai B'rith.

In 1906, American medical education was revolutionized through the work of Abraham Flexner who helped set new standards for the training of doctors in the United States. The charitable organization, Hadassah, was founded in 1912 and established Hadassah Hospital in Jerusalem in 1934. In 1914, Dr. Joseph Goldberger helped found the field of epidemiology and helped advance public health policy. In the fields of psychiatry and psychology, both Sigmund Freud and Abraham Maslow made important contributions. Psychiatry probably has the highest concentration of Jewish doctors of any field in medicine to this day. Ironically, even Hitler, as a youth, had a Jewish doctor, Eduard Bloch, who escaped Europe and worked with the Office of Strategic Services (OSS) during World War II. After the war, American Jewish doctors including Jonas Salk and Albert Sabin led the fight against polio. More recently, Dr. Judah Folkman made major contributions in tumor research and the treatment of cancer.

Without question, for centuries Jews have played a leading role in medical research, education, and practice. The phrase "a Jewish doctor" generally connotes a synthesis of compassion and brilliance to Jews and non-Jews alike. At present, Jewish communities around the world continue to inculcate a desire to study and practice medicine in their student populations and there is little reason to think that this central old trend will end any time soon. What is changing, in my opinion, is that the number of Jewish women studying to become medical doctors is rising and may already equal the number of male students. Chances are that future rabbis will find more Jewish families seeking them out to make sure their children are assigned a portion on leprosy for their *bar* or *bat mitzvah*. Who knows, the line from a thirteen-year- old's *d'var* Torah on *Tazria* to a Nobel Prize in medicine may be shorter than we think!

Liberty and Freedom from Religion in America

B'har-B'chukotai, Leviticus 25:1–27:34
ReformJudaism.org
May 1, 2017

The Liberty Bell holds special fascination for American Jews, especially those of us who live in Philadelphia. For years, we lived happily with the knowledge that the Liberty Bell had been cast in England and brought to America in 1752 on a ship called *the Myrtilla* owned by two local Jewish shippers, Nathan Levy (the founder of the Philadelphia Jewish community) and David Franks (later one of the city's leading Tories during the American Revolution). For better or worse, recent scholarship has changed all that and we now know conclusively that the Bell was aboard a different boat, the *Hibernia*, captained by William Child but of unknown ownership. Moreover, the *Hibernia's* docking was recorded on September 1 and *the Myrtilla* did not drop anchor until the end of the month.

Although the bell did not pass through Jewish hands on its trip to America, there are still enough Jewish connections to it for us to retain a special pride in one of America's oldest political symbols. While usually not depicted as a Jewish symbol, there is a stained-glass image of the Liberty Bell in the memorial chapel of my synagogue depicted along with Independence Hall, Haym Solomon, and Robert Morris, Superintendent of Finance of the United States during the Revolution. It is also interesting to note that a small replica of the Liberty Bell is on display in Jerusalem's

Gan Pa'amon HaDror (Liberty Bell Park). In addition to local pride, there are a number of solid Jewish reasons to include the Liberty Bell in one of our main worship spaces and in a public park in modern Jerusalem.

First, the verse inscribed on the Liberty Bell is from this week's double portion, *B'har/B'chukotai*: Proclaim LIBERTY Throughout all the Land unto all the Inhabitants Thereof (Leviticus 25:10).

I have long maintained that the fact that the verse is from the Torah, and not the New Testament or Greco-Roman literature, adds spiritual accessibility to the Bell's symbolic value for many American Jews. Second, the verse is part of a larger discussion about the biblical Jubilee, itself "proclaimed" on Yom Kippur on the 50th year of the jubilee cycle with the blast of the ram's horn. Third, the verse was chosen by Isaac Norris, Jr. (1701–1766), a Quaker Hebraist who owned the largest collection of Hebrew books in the colonies. Remarkably, Norris taught his children, boys and girls, to read Hebrew, a highly unusual practice. What is unclear, however, is whether or not the commissioning of the Bell was directly tied to the jubilee of Penn's charter of 1701, also known as the Charter of Privileges. An important document in America's colonial history, the Charter built upon the original Frame of 1682 and extended liberty of conscience to all those who believed in one God, an expansion of religious rights beyond what was first offered nineteen years earlier.

The decision to engrave the word, "liberty," in large capital letters is not without significance. In the original Hebrew, the term for "liberty" is *d'ror*, which specifically means to manumit slaves or indentured servants on the 50th year and, secondarily, refers to the release of land mortgages on the Jubilee. The 18th century Anglo-American context of the word, liberty, clearly imbued the inscription with aspirational political meaning and allowed the Bell to become a symbol of the American Revolution. On the other hand, the more precise meaning of *d'ror* helped connect the Bell to the later American Abolitionist movement. On both these accounts and more, American Jews (at least since the Civil War), can take great pride in the Liberty Bell and how it ties our Jewish and American traditions together in profoundly inspiring ways.

American ideas about freedom and liberty have profoundly impacted the way Judaism is practiced in the United States and other democracies. For example, many Jewish holidays in the United States have become as much expressions of our belief in liberty as they are expressions of Jewish values. Both Hanukkah and Passover, our two most widely observed home-based festivals, have become "freedom holidays" more than celebrations of miracles or divine redemption. The Maccabees have become righteous Minuteman fighting for freedom of religion. Internecine conflict, political squabbles over the control of the Temple, even the debate over assimilation into Hellenistic culture have all been glossed over, and the miracle of the oil and its unlikely supernaturalism is viewed as a symbol of uncoerced faith burning in the temple of freedom.

The Americanistic rewriting of Passover is even more dramatic. In the Torah, the Passover story is mostly about the God of Israel battling the Pharaoh to gain the affection and support of the Hebrews. Everything is done to win the hearts of a stiff-necked people who barely seem worthy of the divine attention given to them. Ultimately, both Pharaoh and nature itself are upended, the people go free, they celebrate for a moment, and then they go back to their interminable whining! We are taught to remember what "God did for us" and to remain true to a vision of future, greater divine redemptions. Instead, we have created a memorable family night, fun activities for young children, some very good songs, and a challenging seasonal culinary tradition. The deep message for most of us is probably not "God is our Redeemer" but that "freedom is good" and "to proclaim it throughout the land."

Digging down still deeper, I would argue that for many American Jews "freedom from religion," not "freedom of religion," is the most important aspect of separation of church and state in the United States. In America's constitutional system we are guaranteed both the disestablishment of religion and the right to free exercise. In short, that means the United States does not have an official state religion nor should the political state interfere in the personal practice of one's religion. However, neither proposition is straightforward and very often how they translate into actual practice is contingent on the last ruling of the Supreme Court on either principle. Today, we even have inverted situations in which conservative religious interests argue that LGBTQ laws of inclusion actually violate their constitutional right to free exercise. On the other hand, we also have seen cases determining that the display of large *hanukkiyot* in public spaces does not constitute an establishment of religion but is merely a cultural activity.

In the midst of this increasingly complex storm of church-state litigation is a widely held view among American Jews that religion in the United States is wholly a personal and voluntary activity, that is, so to speak, free from religion. In this scenario, Judaism becomes the religion they are at liberty not to practice, a position maintained by the majority of American Jews at least with respect to synagogue affiliation. From this perspective, the inscription on the Liberty Bell functionally means "in America, I am free to not practice any religion at all as a right and by law." In many ways, that freedom is American Judaism's greatest blessing and most daunting challenge.

The question of religious liberty is even more complicated in Israel than it is in the United States, especially for Reform Judaism. Although Israel's Declaration of Independence speaks of democracy and freedom in lofty terms, the Jewish State does not have a proper constitution. A consequence of not having a constitution is that the relations between government and the institutions of religion in Israel are defined in terms of political expediency and not the rule of law. As a minority community, Israeli Reform Judaism has been placed at a terrible disadvantage by the *de facto* established Orthodox community. Ironically, Israeli Reform Judaism is also compelled to gain access to establishment benefits and not fight for an American style separationism. In Israel, the mandate to "proclaim (religious) liberty throughout all the Land" is muted twice.

The inscription on the Liberty Bell sourced from Leviticus 25:10, "Proclaim liberty throughout all the land unto all the inhabitants thereof," is one of the most powerful, challenging, and important Torah teachings in our time. For American Jews, it defines the essence of our relationship with both our country and our religious heritage. For Israeli Reform Jews, it is an aspirational goal that gives us hope and renewed strength for the ongoing fight against the Orthodox "establishment." Embracing, celebrating, and working with the many challenges of liberty is the essence of what it means to be a modern Jew today in America, Israel, and around the world. In that struggle, and as we complete our study of the Book of Leviticus, let us proclaim: *Chazak, chazak v'nitchazeik*, "May we be strong, may we be strong, and may we continue to strengthen one another!"

Finding Our Moral Compass: Reflection on Charlottesville

August 18, 2017

Two years ago, I received a phone call from my daughter-in-law, Kelly, and she asked if it would be possible for me to drive our older granddaughter, Sophie, to school a couple days a week. Of course, I said, "Sure. It'd be a great opportunity." I was thinking, what is it that I needed to do to do a good job of this? So I decided to get some great music in my car, and I loaded up the disc player, with songs from *Frozen*. I thought to myself, "Well, I really am going to impress my granddaughter with *Frozen*."

"Get in the car and buckle up," I said. "You want to hear some great music?"

And she said, "No."

I said, "You've got to be kidding! I got your music. Why don't you want to hear it?"

She said, "What I really want to know is does your car have a compass?"

I said, "You want to know if my car has a compass?"

She said, "Yeah, we learned about compasses in school, and I was wondering if your car had a compass."

Well, built in to all the bells and whistles of my car was a compass. It's actually on the rearview mirror. We drove to school following all the changes in the compass. We learned that SE was *southeast*, and we had a debate as to whether or not the compass could ever say NS or could it ever say EW or could it say SS. And she became very proficient in the compass. And, in fact, at another time, some other of us were driving together; and

Sophie announced from her seat, "We are now driving southeast." She knew her compass.

Learning about the compass and setting one's direction is important. It also supplies us with a very important analogy to what is called a moral compass. How do we set our moral compass? Almost weekly during the school year as bar and bat mitzvahs get under way, we talk about "What's the meaning of becoming an adult?" One of the answers is, as you become an adult, you learn more and more to set your own moral compass! You learn how to begin to make decisions about right and wrong on your own.

This was a week, unfortunately, in which we as a nation were challenged to make sure that our personal and national moral compasses were set correctly, that we had a true North Star to guide us from a point of view of fundamental beliefs as a society. It wasn't just because of the viciousness of the white supremacist demonstrations and violence that took place but because, unfortunately, of the moral confusion that emanated from the highest sources of this country, in which there was a moral equivalency drawn where there is no moral equivalency. The fact of the matter is that Nazism and all its doctrines and its allied causes, whether it's in the form of the white-robed Ku Klux Klan (KKK) member or some other nationalist or supremacist, is always wrong; and there is nothing to compare it with! It represents a kind of absolute evil, and it represents the moral opposite of what this country is founded upon and the moral opposite of what has been the foundation of our faith for almost four thousand years.

The Torah begins, among other things, with the statement that the human being is created in the image of God. It doesn't say that white people are created in the image of God exclusively, or black people are created in the image of God, or Asian people are created in the image of God and others aren't. It simply says the human being—from our distant, distant ancestors to today—all reflect the divine. All are entitled to our ultimate respect.

When this country was founded in 1776, ten miles from where we're sitting, the American Revolution was summed up in a terse phrase that said that certain rights are inalienable—life, justice, the pursuit of liberty—and that every human being is granted those rights by their Creator. The reality is our experiment in democracy—our experiment in extending rights, equal rights to all our citizens, of all shades and all faiths—has been less than perfect. It's been a very rocky road. But at the end of the day, supposedly, our ideals are in place. The rock upon which this nation was built was meant to be unshakable.

There is no debate, ultimately, as to the truth of all men are created equal. Yet all of a sudden, the moral compass is no longer clear. There was a false equivalency between those who hate that principle and deeply hate and resent that principle and those who stood up to resist those who were saying all men are not created equal, that some are superior and some are inferior. Some are to rule, and others are to be ruled over. And it was indeed a difficult and depressing and challenging week, I think, for all of us.

To get a sense of how bad it was on the ground in Charlottesville, I shared online with the congregation. I know some of you have seen it and others not, so I'll take the liberty of repeating a letter written by the president of the Reform Synagogue of Charlottesville, Virginia. What happened there, beginning this time last week, on Friday night, when worshippers came to the synagogue and people began passing by the front of the synagogue with torches, with automatic weapons, with long guns, with swastika flags, with the banner battle flag of the Confederacy, with white supremacist messages spewing from them. He reported how men with guns stood on the other side of the street from the synagogue and leered at the synagogue, of how messages were being burned, were being sent across the Internet and on Facebook that if you're in Charlottesville, and you march by the synagogue, burn it down.

The members of the synagogue had to make decisions. Do we stay? Do we leave by the back door? Do we wrap our Torah scrolls up in blankets and smuggle them out? Do we have an off-site *havdalah* service for our members tomorrow night, or should we cancel it? Because we put the address online and the bad guys knew exactly where they were meeting? And we learned that the local police were so stretched in their obligations and the situation that the local police department was unable to put a policeman or a squad car in front of the building. It was just too overwhelming a moment for the congregation. Over and over again, in his letter Mr. Silverman wrote, "And this is America 2017."

I know from my own family's story from Germany in November of 1938 that long lines of Nazi demonstrators and marchers with torches went through the street of their city in Bavaria, Bamberg, and ultimately took the Torahs out of the ark, tore them to shreds, used them as kindling, and then burned the synagogue down. But something happened in Charlottesville that did not happen in Bamberg. Other people—old and young, male and female—also showed up at the synagogue. A thirty-year veteran of the United States Navy with a Spanish name and not Jewish went to the synagogue, talked to the president of the synagogue, and said, "Would you mind if I stand in the door of your synagogue? I need to protect you." And an elderly woman who was Christian came and said, "I need to sit here and worship with you. And would you explain to me exactly why these people hate you? Because I can't figure it out."

That did not happen in Germany. Also, what didn't happen in Germany were thousands and millions of voices that rose up, not because word went forth from an opposition political party that said, "Go and demonstrate" but because people simply couldn't contain themselves in the face of this abuse of our national ethos.

Here in Elkins Park, last Sunday night, as we were coming back from our summer vacation, we got some email from KI families. Not even Jewish families at the preschool saying, "There's been a message on Facebook that there's going to be an anti-racist gathering in the park at High School Park. Just come." There was no organization behind it. There was no program. There were no speakers that had prepared in advance. It was simply people rising up out of the grassroots, out of their homes, and proclaiming, "We have a moral compass. And our moral compass is not confused, and we're going to hold that moral compass up, and we're going to say, 'We have a true North Star in this country. And that North Star says all men, all people are created equal, and that is inalienable, and that is self-evident, and we are not going to allow anybody to intimidate us. We're not going to back off because thugs with torches and shields thinking they're some kind of medieval warriors are going to tell us that that is no longer true and that's not America. What they are saying is not America. We know what is America.' We know the direction that our moral compass points."

And that letter explained to me, illustrated to me, very, very deeply what it must have felt like to be on the ground where there was no question whatsoever about moral equivalency. People were yelling 'Sieg Heil,' 'America is for white people only,' 'Jews will not replace us' and 'blood and soil;' these are things that are totally foreign in American political life and were being shouted, supposedly, in the name of patriotism. But that is not patriotism! That's treason. That is confusion. That is having a broken human compass.

Shabbat Shalom.

Personal Strength: Am I Strong Enough?

September 20, 2017 Rosh HaShanah

Every time we finish reading a book of the Torah, there is a wonderful custom in the synagogue for the congregation to proclaim: *"Chazak, Chazak v'nitchazeik,"* which means "Be strong, be strong and let us strengthen one another."

In the year ahead, I am hoping that these words will serve as KI's motto. They embody where we have been as a congregation, where we are today and where, hopefully, we will be in the future. There can be no question that historically KI was a strong congregation, the leading synagogue in Philadelphia and a powerful house in the Reform movement. Today, too, KI is a strong congregation, unsurpassed in its programming, art, music, youth education, preschool and use of technology, to share its vital message of peace, justice and compassion for all. *"Chazak, Chazak v'nitchazeik"*—"Be strong, be strong and let us strengthen one another." So, too, we are resolved to remain strong for the future, for the rising generation and beyond. We must continue to strengthen one another.

What is strength? If you check the dictionary, you will see that strength, being strong, has many meanings and applications: being able to lift 250 pounds means you are strong. The power to resist an outside attack means being strong. If a company is showing solid profits, it is strong.

There are many famous sayings about strength: Thomas Paine said, "The real man smiles in trouble, gathers strength from distress, and grows brave by reflection." Confucius wisely observed that "the strength of a nation derives from the integrity of the home." Ernest Hemingway, known for his admiration of strength, wrote "the world breaks everyone and afterward, some are strong at the broken places."

To a certain extent, I think that the whole world stands on strength. A lion without strength will starve. An NFL lineman without enough strength will be trampled. A woman in business without inner strength will be crushed by a male-dominant culture in the work place. The world needs genuine strength to function but not so much strength that it smashes everything in its way. By contrast, the false romanticization of strength can lead to a Nazi state or a North Korea or an Iranian theocracy.

We need and admire strength. Maybe that's why we created superheroes with abnormal strength, capacity to fly without the normal aerodynamics and conquer evil with their hands. Many of the greatest movies of all time are about strength, movies about war, death-defying love, moral courage in the face of great evil. From *Hacksaw Ridge* to *Saving Private Ryan* to *Hidden Figures* and *Loving*, they are all cinematic tributes to that inner strength called courage.

Courage is a tricky business. Courage is not recklessness or foolishness. Courage means recognizing one's fear and rationally overcoming those fears for a higher purpose. The great philosophers of antiquity from Aristotle and Plato to Cicero speculated on the nature of courage. Perhaps one of the greatest theological works of the 20th century, Paul Tillich's *The Courage to Be*, defines courage as "the self-affirmation of one's being in spite of the threat of non-being." According to Tillich, fear of death, moral inadequacy, and meaninglessness posit the central anxieties we all face, and it takes deep, personal courage just to exist as human beings.

What about strength and courage in Jewish tradition? *Chazak* means strength in Hebrew as does *Ometz*. There is also the word *Ohz* as in "*adonai ohz la-amo yee-tain*," the Lord will give strength to his people," recited at the end of the grace after eating. Most of the Bible's teachings about strength are tied to personal faith. In Deuteronomy 31:6 we are encouraged "to be strong and of good courage, fear not nor be afraid [of your enemies], for the Lord your God will go with you." Of course, we all know the words of the 23rd Psalm, "even though I walk through the valley of the shadow of death, I will fear no evil for You are with me." A song based on the prophet Zechariah asserts "not by might and not by power but by spirit alone" is a spiritualized understanding of strength. Following Tillich's "courage to be," a popular Hasidic song teaches "the whole world is a very narrow bridge and the main thing is not to be afraid."

As the new year begins, I want to address a different kind of strength: personal strength. Strength of person, moral strength, strength of character, strength in the face of personal adversity, illness, family conflict, unbearable loss, failure, pain, abandonment and betrayal.

Many years ago, while serving Temple Concord in Binghamton, New York, it occurred to me one morning while driving to work that despite the fact I was serving a relatively small community, I experienced life from birth to death and everything in between on a regular basis. Intervention in life's most important moments is something congregational clergy do as part of their calling. Happy, sad, tragic, victorious, anxious, catastrophic, joyful and overwhelming are almost daily fare in what I do. The same and more are true for me here at KI for sixteen years. A few years ago, I even asked a psychologist to work with me and my staff, to better process the huge range of emotions and situations we experience so we can do our work better and better manage how these experiences affect us as people. Pastoral work is never easy, always important, always impactful.

I have come to a realization that at the core of this shared experience is the issue of personal strength. Very often we are called upon to be strong and to help others summon their personal strength exactly at those moments in life when we are least confident that we are strong enough to meet our challenges. Problems with our kids, family disputes, the breakup of a promising relationship, a broken marriage, betrayal by a friend or rejection by a school, are all hard times and unrequested tests of character. Life is filled with unfair challenges. The death of the unborn and the very young, car and motorcycle accidents, murder, suicide, fast-moving, murderous diseases are all impossible moments in life.

So, too, the loss of a loved one, even under the best of circumstances, is so final, so intractable, and so permanent that we are shook, challenged and wounded to our very core. And then, what does it mean to live alone after forty, fifty or even sixty years of marriage?

These are just some of the times and challenges which test us, and force us to dig deeper than we thought possible. "*Chazak, Chazak v'nitchazeik.* Be strong, be strong and let us strengthen one another." What is it that makes us strong, even when we think we don't have the strength to carry on? Ask yourself, where does my inner strength come from?

Perhaps our first source of strength are our oldest and deepest relationships. Parents, grandparents, siblings, aunts and uncles and cousins are our earliest social constellations. Early in life, friends become an important part of our world. Little things like learning how to climb a tree are tests of courage we face outside of our homes. Later, school friends give us strength, sometimes tested by bullies or mean-spirited cliques. We join teams as kids to learn skills, to learn to cooperate and take shared risks. Some of us serve in the military, where courage and strength are demanded of us.

Spousal relations are tremendous sources of strength. As we grow and share life together, our soul mates can provide us new strength and purpose. Becoming a parent gives a unique and profound reason to strengthen ourselves, and find inner courage to protect or advance our children's interests. Being parents can make us stronger than we ever imagined we could have been.

As we grow older, we join all types of organizations and affiliate with institutions to further common causes and interests. They also have social dimensions, which help define who we are as individuals. Being part of an organization can make us stronger as individuals.

What about Judaism and synagogue life? To what extent do they help me be a strong person? I have probably conducted 1,500 funerals and I am amazed by the power of the Psalms, of *El Malei Rachamim* and especially of the Kaddish to help bring "balm to Gilead." At the worst possible moment in life, frozen by grief, the sure, familiar, rhythmic words of Kaddish seem to give most some respite from the pain of the moment. Feeling the earth in our hands somehow marks the beginning of the next cycle. Lighting the shiva candle at home reminds us that there is still light in the darkness. Sitting with family and friends allows us to form eternal narratives about finite lives. Judaism has tremendous power, if we allow it into our lives.

Judaism cannot exist in a vacuum. Like any great structure, it needs a sure foundation. Judaism is built on the pillars of self, family, tradition and synagogue. Each pillar helps support us. Each pillar is necessary and mandated and trustworthy.

I have spent most of my life inside the synagogue, the last sixteen years in this one. KI has become more than a building in my life. It has come to define me. Its history and traditions inspire me. It has music and art that reflect the core of my being. Most of all, it has people who ask me to help them to be strong. It is a reciprocal relationship. So many people here have been strong and fair and wise to me when I needed their support.

Perhaps the ultimate question about strength is whether or not strength has a transcendent source. For some people it is an easy question: "my help comes from God, Maker of heaven and earth." Others have more philosophical answers. Others believe we are on this earth alone and that each person must be the source of their own strength.

In this new year, 5778, I need to ask a very basic question as I go forward: what makes me strong? It is one of the great questions of human existence. In the end, I make me strong but I need help. I can't be strong alone. I need my family close to me, my friends, my congregation, my heritage. I need my community, my country and its magnificent ideals, and I need my God to be strong. And I need to be strong for all of them, for they can only be as strong as I help them to be strong.

Throughout this holiday period, I have heard my tradition calling to me: "*Chazak, Chazak v'nitchazeik.*" "Be strong, be strong and let us strengthen one another." Let us resolve to try to be strong as individuals, to help one another, to be a strong community of faith and to move forward into the new year with hope and with renewed confidence. Amen!

Jewish Unity

September 21, 2017, Rosh HaShanah Morning 5778

Our theme for the High Holy Days, 5778, is "strength." Last night, I talked about "What makes me strong as an individual?" Today, I want to talk about strength derived from Jewish unity, or lack thereof. On Kol Nidrei, my theme will be Faith and Strength; and finally, on Yom Kippur morning, we will explore the topic what makes a synagogue strong.

My choice of the theme of strength comes from a wonderful synagogue custom enacted five times every year with the completion of the reading of each book of the Torah. When we finish reading Genesis, Exodus, Leviticus, Numbers, and Deuteronomy, we proclaim, "*Chazak, Chazak v'Nitchazeik,*" which means "Be strong, be strong, and let us strengthen one another." The Hebrew word *chazak* is an imperative. It means "Be strong!" The Hebrew word *v'nitchazeik* is a reflexive verb and means "Let us strengthen one another." "*Chazak, Chazak v'Nitchazeik* [Be strong, be strong, and let us strengthen one another]."

At noon on March 2, 2017, Liz and I went into town to participate in a rally against hate. Here in Philadelphia, as in other places around the country, Jewish cemeteries had just been vandalized, and the police suspected that hate crimes and not just vandalism were involved. In my opinion, the situation was clouded by the fact that a number of local Jewish cemeteries are in terrible condition and that some stones had fallen over because of neglect and lack of proper maintenance, a situation documented multiple times over the years by the local print media. Still, it seemed, foul play was involved this time; and the community, led by Federation, went into action. A crowd of five thousand to six thousand gathered in front of Independence Hall. A number of Jewish organizations and schools brought signs and banners. Non-Jewish groups and individuals were also present, self-identified and supportive. It was an impressive display of unity by and with the Jewish community. A crime had brought us together, and the simmering differences in the local Jewish community were bridged, at least for the moment.

My first experience of such communal solidarity took place in May 1967. At the time, we didn't know it, but it was about a month before the fateful Six-Day War. Egypt and Syria had combined politically and militarily and were poised to strike Israel. Their goal was the total destruction of the Jewish State. My home Jewish community in Baltimore, like other Jewish communities, mobilized. The anxiety was palpable and growing.

I remember going to the Pikesville Armory with my mother. At the time, it was the largest crowd of people I had ever seen other than at a Baltimore Colts home game, may they rest in peace.

Across the front of the armory was a huge banner that said Never Again, and under it was a massive reproduction of the tragic scene from the Warsaw Ghetto in 1943 with a frightened little boy holding his hands up in the air as a Nazi soldier with a rifle looked on. Everyone in that photograph looked terribly afraid and eerily aware that a terrible fate awaited them. "Never Again" we repeated over and over. The crowd eventually broke up, but the anxiety didn't. It wasn't until the war started, and it became clear Israel was headed to victory that the fear broke and quickly turned into jubilation. It was one of the proudest Jewish moments of the twentieth century. Israel survived. Jerusalem was reunited. The Sinai and the Golan were ours. The Arabs were vanquished.

At that moment and for decades, no one fully understand the deeper implications of the moment. What would Israel do with the Sinai, with the Golan, with the Gaza Strip? How would the international community accept Israeli control of all of Jerusalem? What were Israeli defense needs in the West Bank and in the Jordan Valley? Which sectors would be annexed, and which areas would go under military control? What would happen to all the Arabs Israel now controlled? Who among them could vote in Israel? Who were stateless? Who were Jordanian? In June 1967, only the feel of victory was in the air, and the Jewish people was an internationally united community of destiny!

That was fifty years ago, and that sense of elation and unity would last but not for long. The 1973 war came along. Then an increase in Arab terrorism. Then wars in Lebanon and Gaza. Israel made peace with "Egypt and Jordan" but not with itself. The low point came with the assassination of Yitzhak Rabin on March 28, 1996, by a fellow Jew and not by an Arab terrorist. Moreover, a whole series of developments, including the decision by the Reform movement to accept patrilineal descent and uncertainty about the Jewishness of Russian immigrants to Israel, led to the "Who is a Jew" crises, which threatened to tear the whole Jewish world apart. As the twentieth century drew to a close, the old United Jewish Appeal (UJA) slogan We Are One seemed more aspirational than real.

The question of Jewish unity is both ideological and historiographical. Some Jewish ideologies emphasize a broad, inclusive approach to Jewish life. Others draw narrow boundaries around Jewish peoplehood. Some ideologies of Jewish life believe we should cooperate with one another despite our differences; others say that only certain types of Jews are real and other are literally "outside the camp" of Jewish life. The same is true of historians. Some believe the general Jewish experience is essentially a single story; others argue that the idea of a Jewish consensus has also been more of a myth than a sociological or historical reality.

Jews and Judaism are not unique in this regard. Is American history mostly the story of a unified nation with a solid core of shared values; or is it a story of regional, racial, and economic conflict? Does America have a single "manifest destiny"; or are we the boiling cauldron of Jeffersonians and Jacksonians, slave holders and abolitionists, isolationists and democratizers of the world, integrationists or segregationists, a rural nation or an urban nation, states' rights advocates or Washington-centric, big business or big labor, pro-life or pro-choice? The list goes on; the question of the centrality of either consensus or conflict remains.

Viewed broadly, Jewish tradition understands itself internally as a consensus tradition. We began as a single family that expanded into a family of tribes. We left Egypt together, and together stood at Sinai. For centuries, we were bound together as a community of destiny and purpose. And for all its terrible consequences, the long history of anti-Semitism bound us together, sometimes in the most awful of ways.

However, if we think of Jewish history more critically and think of in empirical and not mythic terms, a very different narrative emerges. Our ancestors probably belonged to disparate tribes who struggled to find common cause. The first Jewish kingdom split into a northern and southern set of monarchies who were not always fond of one another. Prophets railed against biblical Israel and its waywardness and rarely praised the Jews for their lifestyle. The real Hanukkah was as much a civil war as it was a war of independence. Judaism two thousand years ago, like today, was made up of different feuding groups. A large percentage of the Jewish community of the eighth century rebelled against the rabbis in the Mesopotamia of late antiquity and formed their own Karaite community. The Hasidim were bitterly denounced by the Yeshiva-based Misnagdim in the eighth century, a split that still affects the ultra-Orthodox community. Zionism was fiercely rejected by anti-Zionists, secular Jews clashed with religious Jews, and Sephardim resented Ashkenazic power in the new State of Israel. In this light, the Jewish experience becomes more a tale of discord than harmony, of inner conflict, not inner unity.

Remember the scene from *Fiddler*: it was a horse, it was a mule? The only forces able to resolve that split in Anatevka were the Czarist police and rioting Cossacks.

In my opinion, Jewish history—all history—is a mix of consensus and conflict. Indeed, I would suggest that Jewish history, ancient and contemporary, is broadly a story of consensus internally riddled with conflict. Today, sadly, it is no different.

Although we gather every year on Rosh HaShanah to reaffirm our covenant with our ancestors, the contemporary Jewish world, and one another, I think we have to admit that there are issues that not only unite us but also divide us, especially the relationship of the Reform Jewish community with Israel. It is not a happy moment. As much as most of us support Israel, we know beyond concern for the defense of the Jewish state and our desire to share its modern culture that we have problems. Indeed, we have very deep problems.

For Reform Jews, during the last year, the first issue that worried us most is the situation at the Western Wall. The Western Wall, or Kotel, is a surviving remnant of the Second Temple, reconfigured and enlarged by Herod the Great and his family beginning in the year 19 BCE. Following the destruction of Jerusalem in 70, Jewish access to Jerusalem and the Wall became problematic. Special permission was given on occasion to go to the Wall, largely blocked by the so-called Moroccan Slums, especially on the Ninth of Av. The crying sounds of the prayers of that holiday led to the name Wailing Wall. Numerous attempts were made by rabbis and Jewish businessmen to buy the Wall from

Muslim leaders. None succeeded. It was only under the British after WWI that Jews secured the right to worship at the Wall, a right quickly challenged by the Muslim authorities. From 1919 to 1948, access to the Wall was regularly contested until Old Jerusalem fell into Jordanian hands. It was only in 1967 that the Wall was liberated by the Israeli army.

The fight over the Wall then shifted from Jews versus Arabs to Jews versus other Jews. As early as 1968, the Reform movement attempted to run services at the Wall with men and women standing together. Despite the Reform movement's rejection of praying for the rebuilding of the Temple, there was still a strong feeling that Progressive Jewish services should be permitted at the Wall as a symbol of Jewish unity and Israeli democracy. It also reflected a broader desire to keep Jerusalem united under Israeli control. Then in 1988, twenty years later, the Women of the Wall or WOW formed and quickly gained Reform support. Respecting gender segregation at the Wall, only Women prayed in the women's section. But when WOW began reading Torah and wearing prayer shawls and tefillin, the ultra-Orthodox pushed back. In 2003, Israel's Supreme Court sided with the Orthodox, but the struggle did not end. While public opinion in Israel split almost evenly over the Wall, the non-Orthodox movements in the Diaspora, especially the United States, made continued efforts to secure an egalitarian section of the Kotel. Victory seemed close at hand in January 2016 when the Israeli Cabinet announced that a new section of the Wall, south of the Kotel Plaza, would be developed for egalitarian worship. Progressive Jews claimed victory. But the traditional community went to work to undermine the deal. At the beginning of this summer, the Netanyahu government announced the deal had been suspended. Protests were loud but ineffective. Tensions remain high, and Reform Jews the world over who followed these developments and cheered for the Women of the Wall were roundly defeated.

To date, fears of an Israel-Diaspora rift have not fully materialized, although calls have been made to limit travel to Israel, boycott El Al, and refocus liberal Jewish support of Israel to specific causes that promote pluralism in Israel. Others maintain that the defeat of Reform over the Wall signifies either the decline of its political importance in Israel or a calculated move by the Netanyahu government to realign itself with the right wing of the American Zionist movement and the Orthodox. However you look at it, it is not a happy outcome for Reform Judaism, although it is clear that the struggle for egalitarian rights at the Wall will continue.

A second issue developed just a month ago in the wake of the Unite the Right Nazi-KKK rally in Charlottesville, Virginia, in mid-August 2017 over the fate of that city's Robert E. Lee memorial. The sight of hundreds of American Nazis marching through the night in an American city with tiki torches disgusted American Jews and others devoted to inclusion and racial harmony in this country. The failure of the American president to unequivocally condemn White Supremacy threw gas on the political fire, which is still smoldering in much of this country. For many, it was an unforgivable offense to give sanction to hatred and bigotry and fail to work to stem the rising tide of hate crimes in this county.

Then, the unthinkable happened. To the surprise of many American and Israeli Jews, the prime minister of Israel was both slow to condemn the Unite the Right rally; and when he did so, it was less than forceful. Others on the Israeli Right went as far to say that the Right was not a real danger to American Jews. Prime Minister Netanyahu's son, Yair, then posted Nazi-style cartoons on Facebook in an attempt to denounce his father's enemies. American Nazis leaped to his defense, including David Duke, declaring the young Netanyahu a Nazi hero. The whole episode was maddening and deeply disturbing. It further complicated internal Jewish politics for Reform, Conservative, and Reconstructionist Jews.

The third issue creating "degrees of separation" between Progressive Jews and Netanyahu is the West Bank and the Jewish settlements there. The question of the West Bank is one of the most difficult, complex, and emotional issues facing Israel, the Middle East, and the world. On the one hand are concerns about Israeli national security. Israel is a small country. Across from the city of Netanya, it is only eight miles wide. Defending its borders and creating even a fraction of strategic depth is no small issue. On the other hand, the civil rights of the Arab inhabitants of the West Bank and the national rights of the Palestinian people are also important to consider. The West Bank, excluding Jerusalem, is divided up into three administrative zones. Section A is Arab and urban. It was where most of the Arabs live in the territory, and it is under Palestinian control. Area A makes up 18 percent of the West Bank. Section B, which surrounds the A areas, is under mixed control with Israel in charge of its security. Section B accounts for 22 percent of the West Bank. A and B together have a total of 2.8 million Palestinians but also almost 400,000 Israeli settlers. Section C, made up of more remote areas, was originally intended under Oslo II to return to Palestinian control in 1999 but remains under Israel. Area C is also the site of the greatest numbers of building demolitions and other conflicts.

The Reform movement, along with the American government and the State of Israel, have long supported the idea of a two-state solution, which means the creation of some kind of Palestinian state in the West Bank and Gaza. The growth of Israeli settlements, widely favored by the Netanyahu government, is leading many to conclude that the window of opportunity for a two-state solution is closing.

There are proposals for land swaps inside of Israel proper, but no one knows if they are serious. Meanwhile, the tension between Palestinian human rights and Israeli security needs intensifies. For the Reform movement, and probably the majority of Reform Jews, confidence in the Netanyahu government continues to diminish. At the same time, confidence in the government of Mahmoud Abbas is minimal or nonexistent. Ultimately, the collective wisdom of our movement is that Netanyahu's policy of creeping annexation does not bode well for the future of a democratic Israel.

Sadly, 5778 does not begin in a good place for Reform Jews and Israel. Betrayal at the Wall, angry disappointment over Charlottesville, and deepening concern over the political realities of the territories have put us at odds with the government of the Jewish State. It does not mean that we don't love Israel or support it. *Chazak, Chazak v'Nitchazeik* (Be strong, be strong, and let us strengthen one another) is complicated business for us and Israel. The burden of unity is on all of us, and it is difficult.

Despite rejection, frustration, and disappointment, we need to both embrace and challenge Israel. In doing so, we need to make sure our bastions of strength, our Reform synagogues here and in Israel, are as strong as possible. If we weaken in any way, the fight for pluralism, democracy, and justice inside of Israel will be lost. In that scenario, Israel would lose, we would lose, and the Jewish people would lose. We were taught to be a light to the nations by our prophets. That battle continues here in America and in Israel. That battle requires unflinching strength and unity.

Chazak, Chazak v'Nitchazeik (Be strong, be strong, and let us strengthen one another) as we enter a new year. We pray it will be a Shana Tova, a good year and a year of renewed strength. Amen.

Staying Strong: American Anti-Semitism Today

September 29, 2017, Yom Kippur Evening 5778

I grew up in Pikesville, Maryland, just outside of Baltimore, in the late 1950s and early 1960s. Twenty years earlier, that corner of Baltimore County was still largely a rural area with working farms and small villages. New suburbs, almost entirely Jews moving out of the city, quickly enveloped the smaller non-Jewish community. The ratio of Jews to non-Jews, especially in the schools, was tremendous, perhaps 10:1, maybe 15:1. In elementary school, so far as I remember, I had no non-Jewish classmates. I didn't meet the so-called locals until junior high school. At first, I went to Sudbrook in old Pikesville, conveniently located in the middle of the Jewish neighborhood and in walking distance to my house, while waiting for the new junior high school to open.

At Sudbrook, I met non-Jews for the first time in my life. In fact, I even had a Mormon friend with corn-blond hair. Kevin Jensen accidentally broke my nose by heading me in a soccer game, but we stayed friends anyway. He even taught me about Postum and other non-caffeinated drinks.

But there was another set of kids who were not so friendly. They were rural. We called them hicks, a class-based substitute word for *goyim*. They dressed tough and kept their distance from the better-to-do Jewish kids. My first encounter with anti-Semitism came from within this group.

I remember two incidents. The first was penny pitching. They used to flick pennies at us. I didn't understand it at first. We were supposed to dive to the ground to retrieve the small change but didn't know enough about anti-Semitism to do so. The other incident was worse. I got off the bus one sunny day, and another student jumped in front of me and punched me—hard—in the stomach. In a mean-spirited whisper, he said "Jew" and disappeared into the swirling crowd of students. He never bothered me again. We never had a class together.

There are other random stories to report. Nothing noteworthy. No pogroms. No expulsions. In Cincinnati, Liz and I encountered sales help in a Sears who used the expression "Jewing down." Our kids also had a few experiences when we lived in Binghamton from other kids and school officials alike. No Cossacks or Nazis. Just enough to drive home the reality that we were members of a small religious minority that had a long history of rejection and oppression.

Although anti-Semitism has existed since Abraham and Sarah, the term itself is modern. It was coined in the middle of the nineteenth century reflecting the then-new racialized meaning of hatred toward Jews and Judaism but quickly expanded to all forms of animus against us and our tradition. Technically, there are several different types of anti-Semitism: simple inter-ethnic tension; religious anti-Judaism, which has existed from ancient times and continued through Christian and Islamic anti-Semitism; racial anti-Semitism, including Nazism; and now, political anti-Semitism or the kind of anti-Zionism, which seeks the annihilation of the Jewish State.

Compared to almost any other country in the world, anti-Semitism in America has been relatively light and rarely lethal. On the other hand, anti-Semitism has been a constant factor in American history—sometimes strong and threatening, sometimes at low tide, but there nevertheless. Unfortunately, and incontrovertibly, we are now witnessing a measurable uptick in domestic anti-Semitism; and it is critical for all of us to be informed about and to be prepared to counter it through education, legal efforts, and legislation.

Jewish life in the New World began as a function of vicious anti-Semitism in Spain and Portugal. Seeking to flee the flames of the Inquisitions, Marranos were the first Jews to move to the Western Hemisphere. They settled in distant corners of the Iberian Empire and as far north as New Mexico to live out their secret lives in safety. Dutch, then English, colonies were the first to accept practicing Jews in their colonies but not without discrimination. The embittered governor of New Amsterdam, Peter Stuyvesant, unsuccessfully tried to block the permanent settlement of Jews in his jurisdiction. Rhode Island, one of the more inclusive colonies, denied naturalization to Aaron Lopez, its most illustrious Jewish resident, in the days prior to the American Revolution. The majority of colonies did not allow Jews to hold public office, and the fight to drop religious oaths of office continued throughout the nineteenth century in the original thirteen states. Perhaps the most dramatic display of American anti-Semitism took place during the Civil War when Jews, as a class, were temporarily expelled from the Southern states by the United States Army. Had Lincoln not reversed that 1862 order, the civil status of Jews in this country would have been deeply damaged.

A turning point in the history of American anti-Semitism came in June 1877 when Joseph Seligman, a leading Jewish businessman, and his family were denied a hotel room at an upscale resort in Saratoga Springs, New York. A nationwide boycott of the hotel's parent company followed, leading to it going bankrupt. The incident was symptomatic of the sharp upturn of American anti-Semitism during the Gilded Age, leading to thousands of restrictive covenants against Jews and their ability to do business, belong to organizations, and live in neighborhoods of their choice. On August 15, 1915, a mob lynched Leo Frank in Georgia. Less known, but still real, was the street violence even in pre-WWI Philadelphia against Jews, particularly in South Philadelphia. Following WWI, racism, anti-Semitism, and xenophobia again rapidly increased in the United States; and the Ku Klux Klan reached the apex of its power and popularity. In 1924, the Congress of the United States all but closed America to Jewish immigration. While Jews were not the only group to suffer because of the Johnson Acts, the consequences of the restrictive legislation for European Jews during the 1930s and World War II was catastrophic. Individuals like Henry Ford and Father Charles Coughlin railed against Jews through various media.

Anti-Semitism in the United States did not begin to wane until after World War II. Numerous factors figured in the change. Over five hundred thousand Jews served in the American military during the war. Bravery and mere social contact played an essential role in the shift in American culture toward inclusion. Jews also were becoming more Americanized as they entered into their second and third generations and moved away from their immigrant culture. The new suburbs played a role in the Americanization process, as did upward economic mobility aided by the GI Bill and education. The establishment of Israel also gave American Jews a lift as an increasingly respected minority as did the conspicuous rise of Jewish artists and entertainers in popular American culture. But most of all, it was the Civil Rights movement that challenged the deepest structures and practices of anti-Semitism in America as part of its drive to break Jim Crowism in this country. Widely ambivalent about their own relations to African Americans, American Jews nevertheless supported the drive toward social inclusivity in the United States.

One by one, previously closed industries began opening up to American Jews. New neighborhoods were increasingly more diverse than old urban neighborhoods, at least with respect to groups whose ancestors came to America from Europe. By the early 1960s, the first statistical evidence of mixed marriage in a century was detected by demographers of the Jewish community, signaling a new kind of social acceptance in this country. Remarkably, within fifty years, mixed marriage would become statistically normal in the American Jewish community, and tens of millions of Americans now found themselves with Jewish relatives. The results were outstanding. Shops in towns in Northern Idaho without any Jewish residents began carrying Rosh HaShanah and Hanukkah greeting cards. Jews had become part of Main Street America.

Of course, there were still pockets of resistance. In the Fifties, antiblack racists resisting the Civil Rights movement were also anti-Semitic. Synagogues, along with black churches, were bombed in the 1960s. A small neo-Nazi movement appeared.

With the breakup of the Civil Rights movement and the rise of a protest movement against the Vietnam War, a new anti-Semitism began to appear on the margins of American society. Black Nationalists, Louis Farrakhan's Nation of Islam, and parts of the American Left saw American Jews and their support of Israel as part of American and European colonialism. Tension between the Jewish and African American communities increased and received considerable media attention, but at the same time, both groups largely remained inside the National Democratic Party. Anti-Semitic comments by President Nixon, Charles Colson, and Patrick Buchanan, among others, generally reinforced American Jewry's traditional distrust of the political Right.

Remarkably, at the same time, in the final quarter of the twentieth century, Jews and Judaism were increasingly accepted in a broad spectrum of areas of American society from hospital boards to museums to the administration of Ivy League schools. Israel, following the 1967 war, forged a special relationship with the American government, and military and organizations like the American Israel Public Affairs Committee (AIPAC) were increasingly able to span both sides of the aisle in the halls of Congress.

Hate in America began to spike again after the 2000 census predicted that white Americans would no longer be the majority group in this country after 2040 as a result of increased Hispanic immigration, in particular. The number of hate groups in 1999 was estimated at 457. By 2005, that number doubled and peaked in 2011 at 1018 according the Southern Poverty Law Center. The rise of Internet activity after that scrambled the number of groups, which again is over 900.

The Anti-Defamation League began tracking anti-Semitic incidents in the United States in 1979 and claims that number peaked in 2006 at 1,154. An increase of one-third was reported by ADL in 2016 with the biggest jump in November and December 2016. So far in 2017, the rate is up 87 percent over the year before. Millennials, born during the low point in American anti-Semitism, are now witnessing its greatest resurgence since WWII. How it affects them is still largely unknown.

At the same time, Jews are among the most respected groups in the United States according to a Pew poll form earlier this year. More than half of Americans are concerned about the well-being of Jews in this new environment and believe that anti-Semitism has increased since the 2016 elections. Eighty percent believe that the government should sponsor anti-anti-Semitism programs.

What are the new sources of anti-Semitism in America today? Extreme elements on the American Left bear some responsibility. Witness the exclusion of Jewish lesbians from a gay march in Chicago earlier this summer. However, figuring out exactly who is on the Far Left in the United States is difficult. There is no central organization or ideology other than a loosely defined anti-fascism, anti-racism, anti-globalist core, which is broadly anti-globalist and anti-capitalist. There may be as many as two hundred so-called Antifa groups, many of which are either communist or anarchistic or both.

However, many conservative and libertarian groups agree that the Far Right is more dangerous than the Far Left in the United States. According to a recent twenty-five-year study by the Cato Institute, nationalist and right-wing terrorists have killed about ten times as many people since 1992 as left-wing terrorists, which may or may not include those who identify with Antifa, the total number of casualties coming to about four hundred.

Information about anti-Semitism and the American Muslim community is often contradictory. On the one hand, Jewish and Muslim groups, including the local and national American Jewish Committee, have forged impressive alliances in the last few years. Here at KI, we have been exchanging programs with a Turkish Muslim group Peace Islands for over five years. The Reform movement, especially in connection with the Los Angeles campus of the Hebrew Union College, has been working closely with Muslim religious leaders for a similar amount of time.

Distinguishing between anti-Semitism and anti-Zionism is no easy feat. Some American Muslims insist there is a difference. The same is true on the so-called alt-right that displays considerable anti-Semitic tendencies while at the same time often favors Israel in the war against Islamist terrorism. Trying to figure the landscape of American hate today is like doing a one-thousand-piece puzzle in which all the pieces are different colors. It is no easy task.

For most American Jews today, the biggest concerns about anti-Semitism are the alt-right and random violence against Jewish property, organizations, and persons. In Europe, by contrast, the Muslim threat to Jews is seen as greater than the threat from the traditional right wing, although those worries are growing as well.

By far, the greatest concern in the country has recently focused on groups responsible for the Unite the Right rally in Charlottesville, Virginia, this past August. The local person who started the ball rolling was Jason Keller, who was joined by Nathan Damigo from Identity Evropa; Richard Spencer, a major national leader of the Alt-Right; and David Duke from the Ku Klux Klan. The Daily Stormer, the League of the South, and several militias all joined in. At the height of the demonstration, there were approximately five hundred white supremacists and one thousand counterdemonstrators. With Virginia's right to carry law in place, the presence of a large number of automatic weapons was clearly evident; and although shots were fired, only three died: one woman, Heather Heyer, by vehicular assault and two policemen operating a helicopter. A large interfaith protest preceded the actual demonstration and counterdemonstration.

The shock of seeing tiki-torch-carrying white supremacists and Nazi demonstrators in Charlottesville was further compounded by the president of the United States who made equivocal statements about the failed Unite the Right rally. Many in the Jewish community felt that the president's remark helped normalize racism and anti-Semitism in this country. Others pointed out the contradiction in his defense of protests involving the American flag at NFL games and his lack of clear-cut condemnation of Nazi flags, KKK symbols, and other open displays of extreme racism. In the wake of Charlottesville, the American Jewish community seems more unnerved than in any time in the recent past, and donations to the ADL are coming in at 1,000 percent the normal rate.

In my opinion, the fear in the Jewish community is *not* so much that vast majority of their American neighbors have become anti-Semitic overnight or that a deeper dormant anti-Semitism in America has awoken from its slumbers. Rather the real, rationally derived concern is that dangerous, fringe elements are being legitimized as true players in our essential national discussions. The fear is real. Less than 3 percent of Germans supported Hitler before the crash of 1929. In 1932, that support spiked to 40 percent, and when it fell dramatically the following year, the Nazis staged a coup and seized power in Berlin in 1933.

The long global history of anti-Semitism has taught Jews to take any uptick in its popularity seriously, especially any sustained effort to legitimize it as a responsible basis for political action or governance. That anxiety has been, for better or worse, triggered in the minds of the majority of American Jews. We are not wrong to be concerned. Supporting the ADL; strengthening Jewish life, especially our synagogue; working with non-Jewish friends; and being vigilant are all the order of the day.

However, deep down, I personally do not believe the United States is about to go over the edge and that anti-Semitism here will resemble Germany in 1932 or Russia in 1832 or Spain in 1432. We do have a problem, but we have other internal problems too. You know the list: lack of Jewish education, declining rates of synagogue affiliation, generational continuity, adequate funding, and so on. I also believe we will be OK.

For centuries, we have said the following in the synagogue as we complete each book of the Torah: *Chazak, Chazak, v'Nitchazeik* (Be strong, be strong, and let us strengthen one another)! We were strong before when it seemed our strength was inadequate. We will be strong again today because we must, and we will be strong again in the future because our work is not done.

As we enter into this New Year, let us consider the threats against us, let us take stock of ourselves, and let us resolve to move forward with renewed strength.

Amen. Shana Tova.

CHAZAK, CHAZAK V'NITCHAZEIK: KEEPING OUR SYNAGOGUE STRONG

September 30, 2017, Yom Kippur Morning 5778

Our theme for these High Holy Days has been *Chazak, Chazak, v'Nitchazeik* (be strong, be strong, and let us strengthen one another)! The phrase comes from a wonderful synagogue custom. Each time we complete reading a book of the Torah (Genesis, Exodus, Leviticus, Numbers, or Deuteronomy), we say, "*Chazak, Chazak, v'Nitchazeik* [Be strong, be strong, and let us strengthen one another]!" It's a joyous moment of victory, continuity, and accomplishment, both communal and personal.

The phrase "*Chazak, Chazak v'Nitchazeik*" (Be strong, be strong, and let us strengthen one another) can obviously also stand on its own, independent of its origins. In fact, it would work for any organization or cause. A school could use it. A bank could use it. A sports team could use it. It's a great line that summarizes just about everything we do collectively as people and as a community. That is why we are using it this year as the KI motto. *Chazak, Chazak, v'Nitchazeik* (Be strong, be strong and let us strengthen one another)!

The specific origin of the *Chazak* response grows out of the Jewish tradition and the world of the synagogue as the home of Torah, its study, and its practice. I have spent most of my life in the synagogue—first as a small child and a member of a synagogue-based family; then as a college and rabbinic school student and since ordination in four pulpits (Middletown, Ohio; Endicott, New York; Binghamton, New York); and here at KI. It has been an extraordinary run. The synagogue is not only my professional habitat, but it is a cause I truly believe in.

No one knows when and where the synagogue came into being. One theory is that it started in Jerusalem and was a "small sanctuary" in the courts of the ancient Temple of Solomon. A second tradition places it in Babylonia in the sixth century BCE. "By the water of Babylon," a grief-stricken people lamented, "we sat down and wept." A third hypothesis says that the synagogue began in Hellenistic Egypt, and a fourth theory suggests it was not until the first century, in Roman Palestine, that we had synagogues.

Whatever the origin of the synagogue, it quickly emerged, after the year 100 CE, as the central institution of Jewish religious life. Over the centuries, most synagogues have been relatively small places, cradles of Jewish life. Ecclesiastical law both under medieval Christianity and Islam required that synagogues be modest and located in the back-alleys of Jewish neighborhoods. First in Holland and then in other emancipated lands, synagogues became grand structures, proudly proclaiming the place of Jews in modern society and role of Judaism in shaping Western civilization.

The synagogue is truly the sanctuary of Israel. It has also been my personal sanctuary for my entire life. Along with the family, it is the foundation of Jewish life in this country and most of the world. There are all types of Jewish institutions and organizations, but only one is indispensable, and that is the synagogue. I am sure all of you have memories of synagogues from your past. Here are some of mine:

As a little boy, I loved my home synagogue. It was a lot like KI—big, Reform, and busy. I had a wonderful teacher in second grade who suggested I might think about becoming a rabbi. At the time, I wanted to be an architect, but she planted a seed that later grew. I had good rabbis. The senior rabbi was Abraham Shaw, a contemporary of Rabbi Korn here at KI. Typical of that generation, he had a godlike voice and seemed infinitely wise to me. One of his assistants, Martin Weiner, was the rabbi of my adolescence. He spoke well too but was more *haimish* and made me feel comfortable at Temple Oheb Shalom. I had a wonderful youth group adviser too and a couple of good synagogue friends.

At one point before graduating high school, I had a dream that I was exploring the blackened wet ruins of a synagogue that had been destroyed in a massive fire. In my dream, I was looking for prayer books, *tallitot*, and Torah scrolls that were still usable. Curiously, there were no people in my dream. It may have been a kind of "calling dream" for me because, thereafter, I decided my professional goal was to be a rabbi.

Many years later, following ordination and working on a doctoral (PhD) thesis, I found myself here in Philadelphia in the charred ruins of the old Dropsie College Library at York and North Broad. On November 9, 1981, the forty-third anniversary of Kristallnacht, and early in my second year of graduate school, a fire destroyed one of the oldest collections of Jewish books and manuscripts in the world including the materials I needed for my own research. There I was, literally in my own dream, crawling under displaced burnt beams at Dropsie and wiping water off sacred books I had determined to study.

As a rabbinic student, I served two small communities: first Harlingen, Texas, and then Richmond, Indiana. The two towns together had about one hundred Jewish families. They had enough people each for only one Jewish institution, and that was the synagogue. Without their synagogues, they would have had no real sense of community, no place to gather, no place to teach their kids, and no place to celebrate the holidays. What they did have was a lot of spirit, a true sense of community and purpose, and a great deal of pride that they could represent Judaism to their fellow citizens. I too was proud to be part of their lives. Forty years later, I am still in touch with several of my Hebrew Hoosiers.

Preparing myself for a life of sacred study and service was my dream, and I was fortunate enough to see it become my reality. I haven't seen everything, but I have seen a lot. My first *bar mitzvah* student from Indiana died in a fire during his freshman year at college. On my first day on the job in my pulpit in Middletown, Ohio, a six-year-old was killed in a bizarre accident. It was like a scene out of Milton Steinberg's classic novel *As a Driven Leaf*.

In Endicott, New York, a Reconstructionist synagogue, Beth El, was ready to close and had to make a decision to hire me as a part-time rabbi (I was full-time at SUNY) or shut down. They stayed open, and the synagogue flourished for the four years I was there. It was my dream—again—playing itself out.

By 1990, I was ready for a full-size synagogue. First, Temple Concord in Binghamton and then, eleven years later, here at KI. Temple Concord was a wonderful congregation, which had a modern sanctuary and an old gingerbread mansion to house its school. There, I created the Hanukkah House Museum, still going strong, and a licensed Elder Hostel program, and wrote a history of the local Jewish community called *Beyond the Catskills*. The title came from an undergrad who exclaimed about Jewish life in upstate NY that "I didn't know Jews lived beyond the Catskills."

Life in Binghamton was good. It was a good place to raise a big family. The synagogue, which grew from 175 to 300 families on my beat, felt like a big a family too. I wasn't really looking to move when the Director of Rabbinic Placement called me. KI was looking for a new rabbi. It was being served by an interim and needed to move on.

Everyone in the world of Reform Judaism knows about KI. It's a flagship congregation. It was the spiritual home of Rabbi David Einhorn during the Civil War. Einhorn was the first major theologian and liturgist of Reform Judaism in America. He brought the music of Reform Judaism to this country, and he was a raging abolitionist at a time when most American Jews, largely Central European immigrants, were unwilling to risk public political opinions. More recently, KI was the home of Rabbi Korn, my personal role model rabbi-scholar, and Rabbi Maslin, who was the President of the Central Conference of American Rabbis during my early years as an ordained rabbi. I even came here to KI to hear Rabbi Maslin speak in this sanctuary to about one thousand rabbis in the late 1990s, never imagining I would end up in his pulpit.

This is now the beginning of my sixteenth year at KI. At the time of my arrival, I did not fully realize it but it was my job to help transition KI from the twentieth to the twenty-first century. KI is rich in history and its own customs and cultures. It needed to stay true to itself as a flagship synagogue and to move into unchartered new waters.

So much has changed: an Israeli flag on the *bimah*, a *shin* over the Ark, a lower *bimah*, retractable screens in the sanctuary, live streaming of services, new prayer books, a collaborative of three religious schools headed by our education director, a new playscape for the preschool, a Conservative congregation living in our Rothschild Auditorium, one less rabbi and a second cantor serving as our choirmaster, Cantor Amy's experimental worship, chairs in the chapel, value banners in the lobby, a Torah scroll handwritten by our own congregation, an incredible expanded adult education program, a professional music arts program bringing rising young stars here several times a year, outreach programs to "seniors and the elderly" on- and off-site, and a social action program that includes working with an elementary school in Logan and providing free hot meals here at KI on a monthly basis including vegetables grown in our own garden.

Never in my wildest dreams did I ever imagine this level of activity and engagement. And I have only mentioned some of the newest features of this synagogue and none of the older established traditions.

However, the realist in me also knows that not everyone in the Jewish community shares my views of synagogue life. For sure, it doesn't take much to turn people off to synagogue life. There can be a lot of politics in a synagogue. Sometimes congregants are not welcoming, sometimes downright cold. Some rabbis aren't very good either and repeatedly offer long boring sermons at long boring services. Then there are those terrible Hebrew school teachers. I had one. It was my second year of midweek Hebrew. He screamed for two hours every Monday and Wednesday afternoon and walked around his room with a yardstick he would smack on a desk when we misbehaved or didn't do our assignments, which was often. Thankfully, he never hit us.

In college, I was fired from my first job as a Sunday school teacher. My roommate and I were in charge of leading music at the closing assembly every week. None of the kids would sing the usual Hebrew songs. So we decided to open the program with "Feeling Groovy" by Simon & Garfunkel. Everybody sang, but when the rabbi heard it, he wanted to know who was responsible for bringing that garbage into his Temple. We were canned and then rescued by the PTA.

I really didn't mind the old Reform prayer book as a kid. The *Union Prayer Book* was kind of Shakespearian, but it was mercifully short. As teenagers, we tried writing our own services but really didn't know enough to do that correctly. So we read from Khalil Gibran, a Lebanese poet, and sang the music of the Civil Rights movement and called it Jewish. At my Confirmation in 1970, our closing song was "The Great Mandala" by Peter, Paul and Mary. At lunch, a family member angrily accused me of being a pacifist while our country was at war.

The new prayer book introduced in the late 1970s was massive. At the time, I was already in rabbinic school and was assigned to lead services in a nursing home in Cincinnati. Most of the residents there were in wheelchairs. I handed out the prayer book and started services. Within five minutes, I heard a steady *thump, thump, thump* in the room. The patients were dropping their books—too heavy to hold, print too small to read. Sometimes rabbis miscalculate.

I guess the official Jewish world began to figure out we had a synagogue problem in America in the mid-Seventies. They started creating synagogue alternatives. Coffee houses were big for twenty-somethings. Nature retreats were another alternative. The *Chavurah* movement moved services from the sanctuary to the living room. Brotherhoods tried cigar and whiskey nights for middle-aged and older gentlemen. One day, all-day adult study programs from the UK challenged more conventional synagogue-based adult education. Anything was better than actually coming to synagogue. Today, many Jewish foundations have decided they would fund anything but synagogues. In some corners, the crisis in the American synagogue became a "war on the synagogue."

Surveys of Jewish life began to report that an increasing number of young Jewish adults began demonstrating that they were ethnically Jewish but had no religion. They became known as the Nones Jews. Questions about the basis of Jewish identity showed that the Holocaust, not Judaism, was the foundation of Jewish life for the rising generation although they didn't go to Holocaust programs, services, or museums.

Birthright Israel was originally designed to transform young Jews by sending them to Israel for free during their college years. The program clearly worked. Young people were feeling more Jewish, but Birthright did not lead many back to the synagogue.

Summer camps were effective identity builders too and literally reversed the standing pattern in American Jewish life, making summer the most, not the least, Jewish time of year. Shabbat every week at camp—great! Shabbat once in a blue moon at home, maybe, but only if the music sounded like camp.

Interestingly, a Jewish-Buddhist movement began, known as Ju-Bu-ism. Before JUBUs, almost no one liked silent prayer in the synagogue. The silent prayer was a chance to check your watch, ask if anybody knew the score in the Phillies game, and return to the conversation you were having before you got to Temple. But with the Jewish mindfulness movement, silent prayer became serious business. I remember learning to count to fifty before signaling the organist to end the silent prayer: long enough for some to mediate, short enough not to frustrate the rest of the congregation. But something positive was starting to happen.

Maybe, just maybe, a path or paths back to the synagogue could be found. Maybe, just maybe, the synagogue itself could adapt to the new digital world of selfie photos, cell phones, endless apps, and pop music on demand. Maybe being part of a real community had some benefits. Maybe meeting kids from different schools could be socially valuable. Maybe creating an environment in which non-Jewish partners and spouses would feel not only welcome but also enfranchised would be appealing. Maybe a synagogue that communicated digitally would be more accessible. Maybe real community service projects that helped real people would create a sense of sacred purpose in life. Maybe, just maybe, we could hold on to the best of the past and simultaneously embrace unprecedented new expressions of the Jewish spirit. Maybe, just maybe, there is a place and a reason for a synagogue in the twenty-first century in the life of modern Jewish people.

There are so many obstacles to overcome in synagogue life today. In the Talmud, there is a teaching that without wheat, there is no Torah. In other words, we need to resolve the challenge of synagogue financing. Some people are satisfied to have rent-a-rabbis to teach their children, marry them, and officiate at family funerals. Others just have too many bad memories to cross the threshold of a synagogue, and others can't find a synagogue that respects their belief system or lacks of a belief system.

In many ways, synagogue life in our time is like the burned-out synagogue of the dream of my youth. It is a ruin for too many Jews today. But in it are also the seeds of its rejuvenation—if we try hard, are creative enough, and are open enough.

The synagogue has served the Jewish community well for at least two thousand years. It has adapted, grown, shrunk, and repositioned itself many times in history. Microchips and wireless communication are not the greatest challenges it has ever faced. In fact, they are part of the answer.

KI is an old synagogue, boldly entering the twenty-first century. It is determined to succeed because it knows it has a vital role to play in the lives of its people. We have always been strong as a congregation. We are strong as a congregation today and will continue to strive to meet the Jewish and religious needs of our members for a long time to come.

"*Chazak, Chazak, v'Nitchazeik* [Be strong, be strong and let us continue to strengthen one another]!"—that is our motto. That is our promise. That is our future.

May we all be inscribed and sealed for a good year in a strong, renewed KI.

G'mar Tov and a Happy New Year!

Amen.

Yizkor: Staying Strong in the Shadow

September 30, 2017, Yom Kippur 5778

We are all familiar with the words of the Twenty-Third Psalm, "The Lord is my Shepherd."

It is the most familiar of all the 150 psalms. Only fifty-six words long in the original Hebrew, it has a natural, soothing flow in English, especially older English translations, and somehow helps us transition from fear to faith, from anxiety to hope, from uncertainty to inner peace. Recited in funeral home chapels, gravesides, and houses of worship of all types and styles, it is a familiar and comforting text.

Somehow, the Twenty-Third Psalm's ancient pastoral images of a young King David wandering the fields of Judea, surviving repeated life-threatening events, one after another, and ultimately dreaming of a time of restfulness "in the house of the Lord" in Jerusalem helps calm the stirred-up spirits, even of modern, contemporary people like us. Basically, the Twenty-Third Psalm portrays how spiritual strength, like a rod and staff, helps support us and even guide us in our most sorrowful of times.

Looking at a casket of a loved one or staring down into an earthen grave or simply closing our eyes at a funeral and feeling the torn-ness of our hearts all seems overwhelming to us. How am I ever going to get through this moment? How am I ever going to endure words that too often, no matter how well intentioned or spoken, fail to bring comfort? How am I going to continue without my loved one? How am I even going to get through the funeral rites? These are real and sometimes bitter questions.

And then come the familiar words of the Twenty-Third Psalm, like an old friend or a well-worn pillow or a familiar soft blanket. Tenderly, it allows us some repose, some peace, some safety, in the unknown and bitter world of mourning. These words "They comfort me . . . even when I walk in the valley of death" cast light even in the deepest darkness of primal loss and pain.

I regularly tell mourners there is no magic in our ritual or other secret cures to the pain of mourning. But then I think of the Twenty-Third Psalm and *El Male* and *Kaddish*, and I remember that tradition does have some curative power—sometimes temporary, sometimes longer. Often these words give us strength when we have no strength. Often they help us stand when our legs can no longer support us. Often they hold us even when the gravity of the loss of the moment overwhelms us.

Where does strength come from in the shadow of the valley of loss? Strength comes from the love of those who know and love us most. Strength comes from the deep inner recesses of ourselves, strength we do not always know we have. Strength comes from tradition and its paved paths through grief and joy alike. For some of us, strength comes from a transcendent source, from music and art, from poetry, from the sky and trees, flowing streams, and crashing waves. For some of us, strength comes from an unknown transcendent source further away from us than the end of the universe but still close enough to our hearts to help us. For some of us, strength comes from God, Maker of Heaven and Earth and Consoler of the Brokenhearted.

Staying strong in times of loss is not an easy matter. Sometimes it's all too much, and we simply have to wait for another day, a different time, to begin to repair ourselves. Meanwhile, there are loving friends and family, sacred memories, and sacred texts to help us limp until we become strong enough in the broken places of our lives.

Today, this service is one of those times dedicated to remember, cry, test old wounds, and look for new sources of strength. *Chazak, Chazak v'Nitchazeik*. When we are ready, let us try to be strong and then try again and then remember to help others be strong, who, like ourselves, are bowed with sorrow and reduced by tears. "May goodness and mercy pursue you until you find peace in the sanctuaries of your hearts and homes for a length of days." Amen.

I Still Believe: Rereading Anne Frank

2017

I spent part of my winter vacation rereading *The Diary of Anne Frank*. I returned to this classic because I would be teaching it as an elective in our KI Confirmation program or Quest Noar this coming semester. It had already occurred to me to reread *Anne Frank* last summer after teaching a graduate seminar at Gratz College on Holocaust and Art. Most of my students were teachers; and many, if not most, teach Holocaust curricula, which include *Anne Frank*, despite the fact that many scholars of Holocaust literature are urging Holocaust educators to try other primary sources. The problem is, despite the desire in the "academy" to move beyond Anne Frank, in the real-world, *Anne Frank* still captivates people, especially young people. The Anne Frank House in Amsterdam attracts more visitors than any other site in Holland, over two million a year. Now in 2017, humanity, in its full diversity, still easily relates to Anne Frank, her diary, and her iconic image. So I decided to reread *The Diary of Anne Frank* after nearly fifty years.

Of course, how I read *Anne Frank* today is much different than how I read her the first time. For one, I know the story and have seen play and screen versions of it. Second, I now relate to the Diary not through the eyes of an adolescent but through the eyes of a parent who has raised five teenagers and as a grandparent wondering what the next round of adolescence will be like as my grandchildren grow up. I now also read *Anne Frank* critically as a trained and experienced historian. Moreover, I am aware of the complex editing process that took place both in the

Secret Annex and when Otto Frank and others prepared the Diary for publication, including both deleted and added passages. I have even looked at the magnificent critical edition and its masterful treatment of the original texts.

Finally, I now read *Anne Frank* contextually with the help of other books like Melissa Mueller's 1998 *Anne Frank: The Biography*, a very readable text that includes lots of Frank family history from both before and after the war. Mueller's knowledge of the story of the Frank family is incredible. I think she has every receipt from stores they frequented, has learned about everyone in the Frank family tree, and is an expert on life in general in Holland and Germany since 1900. I have also learned about how extensive Dutch-Nazi collaboration was and studied the question as to why Holland had the highest number of Jews killed in the Holocaust on a percentage basis than any other Western country. I've even read up on Bergen-Belsen concentration camp, where Anne and her sister, Margot, died and about the struggle against the Anne Frank deniers who claimed her Diary was a forgery.

For sure, my perspective on Anne Frank has changed. Anne is now much smaller, so to speak, a dot in the vortex of the Shoah, a hidden child in an occupied country, an adolescent with a natural talent for writing, and a teenager who had many typical issues with her own mother. In other words, I think I can now see Anne as a real person and not just as a symbol. I even understand how her own reduced interest in Judaism makes her more universally appealing. In short, Anne Frank has become an incredibly real person for me at this time. Her diary now shines in its specificity as much as it does as a universal symbol. At the end of the day, she was just a kid but a kid with an ability to look inward (she had nowhere else to go) and explain her adolescence in its fullness in her diary. And that is why *The Diary of Anne Frank* is even more compelling to me than before.

To my delight, my Confirmation elective quickly filled up; and not surprisingly, the girls outnumber the boys. Some of them have already read the Diary. Others are studying it in school as well as at KI. One student is in the class because she hopes to go to Amsterdam over Spring break and wants to prepare for her visit to the Anne Frank House. What is so wonderful to me is that the level of enthusiasm in the class to learn about Anne Frank is very high. No PC kvetching here. That they want to read and discuss every word is not only fine with me—it is inspiring.

I hope that I will have an opportunity to teach *Anne Frank* at the graduate level one day. We will be in good shape because I will have read it several times by then. Even more, I will have analyzed it with a group of devoted teenagers who feel drawn to her like one feels about a stranger who you just know is going to be your friend. That's the power and horrible tragedy of Anne Frank. She was real, and she was murdered because she was a Jew. But it does seem like her spirit is still alive in the millions of people who continue to love her.

Mazal Tov: The KI Puppets are 13!

February 15, 2018 Bulletin

Sixteen years ago, when I first started at KI, I faced a new challenge. I had never worked in a synagogue with a Preschool. How was I going to communicate with three- and four-year-old children, let alone one- and two-year-olds? I decided to do some online research and it instantly became clear that there was only one thing to do: puppets! Seeing that I personally did not own any puppets, I immediately began searching for them. Everywhere I went, I checked stores for puppets. Even on trips to Europe and Israel, I always looked for puppets. Online resources were improving at the time, so I looked for "puppets" in Google, too.

Well, before I knew it I had a small collection of hand puppets. I had animals, insects and birds of every kind. I even had imaginary beings with many eyes and strange colors. I had to buy large boxes and mesh nets to store them in my office.

I quickly learned that marionettes with complex strings were way above my abilities to control them. I began reading about puppetry and the history of Puppet Theater. After I while, I realized I had an affinity for several different animal puppets: turtles, monkeys, bears and lambs were quickly becoming my puppet friends.

About a year later, maybe 2002 or so, I settled on a couple of puppet names. The puppets' personalities were based on the personalities of staff and their jobs at KI. I was Torah Turtle. Rabbi Peter Rigler was Mitzvah Monkey. The administrator was Chaim the Crow. The Cantor created her own puppet character—Shira Salamander. On and on it went. But something was missing. We needed songs to help define their characters. So, I contacted a friend from New York who writes commercial music professionally. Paul Suchow had a lot of questions for me and grilled me on the puppets' characters. Before I knew it, Paul had produced a theme song, and songs for several of the characters.

Now, I was ready to create my own puppets. With the help of Robyn Miller, a KI member and artist, I contacted Glen Lash, who was able to draw sketches of the puppets I was dreaming of and then actually create them. We decided to go up to *Avenue Q*-sized puppets, which Liz and I had seen on Broadway. It only took a few weeks. Torah Turtle in green, Mitzvah Monkey in purple and orange, Shema Sheep in white, Bracha Bear in brown and Shira Salamander in red, were ready to go. Later, Teva Tiger in green, black and orange was created.

The KI Puppets were an instant success, except for "Chaim the Crow who only says 'no.'" All the kids were afraid of Chaim, so we put him away. We started doing little skits acting out the Torah portion of the week and teaching a Jewish value. They were added to Friday morning Tot Services and the once-a-month Tot Shabbat. Family and holiday services were soon featuring a puppet show. Artists Rhea and Robert Dennis created huge wall displays featuring the puppets in the Preschool. I was invited to show a national association of Preschool Directors how our puppets worked. Confirmation Class made a few short puppet movies and put them on YouTube. "Who would have ever thought," Rabbi Rick Jacobs, President of the Reform movement, once said to me in his NY office, "that you (Lance) did puppets. You're a historian, no?"

I guess we can be a lot of different things. I am a rabbi and a historian, but I am also Torah Turtle, and that part of me is almost 13 so it is time for a Bar Mitzvah, and a Bat Mitzvah for Shira Salamander and a B'nai Mitzvah for the rest of the gang. We will celebrate our simcha on Friday morning, February 23 with the Preschool and that night with the congregation. We are going to have a KI Puppet B'nai Mitzvah and I hope you will be here to celebrate with us.

I must say that my initial research on puppets failed to indicate something really important. It's not just three-year-olds who like puppets! Thirty-three-year-olds like puppets! Fifty-three-year-olds like puppets! Eighty-three-year-olds like puppets! In fact, everybody likes puppets. So join us on February 23 for a KI Puppet B'nai Mitzvah. It's fun, it's unique and, who knew, it's even educational!

MARINES

April 2018 Bulletin

Last Sunday, April 15, 2018, I officiated at the funeral of USMC Captain Samuel A. Schultz (28) z"l of Huntingdon Valley, PA. It was the first time I officiated at a funeral with full military honors for an active serviceman in my thirty-eight years as an ordained rabbi. Sam was the commander of a four-man crew, all of whom perished in a training accident on the US-Mexican border east of San Diego on Tuesday, April 3, 2018.

By all accounts, Sam was a remarkable young man who graduated from Abington Senior High School and Penn State. From a family of pilots, Sam enrolled in ROTC and subsequently earned his wings before rising to the rank of Marine Captain. The Corps was investing deeply in Sam at the time of his death as a flight instructor with multiple military specialties and active deployment experience. A four-star general attended his funeral. Our deepest sympathies go out to his dear parents, Julie and Mitchell, his older brother Eric, and his entire family.

Officiating at the funeral of an active-duty Marine was a new and profound experience for me. I have led many funerals for veterans in the past complete with a flag folding ceremony, a three-gun salute and taps. But this was different, really different. Not only was Levine's chapel in Trevose "Standing Room Only," but also whole families lined the processional route standing with flags, their hands on their hearts in the wind and rain. Entire firehouses and police squads stood saluting his casket. Sam also had a 21-gun salute. But even more, there were hundreds of Marines in full-dress uniform who came to his funeral voluntarily and at their own cost.

Most of the Marines were officers, largely Captains as he was, as well as dozens of USMC Sergeants and Navy officers, including an Admiral from the Department of Navy. They were "Friends of Sam."

Honestly, I have never been more impressed with a group of young people, especially the Marine Captains, who I met on Sunday. Every possible assumption and stereotype I held was wrong, way wrong. The men and women were intelligent, polite, respectful, engaging, humane and fit as fiddles. They wore their uniforms perfectly. The bonds of friendship among them were palpable.

When the Artillery Captain assigned to the family in a temporary pastoral role presented them with their Gold Stars, he shook with emotion as he pinned them. When another Captain presented the folded flag, which had draped his coffin to Sam's mother, tears streamed down his face even as he maintained perfect military posture. Many, if not most, of these twenty-five, twenty-six- and thirty-year-olds had already seen combat in the Middle East but they were not robots or cynical. They were real people, magnificent people doing their duty with love in their hearts.

We have all heard politicians say our military people are "the best" we have to offer. Whether you believe that or not, I will tell you, the Marines I met, one step chronologically above being kids themselves, were truly the best I have witnessed collectively in my life. My father and father-in-law were both soldiers who earned Bronze Stars under fire and never bragged about their time in the Army. This Sunday, I had an opportunity, for all the wrong the reasons, to glimpse into the heart of the military they served and respected.

I was truly impressed as a rabbi and an American citizen and although I grieve with Sam's wonderful family over his death, I am so proud our faith was represented so gallantly in the midst of the Corps. If you have ever worried about the soul of this country, I hope you get to meet a Marine Captain for a happier reason than I did. Yet again, I was reminded that freedom does not come cheaply and again, sadly, shows how dear a price we have to pay to be truly free.

Semper Fi!

Shabbat Shalom.

The Final Review: Philip Roth, 1933–2018

June 1, 2018 eKI

Phillip Roth has been one of the most important literary figures in my life from the minute I began to read adult literature, sometime in my teens. He served as a significant social commentator on Jewish life in America for me who held a mirror up to Jewish life without apology and usually with devastating effect. I eagerly awaited each new Roth book and later as a rabbi probably reviewed most of them since the 1980s either in writing or in live synagogue programming. I never cared an iota about the debate as to whether or not he was a Jewish or an American writer. The fact is that for me Roth wrote about Jewish life, my main personal interest, with a sharp eye for the contradictions, complexity, and neuroses which makes everyday life "real."

I first encountered Philip Roth when I saw the 1969 movie version of *Goodbye, Columbus*. I was fifteen at the time, growing up in Jewish suburbia in a family that a generation earlier had been totally urban and therefore understood his frame of reference. Richard Benjamin and Ali McGraw were perfectly cast as the protagonists for me as I was becoming aware of the class conflict in the Jewish community, familial aspirations about college and, of course, girls. As much as the movie was entertaining, it was also intellectually challenging for a young man already interested in the rabbinate who was thinking about serving a community with a specific sociology so different from the world Jewish sacred books. For me, Roth was already the teller of cautionary tales I would come to appreciate more and more with each new addition to his massive body of literary work.

In 1969, the year that Roth's most controversial work, *Portnoy's Complaint* came out, I guess you could say it was my introduction to "dirty literature." My parents had a policy of no censorship, but it certainly was not discussed at home nor at school, although I did receive tacit approval for having serious literary interests. At the time, I was unaware that the book had precipitated a huge uproar in the Jewish community and the world of literature in general. Instead, it seemed like a clandestine peek into reality as I was experiencing it but was left alone to process. Looking backward, perhaps it was my first encounter with psychiatry and therapy.

Neither time nor space permits to me to go through each major Roth publication nor comment on every single theme he explores. However, his 1997 non-fiction work, *Patrimony*, was of instant and enduring interest to me. *Patrimony* explores the last year of Roth's father's life and how the literary star took off a year to be with his Dad to the end. As a rabbi deeply embedded in congregational life and with hundreds of funerals behind me, it was an incredible report from the inner world of another person's family we are rarely privileged to enter. His discussion of how to dress his father for "eternity" and his encounter with groundskeepers in the cemetery were both particularly illuminating. As a son, it challenged me to think about my own relationship with my own aging father and helped pave the way to an intensification of my own exchanges with my Dad.

Roth's 2004 *Plot Against America* was a remarkably creative way to explore the world of anti-Semitism in America, especially from the perspective of someone born before World War II. As a veteran professor of American Jewish history, it offered me an opportunity to present to my students, who basically never encountered anti-Semitism directly, an imaginative account of the hidden fears, real and imagined, of their grandparents and more remote ancestors. The "what if" approach to history almost always succeeded in provoking serious classroom debate about anti-Semitism, the American experience of animus, and prejudice in general.

Two years, later Roth produced a short novel, *Everyman*, modeled after a 15th century English morality play. In it, he explores in an essentially autobiographical fashion, the musings of an ordinary, elderly man reviewing his life, his shortcomings, and his physical decline. It is a sobering work and a philosophical bookend to *Patrimony* I find helpful in thinking about the inevitability of aging and death. Whatever neuroses may have animated the young author of *Portnoy's Complaint* are all burned out in *Everyman*, which perhaps is also a shelf-mate to the Biblical classic, *Ecclesiastes*, attributed to the elderly King Solomon three thousand years ago.

Finally, a word about Roth's 2008 *Indignation* (and a 2016 movie), a bitter look at a Jewish college student during the Korean War who ends up in the front line facing a brutal Chinese enemy instead of attending fraternity parties back home. Indignation brings together several themes typical of Roth including sexuality, anger, atheism, Jewish marginality and academia. In the end, the main character dies a brutal death in a trench in Korea and his life of anger comes to a tragic, unredeemed end.

Unable to secure a grave near his parents, Roth arranged to be buried in a non-denominational college cemetery without, at his insistence, any Jewish ritual. He never claimed he practiced Judaism and this final act proved it. I would also say we should allow him to label himself as any kind of writer he wanted to be. Personally, I don't care. What I do care about is that he wrote truthfully, even harshly about being a Jewish person in 20th century America. I cannot ignore his words. They remind me of how much work we must do in the real world of Jewish life today and that is not going to be easy to construct, maintain and nurture meaningful Jewish lives in an unredeemed world. Shabbat Shalom.

An Emblem of the Land I Love: Reform Jewish Reflections on Flag Day

June 13, 2018

About a dozen years ago, I was involved in a German Jewish teen exchange program. German students from Frankfurt-area high schools stayed with the families of teens in our synagogue, Reform Congregation Keneseth Israel, in Elkins Park, Pennsylvania, and then our students went to Germany to stay with their counterparts' families. Everything was going well until we took our guests by bus to Independence Hall. As we drew near to the cradle of American democracy, the usually festive German kids became strangely quiet. When pressed, they told us they expected to see banners about freedom and not dozens of American flags surrounding the home of the Declaration of Independence. "It's so nationalistic," they said, "and we are Germans!"

It was a shocking, eye-opening experience for me who instinctively viewed the American flag as a symbol of freedom and hope, especially at its point of origin. Somehow, the Stars and Stripes were both patriotic and above narrow patriotism at the same time. This year, America's Flag Day provides a special opportunity to reflect on the intersection of faith and patriotism given the ongoing controversy in the United States about flag etiquette for the last few months.

Flag Day commemorates the adoption of the Stars and Stripes by the Second Continental Congress on June 14, 1777. President Woodrow Wilson proclaimed Flag Day a national holiday in 1916, and thirty years later, Congress did the same but did not raise it to the level of Memorial

Day or July the Fourth. Meanwhile, the "Star-Spangled Banner" became the national anthem in 1931 and by early in World War II was played before professional baseball games and, about ten years later, before National Football League games.

For American Jews, it is important to point out that the legend of Betsy Ross can only be traced back to the Centennial of 1876 and that the story of George Washington suggesting six pointed stars on the flag is equally apocryphal. The earliest-known displays of the American flag in synagogues were during the Civil War, especially during the period of mourning for Abraham Lincoln, and then again in 1898, during the Spanish American War.

However, not until the 1930s was it typical for synagogues to display American flags in their sanctuaries. As in many church communities, there was a widespread view that worship space was for God and that the American doctrine of the Separation of Church and State precluded showing the colors in church or synagogue from a secular perspective. To this day, Haredi synagogues generally do not display flags. Early in my own career, I regularly heard the admonition "No flags in the sanctuary" perhaps reinforced by the politics of the Vietnam War.

The first responsum by the Central Conference of American Rabbis (CCAR), the professional association of Reform rabbis, on having a flag in a synagogue was issued in 1954 (perhaps as a reaction to the addition of the words *under God*, which were inserted into the Pledge of Allegiance on Flag Day in that same year). Written by Israel Bettan, the responsum affirmed the appropriateness of having a U.S. flag in a Reform temple but also maintained that Israeli flags should only be displayed on special occasions such as Israel Independence Day. Israeli flags became increasingly popular in American synagogues after 1967, and in 1977, the CCAR weighed in and rescinded all limitations on the Israeli flag.

Promoted by a question I raised twenty years later, the CCAR ruled it was permissible to sing "*HaTikvah*," the national anthem of Israel, during Reform worship services without a parallel national anthem in the United States or Canada. The CCAR also hesitated before including the "Star-Spangled Banner" and "O Canada" in *Mishkan T'filah*, the newest Reform prayer book. As far as I know, there have been no attempts to compel individuals to remove their *kippot (yarmulkes)* while saluting the American flag. In France, however, there are laws that regulate the use of religious head coverings in schools and other public places.

For sure, the current debate about football players kneeling during the national anthem is controversial and, upon analysis, very complex, especially with respect to the First Amendment, municipal ownership of stadiums and teams, and the rights of business owners and employees. The debate may give faith-based communities pause to rethink their own flag policies, views of Church and State, and even their theologies.

Personally, I do not object to flags in our sanctuaries and would not kneel before a flag in protest, a practice that is foreign to both my faith and my political beliefs. On the other hand, abolitionists burned copies of the Constitution as "a pact with [the] Devil." This year, Flag Day requires more of us than parades and conventional displays of patriotism. It challenges us to think deeply about what it means to be Americans and Jews in our time.

THE WINE WAS GOOD:
ANOTHER LOOK AT THE *TREFA* BANQUET

July 10, 2018

On July 11, 1883, a large group of about two hundred American Jewish VIPs sat down to eat a festive meal to celebrate the ordination of the first graduating class of the Hebrew Union College (HUC) at the elegant Highland House in Cincinnati, Ohio. For Isaac M. Wise, president of HUC, it was a sweet moment validating four decades of tireless work to unite American synagogues with the primary purpose of pooling resources to create a rabbinic school for the Jewish community in the United States. His students were now ordained rabbis, and the time to celebrate had arrived.

Ten years earlier, dozens of laymen responded to Wise's call for unity by establishing the Union of American Hebrew Congregations (UAHC, now the Union for Reform Judaism); and then just two years later, in 1875, he officially opened HUC in Queen City. It seemed that Wise's many detractors, both among Jewish traditionalists and radical Reformers, were finally proven wrong as the four-member HUC class of 1883 ascended the pulpit of his own Moorish-styled Plum Street Temple.

However, the moment proved fleeting as word of a massive culinary *faux pas* at the ordination dinner slowly spread throughout the American Jewish community. With the exception of serving pork, nearly every category of *kashrut* (Jewish dietary laws) was violated, including serving three types of seafood, at the ordination dinner. On the other hand, the wine was good, beginning with Amontillado sherry and concluding with Martell cognac, as were many of the dishes at Wise's great repast.

By 1884, the Highland House event had already become known as the *Trefa* Banquet, a double entendre not only descriptive of the original menu but also an attack on the integrity of Isaac M. Wise and, by extension, the entire Reform movement. By contrast, the myth of the Trefa Banquet grew slowly. First was the account of the meal in David Philipson's 1940 memoir, *My Life as an American Jew*. Philipson was one of the four ordainees but inexplicitly falsely maintained that a number of distinguished rabbis rose in protest at the banquet itself. Second was an incisive 1966 article in *Commentary* magazine by immigration historian John J. Appel, which revived controversies surrounding Wise's role in planning the dinner, as well as its bitter aftermath, which nearly closed HUC.

While there is no question that *treif* was served at the Highland House banquet, 135 years later there are still a number of historical questions that need to be addressed. First, the dinner itself was not disrupted by protests, which led directly to the founding of the Jewish Theological Seminary in 1886 like a Boston Tea Party igniting the American Revolution. The daily press in Cincinnati reported on the ordination service and the banquet in detail, and no protests were recorded. It took two weeks for editors of Jewish papers hostile to Wise to pick up on the story and amplify it. Mostly likely, a young Henrietta Szold—who had accompanied her father, Baltimore's Rabbi Benjamin Szold—to Cincinnati spilled the beans when she lamented in a letter to a New York paper, using a pseudonym, that she had personally failed to protest at the dinner.

More important, the banquet dinner itself was not unique or exceptional among American Jews in the Gilded Age. Two weeks after their ordination, two of the newly minted rabbis served a nearly identical meal at their double wedding when Rabbi Joseph Krauskopf married the sister of Rabbi Henry Berkowitz. Later, the two worked side by side at Philadelphia's two large Reform synagogues on North Broad Street, Keneseth Israel and Rodeph Shalom, during the Progressive Era. In October 1883, four months after the Highland House dinner, the B'nai B'rith organization held its national convention in Cincinnati; and again, *treif* was served. It was an age of excess, and fresh seafood, especially oysters, was available in Cincinnati overnight in newly refrigerated cars on the Baltimore & Ohio Railroad. Without question, the menu of the *Trefa* Banquet was typical of its time in upscale American culinary culture of the time—with the exception of pork, which was losing ground to the expanding American beef industry.

Finally, the changing nature of American Reform Judaism at the end of the nineteenth century needs to be considered in any discussion of the Trefa Banquet. Ironically, when the UAHC was first formed in 1873, it required all member congregations to keep kosher, perhaps a compromise by Wise to create a religious organizational umbrella for all American Jews. In reality, his congregational union quickly morphed into what would become part of the Reform denominational structure in which increasingly radical views prevailed. In 1885, a group of Reform rabbis promulgated the Pittsburgh Platform, explicitly rejected all aspects of kashrut, and labeled Jewish dietary practice a relic of a different stage in the history of Judaism and no longer spiritually meaningful for modern Jews. Although Wise was chairman of the Pittsburgh Conference, he ambivalently labeled the radical platform as a "Declaration of Independence."

Much of the legacy of the Trefa Banquet was shaped by Wise's exchanges with his detractors in the months and years that followed. He was quick to point out inconsistencies, hypocrisy, and fraud with respect to keeping kosher both at the personal and commercial levels. At other times, it is hard to know if Wise saw any humor in the situation. At one point, he defended serving seafood on the grounds that they were "ocean vegetables," perhaps a play on the French term for seafood, *fruit de mer*, while at other times he employed "scientific" evidence about reclassifying oysters. Wise, who lived on a farm and personally kept kosher, even had two pet pigs that, according to family sources, were named Kosher and Treif.

Food policy is much discussed in contemporary Reform Judaism. The ethics of food production, animal rights, sustainability, tradition, and health are all important topics among Reform Jews today. The dinner at the Highland House was but one instance in which Reform Judaism was struggling to keep Judaism alive in the hearts of followers more than a century ago. There is much we can learn from their decisions, goals, failures, and successes and, by extension, our own.

Bibi: The Cheltenham Years

August 16, 2018 eKI

One of my many projects this summer (2018) was to learn more about the place of Cheltenham, PA in the life of Benjamin Netanyahu, the second longest serving Prime Minister of Israel. As is well known, Bibi lived in Cheltenham twice, once as a little boy and then as a teenager during his high school years. Numerous people in the community and at KI have clear memories of Bibi as smart, athletic and "different." What if anything could I learn about him.

First and foremost, I concluded that by his high school years, Bibi had a fully constructed worldview. He was ideologically a product of his father and his father's family. Bibi's paternal grandfather already was a Revisionist Zionist who brought his family to Palestine early in the history of the British Mandate. While his grandfather was a religious Zionist, Bibi's father, Ben Zion Netanyahu, was a secular Jew and a follower of Jabotinsky, the founder of Zionist Revisionism, which believed both in a "Greater Israel" and capitalism. Ben Zion was also an academic famous for his work on the Spanish Inquisition, including his unusual approach to the motivation of the Conversos who he saw as compliant but then shocked by the Inquisition authorities. His critics accused him of writing Jewish history "with the Holocaust in the rearview mirror." Ben Zion believed that the Inquisition was motivated more by race than by religion.

Like father like son, Bibi Netanyahu held the same beliefs as his father with respect to a greater and well-defended Israel and a negative view of the Diaspora. As such, Bibi (as well as his mother and brothers) were not happy with Ben Zion's decision to work in America. Ben Zion's loss of influence in the Israeli Right was compounded by the rise of Menachem Begin and his followers within the Israeli Right, leaving the Netanyahus on the margin of the Herut, then Likkud, for many years. Ultimately, Bibi regained political control of Likkud, completing his family's return to power.

My take-away from this history is that Bibi Netanyahu is a consistent ideologue and in trying to understand him and his policies, it is critical to remember how deeply anchored he is in the Betar-Herut-Likkud spectrum in Zionist politics. So much of what he does and says is Revisionism blended with political pragmatism and more than a touch of Machiavellianism. On the other hand, the question remains as to whether Bibi's years in the United States as a child, college student, and diplomat also affected him. This question is particularly important now at a time when Israeli-Diaspora relations are so problematic.

My conclusion is that although Netanyahu remains a Revisionist, he has not entirely written off the Diaspora or at least the American Jewish community. Unlike his view of the Jews of France who he believes should pack up *en masse* and move to Israel, Netanyahu does a kind of dance with the American Jewish community. For example, although most believe he has failed Reform and Conservative Judaism with respect to legal equality in Israel as well as representation at the Western Wall, he has also not entirely squashed the efforts of non-Orthodox Jews in Israel for public recognition. Is his hesitation in this regard purely political or does it suggest a hint of enduring "connectedness" with his classmates at Cheltenham High School?

Of course, it is well known that Bibi's brother and the idol of his life, Yoni, wrote bitterly of the shallowness of teenage life in Cheltenham. Bibi himself did not attend his high school graduation and left early to join the Israeli Army. For the record, he served with bravery and distinction. But was there more, even a sense of global Jewish solidarity? Are his ties of friendship with a handful of Cheltenham families a hint to something more? We will never know as Netanyahu is complex and enigmatic. My sense is that deep down there is a tie between Netanyahu and the American Diaspora. Much of that tie is practical and provides for political support in Washington. More broadly, is a longitudinal, nearly messianic view that ultimately the whole Jewish people will see the light and pack up and head to Israel. In the meantime, it does not hurt to stay in touch with cousins who also fray your nerves. They remain family, as difficult as that may be at times, for everybody.

Shabbat Shalom.

Why We Need Good Sermons Now More Than Ever

Reform Judaism Magazine
August 20, 2018

Preaching from the pulpit is a real challenge these days. With few exceptions, rabbis have had to trim their sermonic sails, even during the High Holidays, sidestepping politics, throwing in autobiographical snippets and a joke or two, and ending gracefully, like docking a family boat.

In contrast, when I was growing up in the 1960s, sermons were among the most anticipated events in synagogue life, especially on the eve of Rosh HaShanah and Kol Nidre night. At Oheb Shalom Congregation in Baltimore, MD, our senior rabbi, Abraham D. Shaw, dressed in a majestic white robe and a pillbox-style *kippah* (yarmulke), regaled us with his powerful oratory.

For more than a century and a half in the Reform Movement, High Holiday sermons were consequential both for the rabbi and the congregation, as hearts were receptive and the pews packed. It is fair to say that many congregants came just to hear their charismatic rabbi preach on the pressing issues of the day. It was also customary for High Holiday sermons to be printed and distributed for further review, even compared to rabbinic discourses of neighboring synagogues.

So why has the Reform preaching tradition gradually waned over the past half century? I surmise the following three factors may have played a role:

1. The prominence of prayer or *davening* in synagogue services has increased, leaving less time for preaching. Several years ago, I found myself in a public disagreement with the president of a non-Reform, progressive rabbinic school. When asked how his school trains rabbis to preach on the High Holidays, he said his students are urged not to speak, but rather to concentrate on the *davening*. "People no longer want sermons," he insisted.
2. The American Jewish community is today more fragmented and less tolerant of those holding opposing views than at any time since the Vietnam War. Reform Jews are not immune to the lack of civility that is plaguing public discourse, making preaching from the pulpit on divisive issues tricky, even risky. One congregant insists on boldness from the pulpit, another steadfastly aims to block any attempt by the rabbi to question his or her political views, and still another wants only comforting and spiritual words.
3. Feminism and the ordination of women have had a transformational impact on Jewish preaching. Women rabbinic preachers have demonstrated that charismatic male-ness is not the *sine qua non* of success in the pulpit. In an effort to overcome gender inequality in Jewish life and to promote the egalitarian ideals of Reform Judaism, they boldly used examples from their own lives. It would not be an exaggeration to say that women rabbis may have saved preaching in the Reform pulpit from extinction.

While the grand oratorical sermon style practiced by charismatic male rabbis is a thing of the past, I believe that preaching from the pulpit remains an indispensable part of the modern synagogue experience.

Here's why:

1. Nothing can replace the immediacy of well-chosen words in speaking truth to power and empowering the powerless.
2. Meekness on the pulpit does not inspire audacious hospitality, the welcoming of spiritual seekers into our synagogues.
3. At a time when powerful and dark forces, such as religious fundamentalism and political authoritarianism, threaten the

future of democracy in the United States, Europe, and Israel, it is rabbinic malpractice, or at the very least a shirking of rabbinic responsibility, not to rally the Jewish people around the prophetic tradition to pursue peace and justice.

If rabbis cease boldly voicing the living words of our prophetic tradition, the spirit of Reform Judaism surely will wither.

I Cannot Forgive You

September 18, 2018, Yom Kippur Evening 5779

You are in your family room. The TV show your kids have been watching is over, and the credits start running. The quicker of the two kids grabs the remote purposefully, instantly changes the channel to the show of his choice, and cradles the remote controller like a fullback clutching a football on a short yardage play up the middle. The other child is physically unable to dislodge the remote but, in fact, had been promised the remote and loudly begins to protest. Number one won't budge. Number two escalates his ever-louder protests, and the quiet of your home descends into the Battle of the Alamo.

Then it's time for parental intervention. A parent secures the remote from child one and hands it to child two and then orders the aggressor to apologize to the victim. The command is followed by a half-hearted but rather snotty sorry, which draws a bitter grunt of disgust from the new owner of the remote. Battle over. Parent wins. Both kids are sore, and it's back to television for a maximum of thirty minutes of *shalom bayit* (family peace) before the warriors of discontent shift their positions on the remote-control TV battlefield.

Sounds familiar? Of course, it does! We all have these moments of ephemeral crises or something like them. All of us have been compelled to make insincere apologies to our siblings and say "I am sorry" just to maintain the appearance of civility, only to be met with the snide rejection of the winner of the battle, knowing full well that round two, or twenty-two, is only a half an hour away.

We learn to say "I am sorry" and even "I forgive you" early in life, just like we are taught to say "Thank you for the candy" when all we really want to do is rip the wrapper off and sink our teeth into a welcome piece of chocolate. Saying "I'm sorry" is the price of civilization, and eventually, most of us learn how to play the game.

There are many famous quotes about forgiveness. Alexander Pope taught, "To err is human, to forgive is divine." Gandhi said that "forgiveness is an attribute of the strong." Norman Cousins said, "Life is an adventure in forgiveness." Hannah Arendt observed that "forgiveness is the key to action and freedom." As a young person, I was deeply impressed by a quote attributed to Golda Meir that "we can forgive you for killing our sons, we cannot forgive you for forcing our sons to kill yours."

Judaism, like all the great religions, recognized a long time ago that without some kind of forgiveness, the world would be a lot tougher place than it already is. Thus, forgiveness is at the very heart of Yom Kippur, our most sacred of days. It is our divinely sanctioned amnesty day. We offer God our deepest prayers of supplication and remorse for our offenses, and then we are clean, *tabula rasa*, until we ourselves begin to sin again the next day or even that night. We don't need an interlocutor, an agent, a priest, a sacrifice, or anything other than sincerity. In Judaism, we are forgiven by God and enter the New Year in a blameless state.

Sounds great, even easy, whether you believe in God or not. Who wouldn't take this kind of deal? But there is a catch. In the Talmudic discussion of Yom Kippur, it is stated in Yoma 8.9 that for sins between God and people, Yom Kippur atones. But for sins between people, Yom Kippur does not atone until the perpetrator seeks forgiveness from the victim and the victim forgives him or her.

In light of this teaching, a tradition developed in Judaism that at this time of year we approach people we have hurt, in any way, during the course of the last twelve months and sincerely ask them to forgive us. In more serious cases, asking for forgiveness may require payment for actual losses and then punitive damages. In still more serious cases, punishment, even jail, may be required before all accounts are squared. But what happens when the victim simply cannot forgive the perpetrator? What if we can't just turn the other cheek? What if a person hurt us or hurt a loved one so grievously that we have no forgiveness in our heart? What if you were betrayed in a way that there is no end to your suffering? What if what they did to you was so bad you could never forgive them?

What do you do then? Do you take your anger to the grave with you and hope your enemy takes it to the grave too but before you? Do you refuse to talk about it, negotiate, or coexist in any way? How will the grudge ever end? How can there ever be peace again in our heart or in the social dimension of your life?

In the news last week, it was announced that the woman Wanda Barzee involved in the kidnapping and torturing of Elizabeth Smart from her childhood home in June 2002 was getting an early parole for good behavior! Elizabeth Smart, from a passionately Mormon religious home, went on the air and stated that this is wrong and her tormentor should not be released at this early point in her sentence! Can you really blame Elizabeth?

On the other hand, what are we to make of the surviving members of the 2015 Charleston Church shooting in which a young white supremacist murdered nine people at a Bible study at a Black church in the South Carolina port city, standing up at a bond hearing and forgiving him? Some qualified their comments by adding, "May God forgive you." Others said they forgave him but still sought justice. Is it possible to automatically forgive even the most heinous crime without preconditions?

The most poignant treatment I know of the question of forgiving the unforgivable was raised by Simon Wiesenthal exactly fifty years ago in his book *The Sunflower* in 1969. Wiesenthal was born in Austria and survived the Holocaust. He became a renowned Nazi hunter and was involved in the capture of both Adolf Eichmann and Josef Mengele. He was prolific and wrote nine books and many articles.

In *The Sunflower*, Wiesenthal recounts how he met and was asked by a twenty-two-year-old SS soldier who was dying of his wounds to be forgiven for his personal role in massacring a large number of Jews in a hideous manner. The dying German explained that he had been raised as a practicing Catholic although his father was secular and an anti-Nazi. The dying soldier also asked Wiesenthal to deliver a letter to his mother.

In addition to telling his story, Wiesenthal also asked thirty-two distinguished individuals to reflect on the question of forgiving the unforgivable. Among the respondents were Rabbi Abraham Joshua Heschel, Primo Levi, philosopher Herbert Marcuse, and novelist Cynthia Ozick. Each provided a serious, thoughtful answer. Some urged forgiveness to break the cycle of hate. Some said the dying soldier was wrong to ask to be forgiven. Some said they could not forgive. Others said they could forgive but could not forget.

I remember back in the mid-1990s, fifty years after the end of World War II, I read that some of the German army divisions my own father had fought against in the Battle of the Bulge were having reunions at the same time as some of the American military units. Both were scheduled to go to Metz, France, for the event. "If you went," I asked my father naively, "would you greet former German soldiers if you bumped into them?"

"I would acknowledge them," he answered, "maybe a nod." Then, unexpectedly, he added to his answer, "But if they were SS," he said with a much darker voice, "I would not acknowledge them in any way."

"Why?" I asked. "What's the difference?"

"Snipers," he said tersely, "snipers."

"I don't understand," I replied.

"Well," he continued, "many times after we attacked a village and took it, the German Army would pull out and retreat, but the SS left suicidal snipers behind, and they killed more Americans than we would lose in the battle. They can never be forgiven," he ended the discussion conclusively. His words stuck.

"They can never be forgiven," I thought to myself. "I guess they can't."

On the other hand, with the passage of enough time, forgiveness can be achieved between groups of people and between nations. Even though the British burned down the White House, America and the UK reconciled a long time ago. And how many wars took place between the English and the French? Seventy-three years ago, the United States dropped two atomic bombs on Japan to hasten the end of World War II, and for the most part, American Japanese relations are fine today. I don't know of too many American Jews who will not go to Spain because of the Spanish Inquisition, although feelings about places like Germany and Poland are both mixed and ambivalent. Given enough time and the right circumstances, it seems even the bitterest of enemies at the national level can find common ground, if not true forgiveness.

However, the collective and the interpersonal clearly do not work the same way with respect to forgiveness. In his answer to Wiesenthal, Rabbi Heschel told a story about the rabbi of Brisk. The Brisker Rav was riding on a train on the way home from a business trip. On the train, he was mocked by a group of businessmen. Days later in the synagogue, one of the traveling salesmen saw the rabbi in shul, felt mortified, and went up to the rabbi to ask for forgiveness. The rabbi said, "No, I can't forgive you. You are asking forgiveness from the Brisker Rabbi, but the man you mocked in the train was, in your view, a *nebesh*, a nobody, an unimportant man. You must find him and ask him for forgiveness." In other words, no apology was possible the same way the sunflowers that Wiesenthal saw on the graves of Holocaust victims could offer forgiveness. They can only remind us, the author is teaching us, not to excuse the inexcusable. In Judaism, personal offenses between people can only be forgiven personally.

Remember the 1969 movie *The War of the Roses* with Michael Douglas, Kathleen Turner, and Danny DeVito? The two main characters, Oliver and Barbara Rose, are locked in a grueling divorce battle. It was the ultimate case of irreconcilable differences, and it ended tragically with couple lying dead in the entry hall to their elegant home under a collapsed crystal chandelier. But many broken relationships, marriage or friendship, can be fixed; and usually, forgiveness is a big part of the healing. Surprisingly, the concept of forgiveness is only marginally used in modern psychology. Other terms like *reconciliation* might be used; but in general, with the exception of a branch of psychology called positive psychology, forgiveness has not attracted much empirical research.

There are also alternatives to total forgiveness that involve an active suspension of guilt. One alternative to forgiveness is just letting something go. No one says, "I am sorry." No one has to say, "I forgive you." You just let it go and let the cauldron of anger simmer down. Sometime this strategy works; sometimes it is the only thing that works. Sometimes an emotional "time-out" is the best we can hope for.

On the other hand, the opposite of non-forgiveness is revenge. What if you not only cannot forgive but also need to take revenge? Revenge means punishing the one who has offended you. Revenge is a ubiquitous theme in human culture. We see it in the Bible. We see it in the arts. *Hamlet*, one of the great works of world literature, is a dark story about revenge in which revenge is given a supernatural mandate by the ghost of Hamlet's murdered father. In the end, Hamlet himself dies, slashed by a poisoned sword. "The rest is silence," the bard concludes the tragedy.

We use revenge at every level of life. Your team loses a game to a "historical" rival. "Next year," we proclaim, "we will get our revenge and win!" "An eye for an eye," the eighteenth-century BCE Babylonian emperor Hammurabi proclaimed. Blood feuds, vendettas, honor killings, and cycles of violence are all part of human culture and maybe even part of our animal nature. Even some animals like elephants, camels, and chimps are known to take revenge on those who hurt them or their families.

However, normative morality warns against revenge as a mode of justice. The world-class entertainer Frank Sinatra and several others taught that "the best revenge is massive success." Douglas Horton warned, "While seeking revenge, dig two graves, one for yourself." "In taking revenge," Milton wrote, "one keeps his own wounds green, which would otherwise heal and do well." And Gandhi wrote, "An eye for an eye and soon the whole world will be blind."

Finally, it is important to also consider the challenge of forgiving oneself. The need to forgive oneself is based both on the possibility of having actually having done something wrong and feeling guilty for it. Feeling guilty is a complicated subject. Guilt can also be based more on perception than fact, but nevertheless, we punish ourselves and cannot forgive ourselves. If we are overwhelmed by guilt, we cannot function. Conversely, if we have no sense of shame, we can become a danger to ourselves and others. What happens if we cannot forgive ourselves?

Probably the most famous story there is about guilt is *Macbeth*. In this dark tragedy, both Macbeth and Lady Macbeth are destroyed by guilt. Guilty of an actual murder, they descend into madness and perish. A similar plot is provided by Edgar Allan Poe in his *Tell-Tale Heart*, in which the narrator-murderer too descends into madness and his crime is revealed. Emotional guilt, however, is not always tied to a crime or even wrongdoing, but it can tremendously destructive.

Jewish culture is often tied to the idea of guilt. The paradoxical myth of Jewish Momism includes mothers who are endlessly narcissistic about their children's achievements and at the same time seek to control their children through strong doses of guilt. I am sure you know the one about the man who calls his Jewish mother and asks how she is doing. "OK," she sighs.

"Mom," the man replies, "that doesn't sound right. What is wrong?"

"Well, son, honestly," she says in a weakened voice, "I lost ten pounds."

"You lost ten pounds?" the son exclaims. "Why? What's wrong?"

"Well, son, honestly," she replies, "I didn't want to have food in my mouth when you called."

Guilt is serious business, especially when you are your own accuser and you cannot forgive yourself for some offense, real or imagined. It can lead to depression, social isolation, loss of self-esteem, even suicide. I have not heard of an anti-guilt medication. Maybe a Big Pharma company could invent Forgiv-a-nex. It would be a bestseller. Sometimes, it seems, we need to "let it go," forgive ourselves, and move on.

Forgiveness, in all its dimensions, is a central part of most of the world's great faiths. In Judaism, it is so important that our most sacred day of the year, Yom Kippur, is basically about forgiveness. We begin our High Holy Days with prayers of *selichot*, prayers asking to be forgiven. We come to synagogue on the evening of Yom Kippur to hear the chanting of Kol Nidrei, in which we ask God to forgive us for all the false promises we may have made to ourselves during the last twelve months; and we end with *neilah* and its message of confidence that, indeed, we are forgiven for all the forgivable trespasses we may have committed. It is a cleansing, uplifting and restorative process.

But there can also be a class of offenses beyond forgiveness, things done by others against us and things we have done to others. For these offenses, Yom Kippur does not atone for; but the Day of Atonement does chasten, refine, and define. It helps us see what is possible in the realm of forgiveness and what is not. It helps us to be better people. It cannot make us perfect because moral, emotional perfection is beyond our human capacity. Sadly, in that regard, we cannot forgive everything.

Yom Kippur teaches us that God is eager to forgive and that we should be likewise be prepared to forgive and move on, whenever and wherever that is possible. We are told that sometimes we need to work harder on ourselves going forward. We are told that God does not want the death of the sinner but that we should atone and live. We are also told that sometimes forgiveness is not possible even as it remains desirable in other parts of life. Sometimes justice weighs heavier in the scale of life than forgiveness, but justice must also be proportional.

May the power of this sacred night help us to forgive others and forgive ourselves; and whenever we cannot forgive, let us strive for self-respect, fairness, and proportionality.

G'mar Tov. May you be inscribed for a good year.
Amen.

THE VOICE FOR JUSTICE

September 19, 2018, Yom Kippur Morning 5779

Of all the different types of natural disasters, the one that holds the most weight for people in our region of the country is the hurricane. The word *hurricane* is actually derived from the name of a god of the indigenous people of Puerto Rico and entered the English language through Spanish. Hurikan was the god of weather and storms among the Taino. Tragically, the people of Puerto Rico still know of the relentless power of Hurikan in the most tragic of ways.

While living in Ohio, Liz and I experienced, separately, both an earthquake and a tornado. The earthquake literally caused the hills to roll, and the tornado was preceded by the most threatening sky I have ever seen and was followed by incredible localized destruction. In northern Israel, I once found myself driving through a wildfire. Flames of twenty feet leaped up in front of our vehicle and then to the side and then back in front of us like a multiheaded dragon. The heat was tremendous. For a few minutes, I feared for my survival.

But it is the reality and effects of the hurricane that speak to most of us. Hurricanes are immense, powerful, relentless, and unforgiving. The wind can roar day and night, breaking and cracking things everywhere. Unprecedented rain, like a horizontal waterfall, furiously drenches everything, and floodwaters rise quickly and then recede slowly like in the Noah epic in the Torah. Will we have electric power? Will we be trapped? Will our property be destroyed? The howling and the beating of the storm don't seem to stop if you try to ride out a storm. And then, your family needs to wait to hear if you have survived the storm as communication is restored block by block, neighborhood by neighborhood. Rebuilding seems overwhelming, if not impossible. In some places, rebuilding takes somewhere between forever and never. Hurricanes are powerful, terrible experiences.

For many of us, the news cycle during the course of the last year has been like living in a hurricane that landed onshore and then just didn't move. The rains and winds of controversy and injustice constantly rattle the protective shutters of our lives. The flood of concerns about reproductive rights keeps rising. The damage to human life because uncontrolled gun violence gets bloodier and bloodier. The storm surges of new policy sweep away immigrant families and leave children cut off from their parents and trapped in government housing with no hope of reunification. Who would ever have imagined that we would actually be discussing white nationalism again in this country as a current reality in 2018?

For many of us, it feels we are trapped in a howling storm, and we are forced to scurry about stuffing the sandbags of political resistance to save what little seems to be left of human decency in this country. Not since the Civil Rights movement and the Vietnam War has American society been as stirred up as it is now. We have seen activism on the Left and the Right at various moments. For sure, there was a rising tide of discontent from the Right during the Obama years; and now, the reaction from the Left is activated, and a huge political clash, an uncivil war of sorts, has erupted across the land. The political center has all but disappeared, contracted from the constant demonization and name-calling that has replaced most rational discourse. Time-honored legislative procedure has been replaced with brutal, power politics. Labels have replaced discussion of policies. Basic morality is drowning in a sea of pornographic excuses, which literally make one's head spin. International relations are being disrupted. Enemies are treated as friends, and friends are viewed as enemies. In short, we are living in a political hurricane that has come ashore and is tearing us apart, drowning us in anger and not moving on.

How far have we come? Two years ago, when the Colin Kaepernick story broke, I was at my gym, dressing after a very modest workout. Several older gentlemen were having a discussion about "the knee." They all agreed, if Kaepernick didn't want to respect the flag, he should move to Russia. Everyone who had been talking nodded in agreement, and the locker room went silent.

Equally perplexing is the latitude extended to the White House by Protestant, evangelical churches in this country, which, simultaneously, take on harshly xenophobic attitudes and are endlessly forgiving of any sin, no matter how salacious, by the president. It is almost impossible to understand the moral and theological calculus used to reach these conclusions other than raw Machiavellian politics.

There is a Chinese curse, "May you live in interesting times." We apparently are cursed. We live in a stalled hurricane and are being pounded by the constant swirl of the storm.

How do we ground ourselves in such a storm? To what can we tether our ship of life? How do we navigate and keep our bearings in these trouble times?

My answer will not surprise you. Judaism is a prophetic faith. Its goal is peace and justice and rejects retreat from the world, the search for private cocoons of harmony. Judaism is all about keeping the moral high ground and fighting for human dignity.

Judaism began with a protest against injustice, a protest again God sweeping away the good people of Sodom and Gomorrah along with the bad because they were in the wrong place at the wrong time. Even God is called to moral account in Judaism.

Moses stood up in front of the people and told them in no uncertain terms, "Justice, justice you shall pursue" and added, "Do not favor the rich or the poor in justice," "Use honest weights in all your business dealings," and "Love your neighbor as yourself."

The eighth-century BCE prophet Amos, who we honor with a full window in this sanctuary (middle window, my right, your left), prophesied in the northern kingdom of Israel in a time of general prosperity and reprimanded the wealthy of the realm "not to sell the needy for a pair of shoes," lest their success be derived from exaggerated economic inequality.

The prophet Isaiah in this morning's powerful *haftarah* rejected religious hypocrisy as unacceptable in God's eyes: do not come to the Temple and offer your prayers and songs and then cheat and defraud people in other parts of your life. What is it that God wants? The fast from injustice! In Isaiah 58, we read,

Is this not the fast that I have chosen . . .
Is it not to share your bread with the hungry,
And that you bring to your house the poor who are cast out;
When you see the naked, that you cover him,

And not hide yourself from your own flesh?
Then your light shall break forth like the morning,
Your healing shall spring forth speedily.

In his Second Inaugural in the waning days of the American Civil War, President Lincoln also quoted Isaiah and told the people that healing the nation and caring for the widow, the orphan, and the wounded veteran were our highest national responsibilities. Helping our neighbors, not endlessly punishing our domestic rivals, was his creed.

Reform Judaism, especially Reform Judaism in America, is distinguished by its concern for social justice, and KI has always been at the center of this effort. The first American Reform rabbi to make social justice the centerpiece of his theology was David Einhorn, who served KI during the Civil War. Courageously, Einhorn condemned slavery as immune and a function of greed above justice. Einhorn's son-in-law, Rabbi Emil Hirsch, who served in Chicago, was responsible for adding the social justice plank to the Pittsburgh Platform of 1885. It read, "In full accordance with the spirit of the Mosaic legislation, which strives to regulate the relations between rich and poor, we deem it our duty to participate in the great task of modern times, to solve, on the basis of justice and righteousness, the problems presented by the contrasts and evils of the present organization of society." Rabbi Krauskopf heard that call when he established his farm school in Doylestown in the 1890s.

After Lincoln, the president who probably had the greatest impact on Reform Judaism's view of social justice was Teddy Roosevelt, first a Republican and then an independent Progressive. So powerful were Roosevelt's views that when he died in 1919, KI commissioned a memorial window in his honor. It still stands in our lobby, next to the entrance to the chapel. Take a look. It is beautiful!

Roosevelt's 1912 Bull Moose Platform, which he called A Contract with the American People, called for, among other things:

1. The dissolving of the unholy alliance between corrupt business and corrupt politics
2. Strict limits and disclosure requirements on political campaign contributions
3. Registration of lobbyists
4. A national health service to include all existing government medical agencies

5. Social insurance, to provide for the elderly, the unemployed, and the disabled
6. Limited the ability of judges to order injunctions to limit labor strikes
7. A minimum wage law for women
8. An eight-hour workday
9. A federal securities commission
10. Farm relief
11. Workers' compensation for work-related injuries
12. An inheritance tax
13. Women's suffrage
14. Direct election of senators

As the Bible says, there is nothing new under the sun.

Exactly one hundred years ago, in 1918, combining biblical teaching with American Progressivism, the Reform movement through the Central Conference of American Rabbis issued its first social justice platform. Although incomplete by today's standards, it still stands as the foundation of social justice activism in the Reform movement, in many ways the defining characteristic of our brand of Judaism.

Social justice was subsequently taken up by Reform Rabbi Stephen Wise who helped found the NAACP and the movement's Social Justice Commission, which was created in 1948, and, most importantly, the creation of the Religious Action Center of Reform Judaism in Washington, DC, founded in 1961. To the eternal credit of the RAC, it hosted the group that drafted the Civil Rights Act of 1964, originally envisioned by President Kennedy before his assassination and then championed by LBJ (President Lyndon Baines Johnson) and others.

Today, the RAC is widely known as a vanguard for social justice in Washington. Our own synagogue has deep ties with the RAC. Lay leaders from KI attend its Consultations on Conscience and annually our Confirmation class visits there to learn how to directly lobby Congress in Washington, DC.

So what are the social justice issues Reform Judaism is championing today? The list is long, and the list is urgent. From affordable health care to Me Too, Reform Judaism is providing important leadership in America today. The two national issues I found to be the most impactful this last year were immigration and gun control.

The storm over immigration policy in the United States was whipped up with the revelation of a policy of family separation on our southern border. The decision to blur the criteria for asylum-seeking turned the flight to freedom into a national nightmare for this country. Responding to feelings expressed in this congregation, I wrote a poem last Spring called "My Mommy Is Here" and had it posted on Facebook. More than 100,000 people read it; and many used it at services and programs—Jewish, Christian, and secular—all across the country. Although the furor over this policy has simmered down, there are still 12,800 minors in custody and federal facilities designed to hold children are 90 percent full on our southern border.

No question, immigration is a hot-button issue. It involves race, economics, and security concerns. It has been used as a rallying call for the politics of xenophobia. It flies in the face of Judaism's understanding of the golden rule, to love your neighbor as yourself, in which the word *neighbor* is understood to mean all of humanity.

A second national issue for the year 5778 was gun control. Mass shootings have become a way of life in this country, from Columbine to Sandy Hook and now to Parkland, Florida. On February 14, 2018, the deadliest secondary school shooting in American history took place at Stoneman Douglas High School. Seventeen were killed, including several Jewish kids. A nearby Reform synagogue turned into a hiding place. I know the rabbi there. Brad Boxman is a native Philadelphian. Previously, he was the rabbi of my brother-in-law's synagogue in Connecticut. He lost confirmands in that mass shooting. Our confirmands elected to sing the Parkland song "Shine" at their service this year. We will hear it again in just a few moments. Gun violence is not an abstract problem; it is real, and it is personal.

There are 393 million guns in the United States, 120 guns for every hundred people. About one hundred thousand people a year are shot in the United States; of them, approximately thirty thousand die. Since 1982, there have been ninety-nine mass shootings with assault rifles in this country. Ninety-six people are killed by a gun in the United States every day. Two-thirds are suicides, and 75 percent of suicides are white males. Approximately three million children a year witness gun violence. Forty-four percent of Americans know someone who has been shot. Statistical information is endless and sickening. No other advanced country behaves as we do with our guns.

What do we need: gun registration, removing assault rifles from the market, limits on magazine capacity, and tracking of all gun sales? Even if you sell a car to a friend, you have a title and taxes to attend to. In my opinion, the Second Amendment calls for a well-regulated militia, not radically *laissez-faire* gun ownership. Gun ownership is a right, but it is also a responsibility. Gun violence in America is yet another perpetual storm we seem to live in without hope of resolution.

In addition to immigration and gun violence at the national level, there is another storm I believe we are weathering. It is so close and so much a part of our lives it is hard for us to even see. Instead, we just put on the raincoats of denial and go about our daily lives. It is called Hurricane Philadelphia. Philadelphia is the sixth largest city in the United States and is located 2.5 miles from where we are now sitting. Officially, it is also the poorest city in this country. About 25.7 percent of Philadelphia's 1.5 million residents live in poverty, double the national poverty rate of 13.4 percent.

Our poverty is deep, and it is old. It is multigenerational. It is multiracial. It is 50 percent black (double the national rate), 20 percent white, and 20 percent Hispanic. It is overwhelmingly young and in single-parent homes headed by single mothers. We are at the lower end of high school graduation rates in the country. While much of the rest of the country is growing and in recovery, we are sinking ever deeper into the quicksand of urban poverty.

It is easy to wear blinders and not see this cancer. You can drive up and down North Broad Street, stay in the left lane, and never stop. You can bask in the glory of the revival of Center City and the gentrification of adjacent neighborhoods. You can marvel at the growth of the University of Pennsylvania, Drexel, and Temple and not be concerned about the displacement of the impoverished neighborhoods crumbling on their edges. You can drive by the massive central offices of the Philadelphia School District and not stop to think that 70 percent of the students it serves live in poverty and the per-student budget in the city is less than half of that of the suburbs. You can be content to live in your own pocket, pull down the blinders, and blame the poor for their plight.

Permit a local analogy. Next to Abington Friends School, there are no storm drains. When it rains, a lake appears in the street and then drains down to Elkins Park. So too Philadelphia. Urban poverty and its consequences will not be contained; they spill over and cause problems in surrounding areas.

We have two model city-suburb partnership programs here at KI. We send two dozen tutors to help at Lowell Elementary School in Olney, and we have a monthly community dinner, HaMotzi, here at the synagogue. If five hundred or one thousand synagogues and churches did the same, it probably would not move the needle, so to speak, on local poverty. But it would create a different environment, a different ethos, and hope!

Big shiny buildings in City Center are great. Gentrified neighborhoods are great. But the worst urban poverty rate in this country is horrible, and it is growing like a hurricane stalled over land dumping misery on the population.

A partnership between the suburbs and the city will help. But we need creative national policies, we need regional planning, we need business strategies that help improve the general quality of life, and we need city-suburban partnerships. We need to vote with the common good in mind, and we need to work for that good as individuals and as a congregation.

This afternoon, we read about the prophet Jonah. He was sent to save the Mesopotamian city of Nineveh. Can we do less for our own time and place?

Things are not all bad in this country or this region at this moment. Far from it. There is so much that is good, strong, and growing. The problem is that too few of us share in the blessings of our area and our country. Working to share the blessings; helping to provide responsible, self-sustaining opportunities; erasing structural racism; and just being a loving neighbor will go a long way.

Abraham, Moses, Amos, and Isaiah knew that.

Rabbis Einhorn, Krauskopf, and Wise believed that.

Now it is our turn not only to weather the storm but to also man the lifeboats and to work for the day when our light too shall shine forth like the morning.

Amen.

Shana Tova.

An English Hanukkah

December 5, 2018 eKI

During the last month or so I have crossed the Atlantic three times. First, in November, I escorted a large group from KI to Israel. It was a fabulous trip. Arriving home in time for Shabbat, I was off to Germany on the following Monday to participate in a rabbinic mission to Germany for the 80th anniversary of Kristallnacht. Again, I came home for the weekend, only to head to the airport for the third time to fly to Birmingham, England, via Dublin, Ireland.

The purpose of the third trip was to lead a family funeral. My daughter-in-law's grandfather, Thomas "Tom" Dangerfield (1932–2018) died, and Kelly's family asked if I would help lead a non-denominational service. For me, it was a great honor to be asked and before I knew it, five of us (Benji. Kelly, Sophie [9], Charlotte [7], and I) were headed again to the airport.

To say the least, it was a very special trip. I stayed with family members in the English countryside on the "Fosse Way," the ancient Roman road that connected London to the north 2,000 years ago. The farm-style ranch itself was between Stratford-upon-Avon to the north and Oxford to the south. The area is characterized by green rolling hills, flocks of sheep and horse-riding in full English gear. On a scale of natural beauty of 1 to 10, it was a 20. The family gathered from all around England and my grandchildren were surrounded by their English cousins, eager to be with them, play, share, compare words and bond.

Everyone knew I would want to spend time touring and doing my Jewish history thing. On the day after the funeral, we divided up into

477

groups and my group went down the road to Oxford. Oxford University is an 11th century institution and although it did not officially allow Jews to study there for centuries, Hebrew was always a part of the curriculum and for years prior to the expulsion of Jews from England in 1290, Oxford scholars and local rabbis regularly compared notes.

In the 20th century, the greatest British Jewish historian, Cecil Roth, taught at Oxford where his best friend was J.R. Tolkien. Who needs fiction when life creates scenarios like that! Not surprisingly, Chabad had a large Hanukkah Menorah in the Town Square and, ironically, Christmas carolers gathered and sang in front of it, including a rendition of *"White Christmas"* by Irving Berlin. Among other works, a fabulous 1850s oil landscape of Jerusalem was on display at the Ashmolean, Oxford's grand art museum.

The next day, we headed north to Stratford-upon-Avon. The whole way up a lively discussion ensued about Shakespeare's "Dark Lady" and whether or not she was an Italian woman of Jewish descent. We also briefly discussed Shylock and anti-Semitism in English literature.

Surprisingly, we happened upon a large lamppost behind the Shakespeare Theater decorated with characters from Shalom Aleichem plays. Before leaving town, we visited both Shakespeare's birth house and his grave along with the graves of his immediate family in a large Anglican church where he attended services. I had never really thought of Shakespeare as a Christian before. but it did help place him in the England of his day and place.

Kelly and Benji brought *m'norott* with them for the first two nights of Hanukkah. The first candle was in the country house and second candle in Birmingham. None of the family there is Jewish, but everyone, children and adults, was present. We lit our candles in front of large windows, made all the blessings, sang *"Rock of Ages"* in Hebrew and English, exchanged small gifts, played dreidel and did Hanukkah crafts. It was warm and loving and Yorkshire pudding served as an adequate substitute for latkes. Interestingly, the TV news on the second night focused on the 80th anniversary of the kinder transport which brought German Jewish children to the UK in the wake of Kristallnacht.

Jewish life in England is nowhere as near as strong as it is in the United States, especially in the Midlands. But it's still there and an ember of Judaism continues to glow in the heartland of the English countryside. Family and friends had many questions about our tradition and others wondered why there wasn't more Jewish life in their area. It's a long story. England and the UK today are struggling mightily with issues of diversity and it's not going very well. But at least for this Hanukkah, wrapped in the protective embrace of family love, we were able to tell the story of the Festival of Lights and continue the miracle of Jewish survival for another year. Wishing you a Happy Hanukkah with family and friends.

Shabbat Shalom.

WALLS: AMERICAN, ISRAELI, AND MEXICAN

January 31, 2019

In 1914, the beloved American poet Robert Frost wrote a poem simply called "Mending Wall." It begins with and repeats the phrase "Something there is that doesn't love a wall." As a country, we are now engaged in a great debate about a wall (or fence or security barrier) that could stretch two thousand miles across our southern border from the Gulf of Mexico to the Pacific Ocean. Debate over this wall has already resulted in the longest government shutdown in our national history. Currently, we are experiencing a reprieve and federal workers are, fortunately, again being paid. Alternatively, a national emergency could be declared; and funds could be diverted from elsewhere in the federal budget, a dramatic move that is sure to stimulate more debate, lawsuits, and a constitutional crisis about circumventing the legislative branch of government.

All of us are painfully aware of the details and political challenges of the wall debate raging in the United States. I want to add two insights, either of which is not reported adequately or not mentioned at all in the news. The first is of specific Jewish interest. Much is made in the American wall debate about the use of security fences in Israel and their effectiveness. No surprise, but this is a complicated business. First, Israel has multiple fence systems, not just one border wall. The best known and most controversial is the security barrier on the western border of the West Bank. Actually, it is a complex weave of fences and walls including controversial sections, which run to the east of Jerusalem. My sense is that this is the wall most referred to in the American press and also is the wall most praised for its effectiveness.

The West Bank Wall, however, is not a valid model for the American-Mexican border because of the massive deployment of Israeli security forces to the east of the Wall. A comparable American plan would require a U.S. military presence at least twenty if not one hundred miles deep into Mexico, complete with road checkpoints. We also have to consider destroying buildings in Mexico, housing leaders of the caravans and others. In terms of security, Israel's West Bank is effective; it is also a major symbol of the Arab-Palestinian conflict and is mainly meant to control everyday traffic and not immigration.

Israel has a second wall system around Gaza. This is nearly a 360-degree enclosure (land, sea, and air) with Egypt responsible for a tiny southern border crossing that is peppered with tunnels. The crossing points into Israel are well fortified. There is also a significant no-man's land to the east of the Gaza border in Israel; the sea is blockaded, and the airspace over Gaza is a no-fly zone. Although there is no border fence with Syria, the area is an active military zone, which relies heavily on electronic surveillance. The same is true with the small Israel-Lebanon border. By contrast, Israel's border with Jordan, its longest border, is protected by a minimal wire fence and dirt-road system. There are only three official border crossings on the Jordanian border.

The border between Israel and Egypt is problematic but maybe the most relevant to the American situation. Israel and Egypt have a peace treaty and mutual security interests in the Sinai. Recently, tens of thousands of African workers crossed the border illegally and settled in Israel. A particularly large community can be found today in Tel Aviv. Israel has adopted numerous laws limiting the economic activity of these workers and has sealed the border with Egypt. Offers of repatriation to Africa have largely failed.

Finally, I decided to look at Mexico's southern border, mostly with Guatemala and Belize. The Guatemalan border, less than six hundred miles wide, is the site of most border crossings, legal and illegal, from Central America, while the Belize border is not highly active. To me, it is the Mexican-Guatemalan border we should be focusing on, perhaps even more than the U.S.-Mexico border. Mexico formerly offered a friendly program on its southern border that is a temporary registration system of migrants including encouraging the immigrants to stay and work in Mexico, principally in agriculture. Those policies—combined with humanitarian aid to Guatemala, Honduras, and El Salvador—should dramatically help the situation on the American border. We also need to be clearer in delineating between illegal immigration and asylum seeking, categories purposefully blurred by the Trump administration. Legitimate asylum seeking is not an immigration crisis as much as it is a human rights crisis.

Most immigrants to America today are from East and South Asia. They arrive legally by planes, as do illegal drugs. Israel's Egyptian border offer both answers and challenges for us. Meanwhile, the well-being of thousands of people including many children is at risk. We need to do better, protect our national interests, and be a moral beacon to the world.

A Bold Centrist: Remembering Isaac M. Wise

on His Two Hundredth Birthday
March 27, 2019

Isaac Mayer Wise is widely recognized as the founder of Reform Judaism in North America. Born in Steingrub, Moravia (Czech Republic), on March 29, 1819, he arrived in the United States in 1846 and immediately went to work to create a nationally united expression of Judaism, a *Minhag America*, under his leadership. Criticized by traditionalists as a reformer and resisted by radical reformers as unprincipled and unrefined, Wise nevertheless relentlessly pushed forward with his dream.

Largely because of his urging, the Union of American Hebrew Congregations (now the Union for Reform Judaism [URJ]), the first national organization of synagogues in the United States, was founded in 1873 followed by the Hebrew Union College (now the Hebrew Union College–Jewish Institute of Religion [HUC-JIR]) two years later and, finally, the Central Conference of American Rabbis (CCAR) in 1889 to complete the denominational polity of what would become the Reform movement in North America. Ultimately, his more traditional opponents created similar structures both for the Conservative movement in Judaism and modern American Jewish Orthodoxy.

Ironically, at the time of his death on March 26, 1900, Wise's national organizations and institutions had been "conquered from within" by radical reformers. However, his unparalleled achievements were understood to be transformative, and the Reform movement he had created went into deep mourning with news of his death. In Cincinnati, ten thousand people attended his funeral. On the two hundredth anniversary of his birth, it is important to reconsider the life and career of Isaac Mayer Wise, his achievements, and his legacy.

First and foremost, it is important to recognize that Wise was pugnacious, a fighter, and indefatigable. His personality, spirit, and energy loom large over all his actions and concerns. Second, he must be understood as a person of his time. Nineteenth-century American Judaism was very different than twentieth-century American Judaism, just as there are many indications that twenty-first-century American Judaism will be remarkably discontinuous from its predecessors. Third, Wise was a bold centrist in much of what he did, and he positioned toward the "right center" of the Reform movement of his time. Of course, the middle is always a tough place to be, particularly when the polar opposites on a spectrum deny the possibility of a vital center.

For example, on the difficult issue of slavery, Wise, as a nineteenth-century American, viewed himself as a moderate. Today, his failure to embrace abolitionism is viewed as a moral failure. On his own, like most American Jews, he accepted slavery as a biblically sanctioned institution, which was unduly harsh in the United States but still was permissible. Wise, the Copperhead Democrat and anti-missionary religious leader, was superior to the abolition of slavery. In his mind, he was a bold centrist.

With respect to the role of women in Judaism, Wise was a reformer but hardly a feminist. He lived before the suffrage movement but allowed men and women to sit together in synagogue, confirmed girls as well as boys, and allowed mixed-voice singing. He even welcomed girls to study at the Hebrew Union College. On the other hand, he did not actively advocate for the ordination of women. He was a moderate modernizer, not a radical.

Wise actively opposed new concepts like evolution and the documentary hypothesis (which argued that the Torah was multiauthored). He believed in a denationalized American form of Judaism and in the value of vernacular prayer. He actively opposed the political Zionism of Theodore Herzl. On the other hand, he opposed Jews becoming Unitarians, thereby abandoning their covenant with the Jewish people, and equally resisted Felix Adler and Ethical Culture, which rejected both God and ethnicity. He invented the late Friday night service to help preserve the historic character of the Jewish Sabbath and opposed the Sunday Sabbath movement late in his career.

Uniquely American, Wise sported bushy sideburns and a clean-shaven chin! Indeed, no rabbi before him looked anything like this Midwestern Jewish preacher. He edited his own newspaper, wrote fictional works in English and German to create new ways of envisioning Jewish life, and edited his own prayer book to create a path for Judaism in America, which was both traditional and modern.

Above all, Wise believed in the importance of the well-trained, well-spoken rabbi. He believed that religious leadership was the key to Jewish success in America and that the Jewish professional who would lead the way was a new type of articulate, confident rabbi-preacher of which he was a leading exemplar. As a congregational rabbi, he built one of America's great cathedral synagogues (Plum Street Temple in Cincinnati, Ohio) and trained dozens of students to follow in his footsteps. In time, he learned to partner with lay leadership but in the end believed that Judaism's fate was ultimately in the hands of a trained, modern rabbinate.

As the late HUC-JIR Professor Samuel Sandmel once cautioned, it would be both unfair and inadequate to remember Isaac Mayer Wise on the bicentennial anniversary of his birth just as an organizer and builder. He was much more than that. He was a bold moderate, a theologian, a literary artist, and a Reform activist. He was the one and only Isaac Mayer Wise. Two hundred years after his birth, we would do well to retell his story, learn from his example, and move forward in the sacred work of creating a compelling modern Judaism for our time.

SIDING WITH SCIENCE: REFORM JUDAISM, EVOLUTION, AND THE ENVIRONMENT

2019

Rabbi Joseph Krauskopf (1858–1923) often said that he had two heroes, Abraham Lincoln (1809–1865) and English naturalist Charles Darwin (1809–1882), and that both were born on February 12, 1809! The fact that a rabbi admired Darwin, the best-known advocate of the theory of evolution, was big news in the nineteenth century. Krauskopf was in the first ordination class of the Hebrew Union College (1883), whose founding president and Krauskopf's teacher was on record as being firmly against the idea that "people are descended from monkeys." Yet just four years after ordination in 1887, Krauskopf gave a series of lectures on Judaism and evolution from his pulpit in Kansas City; he supported Darwin and maintained that the theory of evolution was compatible with the idea of a created universe, although not the Bible's creation story. Science, Krauskopf boldly asserted, leads the way in modern times; and its discoveries, when viewed broadly, do not conflict with the deeper eternally valid aspects of biblical theology.

Interestingly, Krauskopf's later successor at KI, Dr. William Fineshriber (1878–1968), "in response to the attempt by William Jennings Bryan and his followers to ban the teaching of evolution in universities and public schools [in Tennessee], devoted three Friday night sermons in 1922 to discussing it at his synagogue in Memphis. He emphasized to packed audiences the 'inalienable right of free thought and free speech, guaranteed by the Constitution of the United States,' and argued that 'the majority of thoughtful and liberal preachers of the world have found no difficulty in accepting the theory of evolution without discarding their Bibles or their religion.'" Subsequently, Fineshriber and Bryan directly debated evolution face-to-face. Today, not only does the Reform movement in Judaism broadly support science, but it also opposes pseudoscientific theories like creationism.

The theory of evolution, the idea that "the heritable characteristics of biological populations change over successive generations by natural selection," can be traced back to as far as pre-Socratics, but the opposite Aristotelian view of unchanging biological "forms" won out over time and dominated scientific thinking. It was not until the middle of the eighteenth century that theorists in France began to speculate about "modifications" in natural history. Drawing both on his own research and including work by others—Lamarck, Malthus, and, most importantly, Alfred Russell Wallace—Darwin published his groundbreaking *Origin of the Species* in 1859. Darwin's work proved to be a turning point, not only in the history of science but also in all human thought. Rejection of Darwin's ideas was strongest in Protestant circles and led directly to the rise of modern biblical literalism and religious fundamentalism.

The reaction in the Jewish community to the theory of evolution during the last hundred years has been either muted or pro-Darwin, including many leading, but not all, modern Orthodox rabbis. Ultra-Orthodoxy has been another story, with numerous leading rabbis declaring Darwin's theories to be heretical and incompatible with their branch of Judaism. In 1961, the Lubavitcher Rebbe and leader of the Chabad movement, Menachem Mendel Schneerson, wrote that the theory of evolution is "highly speculative and scientifically ... [it] can capture the imagination of the uncritical, so much so that it is even offered as a scientific explanation of the mystery of Creation, despite the fact that the theory of evolution itself has not been substantiated scientifically and is devoid of any real scientific basis."

Today, resistance to scientific theories concerning the origins of the universe, evolution, and, most notably, global warming is not limited to religious literalists. It extends to many different cohorts in society, including industries burning fossil fuels and political nationalists who generally loathe international cooperation. Complicating the situation are the short-term costs of reducing human impact on the environment, which, in part, sparked the recent Yellow Vest demonstrations in France.

In my opinion, although the Reform movement in Judaism is overwhelmingly aligned with modern science, it also maintains an unwavering belief in a higher moral order in the universe, the human need for the construction of a cosmos of meaning, and the reality of personal spirituality. Simply put, science is the key to the physical universe; but as humans, we are more than the aggregate of our biological condition. Defining humanity's place in the universe and how we collectively respond to our finite existence is a different story, including the possibility of metaphysical origins to realities of love, truth, and justice, the emotional and philosophical building blocks of our existence.

The Coronavirus Pandemic and the Future of Organized Religion

March 24, 2020

By now, it is clear that the COVID-19 pandemic sweeping the entire world is changing life as we know it. It is less clear, but certainly as true, that this experience will have long-term effects on how we live on this planet after the pandemic is over. Someone once defined war as "time in fast motion." War accelerates the creation of new technology, new modalities of social organization, new means of production and distribution, and new means of social interaction. Clearly, COVID-19 is a kind of war that is fueling massive change across the spectrum of human activity. On the other side of this crisis after there is an effective vaccine to block the further spread of the disease, full treatment of the disease, and sufficient supplies of all necessary medical equipment, life is not going to go back to the way it was, let's say, in December 2019. Like the Disney song declares, it's a whole new world now, and we need to try to anticipate what the post-COVID-19 twenty-first-century world will look like.

There are so many aspects to this discussion it is hard to know where to begin. What to do about health care, in general, is clearly the number one issue. Second, the enhanced role of technology, particularly the role of technology in communication and business, is changing how we live. My senses are we probably will not reevaluate the question of things like nationalism versus internationalism, although the need for more, not less, global cooperation is clear, at least to me.

The one area I can speak to, but not prognosticate about, is the impact of COVID-19 on organized religion. Organized religion, of course, is not the same as private spirituality. If anything, COVID-19 and its isolating effect has forced people to think about their basic values and priorities and to explore different ways of keeping their spirits up during these trying times. Some pray, some meditate, some exercise, some listen to music, some light candles, some seek out community through the Internet, and some crave maintaining human contact through virtual means.

But what about organized religion? What about houses of worship and congregations and other formal structures built around the concept of a spiritual community? Will they survive the COVID-19 pandemic? Are they part of what, in a different context, government (at all levels) is calling essential business? I heard one unofficial report that as many as 25 percent of all churches and synagogues will close in the United States by the end of the summer for lack of funding. Some will simply shut down and shutter; still, others will find ways to merge and thereby preserve some infrastructure and many basic services. Huge decisions about congregational identity, autonomy, and culture will have to be made at an accelerated rate.

The fact of the matter is that all types of changes were occurring before the pandemic broke out in the world of organized religion. Secularism or no religion at all has been growing, especially among young American Jews. Affiliation rates have been falling across our entire community. The use of technology in religion was also increasing in many different ways before the pandemic. On the other hand, charitable support has been shifting away from religious institutions in the Jewish community and toward general education, health, and cultural concerns. The differential in giving is increasingly pronounced. Meanwhile, some Jewish organizations like the old Philadelphia Jewish Y had already failed; and others, like the National Museum of American Jewish History, announced bankruptcy just before and not because of the pandemic. But these institutions are secular and cultural. What about our synagogues? Can they survive COVID-19, or are they going to be among the permanent victims of this historic pandemic?

My sense is that many synagogues will indeed fail or at least be compelled to merge. On the other hand, I believe that the synagogue as an institution will survive this emergency situation. A synagogue, in real space or online, creates a critical mass of Jewish activity. It also has the capacity to attract and maintain trained, dedicated staff who can do everything from introducing little children in preschool to Jewish life to running a funeral for a family with complex dynamics (and we all have complex dynamics). Synagogues—like the Eternal Light, which hangs in front of the ark—are constant. They are open and available in the summer when people are down the shore and in the dead of winter when people are sheltered at home against the cold.

Increasingly, synagogues are learning how to be both in person and virtual communities. The line between the two is blurring rapidly. You can come to services, or you can participate online. But the reason that it works is that if you belong to a synagogue, when you use it virtually, you have a real human contact to the people and leadership there. In other words, synagogues are living Jewish communities. They are not on-demand, pay-for-service Jewish human resource agencies. Synagogues do not provide rent-a-rabbi but a rabbi who knows you and your family, your joys, and your sorrows. It's not just a question of who can read the prayers in Hebrew; you can actually get prerecorded digital messages. It's who will say the prayers with you and be the living bridge between yourself, tradition, and today with all its challenges.

Finally, this is the biggest question: does religion provide answers to the big questions? That depends on the question. In my view, the question "Why did God create and spread COVID-19?" is based on an unworkable assumption about the nature of a God who is all-powerful, all-knowing, and controlling every detail on every action on earth, the moon, and beyond. God is not the head of a cosmic insurance company that provides protection from all catastrophes, human or natural. COVID-19 is not an "act of God."

An act of God is a compassionate health care worker who goes to work every day in an ICU unit to take care of the sick and dying. An act of God is a dentist who gives away all his or her medical masks to a local hospital in need of protective gear. An act of God is a synagogue that, despite its own financial challenges, makes collecting funds for children's lunches during school closures its first order of business. Kindness, mercy, and justice are all acts of God; and synagogues, among other institutions, are the repositories of goodwill that make acts of God happen locally and beyond. The question is not "Where is God?" but rather "Where is humanity?" Chances are, people linked together in communities of faith will be quicker to answer, "Here we are"—we are here for each other, we are here for you, we are here for humanity. In that sense, yes, a synagogue is an essential business and worth preserving. So if you can, help keep KI alive now, tomorrow, and next year. We have a lot of work to do for the good of all, and together, we will do it.

Shabbat Shalom!

Ordinary Citizens: Lessons from the Pandemic of 2020

March 30, 2020

Many of you may remember Stephen E. Ambrose's book *Citizen Soldiers*, which came out in 1997. At one level, it traced the history of World War II from the beaches of Normandy to the Battle of the Bulge to the ultimate defeat of Nazi Germany. At a different level, it offered a significant thesis that the United States won the war against Nazism not because of its superior industrial capacity or its top military leadership but because of its "citizen soldiers," reared in the culture of a democratic state, who, in the heat of battle, performed in a superior fashion to the generation of German soldiers reared in the Nazi culture of the Third Reich in the 1930s. It was the Citizen Soldier, Ambrose proclaimed, who saved the world for democracy.

Today, we are engaged in a different war. Not a war against a political ideology but a war against an invisible enemy, a novel biological enemy, that has the capacity to destroy life on earth, as we know it. In this war, there are scientists, public health officials, politicians, and others who are shaping, however unclear and uneven, a strategy to fight this battle. But the real battle is being fought in the trenches, at home, and in the ERs. In other words, this is a battle of ordinary citizens called upon to work together in extraordinary times.

There have been many times when I wondered if this generation, my generation, could do what the Greatest Generation did? Could we fight on the beaches of Normandy or in the skies over Midway? I had my doubts.

Now I am seeing something different. I am seeing health care workers go to work knowing that they only have one protective mask for an entire shift. I am seeing the people of New York stand on their balconies and cheer for those health workers. I am watching children happily accept "drive by" birthday parties with no presents and no cake, just their friends holding up signs and cheering them on for becoming ten or eleven or twelve years old.

The Great Pandemic of 2020 is a terrible battle. We do not know how many are going to get sick and how many are going to die. However, we do know that hundreds of thousands of people are volunteering to help take care of their elderly neighbors by shopping for them or calling them on the phone. We know that teenagers are willing to make phone calls to isolated neighbors. We know that seven-year-olds are willing to create artwork and then mail it to total strangers to cheer them up. These acts of support and courage are breaking out all over the country spontaneously and ubiquitously.

The Great Pandemic of 2020 will eventually end, but its legacy will last forever. It has been a moment of truth for all Americans and the whole world. Ultimately, I believe science and social policy based on science will defeat COVID-19. That victory will require the support of ordinary citizens, of people who value life over material advantage, of people who believe in the welfare of the nation and the world as their first obligation as regular people. We are not being asked to join the military and fight on an island in the Pacific with little hope of return. We are being asked to "love our neighbors as ourselves"; to self-quarantine; to practice social distancing; and to provide support for those who are isolated, vulnerable, and at risk.

We are living in extraordinary times; and the lesson I am learning is that our survival as a race, the human race, ultimately depends not on government or industry but on ordinary people doing the right thing for themselves, their families, their neighbors, and everyone else on this planet. I do not know if a new global human consciousness will emerge out of this experience. I hope so, but I am less than sanguine. Meanwhile, like Stephen E. Ambrose, I believe that victory—indeed, survival—depends first and foremost on the "citizen soldiers" among us from the trained health care workers, to the EMS squads, to the police, and to your next-door neighbor doing the right thing 24/7 without wavering. Ultimately, our victory over COVID-19 is up to you!

These are extraordinary times, and extraordinary times require ordinary people to do the right thing. I hope that enough people will get that message in enough time to save the world. Hopefully, they will abandon their small-minded, greedy, conspiratorial theories and let the most important strategic elements of victory prevail: love, wisdom, and courage as practiced by the most ordinary among us.

I do not know what will happen in the weeks ahead, but a bit of hope in our collective ability to simply be ordinary cannot hurt.

Shabbat Shalom.

Lessons Learned: Historical Pandemics and the Philadelphia Jewish Community

April 15, 2020 eKI

By the time this eKI arrives for you to read it, Passover will be over, but what many are calling the 11th Plague will still be raging. We will still be quarantined and the serious discussion of trend curves and economic restarts will continue to rage. Of course, the Coronavirus is not our first encounter with a pandemic in the City of Brotherly Love in general or for the local Jewish community. Maybe we can learn something from our collective past.

Unfortunately, Philadelphia is well known for public health crises from Colonial Times to the present. Full disclosure, I received a request from my dear friend Dr. Gary Zola, Director of the American Jewish Archives in Cincinnati, to help prepare a series of online seminars (including primary documents) for graduates of the Hebrew Union College—Jewish Institute of Religion to learn about how the American Jewish community historically experienced pandemics. What follows is an initial report on the research I started earlier this week.

My first inclination was to look into the Yellow Fever Epidemic of 1793. Sixteen years ago, in 2004, I was invited to participate in the dedication of a historical marker in memory of Major David S. Franks (1740–1793), a Jewish officer who served in George Washington's inner circle and died in October 1793 of Yellow Fever. Born in Philadelphia and

Bar Mitzvah at K.K. Mikveh Israel, Franks left his hometown in pursuit of business opportunities in Canada, as he was fluent in French. But when the Revolution broke out, Franks joined the American side and fought in the losing effort to liberate the Canadian provinces before making his way south, first to West Point and then to Philadelphia.

Unfortunately, Franks was, at times, under the command of Benedict Arnold, which ultimately cast great suspicion on his loyalty to the American cause. Washington himself exonerated Major Franks several times and later gave him a diplomatic assignment in which he helped deliver the American terms for peace with the British to the talks in Paris. Franks, however, never was able to shake the stigma attached to his association with America's most notorious traitor and actually died as a pauper during the 1793 Yellow Fever Epidemic.

Frank's body was placed on a cart bringing plague victims to a Potter's Field in Philadelphia for burial when, according to Dr. Benjamin Rush, a one-legged blacksmith, John Thompson, identified him as a hero of the Revolution. His body was then taken to the cemetery of Christ Church where he was given a single burial although no marker was set over his grave during the emergency. A symbolic marker was finally installed 211 years later. It was my honor to recall his story at that time along with several others and then dedicate a second, larger historical marker on 5th just below Arch on the east side of the street.

However, the Franks' story does not end there. Life is always complicated at times and, sometimes, ironic. The fact is that there was a second Jewish man in Philadelphia during the Yellow Fever Epidemic of 1793 also by the name of David Franks (1720–1793). The second David Franks was an uncle of Major Franks. This David Franks was twenty years older than his nephew, wealthier and, most of all, a British loyalist. In fact, his grand home, Woodford, in Germantown, frequently served as a British officers' club during the Revolution and a Frank daughter, Rebecca, married a British officer, Henry Johnson, who later served in Ireland, rising to the rank of general.

David Franks, the loyalist, left Philadelphia after the war for England but returned to town in 1783 and went into business. Although there are different accounts of his death, one tradition asserts that he, too, died in Philadelphia during the Yellow Fever Epidemic of 1793 just like his impoverished nephew. Pandemics, as we are learning again today, do not respect class, flags or political loyalties. They are a human, medical condition and need to be treated universally. Five thousand people, or 10 percent of Philadelphia's population, died of Yellow Fever in 1793, including two Jewish men both by the name of David Franks.

A second Philadelphia pandemic story comes from 1918 during World War I. The Spanish Flu ravaged the city and Philadelphia was widely viewed as the national epicenter of the pandemic. To make matters worse, the city's political and health leaders made a terrible mistake and agreed to hold a Liberty Loan parade in September 1918 at the height of the pandemic. Two hundred thousand people lined the city's streets in support of the campaign to financially support the American war effort. The results were devastating. Within a few weeks, the mortality rate spiked and thousands died of the Spanish Flu. A total of twelve thousand Philadelphians died of the flu alone; 675,000 in the United States; and perhaps fifty million worldwide. One of the Philadelphia casualties was Joseph Bender, who was the maternal grandfather of our member Sallie Olson. Sallie reports that her mother was only thirteen when her father died; she never overcame the loss of her father.

By contrast, St. Louis cancelled its parade, imposed the strictest rules on social distancing in the country and, consequently, suffered the lowest mortality rate from the 1918 Spanish Flu of any major city in the United States. The architect of public health policy in St. Louis was Dr. Max Starkloff, a graduate of Widener University, and the father of "social distancing." Social distancing remains the first defense against pandemics to this day.

In my own research on KI's history, I discovered that of the five KI soldiers who died during World War I, three died in combat in France, including Captain Frederick David Clair, Lieutenant Edward Benjamin Goward and Private Byron H. Reis, and two, or 40 percent, died of the flu in Philadelphia. A very high price that made the Spanish Flu of 1918 "personal" for our congregation.

Morris Adolph Deutsch was a Storekeeper in the United States Navy. He lived on Park Avenue in Philadelphia. He died of the flu on October 13, 1918. Captain Eugene Rice, who worked for the Philadelphia Rapid Transit Company before enlisting, died in Philadelphia in January 1919 from complications from the flu. The date of his death is disputed.

A total of 116,515 American soldiers, airmen and sailors died during the Great War, just 17 percent of the number who died from the Spanish Flu. Interestingly, Rabbi Krauskopf, who led KI at the time, was a full-throated opponent of American involvement in the war and later prophetically warned that the Allies' unjust treatment of Germany would lead to still greater death and destruction.

In the end, containment and termination of a pandemic comes down to empirical science and human choices. The Philadelphia Jewish experience in 1793 and 1918 shows that the greatest of international, national and regional catastrophes had devastating local consequences. No one is exempt. Everyone is responsible. At this time, let us be wise, safe and humane. We need one another to survive in every respect: physically, fiscally and spiritually. As the good book says, "Love Your Neighbor as yourself" and take it from there!

Shabbat Shalom and wash your hands.

Grant Us Peace: An American Reform Jewish Classic Prayer

The Reform Advocate Volume XI, Number II: Passover 2020
April 21, 2020

For those of us who grew up in the Reform movement or joined it during the course of our adult journey, *Grant Us Peace* is a familiar and much beloved prayer both because of its English language text and its various musical interpretations. What is less known is the surprising history of *Grant Us Peace*. *Grant Us Peace* serves as the final section of the "18 Benedictions" or *Amidah* in the liturgy of the synagogue, appearing just before or as a prelude to the Silent Prayer. Its text, based on two traditional prayers for peace (*Shalom Rav* from the Ashkenazic tradition and *Sim Shalom*), is essentially an original Reform composition combining Judaism's ancient hope for universal peace with prayers for national well-being and personal virtue, the basis of good citizenship.

The origin of the English language text of *Grant Us Peace* is surprising. In fact, it did not appear in the original 1892 *Union Prayer Book I* (UPB I) prepared for the Central Conference of American Rabbis (CCAR) by Rabbi Isaac Moses of Chicago. The Conference withdrew Rabbi Moses' text which they viewed "as a dilution" of Rabbi David Einhorn's radical German 1858 prayer book *Olat Tamid* which had been translated into English in 1872. However, instead of immediately reworking the Moses prayer book, the CCAR proceeded to publish the UPB II, a High Holy

Day prayer book, in 1894. It included the first known version of *Grant Us Peace* before re-publishing a thoroughly revised UPB I.

Thus, the original text of *Grant Us Peace* appears in an "Evening Service for the New Year" under the Hebrew title of "*Sim Shalom*," although the actual prayer for the Evening Service is entitled *Shalom Rav*. Because *Grant Us Peace* was originally written for the High Holy Days it included a reference to the "Book of Life," later dropped when the prayer was added to the Sabbath liturgy.

The first version of *Grant Us Peace*, was originally read by the "Minister" as follows:

Grant us peace, Thy most precious gift, O Thou eternal source of peace, and enable Israel to be a messenger of peace unto the peoples of the earth. Bless our country that it may ever be a stronghold of peace and be its advocate in the council of nations. May contentment reign within its borders, health, and happiness in its homes. Strengthen the bonds of friendship and fellowship between all the inhabitants of our land. Plant virtue in every soul and may love of Thy name hallow every home and every heart. Inscribe us in the book of life, and grant unto us a year of prosperity and joy. Blessed be Thou, O Lord, Giver of Peace. Amen.

The UPB series proved to be immensely popular in the Reform movement and within twenty years it was used by over three hundred congregations which had purchased over one hundred thousand copies of the prayer books. The text of *Grant Us Peace* remained essentially stable in subsequent editions of the UPB series. In the 1940 edition edited by Rabbi Solomon B. Freehof, "all the inhabitants of our land" was broadened to "the inhabitants of all lands." At the same time, a Hebrew text of *Shalom Rav* was provided by Rabbi Freeho, including a request for a blessing on "Your people Israel," perhaps a veiled Zionist reference, as opposed to the use of the name "Israel" in the original UPB II, employed in the more universalistic theological framework of the "Mission of Israel" as "a light to the nations." On the other hand, Freehof did not include the "closing blessing" of *Shalom Rav* in his Hebrew text.

In Service V of the 1975 *Gates of Prayer*, additional subtle changes were made. For example, the original "source of peace" was changed to a name of God with capital letters, "O Eternal Source of peace" and the formal "Thou" was dropped. Also, the phrase "advocate in the council of nations" was changed to "advocate among the nations," perhaps reflecting distrust in the United Nations after its 1975 adoption of Resolution 3379 condemning Zionism as a racist ideology.

The most recent Reform Prayer book, *Mishkan T'filah* ("*Sanctuary of Prayer*"), published in 2007, includes a version of *Grant Us Peace* as an alternative (left side) reading (v. p. 179), in an apparent attempt to define it out of the mainstream of Reform Judaism. The closing, particularistic Hebrew prayer, "Praised are You, Eternal One, who blesses our people with peace" is included in English, Hebrew, and transliteration. Interestingly, the Hebrew version of *Shalom Rav* (right side, p. 178) includes an insert for *Shabbat Shuvah*, the Sabbath between Rosh HaShanah and Yom Kippur in both Hebrew and English, thus restoring the original *Grant Us Peace*'s tie to the High Holy Days.

The enduring popularity of *Grant Us Peace* attracted the attention of one of the leading composers of Reform liturgical music, Canadian born Ben Steinberg (b. 1930) who included a Hebrew version of "Shalom Rav" in his immensely popular 1973 *L'cha Anu Shira: Sabbath Eve Service For Cantor, Choir, Congregation and Organ*. According to Steinberg, "*L'cha Anu Shira* was commissioned by Congregation Emanu-El B'Ne Jeshurun, Milwaukee, Wisconsin, in memory of Cantor Sol Altschuller (1917–1964). The premiere of the work was performed on November 21, 1969 by Cantor Roy Garber and the choir of Congregation Emanu-El B'Ne Jeshurun under the direction of the composer." In the musical text, Steinberg notes that an optional text is inserted "for use with the [1967 British] 'Service of the Heart' Prayer Book," although the more universalistic Hebrew in the British prayer book actually is not included in Steinberg's score.

When asked recently by Hazzan David Tilman of Elkins Park, Pennsylvania about his inspiration for his *Shalom Rav*, Steinberg replied that "the text spoke to me in such a meaningful manner that I felt that I was spiritually speaking to God and actually pleading for Peace for the people of Israel. The piece almost 'wrote itself'as I studied the text." (Communicated to author by email, February 28, 2020) In other words, despite its "Classical Reform" musical quality, Steinberg fully restored the text's ancient particularism. The same particularism was further reinforced in the 1974 post-classical version of *Shalom Rav* by Jeff Klepper and Dan Freelander which, along with Steinberg's version, is widely used in contemporary Reform synagogues on Friday nights. Indeed, the temporal proximity of the Steinberg and the Klepper-Freelander versions of *Shalom Rav* constitute a cultural border between mid- and late 20th century modalities of American Reform Judaism.

Finally, a few observations about Steinberg's *Shalom Rav* as a musical composition, which is a deceptively complex and sophisticated work. According to Hazzan Tilman, the composer set the text in G Major, a key that is calming and soothing. The Major tonality is particularly "Western" and "American" in its affect. Interestingly, Steinberg also uses a "triple meter" which is used in a gentle melody for "Dona Nobis Pacem," Latin for *Grant Us Peace* in the Catholic tradition.

Shalom Rav and its English language rendition, "Grant Us Peace," remain classic prayers in the religious culture of American Reform Judaism. They harmoniously blend Jewish universalism and particularism, affirm the value of the ethical life, and proclaim peace as the ultimate goal of the Jewish tradition. They transcend intradenominational differences and powerfully express what is classic about every expression of American Reform Judaism.

Closing Our Shuls, Opening Our Homes: A Jewish Response to COVID-19

May 27, 2020

I was amazed to learn earlier this week that over six hundred people had viewed and liked my posting on Facebook of the message of Rabbi Rick Jacobs, President of the Union of Reform Judaism (URJ), that Reform synagogues will stay closed for the foreseeable future in response to COVID-19. "The saving of human life," Jacobs correctly said, "is Judaism's highest value." Not surprisingly, with the exception of a small number of ultra-Orthodox groups, the same policy of staying closed has been adopted across the entire Jewish denominational spectrum in the United States and around the world. I know of no rabbi who has stood up and demanded that his or her shul had to be opened because of some misconstrued view of the First Amendment or because of a divine mandate from the Torah itself. In Judaism, we believe in the ultimate value of human life, even in the face of disastrous economic loss for our congregations and beyond.

Without question, I fully endorse the decision of our synagogue and the Reform movement to keep our sanctuaries closed so long as there is a major public health danger to our community. However, there is another angle to this situation that I believe also requires public explication. The fact of the matter is that Judaism has two sanctuaries: the synagogue and the home. The home is the principal venue for Shabbat, Hanukkah, and Passover. For many, it is also the place where we observe Sukkot. We hang *mezuzot* on our doors. We hang Jewish art on our walls. We maintain Jewish books in our personal libraries. We hold on to *kippot* from significant *simchas* in our lives and display pictures of ourselves holding Torahs at *b'nai mitzvah* and under *chuppahs* at recent and distant weddings. The home, in Judaism, is a sanctuary. Now, in my opinion, is the time to make a concerted effort to open our homes, our inner spaces, to Judaism wider than we ever have before.

At the same time, we need to be cognizant of those who are alone and radically isolated during this pandemic. We need to focus more of our efforts on them. We need to work with them and their families to create lifelines of connection and community. In some cases, it may require working with them on technology. In other cases, it may be a return to the use of regular telephone contacts. I am not sure we can return to radio broadcasts—it is very expensive—but we need to think creatively about new and old ways to connect to everyone in our congregation. Truth to be told, we never really closed. We pivoted; and our congregation remains engaged, challenged, and fulfilled.

Finally, we need to remember that one day this pandemic will be over. It may feel like we are living in a zombie apocalypse; and in many ways, we are, but it will end. Between now and then, it is incumbent upon us to keep our eternal light lit with the flame of faith and support our congregational efforts of sustained online outreach. If we allow our eternal light to go out, it will be that much harder to reopen and discover our new post-COVID normal.

Together, we have a sacred covenant to support one another at this difficult time. We need each other in so many ways. Together, we will find unprecedented new paths to care for and lift each other. That process begins at home, our personal sanctuaries, which we can fill with the light of life, love, and the abiding faith that we are strong enough to get to the end of this pandemic intact and ready to embrace the next chapter in our lives. May you be blessed with heath, sustenance, and peace.

Amen.

Shabbat Shalom.

An Old Hatred and New Challenges: Jews, Blacks, and White Supremacy in America

June 17, 2020

At this moment of extreme racial tension in the United States, it is important to reopen the books and recall an almost entirely unknown story involving the emergence of the Ku Klux Klan in 1868 in Tennessee. The Civil War had ended just three years earlier, but smoldering racial resentments among Southerners and veterans of the Confederate Army were widespread. Political violence between anti-Reconstruction politicians and free Black Republicans were rising. Starting on May 1, 1868, a three-day race riot broke out in Memphis, Tennessee, in which more than one hundred twenty Blacks were killed and one hundred Black homes, schools, and churches were burned. Several months later, on July 6, members of Franklin, Tennessee's Black Union League of America were ambushed in a town square by unknown white assailants and returned fire. In all, thirty Blacks were wounded and three died of their wounds, as did one of the white gunmen.

Despite the growing violence, a number of Jews moved to the American South in search of economic opportunity. Many of them publicly took up the cause of the besieged Black community including Prussian-born Morris Marks, who settled in New Orleans, and Bohemian-born Charles S. Kuh, who settled in Beaufort, South Carolina, after the war ended. Kuh subsequently was elected to the South Carolina State Legislature on a pro-Reconstruction platform. However, the story of Samuel A. Bierfield was the most consequential of these stories, in the long view of history, as his death was directly tied to the emergence of the Ku Klux Klan.

Samuel A. Bierfield was born in Latvia, immigrated to North America, and initially settled in Toronto, where he worked for a family business. In 1866, he moved to the United States and settled in Pulaski, Tennessee, near the Alabama border. In Pulaski, where six veterans of the Confederate Army first organized the Ku Klux Klan in the spring of 1868, Bierfield immediately encountered numerous problems, including resentment of his economic success, his friendly relations with local African Americans, and the suspicion that he was a Radical Republican. Unable to overcome his problems in Pulaski, Bierfield moved north to Franklin, Tennessee. Tragically, his problems followed him to his new place of residence.

In Franklin, Bierfield opened a dry-goods store and hired an African American as his clerk. Late on the night of August 15, 1868, gunmen surrounded Bierfield's store, forced him and his clerk outside, and opened fire in an attack, which became a signature action of the nascent Klan. Bierfield was shot five times and died quickly of his wounds. His clerk, Lawrence Bowman, was also injured in the attack and later died of his wounds, although a second Black man escaped. Bierfield thus became the first of a number of American Jews to be lynched in the United States from Leo Frank to the mass shooting at a Pittsburgh synagogue in 2018, while Bowman was just one of the thousands of African Americans to be murdered by White Supremacists in the United States.

As to be expected, a shameful judicial circus followed the 1868 Bierfield-Bowman lynching. A forged letter appeared in the local press two days after the attack, accusing Bierfield himself of an earlier murder. In September, a suspect, John Pogue Jr., was arrested for killing Bierfield after being named by a quickly discredited eyewitness and then released on the testimony of seven people who provided Pogue with a shaky alibi. Letters also appeared in the local press both attempting to exonerate the Klan of any responsibility in the attack and assuring the other Jewish residents of the town that anti-Semitism played no role in the attack on Bierfield. The fact of the matter is that the joint lynching of a Jew and a Black man marked the Klan's historical emergence. The reality is that White Supremacists continue to view Jews, Blacks, and "others" as their common enemy.

Fifty years after the dual lynching of Bierfield and Bowman, an untested young rabbi named William Fineshriber (1878–1968) stood up in his pulpit in Memphis, Tennessee in 1917 to denounce the public burning and dismemberment of Eli Persons, a black man falsely accused of raping a white girl. Rabbi Fineshriber continued to preach boldly against lynching and the Klan, often as the sole voice among the Memphis clergy, until he was called to the pulpit of Reform Congregation Keneseth Israel (KI) in Philadelphia in 1923 as a moral heir to KI's remarkable abolitionist rabbi, David Einhorn.

Racial violence is nothing new in this country, and as Jews, it is incumbent upon us to understand that the same hate that is directed at our Black neighbors is ultimately aimed at us as well. That is how the Klan started. That is what both Rabbis Einhorn and Fineshriber understood. That is what we need to recognize in our own day.

Since 1847, our congregational motto has been love your neighbor as yourself (Lev. 19:18). Today, that message is as urgent as it was when Moses first proclaimed it thousands of years ago. Today, we need to remind ourselves that it has been repeated and affirmed by every generation of our people until today. Now, in these turbulent times, we too need to be cognizant of our heritage both as a people and as a congregation and live our lives in accordance with the central teaching of our faith, "love your neighbor as yourself," and denounce racial hatred with every ounce of our moral and bodily strength.

Shabbat Shalom.

A Long History: American Jews and the NAACP

July 31, 2020

The National Association for the Advancement of Colored People (NAACP) and American Jews have a long-shared history. Last week's viciously anti-Semitic posting by Minister Rodney Muhammad, head of the Philadelphia Chapter of the NAACP, has thrown relations between Americans Jews, African Americans, and the NAACP into disarray. First and unequivocally, Minister Muhammad needs to resign. His invoking of an anti-Semitic, Nazi meme was inexcusable and betrays the mission and goals of the NAACP. In my opinion, the NAACP at the national level needs to secure this resignation to remove any doubt as to their organization's philosophy moving forward. Second, the NAACP needs to affirm its historic mandate of fighting all forms of bigotry and discrimination. The mission of the NAACP (in their own words) "is to secure the political, educational, social, economic equality of rights in order to eliminate race-based discrimination and ensure the health and well-being of all persons." Third, American Jewish–NAACP cooperation must continue and maintain its extraordinary legacy of dialogue. Fourth, the Philadelphia Jewish community needs to recognize the size, strength, and continuing growth of our local African American Muslim community, the largest in the United States, and work to build bridges between us, them, and others.

I think it is important to keep the current controversy in historical perspective, as there are forces in both communities that want to break down the historic ties between American Jews and African Americans and empower anti-integrationist and anti-acculturationist ideologies on both sides of the debate. That would be a mistake. That would be a tragedy that for American Blacks, American Jews, and America itself. At the same time, we need to appreciate there are differences and tensions between Jews and Blacks and the United States; and at the same time, we can and must work together for the benefit of our country.

The NAACP was founded in 1909 in reaction to a terrible race riot the year before in Springfield, Illinois. Among the original founders of the NAACP were Henry Moskowitz, a Romanian Jew who worked as the Executive Director of the Broadway League in New York. Moskowitz was joined in his support of the NAACP by Rabbi Emil Hirsch (son of KI's rabbi, the late Samuel Hirsch); Julius Rosenwald (father of KI's Lessing Rosenwald); Jacob Schiff, who was the leading Jewish philanthropist of the Progressive Era; and the well-respected Spingarn family. To this day, the Spingarn Medal is one of the highest awards given by the NAACP to those who best exemplify its goals and values. The young Rabbi Stephen Wise, a leading voice of American Zionism prior to World War II, supported the NAACP; and via W.E.B. DuBois's Niagara Movement, Lillian Wald of Settlement House fame also supported the newly founded NAACP.

But perhaps the most fruitful collaboration between the American Jewish community—and, in particular, the Reform movement in Judaism—and the NAACP took place in the early 1960s. In 1962, the Union for American Hebrew Congregations (UAHC, now the Union for Reform Judaism, URJ) purchased the old Ecuadorian Embassy at 2027 Massachusetts Avenue in Washington, DC Northwest and launched its Religious Action Center (RAC) there. In 1964, with Reform, NAACP leaders, and others huddled around the table, the historic Civil Rights Act was written. The following year, the same coalition produced the Voting Act Rights of 1965 (gutted by the Supreme Court in 2013). In other words, the most progressive social and civil legislation in American history was born of NAACP–American Jewish cooperation.

It is important to note that the seed money for the RAC was given by a Reform Jew, Kivie Kaplan (1904–1975), in 1959. Kaplan, a Bostonian, joined the NAACP in 1932 (at age of twenty-eight); was elected to its national board in 1954; and, from 1965 to 1985, served as president of the NAACP. He marched and was jailed with Dr. Martin Luther King Jr. on many occasions including the Edmund Pettus Bridge crossing in Selma,

Alabama. Curiously, on the back of his business card, Kaplan always had the words *keep smiling* printed.

There is a saying to the effect that things were never as good between Blacks and Jews as Jewish liberals would have it or were as bad as Black Nationalists allege. Tensions between American Jews and American Blacks are nothing new. As a child, I heard endless coded comments about Blacks and was very aware that Jews were paradoxically part of the white flight movement just as they were largely pro-Civil Rights. Later, I learned that Dr. King, Representative John Lewis, and other African American leaders were hard-pressed by Black Nationalists for their integrationist views. But these tensions are secondary to the need for cooperation in pursuit of civil equality in the United States. Hopefully, at these difficult times, American Jews and leaders of the NAACP will remember our joint heritage and our larger common purpose, and together with Kivie Kaplan and others, we will find a way back to marching and smiling together.

Shabbat Shalom.

Monumental Questions: A Rabbinic Reflection for July 4, 2020

Despite the fact that the Constitution of the new state of North Carolina required that the holding of public office required both a belief in the "truth of the Protestant religion" and the "divine authority" of the New Testament, Jacob Henry (1775–1847), a Jew, was elected to the North Carolina legislature in 1808. However, when he was reelected the following year, his eligibility to take his seat in the House was challenged. Henry rose to his own defense on December 6, 1809, and asked that he be judged on the "content of his character" and not how he privately worshipped God. "The ruler of the universe," Henry maintained, "would receive with equal benignity, the various offerings of man's adoration if they proceed from a humble spirit and sincere mind." Henry's argument was successful, and the House voted he could take his seat in the legislature. For years, Henry's elegant defense of the American view of freedom of religion was widely known and often repeated. For American Jews, he became a genuine hero and recognized as defender of their coveted freedom of religion.

What else do we know about Henry? A resident of the oceanfront town of Beaufort, North Carolina, Henry's 1790 home still stands today and is considered a local "gem." He was married to Esther Whitehurst, and the couple had at least seven children. Further investigation also revealed that Henry owned approximately three hundred acres and was the owner of twelve slaves. Nowhere in the literature on Henry is his status as a slave owner problematized, but that is no longer possible today after weeks of debate and protest about the place of racism and the heritage of slavery in the American experience.

How are we to remember Henry? Is he a hero? Is he an oppressor? Is he simply a person of his time and place during which liberty was a more circumscribed idea than it is today? How shall we remember him?

For American Jews, how to remember Jacob Henry is part of a larger historical controversy now raging in this country. We could ask the same questions about our nation's founders including Washington, Jefferson, and Madison. All heroes of democracy, all owners of slaves. How are we to remember them on this Fourth of July weekend? Should we "forgive them of their sins," or do we remove them from the iconography of our national culture?

For me, there are no simple answers. On the one hand, I agree with those who want to (legally) remove statues of Confederate military leaders from public squares. They were traitors and took arms against the United States. In my view, they have no place in America's public squares. However, the public representation of slave owners who help found the nation is more problematic. Washington was the first President. Jefferson was the force behind so many of our basic rights. Madison was an author of the Constitution. They deserve a place in our public life. But how should they be depicted?

In my opinion, we need to rethink our monuments. Just as we reimagined monuments when the Vietnam Memorial was created in Washington, DC, so we need to reimagine our public iconography in general in America. We need to remember Washington, Jefferson, and Madison as great but flawed men. We also need to remember the slaves who helped build this nation and the native population who were decimated and removed from their ancestral lands. Some monuments need to come down, others need to be modified, and still others need to be created. History is not a done deal. It is not a neutral collection of facts. History, ultimately, is a narrative about our national past and purpose.

On this Fourth of July, our past has literally become a monumental challenge for all Americans, including American Jews. How shall we tell our story? What do we mean when we use words like *liberty* and *freedom*? How can we become a more perfect union? These are questions I urge you to discuss as Americans and as Jews. Perhaps we may not find all the answers in the next few days, but in my view, we are obliged to ask the questions.

Shabbat Shalom and a happy, safe July Fourth!

What Is Being Asked of Us?

The COVID Pandemic and Personal Responsibility
August 7, 2020

Yesterday, I met Cantor Amy, Ross Levy (videographer), Adam Guth (sound engineer), Jeff Miller (trumpet and shofar), and Marlene Adler (photographer) to tape the shofar segments of the High Holy Day services and take pictures for the Holy Day videos. It was just six of us in our giant nine-hundred-seat sanctuary, trying to create the experience of the holidays and a full house all in the "beauty of holiness" and in the middle of an empty house. The room was warm and bleached with the afternoon light so many of us love and associate with the High Holy Day experience at KI. We worked hard. Jeff's shofar notes were on the mark. We were filled with high purpose, and now we pray that we created a moment you will experience on Rosh HaShanah and Yom Kippur that will be authentic and moving. We gave it our all: strong voices, sweat, and a lot of heart.

These taping sessions will be going on for much of the month of August. They are complex but necessary. They are "what is being asked of us" at this extraordinary moment, months deep into the pandemic with no light at the end of the tunnel.

But the true poignancy of the moment did not hit me until our taping session was over. It was when I walked outside and looked at our empty playground that a deep sense of loss overcame me. You see, we had to make a decision about our preschool, and we decided we could not safely open this Fall. It is simply too dangerous for our kids, their families, and our staff. No matter how many precautions we take, COVID-19 is too vicious an enemy for an institution to combat. We are not a hospital. We do not have the resources of a highly endowed private school. We provide enrichment, joy, and happy memories. Hopefully, a vaccine will be developed, and our whole population will be inoculated in the coming months or year, and we will go back to a new normal.

I hope so. Shofar sounds in an empty sanctuary and the striking image of a childless playground are not what I want. But I believe that they are what we need to keep our community safe.

In this week's Torah portion, *eikev*, there is a powerful message in Deuteronomy 10:12. It asks, "And now O Israel, what does the Eternal your God ask of you." A very similar verse appears in the Book of Micah, an eighth-century BCE prophet from the Kingdom of Judah. Like Moses, Micah taught, "It has been told you, humankind, what is good and what the Eternal seeks of you?" Judaism's response to Moses and Micah is clear—"to do justly, to love mercy and to walk humbly with your God."

Right now, at this moment, each one of us as individuals, as members of synagogues, as members of the Jewish community, as citizens of Philadelphia and the surrounding counties, as Americans, and as human beings are all being asked, "What is being demanded of you? What is the right path? How should I quarantine? When do I wear a mask? What is best for me? What is necessary for my neighbor? What do I have to give up? How I am supposed to deal with my sense of disconnection and personal loss? When will I enjoy the full physical embrace of a friend, a grandchild, or a distant sibling?

All of us are being addressed personally and collectively by our tradition, by our country, and by our consciences, "What is being asked of me right now?" None of us have ever lived through anything like this before. There are, thankfully, public health policies based on science and the hope that we have enduring spirits and personal emotional reserves that will get us through the tunnel of darkness that we are in and back into the light of life! But until then, we need to be strong, to be willing to sacrifice, to show love by pulling back from life and finding ways of staying together while existing apart!

"And now, what is being asked of you?" In a word, a great deal. Empty sanctuaries, childless playgrounds, masks, and lots of personal hygiene. Most of all, we are asked to remain loving, kind, merciful, and humble. We are asked to remember our foundational values and to be strong.

We are asked to remain human, humane, and giving. We are asked to persevere with faith, neighborly support, and inner strength. Together, we will endure!

Amen.

Shabbat Shalom.

THE RIGHT TO VOTE—SHOF'TIM 16:15–21:9

August 19, 2020

The first part of this week's Torah portion, *shof'tim* (magistrates), begins by providing a constitution for the state, which our ancestors were instructed to set up in the Land of Israel at the end of the Exodus. It provides for two branches of government: executive and judicial. On the other hand, the legislative branch is based on the revelation of law through prophecy. The Torah's discussion of government focuses primarily on the issue of integrity. The king is to keep a copy of the Torah with him at all times and is admonished not to indulge in excessive government or personal spending. Judges are warned to be fair and impartial in their rulings, and prophets can only speak in the name of the one God.

Perhaps the biggest difference between the theocratic monarchy of ancient Israel and the government in the United States is that our ancestors only had the right to choose their judges. The other appointments were to be made by God. In our republican form of government, the people chose their leaders both directly and indirectly in all three branches of government. The right of the people is based on their constitutionally guaranteed right to vote, the key element in the social contract which defines the United States. Significantly, in the history of our democracy, this week marks the one hundredth anniversary of the ratification of the Nineteenth Amendment, giving women the right to vote.

The most important statement on voting as the foundation of democracy was issued by Chief Justice Earl Warren in *Reynolds v. Sims*, 377 U.S. 533, 555 (1964): "The right to vote freely for the candidate of one's choice is of the essence of a democratic society, and any restrictions on that right strike at the heart of representative government. [. . .] Undoubtedly, the right of suffrage is fundamental in a free and democratic society. Especially since the right to exercise the franchise in a free and unimpaired manner is preservative of other basic civil and political rights, any alleged infringement of the right of citizens to vote must be carefully and meticulously scrutinized." Similarly, Justice Hugo Black shared the same sentiment in *Wesberry v. Sanders*, 376 U.S. 1, 17 (1964): "No right is more precious in a free country than that of having a voice in the election of those who make the laws under which, as good citizens, we must live. Other rights, even the most basic, are illusory if the right to vote is undermined."

As a country, we are only about seventy days away from our national elections this fall. Sadly, but consistent with the long history of voter suppression in the United States, fierce debates about voting are currently raging in our country. The most important concerns the role of the post office in the election process this year because of the COVID pandemic and the dangers involved in voting in person for people with underlying medical conditions. A related issue involves the availability of volunteers at the polls. Traditionally, poll workers tend to be older and are unavailable for this year's voting because of health concerns.

Two other issues are of concern both nationally and in the American Jewish community. First is the need for support for our elderly population who are unfamiliar with the new technologies involved in registering for mail-in voting. Second is the lower level of voting among the youngest cohort of voters. The American Jewish community, well-known for its high voter turnout, is not immune to this downward trend.

At Keneseth Israel, our Social Justice Policy Committee is correctly focusing much of their efforts on getting out the vote this year and will be providing information and voter support. The synagogue will be running voter information links in its electronic communications. Everyone is encouraged to vote and to encourage others to vote as well. As Chief Justice Earl Warren wrote fifty-six years ago, "The right to vote freely for the candidate of one's choice is of the essence of a democratic society."

This week's Torah portion begins with the words, "You shall appoint magistrates and officials for your tribes, in all the settlements the Lord your God is giving you, and they shall govern the people with due justice." In our time, those "appointments" are "of the people, by the people and for the people" through our ability to vote freely, fairly, and securely. This year please do your civic duty and vote!

Shabbat Shalom.

Rest in Peace: Remembering Justice Ruth Bader Ginsburg, a"h September 24, 2020

Along with Louis Brandeis, Ruth Bader Ginsburg shares the distinction of being one of the most important Jews in American history. While Brandeis was the first Jew appointed to the Court, was the leading champion of Progressivism, and led the American Zionist movement, Ginsburg was the judicial pioneer for women's rights in America and the first Jewish woman to serve on the Court. Her untimely death just weeks before a presidential election will make the fight for her successor a historic debate without precedent and could potentially lead to the tipping of the Court for another generation. Small in stature, Ginsburg, like Brandeis, will forever remain a giant in the history of American jurisprudence.

The first Jew considered for service on the High Court was Judah P. Benjamin, who declined the offer and went on to serve as the Secretary of State of the Confederacy. Brandeis served the Court from 1916 to 1939. Brandeis helped develop a broader approach to argumentation in the Court and was a relentless foe both of big business and of big government. Benjamin Cardozo served the Court briefly from 1932 to 1938. A Democrat, he was nominated by a Republican President, Herbert Hoover, and was unanimously confirmed by the Senate. The third Jew to serve on the court was Felix Frankfurter, who replaced Cardozo. He was known for his philosophy of judicial restraint. His term extended from 1939 to 1962.

The other Jewish Justices include Arthur Goldberg (1962–1965), Abe Fortas (1965–1969), and two current Justices, Stephen Breyer (1994–) and Elena Kagan (2010–). Interestingly, despite the predominance of

Protestantism in American religious life, the Supreme Court in recent years has been served by Jews and Catholics.

Ruth Bader Ginsburg was born in Brooklyn on March 15, 1933. She first attended Harvard Law School but later graduated from Columbia to meet the needs of her growing family. Unable to find a position in a major law firm, Ginsburg became a professor of law and volunteered for the American Civil Liberties Union (ACLU). In both areas, she pioneered research into "gender and law" and emerged as the leading advocate for women's rights among legal scholars in America. In 1980, Ginsburg was appointed to the U.S. Court of Appeals in Washington, DC by President Jimmy Carter and thirteen years later was successfully nominated to the Supreme Court by President Bill Clinton. Ginsburg viewed herself a judicial moderate, "a rational minimalist, and a jurist who seeks to build cautiously on precedent rather than pushing the Constitution towards her own vision." During her term, the Supreme Court generally shifted to the Right. By simply holding her ground, Ginsburg is generally perceived as having shifted to the Left during her years on the court; and in fact, it may be true in some instances.

Ginsburg, known as RBG and even The Notorious RBG, was an immensely popular figure in American society among women, liberals, pro-choice activists, and American Jews. Her extraordinary, egalitarian marriage to Martin Ginsburg, a tax attorney; her lifelong love of opera; unprecedented friendship with fellow jurist Anthony Scalia; and her sustained efforts to remain fit and healthy made her a hero among heroes for tens of millions of Americans. Locally, she was honored by the National Museum of American Jewish History. In recent years, she was the subject both of documentaries and a full-length motion picture. She is the first woman to lie in state in the U.S. Capitol. Her final resting place will be in Arlington National Cemetery.

Ultimately, in my opinion, the best way to remember and honor Justice Ginsburg is to let her speak for herself. She was a precise wordsmith, unhurried in her delivery of words, honest, and animated by a healthy mix of seriousness and humor. First, in her own words, Justice Ginsburg believed that the Jewish ideal of justice was essential both to her ancestral faith and personal identity. "I am a judge born," she wrote, "raised, and proud of being a Jew. The demand for justice runs through the entirety of the Jewish tradition. I hope, in my years on the bench of the Supreme

Court of the United States, I will have the strength and the courage to remain constant in the service of that demand."

Justice for Justice Ginsburg was both a universal and specific concern. Her lasting legacy will be her work on law and gender. "Women's rights," she argued, "are an essential part of the overall human rights agenda, trained on the equal dignity and ability to live in freedom all people should enjoy." Finally, did she have any regrets? My sense is she lived and died with a clear conscience. However, "if there was one decision I would overrule," she once reflected, "it would be Citizens United. I think the notion that we have all the democracy that money can buy strays so far from what our democracy is supposed to be."

During this period of mourning for RBG, let us take a moment to remember her and her tremendous contribution to the American pursuit of redefining and expanding the meaning of "equal justice under law," the essence of American democracy. Justice Ginsburg's life was a blessing to her nation. May we continue to work in her footsteps and secure the blessings of liberty and protection of law to all our citizens.

Shabbat Shalom and an easy fast!

The Attack on America

January 8, 2021, Shabbat

Shabbat Shalom.

This week has been a traumatic time for the American people. On our televisions and cell phones and iPads, we have seen images that previously would have been unimaginable, with the Capitol building in Washington, DC being attacked and trashed by an unruly and vengeful mob. We've read in history about the storming of the Bastille and the burning of the livestock, but never for a moment could any of us have imagined the storming of the great temple and fortress of American democracy. These are images and acts that will remain in our national and personal memories into the deep future.

January 6 will be remembered as a terrible day of infamy. At the same time, we will also remember that after the building was finally secured after many hours of battle, the Congress of the United States went back to work and the business of our democracy was carried out until the letter of the law, the Constitution, was met. The symbolism of the Capitol Building and its dome is profound. It is iconic.

Like many of you, I remember visiting the Capitol Building as a child, both with my family and my school, and, to use a colloquial term, being wowed by its majesty—by the Statuary Hall, by the great paintings, but, most of all, by the dome, the tremendous majestic dome, which rises above the sixteen-acre complex that symbolizes American democracy and indicates as domes do that there is something transcendent about our experiment in democracy. A dome, especially a big dome, is meant to evoke awe. There are a few buildings, whether they are religious or the Capitol Building in Washington, that invoke greater awe in the transcendent power of great principles like democracy than the dome in Washington. To think that a mob invaded that space, even after we watched it, remains unthinkable. I have wonderful personal memories of being in the Capitol Building. I certainly plan to go back in the future, perhaps with my own grandchildren.

Twenty-two years ago, I was invited to give the opening prayer, the invocation, in the United States House of Representatives. It's a matter of Congressional record. It was one of the proudest moments of my life as I stood in that chamber and gave a prayer on behalf of the United States, its Constitution, and our people. I returned again to the Capitol Building to present a paper on immigration in a Senate hearing room. It was carried on C-SPAN. I spoke about the contribution of a Jewish congressman to the changing laws about immigration in the United States to help the Senate and historians understand where we are on that very, very painful issue today in our history. I've served as a guide and a teacher for our own confirmation class, bringing our confirmands to those sacred halls to teach them the part of their religious duty is also a sacred duty.

I have my own personal memories and connections to that building, but like all of you, I have a national connection to that building. I have the memory that that dome was built during the Civil War, that not even a Civil War could stop the construction of the house of the people, and how ironic that's so much of that work was done by slaves. No sooner had it been completed that an amendment was passed in those halls to abolish slavery forever in America.

The Capitol Building and its dome are not only symbols of American democracy par excellence. They are literally the beating heart of our Republic, and the heart of our republic came under attack this week. Thank God, it survived, and we continue our business now as a people. In our Torah portion this week, we begin the book of Exodus. We begin with the enslavement of the Hebrews and the birth of Moses. We begin at one of the darkest hours of the Jewish people, but embedded in that narrative are the sparks of hope and redemption that even in the darkest hours before the dawn, the possibility of restoration, hope, and redemption are there.

As we move forward, let us commit ourselves to being those sparks, to being those agents of change and redemption of recommitting ourselves to the great principles of our country, which guarantee us our right to live here in freedom and unafraid as Jews, as a tiny religious minority, and go about the work that we were destined and entitled to do by rights, by providence, and by the choice of our own hearts.

Shabbat Shalom and take good care.

Back to Work: Step by Step, Inch by Inch

March 1, 2021

It has been a long time coming. On Wednesday, October 28, 2020, I was scheduled for a regular doctor's appointment, including my annual Fall flu shot. Little did I know that my whole life was going to change and that after a single "listen" on the stethoscope, I would be on my way to Abington Hospital in an ambulance for open-heart surgery followed by a long period of convalescence and cardio rehab. In fact, I was really lucky. My primary physician was "on the ball," and the staff at the hospital were uniformly excellent as were the people in the home nurse program and now "in house" therapeutic treatment. I did not see it coming. I was not being treated for anything in this direction. As they say, this was the "hand of cards I was dealt"; and lucky for me, the deck was in decent order, and I am now slowly returning to my old life. Of course, not everything is going to be the same. The pizza, subs, and other weapons of (body) mass destruction are now gone as are the twenty-hour days and the eight-day weeks. More common sense, better allocation of time, fewer projects, and healthier eating are what are on my plate. I did not come through this storm just to land on a helicopter pad. My goal is a long runway with smooth flying and gentle landings.

But enough of the metaphors. As I pick up the pieces, I am starting to restore parts of my old routine: a weekly meeting with my assistant, Sarah Morrison; weekly senior staff meetings; Shabbat and holiday services; *b'nai mitzvah* lessons; and Confirmation. As best as possible, I am making daily pastoral phone calls and participating in Zoom life-cycle events. However, until a sufficient number of COVID vaccines have been administered, most of my work will remain virtual. I hope that sometime later this year (I do not know which month) "in person" Judaism will resume at KI, probably beginning with our preschool. I look forward to all of it.

Now, my downtime was not a complete loss. With the help of my daughter, Chana, I was able to assemble a collection of my recent poems and put them together in book form, both online and print. *The Kindness Response* (by me, Rabbi Lance J. Sussman) is now available at Barnes&Noble and online at Amazon. With the help, again from Chana, as well as my long-term volunteer assistant, I have also made good progress on a book of my sermons and essays reflecting my twenty years of work at KI. The book will be called *A Portrait of an American Rabbi* and will include nearly one hundred of my articles and reflections. The book will be organized chronologically and will also be available in e- and print editions. I am not exactly sure of the release date yet, but I am hoping this volume, my second book of sermons, will be available by the High Holy Days in 2021. I also have several articles forthcoming this Spring, one on the *haftarot* and the other an essay on our Landau windows in a special art book to be published by the Penn State University Press.

OK, so you are probably saying I really did not take much of a break, but I actually limited my editing time and relied heavily on my helpers.

I truly look forward to getting back to work. One, I love my work. Becoming and being a rabbi is/was a calling for me. Second, when news spread of my medical emergency, I received hundreds of get-well cards (Hallmark must have done well) from you, the congregation. I was overwhelmed by the outpouring of support, concern, and love from so many of you. There is an old joke about how the president of a shul once visited a rabbi in the hospital and reported that she had good news. "The Board voted five to four," the president reported, "that you should get better." Looks like my vote was better than that, and now I feel I must get back to the work of being your rabbinic partner in Jewish and everyday life just as I have been for the last twenty years.

So step by step, inch by inch, I am coming back to my rabbinic vocation; and hopefully, as the rate of vaccination intensifies, it will be in person and not just online. Again and always, thank you for your support during this crazy time in my life. Meanwhile, a happy and healthy Passover to you and your families. May we all be delivered from the plague we are still enduring.

Shabbat Shalom and *Todah*!

The Unbearable Middle: The Public, the Police, and Life in America Today

April 15, 2021

This last week, the news has yet again been dominated by stories and images involving the police in the United States. On the one hand, there are ongoing reports of police departments on trial for the misbehavior of a few cops. On the other hand, there was also the gripping story of yet another police funeral in Washington, DC. Many in the American public are caught in an unbearable middle. We are caught between the realization that there is a real need for police reform in this country and a deep conviction that we need our police in order to save lives and that we are highly indebted to the people in blue who protect us.

Let us start with the issue of police malpractice. This does not mean that all cops are bad and that policing, in general, is out of control in this country. However, it does mean that we have both systemic and individual problems. But we are so polarized that even the slightest of the thin blue line can evoke a furious response from elements from the political Right. Systemic racism, militarization, and undertraining in mental health are more abundantly apparent to police critics; and they see no progress in these sensitive areas.

Then there are the showcase news stories, and there are so many of them. First and most enduring is the George Floyd story. On May 25, 2020, Officer Derek Chauvin restrained a prisoner, George Floyd, in Minneapolis, Minnesota, by handcuffing him, placing him on the ground, and kneeling on his neck for over nine minutes. Today, every day, the trial of Officer Chauvin is on TV for hours on end. Nearby in Brooklyn Center, veteran officer Kimberly Porter shot and killed another black man, twenty-year-old Duante Wright, at point-blank range, claiming she was operating her Taser gun instead of her service revolver. Those legal proceedings on top of a myriad of others are also flooding the airwaves. Then, just the other day, a video was released of two officers in southern Virginia pepper-spraying and handcuffing active-duty Second Lieutenant Caron Nazario after pulling him over on the false perception that his car did not have a proper tag. Their treatment of the army officer was reminiscent of the worst of the Jim Crow era.

There are other examples, equally brutal and appalling and too many to mention here, although the plea of "say their names" rings in our ears. It is gut-wrenching to follow these stories and the protests that follow, often with Black Lives Matter protesters and sometimes, frustratingly, with angry, illegal rioting. It is a mess, it is shameful, and it is wrong in so many ways. It is hard to take, and it takes us back to the awful days of Bull Connor policing in the segregated South. On the other hand, there are stories like the funeral of the eighteen-year member of the Capitol Police, William "Billy" Evans, in the Rotunda of the Capitol Building in Washington, DC. Evans was killed by a deranged individual attacking the seat of our legislative branch of government. During a mournful presentation of "Bridge over Troubled Waters," tears began cascading down the face of his widow, drenching her face mask. Their seven-year-old daughter snuggled up to her grief-stricken mom and with her little fingers wiped some of the falling tears away. It was at once a beautiful portrait of pure, innocent love and a gut-wrenching moment of grief. This, we say to ourselves, is the price of being a cop and the price their families pay. Nor has it been that long since we watched the funeral of Officer Brian Sicknick, a man of our own Jewish faith, killed in the mob attack in Washington on January 6, 2020. Unbearable, unthinkable, emotionally impossible.

So here we are. What is left of the unpolarized American public is caught between police trials and police funerals. We need our police. We want our police to be brave, just, and true to their oaths. We want them to be safe, even when they are in danger; and we want to reset police-public relations, police training, and police service in America. We are in an unbearable middle; and we need to come together peacefully, honestly, and purposefully to get beyond this terrible moment in our collective history.

Shabbat Shalom.

Alaska and the Holocaust: An Unknown Story

July 28, 2021

Like many of you, I spent many hours this week in front of the TV watching the Olympics. In my house, our favorite sports are women's gymnastics and women's swimming, in large because Liz was a competitive swimmer for many years. My interest in the Olympics notched up even further when Lydia Jacoby, age seventeen, unexpectedly won the gold in the one-hundred-meter women's breaststroke. Watching her hometown fans celebrate, literally jumping for joy, was the icing on the cake. For just a moment, all the complexities of the 2021 Tokyo Olympics disappeared. It was the best buzzer-beater high school victory I ever saw, and I have seen a lot of them.

I wondered for a moment, given her last name, if Lydia was Jewish or of Jewish descent. There is even a branch of my own family with the surname of Jacoby. I could not find anything definitive, but one article published by the Jewish Telegraphic Agency (JTA) strongly suggested the family is associated with the Methodist Church. OK, I said to myself, while I am looking things up (a constant for me), I should continue to read about Seward, Alaska, where she grew up. Why not? I said to myself, as I had just watched a rerun of the 2009 movie *The Proposal* with Sandra Bullock, which mostly took place in beautiful Sitka, Alaska, a mere 549 miles down coast from Seward.

Seward was named after the Secretary of State William H. Seward, who engineered the American purchase of Alaska in 1867 from Russia.

Today, Seward only has 2,700 people (and no fifty-meter pool!). It is 120 miles south of Anchorage (which has the largest Jewish community in the state) and is the home of the southern terminus of the Alaska railroad. The climate of Seward, I learned, is surprisingly mild, and the economy is fueled by fishing and tourism. So far, everything about Seward sounded very nice but still nothing of extraordinary interest. Then, as unexpected as Jacoby's first-place victory, I struck historic gold! In 1938, just two weeks after Kristallnacht, the United States Department of State released the Slattery Report, named after Undersecretary of State Harry A. Slattery (1897–1949). Secretary of State Harold Ickes had previously toured the territory of Alaska with several possibilities in mind: improve Alaskan security against the Japanese; further develop the economy of Alaska; and, finally, find a place of refuge for German and Austrian Jews hoping to escape Europe. Because Alaska was not yet a state, the usual immigration quotas of 1921 and 1924 did not apply. In other words, there was a legal possibility of finding a safe haven for thousands of doomed Jews. For its part, the people of the town of Seward eagerly endorsed the plan, one of only three places in Alaska, and were ready to throw their doors wide open to the potential newcomers from Europe.

But it didn't happen. Among American Jews, only the Labor Zionists supported it. Rabbi Stephen Wise, president of the American Jewish Congress and the leading American Jewish spokesman of the day, declared that the Slattery Plan would give people the "wrong and hurtful" idea that "Jews were taking over some part of the country for settlement." Numerous anti-Semites went further and called the plan a Trojan horse, which would allow Jewish Marxists to sneak into the country. For his part, FDR kept the plan under wraps and privately declared that only a maximum of ten thousand people a year should enter the United States under Slattery and that there be a subquota of a maximum of one thousand Jews a year in that group. Thus, the Slattery Plan died without ever seeing the light of day; and Seward, although willing, did not become the Jerusalem of the North. However, the plan did win some support from the Federal Council of Churches and the American Friends Service. Five years later, in August 1944, the United States settled just under a thousand Jews in Fort Ontario near Oswego, New York. It was the only rescue settlement conducted by the American government during the Holocaust while "Jewish quotas" generally were not met.

The United States, FDR, and the American Jewish community all failed miserably to rescue Jews during the Holocaust. That discussion is beyond the scope of this weekly message. However, in the years after WWII, the United States, at the urging of Representative Emanuel Celler (D-NY), did admit over six hundred thousand Holocaust survivors and, by the mid-1960s, overhauled its basic immigration policies. In our own day, too many xenophobic Americans seek to reclose the doors to this country. It seems as if we have learned little since the second Seward Folly, except that there are places in this country like Seward, Alaska, that have met the gold standard of humanitarianism when the chips were down and could have—should have—changed the course of history.

Shabbat Shalom.

HUDDLED MASSES: SANCTUARY FOR AFGHANS IN AMERICA

August 25, 2021

We all saw it. Again. Nearly seven hundred Afghans packed into a C-17 on August 15, 2021, sitting on the aircraft's floor and hoping the giant plane could get on the only working runway in Kabul even as the tarmac was swelling with thousands of their fellow citizens fleeing from the Taliban.

Unfortunately, we have seen it before. A helicopter perched on a tower in Saigon on April 29, 1975, with scores of people trying to get on the aircraft to flee from the victorious communists. American military and foreign policy in ruin and reduced to a tiny perimeter protected by a thin line of indescribably courageous Marines.

These are moments of defeat etched in our mind, which also should remind us that our national humanitarian obligations to our friends, supporters, and collaborators continue despite the horrendous failures of some of our international programs and policies. These moments also remind us of the need for a sane, humane immigration policy, which re-lights the torch of liberty and the obligation to receive huddled masses with open arms.

Today, the United States is a country of over 330 million people of whom about 45 million are immigrants. We have more immigrants per capita than any other country in the world, perhaps with the exception of Israel, which was built on the Zionist dream of a worldwide return of the Jewish people to their ancient homeland. For American immigrants, it is a dream of going to a new homeland unevenly dedicated to the absorption and advancement of its immigrant population.

I was unable to find exactly how many immigrants have come to the United States since July 4, 1776. We did not even keep records of newly arriving immigrants until 1850 at which point there were 2.2 million immigrants in a country of twenty-three million people of whom 3.2 million people were slaves. The largest immigrant group in the United States today is Mexican (11 million), followed by Chinese (2.9 million), and Indian (2.6 million).

Because of multiple factors including immigration, the percentage of white Americans has been dropping steadily for decades. In 1950, nearly 90 percent of Americans were white. As recently as 1980, the white population constituted 60 percent of the national total. Within three decades or less, the majority of Americans will no longer be of European origin.

We can see the changes taking place before our own eyes. When we (the Sussmans) moved to Elkins Park in 2001, I was struck by the large number of Koreans in our area. Nationally, there are about 1.8 million Korean Americans. Near the area where we now live in Center City, Philadelphia, there are also a large number of Vietnamese Americans. Their national total exceeds two million and like with Korean Americans, their move to America was directly tied to American foreign policy.

What about Jewish immigration to America? In this area, we mostly think about the Great Migration of 1880 to 1920, which brought two million Jews to the United States. However, Jewish immigration to the United States is not just a thing of the past. After the Holocaust, about 600,000 Jewish survivors sought refuge in the United States. Today there are also about 500,000 Soviet Jews in this country. There are also about 140,000 Israeli American Jews and another 170,000 American Jews who have at least one Israeli parent, not to mention new Jewish arrivals in America from Colombia, Iran, and South Africa. Indeed, both immigration and Orthodox fecundity are helping to grow the American Jewish communities today.

Now we are looking at the arrival of Afghans (although many are seeking refuge in other countries). Afghans first arrived in the United States in the 1860s but did not receive protected status until the twenty-first century. Right now, given the chaos in Kabul, only a few thousand Afghans have been able to escape. Those numbers will surely grow; and it is possible, in my opinion, that we will have as many as two hundred thousand Afghans here in the United States within a few years, not a huge number by historical American standards.

Not surprisingly, none of them will be Jewish as there are basically no Jews left in Afghanistan, although there are about ten thousand Afghan Jews in Israel. Years ago, I attended an Afghan synagogue in Jerusalem for Purim but did not learn much about their community. As Americans, we are going to learn more about Afghan life and culture in the next few years. America has a tremendous capacity to absorb immigrants, especially immigrants who are well-established friends and supporters of the United States.

At this time, we need to get people safely to the Kabul airport, planes in the air, and valid visas into the hands of our friends and their families. After that, who knows? There will be complex questions about resistance in Afghanistan; Afghanistan as a global center for terrorism; and the fate of the people of Afghanistan, men, women and children. Our dangerous world just became a little darker; and we need to remain strong, courageous, and humane when the chips are down and we are still holding some of the best cards in the deck.

Shabbat Shalom.

In Situ: A View of The Landau Windows from the Pulpit of Reform Congregation Keneseth Israel

2021

During the job interview process that brought me to the pulpit of Reform Congregation Keneseth Israel in Elkins Park, Pennsylvania, one of the themes I constantly heard from congregational representatives was "the windows." "You have to see the windows at the end of Yom Kippur," I was regularly told. "They are beautiful." Sure enough, at the end of my first High Holy Day season in 2001, the sunlight came pouring through the Landau windows in the KI sanctuary, transforming the entire room into a golden sacred space. It was, indeed, beautiful and, biblically speaking, "awesome"!

However, my first experience of the windows on Yom Kippur also awoke a different more complex emotion in me. There was something wrong in the congregants' reports about the beauty of the windows. Were the windows really meant to be beautiful? Were the prophets beautiful? Is the prophetic quest a beautiful message, or is it something else? As a Religious Studies major at Franklin and Marshall College and then again as a rabbinic and graduate student at the Hebrew Union College–Jewish Institute of Religion (Cincinnati), I had been taught that the prophets were challenging, troubling, disturbing, and unsettling—that they were the epitome of good preaching both "afflicting the comfortable and comforting the afflicted." Maybe from a lofty metaphysical point of view, they were "beautiful" but not in any normal aesthetic sense of the meaning of "beauty."

I began to wonder if my congregants' views of the windows were beside the point. That they were confusing the ornamental aspect of the windows with their deeper message, that they saw the windows as the historical completion of their sanctuary (built in 1957 with frosted windows) as a monumental beautification project, not as a set of provocative, upsetting, and teleologically inspiring statements by the artist-prophet Jacob Landau.

Naturally, given my own background as a rabbi and a historian, I decided to learn more about Landau himself and the window project. It immediately became clear to me that there was more to the windows than a sanctuary art project. I knew the prophets had a message. The question became "What was Landau's message?" A second question for me involved how the synagogue leadership and the Senior Rabbi Bertram W. Korn understand Landau's message and, ultimately, "how did the windows reflect the theology of American Reform Judaism in the early 1970s?"

After approximately two years of research, I began to form my conclusions about the worldview of the Landau windows, and they were startling. First, they are essentially secular and humanistic and not inherently religious. Second, with respect to Reform Judaism, they are an historical bookend, almost anachronistic, in their treatment of prophetic Judaism. Third, they are a modernist heresy and codify critical biblical theory. Fourth, they are bibliocentric and barely refer to the rabbinic tradition. Fifth, they are uninfluenced by Herschel's landmark, *The Prophets* (1962), the most important late-twentieth-century Jewish interpretation of ancient Israel's prophets, and, finally, in both American and Jewish ways ultimately affirm the idea of progress and reaffirming a belief in hope in the future! In short, their historical specificity as a 1970s statement about Reform Judaism, not their lucent afternoon colors, became my primary way of relating to them.

My first order of business was to research the life and art of Jacob Landau. Although born Jewish, Landau did not demonstrate any interest in Jewish themes in his art until 1968 when he illustrated the cover of Albert H. Friedlander's *Out of the Whirlwind: A Reader of Holocaust Literature* for the press of the Reform movement in Judaism. By contrast, his friend, neighbor, and colleague Ben Shahn, who was of an equally humanist bent, was recruited by the American Jewish community fourteen years earlier when it celebrated its tercentenary in 1954. When Keneseth Israel failed to recruit Marc Chagall to its stained-glass window project, it turned to Landau—conveniently located in nearby Roosevelt, New Jersey—and a partnership was forged.

The theme agreed upon for the project, The Prophetic Quest, was anything but avant-garde or daring. Although Keneseth Israel had distinguished itself during the American Civil War as an abolitionist congregation, it subsequently became known for its anti-Zionism and largely sat out the tumultuous years of the Civil Rights movement and the Vietnam War. In addition to his work at the synagogue, Rabbi Korn, who served Keneseth Israel from 1949 to 1979, was a Rear Admiral in the United States Navy and eschewed the protest movements of the day. A theological liberal, he neither challenged Reform Judaism as "Prophetic Judaism" nor embraced the "death of God" theology of some of his more radical colleagues. By the early Seventies, it was broadly accepted that Reform was slipping into a kind of malaise, no longer tightly connected to its past self-definition as Jewish Ethical Monotheism and not yet redefined by a mix of neotraditionalism and feminism.

To ground himself in the literature of the Hebrew prophets, Landau surprisingly turned to Martin Buber and his classic 1949 study, *The Prophetic Faith*. Buber, who generally held more sway among Christian theologians than Jewish thinkers, seeks to recover the existential reality of the prophets and their dialogical encounter with the God of Israel.

By contrast, for the more fully humanistic Landau, identifying prophetic themes and tying them to contemporaneous issues was paramount. For Buber, God quested to confront Ancient Israel through the prophets in a specific time and place. For Landau, the prophets' quest was to confront us in our time and our place, literally, our worship.

In many ways, the downward turned hand at the top of the Abraham window is the most important image in the Landau windows. Justice, the ultimate prophetic quest, is ultimately a human quest to Landau, not a divinely commanded goal. Anticipating a later pivot on the Book of Job, the windows are not about questioning God but about trying to discover the highest human aspirations. Like Buber, Landau remained a Hebrew humanist and embraced the challenges of the prophets both for Ancient Israel and for humanity in modern times. In so doing, he made the window project his own "prophet quest," perhaps memorialized in the fusion of his own face with that of the prophet Elijah in the final window.

The most usable image in the Landau windows in my experience is found in the bottom panel of the Amos window. In it, Landau depicts a modern band playing so loudly that *we* cannot hear the prophet's urgent message. One of the band members is shown holding a green electric guitar. Invariably, I begin my tours of the windows by asking new viewers of the windows, especially younger visitors, to find that guitar. As soon as they find it, the windows open for them. I quickly redirect them to the top of the window and the large image of the lion roaring out the prophet's message of justice. At this point, depending on the age of the visitors, I tell them about how the synagogue's Board objected to the ferocity of Landau's lion and insisted he make it smaller. I can only imagine the artist cringing in his effort to compromise with synagogue leadership.

In other windows, Landau clearly pushed the envelope with synagogue leadership. Jewish ceremonial art is highly respectful of the principle of *tzniut* or modesty. Not so, Landau. Both in the Hosea and Jeremiah windows, male and female nudity—breasts and a penis—are displayed following the biblical texts. In this regard, the artist follows the prophets in challenging everyday sensibilities and smashes social convention with impunity.

The bottom of the First Isaiah window contains a second artistic challenge to conservative social convention. To illustrate the discord among the nations, Landau included the flags of the nations including the Soviet Union and Red China. Imagine, in the waning days of the Cold and Vietnam Wars, a synagogue agrees to display in perpetuity the flags of America's communist enemies! Equally sensational was the decision to embed the Israeli flag in the same display. At the time, only the American flag was displayed in the sanctuary of Keneseth Israel, a silent echo of the congregation's pre-1948 anti-Jewish statehood views. In fact, an actual Israeli flag was not installed in the sanctuary until 2002. The other muted reference to Israel in the windows is the weapons being held upward at the top of the Ezekiel window, which, despite its depiction of the Valley of Dry Bones, is not explicit in terms of a Holocaust reference.

Viewing the Landau windows in situ necessitates comment on the Ark in the Keneseth Israel sanctuary. Depicting the life of Moses in gild, the panels were originally fabricated in 1938 for the synagogue's previous temple on North Broad Street at Columbia in North Philadelphia. Designed to "stand alone," the panels now can be seen as part of a broader statement about the supremacy of the prophecy of Moses in the Jewish tradition. Moreover, Landau chose "gold" to represent the divine in his windows at Keneseth Israel. The combination of the Ark and windows in the sanctuary are seamless and powerful. The last window, Malachi, is a statement about the future and boldly modern in its depiction of great skyscrapers. It speaks to a kind of faith in progress untempered by the disasters of the twentieth century and highlights the concluding passage of the Hebrew Bible that the ultimate source of peace is domestic tranquility. The window, like the prophet, merges the personal and the societal with ease and leaves the viewer in awe of the project's majesty and filled with hope.

Finally, a word about what is not in the Landau windows. Had he worked on the same project even five years later, it would be hard to imagine how he could not have included at least one of Israel's female prophets. Buber, in particular, pays a great deal of attention to the prophet Deborah. The windows have few references to rabbinic Judaism and perhaps none to Jewish mysticism. Of course, the late-twentieth-century neotraditionalism of the Reform movement was just beginning to assert itself in the early 1970s. However, the fullness and complexity of the windows as created by Landau are powerful, not only because they are spectacular and beautiful but also because they are truly prophetic.

They speak truth in defiance of social convention. They affirm. They challenge. They inspire, and in the golden light of a Yom Kippur afternoon, they sanctify.

What's in a Name? Thoughts on Jewish Identity

November 17, 2021

This week's Torah portion, *Vayishlach* (Gen. 32:4), includes the story of Jacob's name becoming Israel. Basically, Jacob was returning from years of flight from his brother, Esau. The night before they met, Jacob wrestled with an angel who wounded him in the leg and renamed him Israel or "one who has struggled with God and life and prevailed." The name Israel subsequently became the name of an ancient Jewish kingdom; the entire Jewish people; and, since 1948, the modern Jewish state. In the Talmud, a Jew is called Israel.

In fact, Jews have had many different names. Originally, according to the Bible, our ancestors were Hebrews as in the primary language of the Jewish tradition. Today, we still have the Hebrew University of Jerusalem and the Hebrew Union College–Jewish Institute of Religion, to mention a few. The original Hebrew family expanded into a system of tribes of which only one survived the ancient world, the tribe of Judah, which is the basis of the word Judaism and, etymologically speaking, the word Jew.

In the nineteenth century in the English-speaking world, the name Jew was often avoided by Jews as it carried a negative connotation and was even considered a verb as in "to Jew someone," implying immoral business practices. Instead, Jews self-described as Hebrews (Union of American Hebrew Congregations, founded 1875); Israelites (as in Cincinnati's Jewish weekly paper, The *American Israelite*); and even compound names like people of the Mosaic Persuasion, oy vey! There are, of course, parallel-group name shifts in the African America experience (e.g., Negro, Black, Afro-American, etc.)

Although there was a New York–based Jewish newspaper as early as the 1820s called The *Jew*, the term Jew or Jewish did not come into play until the arrival of Yiddish-speaking East European Jews in the 1880s who referred to themselves as Yiddin, or Yid in the singular, based on the German Jude and Juden (plural). By the twentieth century in English-speaking countries, the term Jew became widely accepted both inside and outside of the Jewish community. Of course, in other languages, there are different names for Jews like Ebreo in Italian, Judio in Spanish, and Juif in French.

Within the Jewish community, there are many subsets of different types of Jews. In Israel, for example, there are Hiloni (secular Jews) and Dati (religious Jews). There are also subethnic groups like Ethiopian, Italian, Sephardi, Mizrachi, and Ashkenazi. Among Ashkenazic Jews, Jews of German origin are called Yeki (literally, *jacket*, implying formality in socio-cultural practice); and, of course, there are denominational names like Reform, Conservative, Reconstructionist, Renewal, and Orthodox. Among the Orthodox, there are Modern, Yeshivish, Hasidish, and Sephardi, to mention a few.

In other words, it is basically inadequate to simply call a person Just Jewish because there are so many types of Jewish people today. That is why I find it somewhat bemusing that there is a significant and growing number of American Jews today who are called Just Jewish. In my opinion, there is no such thing as Just Jewish. Most of these folks are unaffiliated-Ashkenazic Jews, some are agnostic-atheist, and others are spiritual. Some are highly acculturated "American Jews," just one step away from assimilation or total loss of Jewish identity; but then, remarkably, they become "of Jewish ancestry." On the other side, there are also Jews by Choice and Jews of Color, both of whom are increasing in size in the Jewish world today.

What's more important than the label Jewish is the content of Jewishness and the relationship of Jews to their collective past and collective future. One sociologist, Leonard Saxe at Brandeis, understands that Jewishness is best described (and measured) in terms of engagement, not by external labels. For example, his data shows that "mixed married" can actually be correlated in many cases with increased, not decreased, involvement. It is all very complex and challenging.

Ultimately, as a synagogue, we need to be as mission-specific as possible in helping our members become engaged, educated, and energized in their Jewishness. Membership is critical; active membership is the goal. So let us try to move beyond Just Jewish and shift to "engaged Jewish" or "Jewish"! Both the spiritual and cultural qualities of our lives, not to mention our collective future, are on the line. Just Jewish is just not good enough. Together, we can create a meaningful Jewish way of life woven into an active, inclusive Jewish community of our own making. Then, indeed, we will become the New Israel, those who have struggled and prevailed.

Shabbat Shalom.

Anti-Semitism and the Taking of Hostages: A Tragic and Undeniable History

January 19, 2022

The Torah portion for this week, *Yitro*, includes the story of the giving of the Ten Commandments. It is not well-known that in Jewish law, the Eighth Commandment, "You shall not steal," is actually understood to be a prohibition against kidnapping. While this interpretation goes all the way back to the Talmud (c. 200–400 CE, v. Sanhedrin 86a), it is most clearly stated by the great medieval commentator Rashi (1036–1105), who simply notes that the prohibition on stealing in the Ten Commandments "is speaking about a case of one who steals human beings." While the command in Leviticus 19:11, again "You shall not steal," is about stealing money (or property), the rabbis made the distinction based on the premise that there are no redundancies in the Torah.

"Stealing a person" or kidnapping, abduction, and hostage taking are all serious crimes; and all have played a significant role in the tragic long history of anti-Semitism. For that reason, it is most unfortunate that in light of last week's hostage incident in Texas that the FBI concluded that the synagogue's hostage taker's demands were "not specifically related to the Jewish community." In fact, both in this case and historically speaking, the use, or should we say abuse, of the Jewish community by the "stealing of Jewish people" is specifically and intentionally anti-Semitic. Indeed, both the hostage taker and the prisoner he was seeking to free are both flagrant anti-Semites.

Taking Jews as hostages has a long and terrible history, so much so that we even refer to "people stealing" in our daily prayers. The central part of the Jewish service is variously called the *Amidah* (standing prayer), *Tefillah* (the prayer) or the *Sh'moneh Esreih* (the Eighteen Benedictions). It begins with the familiar homage to our founding ancestors (*avot*) and continues in blessing two (*Atah Gibor*) with a praise of God as the One "who frees the captives [*Umatir Asurim*]." Obviously, only a long and bitter experience would have resulted in including such a terrible reference in our daily Jewish devotions including Shabbat.

In fact, "freeing the captive" is considered to be a leading mitzvah in the Jewish tradition known as *Pidyon Shvuyim*, or "freeing the captives." Historically, the entire Jewish community was frequently called upon to seek the release of Jews captured by criminals, slave dealers, and unjust government authorities. Maimonides (1138–1204) wrote, "The redeeming of captives takes precedence over supporting or clothing the poor [and that] there is no greater mitzvah than redeeming captives." To anchor his opinion, Maimonides cites numerous verses from the Torah including "Love your neighbor as yourself" (Lev. 19:18) and "Do not stand idly by the blood of your neighbor" (Lev. 19:16).

The freeing of captives also provides the back story to one of the most important and haunting of our High Holy Day prayers: *"Un'taneh Tokef"* ("Let us speak of the awesomeness of this day"). Its authorship is ascribed by tradition to Rabbi Amnon of Mainz who, in the eleventh century, refused to convert to Christianity on pain of death. Before he died, he was severely tortured and dismembered yet urged his Jewish community not to pay a ransom to save his life. According to legend, Amnon appeared in a vision to Rabbi Kalonymus ben Meshullam three days after his death and urged his colleague to write down the words of his final prayer, *"Un'taneh Tokef."* Its majestic and haunting music and probing words remain a highlight of both Rosh HaShanah and Yom Kippur. Thus, the freeing of captives as a legacy of medieval anti-Semitism remains a powerful memory in the collective Jewish experience.

Unfortunately, there are also numerous modern stories of the kidnaping, ransoming and hostage taking of Jews. For example, the story of the kidnapping of Edgardo Mortara from his home in Bologna in 1857 to be forcibly baptized as a Catholic had a galvanizing impact on the world Jewish community, especially here in the United States. The child was never returned to his family. Nearly a hundred years later during the Holocaust, numerous attempts were made in Greece, Hungary, and Slovakia, among other places, to ransom Jewish lives from the Nazis, mostly to little avail.

Two hostage incidents in Israel represent strikingly different responses to the challenges of P*idyon Shvuyim*. First was Operation Entebbe, which saw the remarkable special operations rescue of over two hundred hostages, held by the Popular Front for the Liberation of Palestine in Uganda in July 1976. By contrast, all of us also remember the capture of a young Israeli soldier Gilad Shalit during an attack near Gaza on June 25, 2006, by Hamas. Years later, on October 11, 2011, with the surprising help of the government of Turkey, Shalit was released in exchange for 1,027 Hamas and Palestinian prisoners as authorized by Prime Minister Benjamin Netanyahu and President Shimon Peres of Israel. At the time, polls indicated that 79 percent of the Israeli public approved of the deal. Not surprisingly, the question of negotiating with terrorists remains highly controversial in Israel and around the world to this day. Sadly, the need to confront the realities of hostage taking remains constant.

Fortunately, in the most recent incident, a positive outcome was achieved, thanks to excellent police work and broad government and interfaith cooperation. Rabbi Charlie Cytron-Walker and his congregants from Congregation Beth Israel in Colleyville, Texas, not only survived but also were physically unharmed. Ironically, Rabbi Charlie, as he is affectionately known, is much beloved not only by his own congregants but also by local Muslims with whom he forged warm personal relations as well as with the local Christian community.

In late breaking news, it is a relief that the FBI finally reclassified the incident at Colleyville as an act of anti-Semitism just as the government of Great Britain did immediately when the hostages were first taken. Indeed, it was classical anti-Semitism at its worst. The Bureau needed to change its policies for the sake of both accuracy and deterrence. For our part, we need to remember that despite our deepest wishes to be an open and welcoming congregation, we must remain vigilant in providing for the security and well-being of our members and guests at Keneseth Israel and, even more importantly, remain active and personally present in our practice of our wonderful Jewish tradition. As the concluding verse of "*Adon Olam*" reassures us, "*Adonai ii v'lo ira*. The Eternal One is with me, and I shall not fear."

Shabbat Shalom.

IN THE CROSSHAIRS OF HISTORY: THE JEWS OF UKRAINE

February 16, 2022

Ukraine is in the news. Daily reports pour in about the buildup of Russian troops, as many as 130,000, to the north, east, and south of the country. Diplomatic activity is also escalating but without a clear path to resolving the situation. NATO is on alert. Ukrainian civilians are beginning to train militia-style to resist a possible invasion. Worst of all are the projections of massive casualties, especially if the capital city of Kiev is attacked. It is a "night of watching" for Ukraine.

In the middle of this storm is Ukraine's Jewish community; and remarkably, although only one hundred thousand Ukrainians are Jews at this moment, the president of the country, Volodymyr Zelenskyy, is Jewish and publicly embraces his identity. Few countries, including the United States, can make that claim. Eight decades ago, members of the Zelenskyy family were murdered during the Holocaust and others fought in the Red Army.

Another surprising fact about the Ukrainian Jewish heritage is that the story of *Fiddler on the Roof* actually took place in Ukraine, not in Russia. At the end of the nineteenth century, Ukraine was in the Pale of Settlement, a vast area established by the czars to quarantine Jews along the western border of the vast Russian Empire. The Pale included not only Ukraine but also Poland and other large centers of Jewish population. Indeed, the territory of the Pale was the site of the largest population in the world until the Shoah.

Today, it is difficult to know exactly how many Jews live in Ukraine, perhaps one hundred thousand down considerably from four hundred thousand before the massive waves of Jewish immigration at the end of the twentieth century. Currently, Ukraine has the fourth largest Jewish community in Europe following France, Great Britain, and Russia but ahead or equal to Germany. Included in that Ukrainian Jewish population are thousands of Israelis as well as Hasidim, mostly Bratslavers, who have returned to their original villages south of Kiev to be near the grave of their Rebbes where they have reestablished Yiddish-speaking communities. Yes, you read that correctly, as crazy as it may sound. There literally are new shtetls in "the old country."

Historians speculate that Jews have lived in the Ukraine since the eighth century and the conversion of Khazars (to the east) to Judaism. Some researchers speculate that Jews were involved in the founding of Kiev itself. By 1648, the Jewish population of Ukraine, then part of Poland, was massive; and as many as 20,000 Jewish civilians (revised from earlier estimates of as high as 250,000) were killed during the Khmelnytsky Cossack Uprising, 1648–1655. One hundred years later, the Hasidic movement in Judaism started among Ukrainian Jews in villages to the south and west of Kiev and quickly spread across much of East Europe. In 1791, the Pale was established on the western edge of the Russian Empire to contain (geographically) the country's vast Jewish population. The region's culturally rich Jewish life is featured in the literary work of the great Yiddish writer Sholem Aleichem (1859–1916). Subsequently, both czars and Soviets targeted Ukraine for Jewish settlement as part of their respective south Russia policies.

Long caught in the crosshairs of history, Ukraine's Jewish population suffered terribly during the pogroms of the late nineteenth century, which led to massive Jewish immigration, principally to the United States. They also sparked the development of the Zionist movement. Odessa became a leading port city for early Zionist pioneers on their way to Turkish Palestine, some of whom trained in Jewish agricultural schools in that region. They went on to help create some of the original kibbutzim. My guess is that as many as 40 percent of Philadelphia's Jews by 1920 came to the City of Brotherly Love from Ukraine and constituted the area's largest Jewish subethnicity.

Subsequently, Ukrainian Jews were again caught in the crossfire of history during the Russian Revolution and the bloody wars, which followed until the founding of the Soviet Union in 1922, five years after the Bolsheviks first sought to overthrow the czar. Soviet Communists then worked to destroy all religious expressions of Judaism in the USSR and control the nature of secular Jewish, mostly Yiddish, culture in their country. In the early 1930s, Stalin's policies of collectivization and political suppression led to the complete failure of the Ukrainian agricultural sector and led to millions of deaths by starvation. During this period known as the Holodomor, Jews increasingly left their villages in Ukraine to look for food and work in the larger cities, intensifying the region's native anti-Semitism.

But the worst was yet to come. In 1942, the Nazis broke their non-aggression treaty with Russia and launched Operation Barbarossa, the largest military operation in history, to create "living space" for Germany in the east and seize the area's rich natural resources. SS Einsatzgruppen followed the German Army and slaughtered as many as one million Ukrainian Jews in mass shootings, including the massacre at Babi Yar in September 1942. Knowledge of Babi Yar was suppressed by the Communists who ruled Ukraine until 1991 and the fall of the Soviet Union.

Since independence, Ukraine has witnessed both massive emigration and a revival of Judaism although most of the country's Jews, who are Russian speakers, are secular. Today there are large Jewish community centers in Ukraine, thirty-some Chabad houses, and other Hasidic communities. The Reform movement in Judaism claims that as many as fourteen thousand Ukrainian Jews identify with it. Reports from Ukraine suggest that the country's Jewish population plans to remain in place as the drama with Russia and a potential military invasion unfolds. Whatever happens, Ukrainian Jews again find themselves caught in the crosshairs of history. As Tevye the Milkman said in *Fiddler*, "May God be with them." Shabbat Shalom.

Spiritual Roadmap: The Hidden Battle for the Soul of Reform Judaism

March 31, 2022

During the last month or so, while our eyes and thoughts have been trained on the war in Ukraine, another battle, a hidden battle, has also been raging over the future of America Reform Judaism. This is not a battle over territory or a war fought with tanks and missiles. It is a silent spiritual struggle, which will determine the future of the Reform movement in America. It is largely a battle being fought in the hidden recesses of the Internet, in Zoom meetings and electronic petitions, but it is a battle nevertheless.

At the surface level, it is about the future of the Cincinnati campus, the original site of the Hebrew Union College–Jewish Institute of Religion (HUC-JIR), established in 1875 by Rabbi Isaac Mayer Wise. But in a larger sense, it is a battle about the shape and nature of Reform Judaism in the twenty-first century. The original Hebrew Union College was founded to train rabbis of all theological flavors for the nineteenth century. In time, it became the flagship of American Reform Judaism and, ultimately, the intellectual anchor for Progressive Judaism and general Jewish scholarship around the world.

No, I am not saying that the "word of the eternal" shall go forth prophetically from Cincinnati, only that two of the greatest and most precious Jewish and American Jewish research institutions in the history of the Jewish people—the Klau Library, with over five hundred thousand volumes and fourteen thousand rare Jewish books, and the American

Jewish Archives, with over ten million pages of documentation—were planted and nurtured and stand on the Cincinnati campus of HUC-JIR. Neither cost nor law will allow them to move elsewhere. Either they remain the premier gardens of Jewish research and intellectual activity tended to by a living community of scholars and students, or they become lifeless warehouses of antiquarian remains.

The administration of HUC-JIR and its Board of Governors have fiduciary responsibilities. That is undeniable. But the future of Reform Judaism, the real issue at hand, cannot be solved by a business plan. It needs a spiritual roadmap planned and provided for by all the institutions of liberal Judaism working together for a transcendent cause. We are at an inflection point in our history as a movement. Although we have impressive pockets of strength in the Reform movement, we are undeniably demographically challenged. We are also challenged by a rising generation that is creating new and unprecedented expressions of Judaism outside the boundaries of congregational and denominational life. Affiliation is shrinking. Jewish identity and spirituality are morphing. Communication inside the Jewish community—indeed, inside the human community—is changing. Downsizing a campus or shuttering a graduate program will not meet the spiritual challenges of the moment or the future.

The true business of Judaism is not to be found in a ledger but in the Jewish heart. The Jewish heart in America is still beating, but it is increasingly nurtured and sustained by a different cultural diet than in the past. We need twenty-first-century rabbis. We need twenty-first-century cantors and educators. We need twenty-first-century lay leaders and twenty-first-century congregants or stakeholders or *chaverim* (members). We need American Judaisms for every region of the vast complex North American continent and not just select metropolitan areas.

The American Jewish heart yearns to sing a Jewish song. The Jewish heart yearns to mourn with an authentic Jewish cry. A Jewish child still wants to stand in front of the Torah as much or more than they want a party eighty minutes later because they already know that eighty years after their final aliyah, they want to stand next to their Jewish grandchildren, children who will be of every complexion, and say that they too once stood at Sinai in their youth and in the fullness of their years.

A business plan for the Reform seminary, no matter how good, will never chart that path for us. Only a serious, sustained, collective, transparent conversation about what makes the Jewish heart beat true can be our path. Moses did not know the route of the Exodus. He only knew the "short path" was not the way. Traveling together, receiving the tradition of Torah together, making mistakes together, and arriving at the border of the Promised Land together is what our ancestors once did and what we too must do. Step by uncertain step, let us find our way out of the wilderness, break the old idols, and embrace the spirit of an ancient living religious tradition with a new song and a new heart!

Shabbat Shalom.

FROM NOW ON, NO DISTINCTION

The Reform Advocate
April 7, 2022

During the last fifty years, it has become typical, if not fashionable, to assess the changing role of women in Reform Judaism in terms of their roles as religious and congregational leaders. In fact, the struggle to incorporate women as stakeholders in the governance and public representation of Judaism's most progressive branch was preceded by a century-long process of redefining women as the religious equals of men in Reform Judaism. Indeed, Reform Judaism itself began with the full inclusion of Jewish girls and women in pediatric Jewish education which was, in turn, followed by a systematic reevaluation of the religious role of women in Judaism. Interestingly, Reform both generated its own paths in redefining the religious status of women and seized on external modernizing trends during the nineteenth century. Subsequently, the "public sphere" of Reform Jewish women was redefined again but this time in response to the external influences of feminism and Progressivism on Reform Judaism. By contrast, earlier religious reforms concerning women were largely products of nineteenth century "modern" or "liberal" religion.

It is interesting to note that even those forces within Reform Judaism that were resistant to the full religious equality of women generally emphasized the Jewish tradition's high esteem of female spirituality. For example, in prefacing his remarks against the ordination of women in 1922, Rabbi Dr. Jacob Z. Lauterbach (1873–1942), a professor at the Hebrew Union College (HUC), included an extended apologia which echoed the

American Cult of Domesticity in praise of women's spirituality. "Indeed," he noted, "the Rabbis of old entertained a high opinion of womanhood and frequently expressed their admiration for woman's ability and appreciated her great usefulness in religious work." "Thus," he continued, "they say: 'God has endowed woman with a finer appreciation and a better understanding than man' (Nidda 45b), 'Sarah was superior to Abraham in prophecy' (Tanchuma Exodus beginning), 'It was due to the pious women of that generation that the Israelites were redeemed from Egypt' (Sota 11b), and 'The women were the first ones to receive and accept the Torah' (Tanchuma Buber, Metsora 18, p.27a)." However, praise, even hyperbolic flattery, is not the same as equality, and it is important to note that Reform Judaism, with its emergence onto the stage of history, immediately began to take practical, if not revolutionary, steps toward emancipating women within Judaism. For example, the year after the first public Jewish and all-male Confirmation service at Israel Jacobson's Seesen Temple in 1810, girls were included in the 1811 ceremony at Seesen. A rationale for the Confirmation of girls was first offered by Isaac Asher Francolm (1788–1849), a German Reform educator and contemporary of Jacobson. There should be, he argued for the first time, a "significant landmark in the life of boys and girls which consists of the knowledge of religion, they have achieved, that is, when they have finished their education ... Such an act ... was not customary in rabbinic tradition. It is something new, but it is in the spirit of Judaism." Thereafter, coeducational Confirmation quickly became the norm in Reform Judaism on both sides of the Atlantic and became the basis for "reforming" Jewish womanhood. It could even be said that on a gender basis, Confirmation was a revolution in Jewish history. It is important to note that early in its history, Confirmation *per se* was not strictly limited to Reform congregations, although the Reform movement did create Jewish Confirmation. Moreover, there were "special events" in which men and women sang together in synagogue both in Europe and the United States early in the 19th century, which were not limited to Reform congregations. Writing in her classic work, *Beyond the Synagogue Gallery: Finding a Place for Women in American Judaism* (2009), Karla Goldman reports that "mixed choirs performed at the dedication ceremonies of both the 1818 Mill Street Synagogue in New York and the 1825 Mikveh Israel synagogue in Philadelphia ... the regular presence of mixed choirs of men and women became a requisite part of such ceremonies, even for the most traditional acculturated congregations." However, Reform synagogues ultimately fully embraced mixed choirs as part of their religious culture, whereas more traditional congregations resisted the practice and reestablished the traditional belief that "the voice of a woman is a sin" and resorted to male-only singing.

The first flowering of Reform Judaism in the United States took place in Charleston, South Carolina in 1824. Triggered by a combination of local circumstances and news of an emerging Reform movement in Germany, a group of young local Jews formed the Reformed Society of Israelites (RSI). Led by Isaac Harby (1788–1828) and Abraham Moise (1799–1869), the RSI produced an original prayer book and plans for a Confirmation service. Included in their proposed worship were hymns written by Abraham's sister. Penina Moise (1797–1880) was prolific. In 1833, she published *Fancy's Sketch-Book*, the first collection of poems written by an American Jewish woman. Penina wrote a total of 190 hymns for her home congregation, Beth Elohim, of which over a dozen were included in the Reform movement's *Union Hymnal*. Moise was also a teacher in Beth Elohim's Sunday School.

The idea that women could serve as teachers of Judaism to young children actually came from outside of Reform Judaism. Influenced by the earlier theories of Swiss educational Reformer Johann Heinrich Pestalozzi (1646–1727) and contemporaneously by American educator Catharine Beecher (1800–1878), Rebecca Gratz (1781–1869) opened the first Hebrew Sunday School in Philadelphia in 1838 taught by women teachers, some of whom also authored their own textbooks. Gratz, it should be noted, was a devoted member of a Sephardic Orthodox congregation, Mikveh Israel. The Gratz Sunday School model, originally pan-denominational, was entirely led by women. It quickly gained traction in the American Jewish community and was widely adopted by Reform congregations. Even more than in the parallel German Jewish schools, the student body was co-educational from the beginning.

In early Reform Judaism in Germany, men and women continued to sit separately in prayer services. The idea of mixed seating, an American Reform adaptation, actually came about accidentally and not initially for ideological reasons. During *Rosh HaShanah* services in Albany, New York in 1850, a physical fight literally erupted between the President of the congregation, Louis Spanier, and its rabbi, Isaac Mayer Wise (1819–1900), the founder of the Reform movement in Judaism in America. Wise was compelled to leave his pulpit and started a new synagogue, Anshe

Emeth, where he remained until moving to Cincinnati in 1854. Under his leadership, Anshe Emeth was able to purchase a former Baptist church equipped with family pews. When Wise's congregation moved into their new digs, families, meaning men, women, and children, all sat together. In 1854, New York's Congregation Emanu-El adopted the same practice and mixed seating then quickly became the norm in American Reform Judaism. Thus, in the years prior to the Civil War, boys and girls and men and women sat, prayed, and studied together in American Reform "shuls" and schools.

Beyond worship and education, another area concerning women's religious status in early Reform Judaism involved weddings, marriage, and divorce. Already in 1810, when his Temple opened in Seesen, Germany, Israel Jacobson streamlined the traditional Aramaic *Ketubah* and rendered it into German. Later, the Reform movement provided for the bride to present the groom with a ring during the wedding ceremony and stating her own vow as a way of symbolizing equality and mutuality in Reform Jewish marriage and lessening the emphasis on the economic and business aspects of arranging marital unions. Previously, as part of the *Ketubah*, only the groom presented the bride with a ring. In 1869, at a conference of American Reform rabbis in Philadelphia, it was resolved that "a judgment of divorce pronounced by a civil court has full validity, also in the eyes of Judaism, if the court documents reveal that both parties to the marriage agreed to the divorce." By contrast, to this day, the problem of the *agunah* ("chained wife"), whose recalcitrant husband refuses to offer a get or Jewish writ of divorce, remains highly problematic in the Orthodox community.

By the middle decades of the 19th century, it was already clear to Reform rabbis that their movement had radically redefined the religious status of women in Reform Judaism. In his anthology of early Reform documents, *The Rise of Reform Judaism* (1963), Rabbi Gunther W. Plaut offers the 1837 summary statement on women in Reform Judaism by Abraham Geiger (1810–1874), the principal intellectual architect of Reform Judaism. "Let there be from now on," Geiger declared, "no distinction between duties for men and women unless flowing from the natural law governing the sexes; no assumption of the spiritual minority of woman, as though she were incapable of grasping the deep things in religion; no institution of the public service, either in form of content, which shuts the doors of the temple; no degradation of woman in the form of the marriage service, and no application of fetters which may destroy woman's happiness." "Our whole religious life," Geiger concludes, "will profit from the beneficial influence which feminine hearts will bestow upon it."

Nine years later, at the Breslau Rabbinic Conference in 1846, the attendees took practical steps to guarantee this new equality. In part, they voted "That from now on, the benediction *Sh'lo Asani I'sha* thanking God that Jewish men "were not created as women" which was the basis for the religious prejudice against woman, shall be abolished." Furthermore, the rabbis agreed "that the female sex shall, from the earliest youth, be obligated to participate in religious instruction and public worship, and in the latter respect, also be counted in a *minyan* (religious quorum)."

Unfortunately, the high-mindedness of German Reform rabbis about women did not translate into social reality in Reform synagogues around the world. Social convention and a deeply embedded patriarchy in the American Jewish community proved highly resistant to change. In her one volume, *The Jews of the United States: 1654–2000* (2004), historian Hasia R. Diner concluded that after he first arrived in America, Rabbi Dr. David Einhorn (1809–1879), the German-born intellectual architect of Classical Reform Judaism in America, "found the role of women in Judaism abhorrent and dysfunctional." "In Judaism," Diner concluded, "women, as understood by Einhorn, remained passive and mute objects rather than active participants in their religion." In other words, rabbinic pronouncements were not enough to truly reform the religious status of women, even in Reform Judaism. Active, practical work still needed to be done and, so it seems, done by women. Ray Frank (1861–1948), a schoolteacher, writer, and lecturer provided a powerful model for the full potential of women in Reform Judaism. Known variously as the "girl rabbi" and the "female messiah," Frank published "a stinging critique" of the American rabbinate in 1890 entitled, "What would you do if you were a rabbi?" That same year, she preached on the High Holy Days to a makeshift congregation gathered in an opera house, and urged the establishment of a truly inclusive, spiritual synagogue. Unfortunately, no congregation was formed and another eight decades passed until a woman was ordained as a rabbi and official spokeswoman for Judaism.

Meanwhile, Reform Jewish women increasingly organized themselves in "sisterhoods of personal service" but mostly along traditional lines. In 1887, a service sisterhood was organized by Congregation Emanu-El in New York City which emphasized social justice, philanthropy, and motherhood. Carrie Obendorfer Simon (1872–1961), wife of Reform Rabbi

Abram Simon, founded the National Federation of Temple Sisterhoods (NFTS) which quickly became the largest Jewish women's organization in the United States, surpassing, in its early years, both the National Council of Jewish Women (established 1893) and Hadassah, the Women's Zionist Organization of America, founded 1912. At first, NFTS's (now known as "Women of Reform Judaism") first priority "was deepening religious observance in the home" as well as to support the work of the synagogue.

Lily Montagu (1873–1963) forged an even bolder path. As early as 1899, Montagu began exploring paths to modernize Judaism, and three years later founded the Jewish Religious Union (JRU) which conducted services along liberal lines. Subsequently, she began founding Liberal synagogues throughout Great Britain. In 1926, she founded the World Union for Progressive Judaism (often running it from her home), which held its first international meeting in Berlin in 1928, at which she preached in the German language. She also served as the lay minister of the West Central Liberal Congregation from 1944 to her death in 1963. In Germany, Regina Jonas (1902–1944), was ordained as a rabbi by that country's Conference of Liberal Rabbis in 1935. She worked in the Berlin Jewish community until she was deported to Auschwitz and murdered along with her mother on October 12, 1944.

In the United States, a century of efforts to reform the religious and public status of women in Reform Judaism came to a head in a 1922 debate at the Hebrew Union College (HUC) in Cincinnati on the question of ordaining women as rabbis. Despite progress, particularly in the United Kingdom and the Central Conference of America Rabbis (CCAR) resolving, "that woman cannot justly be denied the privilege of ordination," HUC failed to proceed with the ordination of women as rabbis. Sally Priesand (b. 1946) did not become the first woman to be ordained as a rabbi by HUC until 1972. Three years later, Barbara Ostfeld (b. 1952) was ordained as the first woman cantor in 1975. Historically, it was necessary for factors outside of Reform Judaism, including the Progressive and Suffrage movements and multiple waves of feminism, to transform the role of women inside the Reform movement. The work of reforming the social, cultural, and religious status of women in Reform Judaism began early in the nineteenth century and, in large part, was a function of the modernism of Classical Reform Judaism. Sixteen decades later, the possibility of a new, fully enfranchised modern Jewish woman which had begun with Israel Jacobson in 1810 in Seesen, Germany was finally becoming a reality in the United States and around the world. However, the work of women's full emancipation and enfranchisement in Reform Judaism is still far from complete. As Rabbi Tarfon taught in Pirke Avot 2:16, "It is not your duty to finish the work, nor are you free to desist from it."

My Last Day at Sunday School (JQuest): A Few Final Thoughts

May 10, 2022

This coming Sunday, May 15, 2022, will be my final day at JQuest. JQuest this year has another week; but because of a family event tied to the KI Spring celebration and two weddings, May 15 will be my last day. I will be in the lobby to say goodbye and even take pictures if you would like a memento.

I probably started attending Sunday School in the fall of 1959. I was in kindergarten at Temple Oheb Shalom in Baltimore, Maryland. That was sixty-three years ago. Since then, I have probably attended Sunday School more than 1,500 times and went every year except the year I was attending rabbinic school in Jerusalem. I always enjoyed Sunday School and, most years, received a Perfect Attendance pin (remember Hebrew School pins?)! Around third grade, I joined the Safety Patrol. Our school was so big we needed a Safety Patrol for dismissal. I rose to the rank of lieutenant (Blue Badge) and then captain (Red Badge).

My favorite teacher was Mrs. Klotzman in second grade. She was an old-fashioned teacher and a believer in Classical Reform Judaism. According to family lore, she encouraged me to become a rabbi. All I can remember is that I admired her devotion to our faith and the unique blend of dignity, seriousness, and fun she brought to the classroom. From her example, I realized (and still believe) that the key to a good Jewish education is a great teacher. Curricula come and go. Educational fads come and go. But a good teacher can make a permanent mark on a child—and she did!

I had a few bad teachers too. One was very mean. He carried a yardstick in his left hand and would hit a desk hard if we misbehaved. I was afraid of him, but fear never motivated me to pay attention or practice my Hebrew. Again, I learned that a good teacher makes all the difference, and so does a bad one. During those years, our school switched from Ashkenazic to Sephardic Hebrew. It was so confusing. All the *oys* and *aws* were officially removed. Even God's name was changed. I never did get it quite right and still speak a kind of *Ashkefardic* Hebrew! More importantly, I learned to love Hebrew and studied it in college, rabbinic school, and ever since. I cannot speak Hebrew like an Israeli, but I am part of that tiny percentage of American Jews who has a basic fluency in Hebrew. Along with the teaching of kindness (*chesed*), I believe Hebrew instruction is one of the two main pillars of Jewish education.

My childhood Sunday School had a beautiful library. We used it regularly, and it also served as a study hall for "regular school." Sitting with my friends and mixing schoolwork and socializing were among my favorite activities. I still believe a synagogue library is important to learning and to community building. At KI, we are very lucky to have a thriving, endowed synagogue library. The "other" activity at Sunday School was youth group. My youth group was part of MAFTY (Maryland Federation of Temple Youth). Our director was a mom of one of the other kids, Mrs. Roz Keane. Junior youth group (middle school) was particularly fun. Our youth group was TOSTY (Temple Oheb Shalom Temple Youth). I went on sleep-away conclaves (to Silver Springs, Maryland) and other special events, mostly at Mrs. Keane's home. It was a good time, and I had good friends (from other schools).

During my college years at Franklin and Marshall (1972–1975), I was a teacher at the local Reform synagogue, Gates of Heaven. At first, the rabbi there did not like me because I had the kids sing songs like "Feeling Groovy" to start our weekly assembly. He eventually came around and realized it was necessary to warm up spiritually before the official prayers and songs of the day started. I did not have a car at the time, so one of my professors' wives, who was also a teacher, drove us on Sunday mornings. There were a few Sundays on which I was totally sleep-deprived from the night before, but with Mrs. Pinsker's encouragement and some real coffee, I persevered. The experience only strengthened my resolve to go on to rabbinic school.

During my third year of rabbinic school to ordination, I served as a student rabbi at Temple Beth Boruk in Richmond, Indiana, halfway between Indianapolis and Dayton. I still hear from some of those students today. One went on to be president of a Conservative synagogue. Another student became a lawyer and an expert in archival law (and a sort of adviser to me in that area), and still others just stayed in touch with me. How satisfying! My very first bar mitzvah student later died in a fire at a frat party while away at college. I will never forget how deep that grief was, and it stays with me every time I work with a family who has suffered a loss.

As a rabbinic student, I taught Sunday School at the Wise Center in Cincinnati. Our director was Rabbi Joel Wittstein. He was a master teacher and deeply committed to values clarification, the educational trend at that time. He taught me the value of good lesson planning and the priority of teaching ethics. I probably learned more about Jewish teacher education from his example than from any class I took on the same. From him, I also learned the need to have a visionary school director.

In Binghamton, New York, Temple Concord's school experienced exponential growth during our years there from 1990 to 2001. At the same time, I was a professor at SUNY Binghamton. At Temple Concord, I worked with an Israeli religious school director, Orly Shoer, who had trained in a teacher's college in Israel. The Binghamton school met on Saturdays and ended with Saturday morning services, which were "standing room only." Hebrew instruction was a high priority, and Confirmation at Concord was a breeze as most of the students were children of professors, and we had wonderful, probing conversations. To this day, the Temple Concord School remains my model of excellence in supplemental Jewish education.

During the last twenty-one years, I have worked in tandem with the directors and teachers at KI, both Hebrew School (JQuest and Quest Noar) and preschool. My unique partnership here has been with my wife, Liz, who not only headed up the music program but also ran a children's choir, Shir Joy, that has galvanized our religious school's sense of community, taught the kids their prayers, and fortified their Hebrew education. We have been an educational team for over forty years, and Shir Joy was among the most effective learning experiences I have ever witnessed in supplemental Jewish education. From Rabbi Stacy Rigler, I learned the importance of project-based learning and the value of informal Jewish education even in a more formal educational structure like Sunday School.

I leave our program in the good hands of Deb Rosen, a forty-year veteran of the KI education program. During the last year, she has overcome the centrifugal forces of COVID, learned to incorporate new educational technologies, and reestablished a sense of community in our school. She has also restored Israel education and Hebrew instruction to a level I happen to like, and I wish her well in the future. I also want to thank Cantor Amy Levy for heading our b'nai mitzvah program for many years and turning the experience into something warm, positive, and memorable for our students and their families. I always love leading a b'nai mitzvah service with Cantor Levy!

I have been going to Sunday school for sixty-three years now. I only have three hours left! It is a bittersweet moment, as I need to retire as a matter of self-care. Meanwhile, I leave with the satisfaction that I have played a role in the Jewish identity development of several generations of Jewish students and even some of their children. The tradition goes on from generation to generation. I am proud to have been a link in the chain of tradition, which links Abraham and Sarah to our generation and our children's and grandchildren's generations. See you on Sunday!

Shabbat Shalom and *L'hitraot*!

Five Special Moments

June 2, 2022

It's June, the final month of my work as Senior Rabbi of KI, and all the big celebrations are behind us. We still have Confirmation (this Saturday night) and a number of *b'nai mitzvah* and baby namings, among other things. But the clock is running, and sometime in the next two weeks, I will be breaking down my office and starting the process of transferring over to my new digs in what has been the gift shop. So it's only natural that I am reflecting back on the last twenty-one years and singling out a host of special moments of particular importance to me.

Here are five of them:

GETTYSBURG: As a little boy, I was taken several times by my late father to visit the Gettysburg Battlefield, where the Union and Confederate armies clashed from July 1 to July 3, 1863. It was the largest bloodiest battle of the Civil War, the "high-water mark" of the Confederacy and later the site of the Gettysburg Address, Lincoln's immortal 272-word speech dedicating the military cemetery. Always fascinated by those three fateful days in July 1863, I decided to do a research project identifying the Jewish soldiers on both sides of the field. As the list of names grew, I decided to go to Gettysburg and, with the help of the thousands of military markers, determine where they stood and, sometimes, died. The list is still a work in progress (with over five hundred names), but even without a definitive count, I thought it worthwhile to organize a bus trip to Gettysburg and share my findings with the congregation "on-site." It was more than a great trip. It was spectacular and resulted in a flood of feelings as we walked the "angle" where Pickett's Charge hit the Union line heavily populated by Jewish soldiers from Philadelphia and then stood in front of a marker commemorating the Gettysburg Address. It was a time of bonding, inspiration, and renewal I will not forget.

SANCTUARY REFURBISHMENT: About a decade ago, when Peter Soloff was president of the congregation, the Board decided it was time to reupholster the seats in the sanctuary. While I agreed that the chairs needed work, I also thought it was the right moment to go large and think about how we would use our sanctuary for the next generation. To my amazement, the discussions were brisk, engaged, and quick! Just thinking about changing the central symbol of a synagogue can take years. But KI was ready. We needed to add technological capacity. We needed to work on the lighting, the sound system, and the color scheme of the room. We needed to think about the use of Hebrew as a visual statement on the bimah. We needed to lower the bimah to get the clergy closer to the congregation and provide handicap access, and we needed to find a new system to help the hearing impaired. In almost no time, a huge amount of money was raised, scaffolding was built from floor to ceiling, and the work began. Remarkably, the new sanctuary looked a whole lot like the old sanctuary, but its functionality had been radically upgraded. We now had sacred space for the twenty-first century. Our biggest and most revered space felt both majestic as always but yet more "heimish." It was a critically important collective accomplishment and, perhaps, a bit of a miracle too.

DOCTOR OF DIVINITY (DD): Unlike most rabbis, I stayed in school for seven more years after receiving my ordination in 1980 to earn my PhD in Jewish history. A doctorate enabled me to have a two-track career, both in the pulpit and in academia. I was lucky because I was able to have both, and even more, one made the other better and deeper. So as I approached the twenty-fifth-year mark in my rabbinate in 2005 and became eligible for my Doctor of Divinity degree, known among rabbis as a Doctor of Duration diploma, I did not think it was going to be "a big deal." I went with my family to Congregation Emanu-El on Fifth Avenue for the ceremony and to my surprise was filled with emotion. My DD, I realized, was not just a piece of paper. It was a hard-earned recognition of twenty-five years in the pulpit, of living a fireman's life and learning how to "pastor" a congregation of all sizes. While I was very happy to be "Rabbi Dr. Dr.," I was even more gratified that my part of celebrating life, comforting the mourner, and just "being there" had official as well as intrinsic value. I decided it was too much to change my letterhead and business card (remember them?)—too many letters! But on the inside, it felt good. In any event, after becoming "Dr. Dr. Rabbi Professor," I was just as content to be called Lance by those choosing to do so. I like all my titles, but I am just as content in just being me.

MISHKAN T'FILAH: In my lifetime as a Reform Jew, I have had three prayer books. First was the *Union Prayer Book* (UPB), a small, beautifully written prayer book that represented the deep root of Reform Judaism from its classical phase. "Grant us peace" and "Let us adore" were two of many passages that became part of my spiritual oxygen as a young person. Next came the *Gates of Prayer* in the 1970s, a massive volume that reflected the growing diversity of Reform Judaism at the end of the twentieth century. It had more Hebrew available than the old *UPB* but was a tad less majestic. It also came out just before the impact of feminism on the Reform movement. Thus, it was dated the day it appeared. In 2007, the movement published *Mishkan T'filah* or *Sanctuary of Prayer*, the third prayer book in my lifetime; but this time, I was not just a user but also a producer of the book. In the production process, something went terribly wrong; and my rabbinic organization contacted me, along with a rabbi-attorney-friend, to take over the process. We worked furiously to fix the many technical problems and oversaw the printing of tens of thousands of prayer books. I was then invited to write a position paper to help frame Volume Two for the High Holy Days. In my mind, the movement was ready to go digital, but it could not find a business plan for the project. That came later. Meanwhile, a new generation of prayer books was out there, serving as the sacred vehicles of Reform spirituality. I am honored that I was part of that process.

EISENSTAEDT TORAH: One last memory. There are thousands of them. But let me end this group of reflections with a remembrance of a very special moment in a little village about fifty miles south of Vienna in Burgenland, Austria. In planning a trip to Central Europe, I wanted to visit a town called Eisenstaedt for three reasons: it had the last surviving door to a Jewish ghetto in Europe (Napoleon's troops forgot to remove it), it was the home of the great composer J. Haydn, and it was the site of the Esterházy Palace, owned by the family who had accused Alfred Dreyfus of treason after the Franco-Prussian War. Any one of these factors would have justified a visit, but as it happened (and maybe why people travel), it was the unexpected that made the day. After touring the Haydn sites and the palace, we went to the old ghetto and worked our way into its narrow, winding streets. We entered into one of the larger residences there (they were all abandoned) and were ushered into a high-ceiling room with an Ark, which, we were told, had been a private family synagogue-chapel in its day. In the Ark was a single fragment of a Torah scroll—a torn, incomplete, single column. "Read it," everyone in our group called out. So we said the blessing on reading from the Torah, and I then read the scrap of parchment and translated it for the group. It felt like the souls of a hundred generations were released into that airspace. For some unknown reason, only a tiny remnant of our ancient tradition remained there, and all the Jews of the town were gone. All that was left was a bit of Torah. But it was enough to wrap our hearts with the complete scroll of our tradition. I went to Burgenland to experience a tiny slice of tradition. Instead, the entire power of our heritage made itself present, and "we were renewed as in days of old."

I am grateful for all my memories of the last twenty-one years. I am glad that I am able to share them with you.

Shabbat Shalom.

Acknowledgments

Although *Portrait of an American Rabbi: In His Own Words* is, indeed, my own words, I could not have produced this book alone. I want to thank everyone who helped me transform a massive pile of unedited material into what is hopefully a coherent collection of select writings.

First, I want to acknowledge my "front line," my synagogue office assistants, Anita Madnick, Sarah Morrison, Pam Saltzburg, and the late Barbara Steinberg, z"l, who steadfastly compelled me to meet writing deadlines and help preserve the record of my written work. Without them, my efficiency rating would have plummeted, and much of the record would have been lost.

Second, I want to thank Joan Myerson Shrager who for thirteen years partnered with me in creating over 120 PowerPoints. Joan not only created each and every slide but also "ran the show" during our presentations and did a massive amount of research and editing along the way. All my illustrated talks were presented with extemporaneous narration, which greatly helped improve my public speaking. On many occasions, I would either write a promotional piece or follow up with a summary of a lecture. Early in our collaboration, my PowerPoints were frequently presented after services on Friday night at the Oneg Shabbat (literally "delighting in the Sabbath" or fellowship hour) in lieu of a sermon, a practice that enabled me to circumvent the time restrictions of regular preaching and "go long." Anyone who only wanted to experience the worship part of the evening and leave was free to go, but happily, the overwhelming majority stayed and listened.

I have named this book *Portrait of an American Rabbi: In His Own Words*. Since the time of Rembrandt, rabbinic portraiture has been an important part of Jewish culture. In the nineteenth century, synagogues began commissioning portraits of long-serving rabbis. I was fortunate that KI chose Deborah Schafer to paint my portrait in anticipation of my retirement. We spent many hours together, studied rabbinic portraits, experimented with open-collar pictures and paintings featuring Jewish symbolic clothing like prayer shawls. In the end, we decided to create a picture of me in my office holding my biography of Isaac Leeser, lowering it just enough so I could greet an imaginary visitor. The subtitle, *In His Own Words*, is offered in the hope that my report of my work for twenty-one years, 2001–2022, will have lasting value or at least constitute an honest report from the pulpit about Jewish life in America in our time.

No words are adequate to thank Lynda Barness who served as my project manager and helped transform my collection of dozens of unedited pieces into a book. Lynda, herself a published author and accomplished businesswoman, was tireless in her efforts in shaping an inchoate collection of unedited manuscripts into a coherent whole. Efficient and indefatigable, she kept the process moving and helped us comply with the requirements of our publisher, Xlibris. Post-publishing, Lynda has continued with the difficult task of marketing and distributing *Portrait of an American Rabbi*, one of the most challenging aspects of contemporary book publishing. I also want to thank Lynda's daughter, Jennifer Urdang Stern, for her support of this project.

To all of you who listened to me speak, read my messages contemporaneously, and have now reviewed my written record, thank you. It has been my honor to work for you and with you to preserve and advance our ancient ancestral tradition.

Finally, I want to thank my family, especially my wife, Liz, for being an essential part of the sermon writing process. It is not easy having a husband, dad, and grandfather who works day shifts, evenings, weekends, and holidays and then stays up almost to dawn researching, writing, and editing; but they did so with grace and understanding. My family was also my first line of supporters and gentle critics, often delighting when I mispronounced words in High Holy Day sermons and offering grades, commentaries, and suggestions along the way. Special thanks to our daughter, Chana, who offered both artistic and technical support to my rabbinic work and the creation of the cover of this book.

I close by dedicating *Portrait of an American Rabbi* to my granddaughters: Sophie, Charlotte, and Celia. I want them to know about their Pop Pop and his work. Perhaps when they are older, they will read this book, reflect on it, and incorporate some of its teachings and values into their own lives. Nothing would make me happier than to make them proud of me because, at the end of the day, their love and approval is my ultimate legacy.

    LJS

About the Author

Lance Jonathan Sussman is a historian of the American Jewish experience. He has served as a college professor, Chair of the Board of Governors of Gratz College (Melrose Park, PA) and until summer 2022, Senior Rabbi, now Emeritus, at Reform Congregation Keneseth Israel (KI), in Elkins Park, PA. Throughout his career, Sussman has been an active scholar, writer and public speaker. He is the author of numerous books and articles including: *Isaac Leeser and the Making of American Judaism* (1995) and *Sharing Sacred Moments* (1999), and a co-editor of *Reform Judaism in America: A Biographical Dictionary and Sourcebook (1993)* and *New Essays in American Jewish History* (2009). Since 2010 he has also published articles on Judaism and art.

Sussman attended Franklin and Marshall College in Lancaster, PA, where he was elected to Phi Beta Kappa and graduated cum lauded with a Bachelor of Arts in Religious Studies. From 1975 to 1987, Sussman attended Hebrew Union College- Jewish Institute of Religion (HUC-JIR) in Cincinnati, OH. He received a Master's of Arts in Hebrew Letters in 1979 and was ordained as a Rabbi by HUC-JIR in June, 1980. While studying for his rabbinical degree, he was awarded the Mrs. Arthur Hays Sulzberger Prize in Homiletics for the Best Short Sermon. After ordination Sussman remained at HUC-JIR where he earned a PhD in American Jewish History in 1987, studying under Jacob Rader Marcus and Jonathan D. Sarna. In 2005, HUC-JIR awarded Sussman an honorary Doctorate of Divinity.

While serving as Senior Rabbi at KI, Lance Sussman continued to teach at the university level. He has been a visiting professor, adjunct professor, or lecturer at, among others, Princeton University, Temple University,

Hunter College (City University of New York), Rutgers University, Gratz College, and the New York City campus of HUC-JIR. Since its founding in 1998, Sussman has been a member of the Academic Advisory and Editorial Board of the Jacob Rader Marcus Center of the American Jewish Archives at HUC-JIR in Cincinnati, OH. He has also served as a trustee of Delaware Valley College (now Delaware Valley University), the Herbert D. Katz Center for Advanced Judaic Studies at the University of Pennsylvania, and the American Jewish Historical Society.

Sussman regularly gives public lectures and presentations and has spoken at, among others, the American Jewish Committee in Berlin, German, Jagellonian University in Kraków, Poland, the (former) Gershman YMHA (Young Men's Hebrew Association) Jewish Community Center in Philadelphia, the Center for Jewish History in New York City, annual conventions of the Central Conference of American Rabbis, and biennial conference of the Union for Reform Judaism. He has served as an adviser to numerous public exhibitions at museums and other cultural institutions and has been involved with several television documentaries.

Printed in the USA
CPSIA information can be obtained
at www.ICGtesting.com
LVHW091734150224
771977LV00006B/25